Yeshivat Har Etzion ישיבת הר עציון
Stella K. Abraham Beit Midrash for Women
Yaacov Herzog College
Israel Koschitzky Virtual Beit Midrash

HONORING

DAVID AND DASSIE SCHREIBER
Dor l'Dor Award

RELLA FELDMAN & MINDY HECHT '04 MO
Gemilut Chasadim Award

RAV MORDECHAI '79 & DEBBY FRIEDMAN
Keter Torah Award

KEYNOTE ADDRESS BY
CHIEF RABBI EPHRAIM MIRVIS '76
*Chief Rabbi of The United Hebrew Congregations
of The Commonwealth*

Wednesday, April 2, 2014
Grand Hyatt Hotel
New York City

Torah MiEtzion
New Readings in Tanach
Vayikra

MAGGID

Torah MiEtzion

New Readings in Tanach

Vayikra

EDITORS

Rav Ezra Bick &
Rav Yaakov Beasley

Maggid Books
Yeshivat Har Etzion

Torah MiEtzion
New Readings in Tanach
Vayikra

First Edition, 2014

Maggid Books
A division of Koren Publishers Jerusalem Ltd.

POB 8531, New Milford, CT 06776-8531, USA
& POB 4044, Jerusalem 91040, Israel

www.korenpub.com

The publication of this book was made possible through
the generous support of *Torah Education in Israel*.

ISBN 978 161 329 008 8, *hardcover original*

A CIP catalogue record for this title is
available from the British Library

Printed and bound in USA

כִּי יְדַעְתִּיו לְמַעַן אֲשֶׁר יְצַוֶּה אֶת בָּנָיו וְאֶת בֵּיתוֹ אַחֲרָיו
וְשָׁמְרוּ דֶּרֶךְ ה׳ לַעֲשׂוֹת צְדָקָה וּמִשְׁפָּט
(בראשית יח, יט)

Dedicated in loving memory of
Dr. William Major *z"l*
אברהם זאב בן יהודה ז"ל

A Holocaust survivor and devoted psychiatrist, Dr. Major was animated by a deep love of Torah, Israel and the Jewish People. Through his personal example of quiet dignity and deep commitment to *hesed* and Torah study, he conveyed these values to his family and made an indelible impression on those who were privileged to know him.

Dr. Major cherished Yeshivat Har Etzion, which in his eyes embodied his loves and commitments, and was deeply grateful for all that his children gained there. It is therefore a singularly fitting tribute that this series – which brings the profound and innovative Torah of Yeshivat Har Etzion to the broader public – is dedicated to his memory.

תהא נשמתו צרורה בצרור החיים

Contents

Preface

The *Torah MiEtzion* series began publication with the appearance of *Bereshit* in Elul 5771 (2011). *Shemot* and *Devarim* were published during 2012, and we have now reached the fourth volume, that of *Sefer Vayikra*.

This volume presents a selection of *shiurim* given on *parashat hashavua* by different lecturers, all of whom are connected in one way or another with Yeshivat Har Etzion. Most of them originally appeared on the Israel Koschitzky Virtual Beit Midrash. But the impetus for publication is not merely a desire to repackage a successful and interesting series of *shiurim*. The VBM series has managed to be itself the catalyst for the written expression of a body of work, from different authors, which represents a distinct approach to *parshanut HaTorah*, one which has been developing over the last forty years in the yeshiva and its affiliated Herzog Teacher's College, and which today is the most vibrant and influential school of modern commentary and interpretation of the biblical text within the Torah world.

One of the unique characteristics of Yeshivat Har Etzion was the inclusion of serious study of Tanach in the curriculum from the outset of the yeshiva. Years before the establishment of an academic affiliate – the Herzog Teacher's College – the yeshiva had regular *shiurim* on Tanach given alongside the traditional *shiurim* in Gemara which occupied the yeshiva's core. Rav Amital *zt"l*, the yeshiva's founder, explained that this was essential to his vision of the yeshiva, to foster an organic understanding of Torah and Torah philosophy, for which it was obvious to him that Tanach was part of the foundation. When, a few years later, the yeshiva established a teacher's college, the Tanach department was one of the two main divisions of the college, and naturally attracted scholars and students, eventually adding to its staff young teachers who themselves had been educated in the yeshiva. Today, aside from the ongoing study of Tanach in the yeshiva itself, and the scheduled curriculum of Tanach studies in Herzog College, the college also sponsors a yearly conference on Tanach (*yemei iyun b'Tanakh*), which attracts tens of scholars and thousands of teachers and students from all over Israel for a week of *shiurim* on all aspects and books of Tanach, and publishes a scholarly journal of Tanach studies (*Megadim*).

This is the fourth volume of the *Torah MiEtzion* series on the Torah to appear, following *Bereshit*, *Shemot*, and *Devarim*. The preface to the first volume on *Bereshit* included a brief summation of the central aspects of the Etzion approach to Tanach. Like many of the readers of the previous volumes, I too have sometimes wondered if a volume applying that approach to *Sefer Vayikra* would in fact be published. The heavy use of literary analysis in the previous volumes, and the prominence of that kind of analysis in the method espoused in the Etzion school, which was highlighted in the preface to the *Bereshit* volume, led many to doubt if the method would be applicable to *Vayikra*, a book nearly devoid of narrative, and almost completely devoted to law – and the rather dry and technical laws of sacrifice and ritual impurity to boot. Could the search for layers of meaning, literary textual analysis, sensitivity to the use of synonyms, leading terms, parallel constructions, psychological hints, and historical perspectives yield the same rich bounty in *Sefer Vayikra* that it did in the other books?

I trust this volume will put those doubts to rest.

On the one hand, the methods that proved so fruitful in the previous volumes were directly applicable here as well. This was true not only for the unusual case of "*Darosh darash*" (Bick), which examines the relatively unique example of a halakhic discussion which forms the crux of a narrative, but for several other cases where the relation of a halakhic section to the overall narrative (the discussions of the "eighth day" and the "Yom Kippur" sections) or to the structure of the Torah in general (Leibtag, Grossman, Spiegelman, and Granot on *Behar-Beḥukkotai*) is examined. But more importantly, the same methods of exegesis, modified somewhat, were put to work on the halakhic sections themselves. The Torah, after all, is not written the same way as the *Shulḥan Arukh*, as a dry legalistic code. The language used to formulate the laws, the placement and relationship of different halakhic sections, repetitions, word associations – all these provide a rich resource for understanding the legal sections of the Torah and explicating their significance and meaning. Consider the following example:

Sefer Vayikra (17:2–4):

> Speak to Aaron and his sons and all of the Israelites, and say to them: This is the matter that God has commanded them, saying: Each person (*ish ish*) from the house of Israel who shall slaughter an ox or sheep or goat in the camp, or shall slaughter outside the camp; and he did not bring it to the entrance of the Tent of Meeting to sacrifice to God before the Tabernacle of God, blood shall it be considered for that man, blood he has spilled, and that man shall be cut off from the midst of his people.

Rambam, *Hilkhot Ma'ase HaKorbanot* 18:3:

> One who slaughters sacred animals outside of the sacred precinct, even though he has not offered it, if he did it intentionally he is liable for *karet* (cutting off), as is written, "who shall slaughter an ox or sheep or goat...blood shall it be considered for that man, blood he has spilled, and that man shall be cut off," and if he did it unintentionally, he brings a regular *ḥatat*.

Legally, the two passages are equivalent. One interested only in the legal implications of the verse will strip from it all the "literary" verbiage, because he is not interested in the introduction, with its appeal to "Aaron, his sons, and all Israel"; the complicated formulation of "in the camp or outside of the camp" is for him irrelevant; the non-performed alternative, "he did not bring it to the entrance to the tent," has no significance; and the part about blood is simply legally meaningless. All of these details, and more, need to be explicated in order to obtain a full meaning of these verses and the halakha included in them, and this is the work of the Torah commentator who addresses the text in more or less the same way he should address the text in any other part of the Tanach.

In this respect, the work presented in this volume is even more revolutionary than in the previous ones. This can be seen even in the first few essays of the book. The essays on *Parashat Vayikra* all deal with purely halakhic topics, and use the methods of Torah exegesis to extract new layers of meaning concerning the institution of sacrifice in the Torah.

This should not be surprising. In the preface to *Bereshit*, I pointed out that I believe that the methods used in this series derive, among other things, from the talmudic background of most of the authors. For legal sections of the Torah, this background and the absorption of talmudic exegesis give our authors a unique vantage and insight. To this must be added a shared belief in the unity of the Torah, both narrative and legal sections. One of the principles of this school of exegesis is reading each *parasha* in light of the entire Tanach, in terms of both terminology and themes, and this naturally engenders a commitment to read halakha in light of narrative (and vice versa). It turns out that this produces fruit, and the volume before you is a pioneering collection of that fruit.

The importance of all these volumes is not so much in introducing a new method, for I am sure that most readers have had some exposure to it, either directly through reading or hearing one of the authors, or through other similar authors. The importance is in the concentration in one place, demonstrating the power and consistency in reading the entire Torah this way. It is not a method of producing a *ḥiddush*, or of solving some particular hitherto unexplained problem, but of reading Tanach as a whole. The book is a recommendation that everyone should read every *parasha* in this way – to read, or perhaps reread, and then reread again – and therefore to understand the message and the meaning.

*   *   *

The majority of the essays in this book were originally published in the "Parsha" series of the Israel Koschitzky Virtual Beit Midrash (*www.vbm-torah.org*). The VBM has been providing an online *beit midrash* for nearly twenty years, creating a worldwide community for in-depth Torah learning, where tens of thousands of readers have already read the essays republished here, as well as thousands of other *shiurim* in all areas of Torah study. The essays have in some cases been shortened for publication in the book. The archives of the VBM have between ten and fifteen excellent essays on each *parasha*. The originals of the essays published here, as well as all the others, can be accessed on the VBM website.

Those essays originally written in Hebrew were ably and elegantly translated by Kaeren Fish, David Silverberg, and David Strauss.

The essay by Rav Breuer *zt"l* is translated from his book *Pirkei Mo'adot* (Jerusalem, 1986). The essays by Rav Yoel Bin-Nun were provided by the author. The essay by Rav Itamar Eldar originally appeared in the *Makor Rishon* newspaper.

Many more studies in all aspects of Tanach can be found in the fifty volumes of *Megadim*, the Tanach journal of the Herzog College.

We thank our partners at Maggid Books for their professionalism and high standards.

In the name of all of the authors, I invite the readers to comment and contribute to the ongoing endeavor *lehagdil Torah uleha'adira*. We hope and pray that these volumes will contribute to the continuous discovery of new and deeper interpretations of Torat HaShem.

Ezra Bick

Erev Ḥanukka, 5774

VBM: *http://www.vbm-torah.org*
VBM *parsha* archives: *http://www.vbm-torah.org/parsha.htm*
Correspondence: office@etzion.org.il

Parashat Vayikra

The Structure of the Book of Leviticus

Rav Tamir Granot

I. A PROPOSED STRUCTURE

Leviticus differs from the other books in the Torah in that it contains little narrative or moral exhortation, but rather pure halakha. Only twice do narratives appear, breaking the continuity of the laws. The multiplicity of details sometimes leads us to a feeling of not being able to see the wood for the trees, and it is therefore instructive to pause for an overview of the book, divided into clearly defined units, so as to reveal its structure and division, and thereby its substance and purpose as well.

How are we to go about dividing up the book and determining its structure? We may divide it by subject – for example: sacrifices, inauguration, the eighth day, etc. This option, however, is inherently subjective, since each reader may offer his own definition of subject. Hence, I shall attempt here to propose a division and structure based on purely internal factors.

I propose that, in defining the structure and parts of the book, we take into consideration the following criteria:

1. Every introductory reference to the speech of God, i.e., "God spoke to Moses saying," shall be regarded as marking an independent unit or item. Altogether there are thirty-seven such

utterances in Leviticus; hence, we start with thirty-seven units (to which we must add the narratives, which do not begin with this opening formula). The assumption is that when God speaks to Moses or Aaron, His speech is not interrupted. Two separate subjects will be treated in two separate utterances. Note that some of the utterances are very long, while others are very short; hence, it is not the length of the speech that matters, but rather the content.

2. General introductions or general conclusions will define larger units.

3. A transition from one genre to another will indicate the end or beginning of a large unit. Therefore, when a story ends, it must be assumed that a subject is now closed. The reason for this criterion is that God's utterances in Leviticus are not presented in any chronological framework (there are no dates provided); hence, there is no reason to assume that the narrative appears in its chronological place, merely on the basis of the fact that it appears after the preceding command. It is more sensible to adopt the literary assumption that the narratives are ordered based on structural considerations.

4. Units within the book which are not part of the continuum of commands (i.e., a divine utterance which is not a natural continuation of the one that preceded it, but which seems to better fit elsewhere) will also represent a criterion for defining the larger units in the book. Thus, we shall distinguish chapters which, we are told, were commanded to Moses at Mount Sinai, rather than in the Tent of Meeting.

5. We shall take note of the recipient or object of each command, distinguishing between the predominant commands, those given to Moses alone, and the less frequent ones, namely those given to Moses and Aaron, or to Aaron alone. Sometimes there is an "utterance" (*vayomer*) instead of a "speech" (*vayedabber*), and we shall address this distinction as well. While awareness of the objects of the speech is not significant for dividing every book, it is generally helpful to frame the discussion with an awareness of to whom it is addressed.

II. DIVIDING THE BOOK

Let us now list the utterances that introduce subject units in the book and their contents, and define larger units on the basis of their beginnings and endings.

1. Leviticus chapters 1–3 – Opening speech from the Tent of Meeting: burnt offering, meal offering, peace offering;
2. 4:1–5:13 – List of sin offerings, including (in chapter 5) an *oleh veyored* offering;
3. 5:14–5:19 – Guilt offering for sin involving holy things (*me'ila*), and a guilt offering in the case of doubt;
4. 5:20–5:26 – Guilt offering for something stolen;
5. 6:1–6:11 – New introduction, "Command Aaron"; subject of first unit: the ashes and the fire, laws of meal offering, pertaining to the *kohanim*;
6. 6:12–6:16 – Meal offering of the *kohanim*;
7. 6:17–7:21 – Laws of the sin offering, guilt offering, peace offering, and thanksgiving offering, as pertaining to the *kohanim*;
8. 7:22–7:27 – Prohibition of fats and blood;
9. 7:28–7:38 – Gifts to the *kohanim* from the sacrifices, conclusion of chapters 6–7 "which God commanded Moses at Mount Sinai";
10. 8:1–10:7 – Command concerning the days of consecration, and narrative concerning the days of consecration and the eighth day, with the death of Nadav and Avihu;
11. 10:8–10:11 – Utterance to Aaron: warning concerning drinking wine, defining the role of the *kohanim*;
12. 10:12–10:19 (no utterance) – Completion of the ritual of the eighth day following the death of Nadav and Avihu;
13. Chapter 11 – Utterance to Moses and Aaron: laws of unclean animals and the prohibition against eating them, followed by a general summary dealing with ritual impurity, obligation of sanctity, and separation of Israel from the nations;
14. Chapter 12 – Ritual impurity of the birthing mother and the accompanying laws;
15. Chapter 13 – Utterance to Moses and Aaron: details of the laws of leprosy manifest on a person and on a garment;
16. 14:1–14:32 – Laws of purification of the leper after he is healed;

17. 14:32–14:57 – Utterance to Moses and Aaron: laws of leprosy manifest on a house and the order of its purification, followed by a general summary of the laws of leprosy;

18. Chapter 15 – Utterance to Moses and Aaron: impurity of the body, followed by a general summary concerning impurity of the body;

19. Chapter 16 – Ritual of the *Kohen Gadol* (High Priest) entering the Holy of Holies, following the death of Aaron's sons, on Yom Kippur;

20. Chapter 17 – Laws of blood, including warning concerning animals slaughtered outside of the *Mishkan* (Tabernacle);

21. Chapter 18 – List of forbidden sexual relations;

22. Chapter 19 – *Parashat Kedoshim*, centered around laws between man and his fellow man;

23. Chapter 20 – Punishment for forbidden sexual relations;

24. 21:1–21:16 – "God said to Moses": impurity of *kohanim*;

25. 21:16–21:23 – Blemishes among *kohanim*; conclusion: Moses conveys it all to the *kohanim* and to the Children of Israel;

26. 22:1–22:16 – Laws of eating sacrificial meat, and gifts (*teruma*) to the *kohanim*;

27. 22:17–22:25 – Laws of blemishes in sacrifices;

28. 22:26–22:33 – Limitations on animal sacrifices: first eight days of life, slaughtering mother animal and its young, requirement that sacrifice be offered willingly; general conclusion regarding mitzva observance and preventing desecration of God's name;

29. 23:1–23:8 – Shabbat and Pesaḥ;

30. 23:9–23:22 – "When you come to the land": *omer* and offering of the first fruits, Shavuot; appendix: gifts of the field to the poor;

31. 23:23–23:25 – Day of remembrance of sounding the shofar (Rosh HaShana);

32. 23:26–23:32 – Yom Kippur;

33. 23:33–23:44 – Sukkot and general conclusion concerning the festivals;

34. 24:1–24:12 – Menora and showbread;

35. 24:13–24:23 – Episode of the blasphemer; following this, utterance and command concerning damages to man and animals, and punishment carried out for blasphemer;

36. Chapters 25–26 – God commands Moses at Mount Sinai: *Shemitta*, Jubilee, and their accompanying laws; the covenant with its blessings and curses; general conclusion: "This is what God commanded at Mount Sinai, through Moses";
37. Chapter 27 – Estimated values and dedications; general conclusion: "These are the laws from Mount Sinai."

III. THE MEANINGS OF THE DIVISIONS

It is easy to see that this division is preferable to both the traditional division into *parashot* or into chapters, since it gives no weight to the length of the unit, focusing instead only on content. In some cases there are large units which, in the traditional division, are divided into several *parashot* or chapters. Now, when they are treated as a single unit, it is easy to perceive their integrity of subject. Conversely, the section on the festivals is divided here into several units, so as to highlight the differences between the festivals when they are not treated as a single unit.

If we focus on the break in the continuity of halakhic commands given to Moses from the Tent of Meeting, and ignore for the moment the chapters of laws whose source is Sinai and which for some reason were inserted into Leviticus, we end up with a simple scheme of the structure of Leviticus:

Section 1 – laws of sacrifices (1–5)
Section 2 – days of inauguration, and the eighth day (8–10)
Section 3 – chapters of laws, statutes, and judgments (11–24)
Appendix – the blasphemer and the laws applicable to him (end of 24).

Perhaps section 3 should be divided into two subsections, based on the same principle, since chapter 16 explicitly relates itself to the death of Aaron's sons – "After the death of the two sons of Aaron." This is true both in terms of content ("that he die not") and in terms of the laws (i.e., the similarity between the ritual of the eighth day and Yom Kippur). We may assert that all of the chapters from 11 to 16 belong to one closed unit. These chapters deal with the details of the laws of the various types of impurity, and the connection between them is clear.

Furthermore, a closer look at these chapters points to their uniqueness and unity, as only in these chapters – and in all of them – does Aaron receive a command together with Moses. This fact alone is enough to provide a common denominator for these chapters. Thus, we may amend our division as follows:

> Unit 1 – Laws of sacrifices (1–5);
> Unit 2 – Days of inauguration and the eighth day (8–10);
> Unit 3 – Chapters addressing the types of impurity and chapters addressing the purification from these forms of impurity: "And atone for the holy place because of the impurity of the Children of Israel" (11–16);
> Unit 4 – Laws, statutes, and judgments (18–24).

In rabbinic literature, Leviticus is also known as "*Torat Kohanim*" – the laws of the *kohanim*. The laws of the sacrifices at the beginning, the laws discussing the various types of impurity, the sacrificial meat and possible blemishes in chapters 21–22, all fit this description. Why then is Moses alone commanded concerning the first set of laws of sacrifices and the last set of laws pertaining to *kohanim*, while the laws of impurity and purification (chapters 11–15) are conveyed to Moses and Aaron together?

The answer is quite simple. When it comes to the sacrifices and the laws pertaining to the *kohanim* themselves, Aaron and the other *kohanim* are nothing but servants; they are the workers in the *Mishkan*, and they must carry out everything that they are commanded to do. From this perspective, there is no real difference between that which is incumbent upon them and that which is incumbent on any other Israelite, qua servant of God, and therefore it is Moses who commands them. When it comes to the laws of impurity, however, their status is different. Here, the *kohanim* are not merely "clerks" or servants. They are entrusted with determining the status of the impurity and giving instructions with regard to it. Here, Aaron and his sons are not there merely to carry out their tasks, but – like Moses – play a role in the molding and application of the actual laws. Since their role here is to be teachers and instructors, God commands Aaron directly.

It is for the same reason that two *parashot* within the laws of impurity are conveyed to Moses alone: the laws of the birthing woman, and the ritual of purification for the leper. The impurity of a birthing woman is a simple determination, with no doubt involved; therefore, there is no need for a *kohen* to issue a special ruling regarding her status. In the purification of the leper, the *kohanim* once again become servants who must perform a certain job – they must offer up the sacrifice, sprinkle, etc. Once again they are not partners in the command, but rather subjects, and so Moses conveys this to them, like the rest of the Torah.

It seems, then, that the section comprising the laws of impurities is placed where it is, not because of the story of Nadav and Avihu which precedes it (as many commentators maintain), but rather as a direct continuation of the chapters describing the seven days of consecration, during which time the *kohanim* were trained and prepared for their service. This training involved practice in offering sacrifices – i.e., the *kohahim* were trained as servants or workers. After the inauguration of the *Mishkan*, the *kohanim* were also commanded to be teachers and instructors, responsible for the impurities of the Children of Israel and guarding the *Mishkan* from such impurities: "To teach when it is impure and when it is pure" (14:57); "And you shall separate the Children of Israel from their impurity" (15:31).

Seemingly, the prohibition against inebriation, commanded to Aaron, likewise arises not from the death of Nadav and Avihu, but rather from the obligation of the *kohanim* to instruct, such that they cannot be drunk: "And to distinguish between the holy and the profane, and between the impure and the pure" (10:10).

The above analysis also leads to the conclusion that the unit discussing forbidden foods is, first and foremost, a unit describing the impurity of those who eat these things; the specifications of the forbidden foods themselves are only a secondary matter here, since the unit belongs to the section addressing the different forms of impurity. At this point there is a clear difference between the chapters of forbidden foods in Leviticus, and their parallels in Deuteronomy (a full treatment of this point is beyond the scope of this essay).

Chapter 16, dealing with the entry of the *Kohen Gadol* into the Holy of Holies, serves two functions. On the one hand, it concludes the episode of the death of Nadav and Avihu and the fears which that event aroused. On the other hand, it concludes the laws of impurities, by means of the general act of atonement for them that is connected to the *Kohen Gadol*'s entry: "And he shall atone for the holy place because of the impurities of the Children of Israel, and because of their transgressions in all of their sins." The essence of chapter 16 is not the details of Yom Kippur, but the atonement for impurities. The command concerning Yom Kippur appears only at the section's end, while the general atonement for sins is almost a fringe benefit, associated with the original context of Aaron's entry into the Holy of Holies, namely, atonement for impurities.

We can now comment on the units that we have skipped, which appear to have been dislodged from their proper place (item numbers refer to the numbering in the scheme above).

Items 5–9 (chapters 6–7): This section contains the laws of the sacrifices, from the point of view of the *kohen*'s role. This section originated at Mount Sinai, and was conveyed – as testified at the end of the section – together with the command concerning the days of consecration. The reason for this is clear – the purpose of the days of consecration is to prepare the *kohanim*, through training and practice, to perform the sacrificial service; therefore, they need to be commanded in advance concerning the details of their service. From this perspective, the command precedes the building of the *Mishkan*, like all the commands that anticipate the *Mishkan* and its service, which belong in Exodus. These chapters are inserted here because Exodus does not deal with the offering of sacrifices at all. The Torah chooses to forego their proper chronological place, preferring to include this list of laws of sacrifices, meant for the *kohanim*, along with a parallel list that discusses the same sacrifices from the perspective of the Israelite who offers them (chapters 1–5), so as to treat all the laws of sacrifices together.

In item 11 (chapter 10), Aaron is commanded concerning the prohibition of wine. This command is inserted in the middle of the narrative about the eighth day, since it is followed – in item 12 – by certain elements that complete the eighth day. Why does the Torah not first finish the narrative, and only then present the prohibition against wine for the *kohanim*? We have already noted that the wine prohibition serves as a sort of introduction to all the chapters addressing the special role of the *kohanim* in the sphere of ritual impurity. If the Torah chooses to place this command to Aaron in the middle of the eighth day, apparently it seeks to relate the prohibition to the event that takes place on that day and to the suspicion that entering the holy place while drunk brings death. It is this juxtaposition that leads Ḥazal to conclude that Nadav and Avihu were punished for entering the *Mishkan* while drunk, since otherwise there would be no need for the Torah to create this break in the middle of the narrative.

Item 20 (chapter 17), dealing with the prohibition against blood, is not part of the preceding units, nor is it part of those that follow. It addresses prohibitions and obligations related to sacrifices and the Tent of Meeting, but also other obligations – such as covering the blood and the prohibition against eating blood – which apply outside of the *Mishkan* too. From the introduction at the beginning of chapter 18, it would appear that the main body of laws begins only after this unit. What, then, is the role of this unit here? It would appear to serve as a sort of bridge between the first three sections of the book, all of which involve – in some sense or other – the *Mishkan* (sacrifices, the days of consecration, impurities) and the rest of the book, which covers statutes and laws that apply throughout the land. The prohibition against sacrificing meat slaughtered outside of the *Mishkan* defines the obligation of serving God through sacrifice only within the *Mishkan*. However, it also connects to more general prohibitions that are not related to the *Mishkan*, but rather to other values – "For the blood is the soul." Since these prohibitions straddle the *Mishkan* precincts and what lies outside of it, the Torah places them in between the first part of the book (the first three sections), dealing with the *Mishkan*, and the second part, dealing with the rest of the territory of Israel.

What is item 36 (chapters 25–26, the section on the Sabbatical and Jubilee years, and the covenant) doing here? The Torah wants the covenant with the blessings and curses, forged at Mount Sinai, to be included along with the lists of laws in Leviticus, even though chronologically those laws were conveyed later on. Therefore, the conclusion of the covenant appears at the end of Leviticus, rather than in Exodus.

Finally, unit 37 (chapter 27), which deals with items dedicated to the *Mishkan*, was also commanded at Mount Sinai. Why is it located here? It would seem that since the subject of this unit is gifts given voluntarily, it is not part of the covenant, all of which is obligatory. Its connection with the subject of *Shemitta* arises from internal halakhic reasons. The calculation of the value of a field that is to be dedicated is dependent on the time remaining until the Jubilee year. Hence, this unit in fact belongs to the laws of Jubilee, which were listed in the preceding unit (chapter 25). However, as mentioned, since the issue here is not an obligation, these laws are separated from the other laws of the Jubilee year (which are included within the covenant), and are appended afterwards.

Sacrifice and Atonement

Rav Avraham Walfish

L eviticus marks a departure from the narrative flow of the Torah through its first two books. The conclusion of Exodus seems to look forward towards Numbers. Concluding the construction of the *Mishkan* with a description of the divine cloud hovering over it, as the Divine Glory fills the Tent of Meeting, the Torah devotes the three final verses of Exodus (40:36–38) to the role of the divine cloud in the travels of the people through the wilderness:

> And when the cloud went up from above the *Mishkan*, the Children of Israel would journey, for all their journeys. And if the cloud would not go up, they would not journey, until the day of its going up. For the cloud of God was upon the *Mishkan* during the day, and fire was there at night, before the eyes of the Children of Israel in all their journeys.

These verses, in fact, are echoed and expanded in Numbers 9:15–23, which serve as a keynote for one of the dominant themes of Numbers, the journey through the wilderness. Seen from this vantage point, the immediate continuation of the end of Exodus is the command, at the beginning of Numbers, to conduct a census, in order to ready the people for their journey towards the promised land (see Rashbam to Num. 1:2). Accordingly we would view Leviticus as a non-narrative interlude between the end of Exodus and the beginning of Numbers.

What is the reason for this interlude, which interrupts the narrative flow of the Torah? Ramban, in his introduction to Leviticus, explains that the commandments of Leviticus are a direct outgrowth of the end of Exodus. The laws concerning sacrifices are the logical continuation of the presence of the *Shekhina* (Divine Presence) in the midst of the people. We may advance textual support for this idea from the wording of the first verse: "[He] called to Moses." Why does the Torah diverge from the normal introductory formula, "God spoke to Moses," by adding the call? The answer to both questions is implicit in the final verses of Exodus, as noted by Ramban on the first verse of Leviticus:

> Scripture says here "[He] called to Moses and God spoke to him," unlike other passages, because Moses was unable to enter the Tent of Meeting [see Ex. 40:35] in order to approach a place where God is present [based on Ex. 20:21] except through being called.

The relationship between the presence of the *Shekhina* and sacrifices may be understood in one of two ways. One is that "sacrifices atone for the people, hence iniquities will not cause the departure of the *Shekhina*" (Ramban, Introduction to Leviticus). A second is that sacrifices may be understood as a positive expression of the relationship between Israel and the *Shekhina* that dwells in their midst. Rav Samson Raphael Hirsch noted that this is the real, literal meaning of the term *korban* (sacrifice): "The *makriv* (he who brings the sacrifice) desires that something of himself should come into closer relationship to God, that is what his *korban* is, and the procedure by which this greater nearness to God is to be achieved is called *hakrava*."[1] Rav David Zvi Hoffmann, in his introduction to Leviticus,[2] writes:

---

1. Rav Hirsch complains that the common translation of *korban* as "sacrifice" is misleading, and distorts the true meaning of the word, which is based on a root meaning "close."
2. *Sefer Vayikra with Commentary by David Zvi Hoffmann* [Hebrew], trans. Zvi Har-Sheffer and Aharon Lieberman (Jerusalem: Mosad Harav Kook, 1976), vol. I, 64.

The sacrificial service is bound up internally with human awareness of God. As soon as man became aware that there is a Supreme
Being in whose hands his entire existence was placed, he immediately felt an inner desire to recognize this Supreme Being as his
master and to give this recognition concrete expression, namely:
first through words, and subsequently, as his emotions intensified
and pressed to erupt into concrete expression, also through palpable and vigorous actions, and not only through evanescent words.

Of course nobody disputes that some sacrifices, such as *ḥatat*
and *asham*, are designed to expiate sins. These sacrifices, however, are
brought as a response to sin, either, in the case of the individual, when
he knows he has sinned, or, in the case of most communal sin offerings,
because we presume that someone in the community must have sinned.
The issue we are investigating is whether voluntary sacrifices, such as *ola*
and *shelamim*, are also designed for the sake of expiation.

Rav Hoffmann supports his understanding of *korban* by sur-
veying the history of sacrifices through Genesis: Cain and Abel (Gen.
4:3–5, *ola* and *minḥa*), Noah (8:20–21, *ola*), Abraham (22:1–13, *ola*),
Jacob (31:54, 46:1, *zevaḥ* = *shelamim*). In none of these cases does the
sacrifice appear to serve as a means of atonement. These sacrifices seem
rather to express in positive and concrete fashion aspects of the God-
man relationship.

The opinion of Ramban, however, is also grounded in scriptural
evidence. Some commentators have proposed understandings of sacrifice similar to Ramban's, in order to explicate those perplexing verses,
such as Jeremiah 7:22–23, Psalms 40:7, which declare that God is not
interested in sacrifices and did not command to bring them. Radak, for
example (Ps. 40:7), explains:

> For the initial commandments of God to Israel were only that
> they should hearken to His voice … and when they began to sin,
> He commanded them regarding the sacrifices: individual sacri-
> fices for the specific sinners and communal sacrifices, such as the
> daily *tamid* offering, because it is inconceivable that there not be
> among all of Israel many sinners daily, many of whom will not

know what they themselves ought to sacrifice, hence the communal sacrifices will atone for them when they repent their sins.

But in order to support Ramban it is not necessary to cast our net as far as Jeremiah or Psalms. I believe Ramban's view is grounded in the language used by our *parasha* to describe the first of the voluntary sacrifices, the *ola*: "And he shall lean his hand (*vesamakh*) on the head of the *ola* and it shall be acceptable for him (*nirtza lo*) to expiate on his behalf (*lekhapper alav*)" (1:4). The term *ratzon*, and especially the term *lekhapper*, would seem to indicate that the function even of this voluntary sacrifice is to expiate. *Ḥazal* indeed assume that the *ola* serves to expiate. According to the Sifra (4:8), the *ola* atones for positive commandments and negative commandments which may be remedied by positive action. According to R. Shimon b. Yoḥai (Leviticus Rabba 7:3), the *ola* atones for improper thoughts.

We may wonder, however, why the Torah does not specify the sin for which the *ola* is meant as expiation. Other sacrifices, such as *ḥatat* and *asham*, have a clear object of atonement. See, for example: 4:21, 26, 31, 35; 5:10, 13, 18, 26. There are however instances where the *kappara* of other sacrifices also seems to be non-specific in nature. See, for example, Numbers 8:12, where the process of consecrating the *levi'im* for their role in the *Mishkan* service includes a *ḥatat* as well as an *ola* "to expiate for the *levi'im*." The term *kappara* also appears in the context of sacrifices which are designed to purify, rather than to atone for sins. See, for example, 15:15, 30.

In order to determine whether the function of *kappara* indeed supports the understanding of sacrifices as a response to sin, we need to examine the etymology of the term. There are three explanations traditionally suggested for the root:

1. "It would appear to me that all uses of *kappara* in the context of iniquity and sin...are all in the sense of wiping and removal, as in the Aramaic usage" (Rashi, Gen. 32:20).
2. "The meaning of 'wiping' for *kippur* is not Hebrew, but only Aramaic usage...for *kappara* never relates to the *sin*, but [Scripture] will say 'to expiate for their *souls*' (Ex. 30:15)...and they are all

[based on] the usage 'and each man shall give *kofer* for his soul' (Ex. 30:12), meaning redemption" (Ramban, Gen. 32:20).

3. "The literal meaning of *akhappera panav* is – I shall cover his face" (Rav Hoffmann, Gen. 32:21).

J. Milgrom (*Anchor Bible – Leviticus*, pp. 1079 ff.) sums up the etymological evidence regarding the verb *kipper*.

In biblical poetry its parallel synonym is usually *maḥa*, wipe (Jer. 18:23), or *hesir*, remove (Isa. 27:9), suggesting that *kipper* means purge…. Other poetic passages will use *kipper* in parallel to *kissa*, cover (Neh. 3:37), giving the contrary notion that *kipper* connotes smearing on a new substance instead of effacing an existent one. Philologists have been divided on the etymology, because evidence from Semitic cognates can be cited in support of either connotation, mainly from Arabic (cover) and Akkadian (wipe). Yet both meanings may go back to a common notion – rub. Because a substance may be rubbed on or rubbed off, the derived meanings, wipe and cover, may be complementary and not contradictory…. The purgation of the impurities from a person…requires the elimination of the wiping material…. This leads to the phenomenon of the substitute or ransom…. This notion of the *kipper* substitute is clearly represented in the Bible in the cases of the scapegoat (16:10, 21–22) and the broken-necked heifer (Deut. 21:1–9).

Which of these meanings of *kipper* best corresponds to the function of the *ola* offering? The key to answering this question lies in the text which served most of the commentators cited above as the base text for their interpretations, the first appearance of this verb in the Torah. Genesis 32–33, in describing the encounter of Jacob with Esau and Jacob's painstaking preparations for their meeting, utilizes several terms which are associated with the sacrificial service: *minḥa* (gift – 13, 18, 20, etc.), *kappara* (20), *ratzon* (33:10), *re'iyyat panim* ("seeing the face" = meeting, encountering – 20, 33:10; compare Ex. 33:17 and parallels), *yissa panai* (20; this term concludes the priestly blessing – Numbers 6:26 – which is associated with the sacrificial service: Lev. 9:22–23; Mishna Tamid 5:1).

The association of encountering Esau with bringing of sacrifices is not accidental, as is clearly indicated by two verses spoken by Jacob. In the second of these verses, 33:10, Jacob implores Esau to accept his *minḥa* because "I have seen your face, as one who sees the face of *Elokim* and you have accepted me (*vatirtzeni*)." *Elokim* here is purposefully ambiguous: Does Jacob mean a powerful man (Onkelos), as Esau is sure to understand it, or does he mean a divine being, as those who have read the account of Jacob's nocturnal wrestling match are likely to assume? The latter understanding is further supported by the earlier 32:30, in which Jacob explains the name Peni'el: "for I have seen *Elokim* face to face and my life was saved." When Jacob addresses Esau, he alludes to a private meaning of *re'iyyat penei Elokim* which only he – and the reader – understand, whereas Esau cannot appreciate it. Only Jacob – and the reader – know that the real point of Jacob's encounter with Esau goes beyond reconciliation with the brother from whom the blessing of Isaac was stolen. The point is to re-obtain the blessing, legitimately and above dispute. Hence the wrestling match concludes with Jacob demanding and receiving the angelic blessing, a blessing which includes a name change in which the name associated with the theft of the original blessing (Jacob suggests trickery, see Gen. 27:36) is replaced by a new name, Israel, suggesting a legitimate struggle and a legitimate victory (32:28). And Jacob-Israel subtly alludes to this underlying purpose in his colloquy with Esau: "Please take my *berakha* (gift – punning on the word for blessing) which I have brought you" (33:11).

The key term in this passage is the frequently-repeated *re'iyyat panim*, which designates the appearance of a supplicant before his superior. The rest of the terminology used divides into two parts, the preparation for *re'iyyat panim* and the desired outcome of the *re'iyyat panim*. In preparation for *re'iyyat panim*, the supplicant offers a *minḥa*, a tribute which expresses his awareness of dependence upon his superior. This *minḥa* facilitates *kappara*, without which the supplicant dare not enter the presence of his powerful, and potentially dangerous, superior. The purpose of the encounter with the superior is to obtain *ratzon*, favor, in order that the superior favor the supplicant with his *berakha*, blessing.

How, then, will we understand the concept of *kappara*? In the case of Jacob, there is a wrong to be expiated (at least from Esau's perspective).

However, the idea of offering a tribute in order to be allowed into the presence of a superior certainly is not restricted to cases where the subject has wronged his lord. If the tribute is always associated with *kappara*, then we may assume that *kappara* comes, not in order to remedy a specific wrong, but rather to render the offerer of the tribute acceptable in the eyes of his lord. Perhaps the idea may be understood by recognizing that the supplicant, mindful of his inferior position (a consciousness much keener in monarchic societies than in modern democracies), feels unworthy of entering the presence of his lord. He fears that his lord will perceive his entry as brazen audacity. The tribute is meant to express his awareness of this anomaly, to reinforce the correct perception of the encounter as a meeting of unequals.

The encounter and dialogue between man and God, while possessing a uniquely transcendent and numinous character, is usually patterned on models of analogous human encounters: subject-king, child-parent, bride-bridegroom. We have already noted the analogy alluded to in the Jacob-Esau encounter, between *re'iyyat panim* of a subject before his lord, and the *re'iyyat panim* of a man before God. This analogy is reinforced by a well-known passage in the prophet Malachi (1:8): "And when you bring a blind animal to sacrifice, there is nothing bad, and when we bring a lame or sick animal there is nothing bad – kindly offer it to your governor, will he receive you favorably (*yirtzekha*) or will he accept you (*yissa panekha*)?"

The terms *kappara* and *ratzon*, associated with the *ola*, suggest that the main function of the *ola* relates to *re'iyyat panim*. The worshiper aspires to enter the Divine Presence, hence he brings a tributary offering before his Lord. The model for this form of religious performance is the mitzva of *re'iyya*, performed on the three pilgrimage festivals. In Exodus 34:23 we are taught that the pilgrimage, the appearance before God, is based on the fact that He is our Lord and Master – "*yera'eh et penei ha'adon,*" "shall appear before the Master, God of Israel." In Deuteronomy 16:16 we are instructed, "And you shall not encounter My presence (*yera'u panai*) empty-handed." Ḥazal learned from here the requirement of offering the *olat re'iyya*, the obligatory *ola* offering that each pilgrim must bring when he enters the *Beit HaMikdash* to encounter his God. The voluntary *ola* may be seen as a spontaneous pursuit of the same goal. The Jew who aspires to enter the Divine Presence, mindful of the awesome nature of this encounter, painfully aware that his human inadequacies render such an aspiration anomalous if not blasphemous, utilizes a tributary offering to achieve *kappara*. The *kappara* may be seen as cleansing the supplicant, as a protective screen between him and the awesome Divine Presence, or as a ransom which stays the wrath which may be expected to ensue from human trespass into the realm of the divine. One way or the other, the purpose of the *kappara* is not to expiate a particular sin, but to facilitate the encounter of the worshiper with his Creator, Judge, and Redeemer.

We have seen two models for understanding the connection between the end of Exodus and the beginning of Leviticus. According to Ramban's model, the Divine Presence achieved at the end of Exodus is volatile and easily lost; hence the need for sacrifices to ensure the continuity of the *Shekhina*. According to Rav Hirsch and Rav Hoffmann, the Divine Presence dwelling in the midst of the people beckons to each and every Israelite. The approach to this Presence is an awesome opportunity and responsibility, requiring sacrifices which give palpable expression to the paradox as well as the spiritual significance of this encounter.

The Meal Offering

Rav Yonatan Grossman

Parashat Vayikra describes three types of voluntary sacrifices, i.e., sacrifices which a person decides of his own free will to bring to the Mishkan. The various options open to a person wishing to bring a voluntary sacrifice are the burnt offering (*ola,* chapter 1), the meal offering (*minḥa,* chapter 2) or the peace offering (*shelamim,* chapter 3). While the *ola* and *shelamim* are animal sacrifices, the *minḥa* is not: "his offering shall be of fine flour (*solet*)" (2:1).

The literary style of the Torah is such that a general rule is usually followed by various details pertaining to that general rule. The formulation is usually in the form of "*ki* (when – יִּ) ... *im* (if – אִם)..." In other words, the general rule opens with the word "*ki,*" and the details are introduced with the word "*im.*" An outstanding example of this is to be found in *Parashat Mishpatim,* where there are several general laws (*ki*) followed by a list of possible specific cases (*im*); for example:

> When (*ki*) you buy a Hebrew servant, he shall labor for six years, and in the seventh he shall go out free, for nothing.

If (*im*) he came in [to servitude] by himself, he shall leave by himself.

If (*im*) he is married, his wife shall leave with him.

If (*im*) his master gave him a wife and she bore him sons or daughters, the wife and her children will be her master's, and he will go out by himself.

And if (*im*) the servant should say.... (Ex. 21:2–5)

A similar phenomenon is to be found in *Parashat Vayikra*, where the Torah again supplies a general introduction using the word "*ki*," and then lists details beginning with "*im*." Thus we find at the beginning of the *parasha* dealing with the sacrifices:

When (*ki*) a person from among you brings a sacrifice to God, from the cattle – from the herd and from the flock – shall you bring your sacrifice.

If (*im*) his sacrifice is a burnt offering (*ola*)...

And if (*im*) his sacrifice is from the flocks – from the sheep or from the goats, as a burnt offering...

And if (*im*) his burnt offering to God is from the birds....

The general introduction deals with a person who wishes to bring an animal sacrifice, and thereafter the text lists the various options available to this person. The first possibility is that of an *ola*, which itself is further subdivided – it may be "from the cattle," "from the flock," or "from the birds."

Now the reader expects to find further options for animal sacrifices, since otherwise the introduction, "When a person from among you brings a sacrifice to God, from the cattle," is not appropriate as a general introduction, but rather represents a single individual law (*ola*) that stands on its own. Indeed, the continuation of the list of possibilities for animal sacrifices is resumed at the beginning of chapter 3:

And if (*im*) his sacrifice is a peace offering:

If (*im*) he offers it from the herd...

And if (*im*) his offering is from the flock....

Thus, there are two categories of possibilities from which the person wishing to offer an animal sacrifice may choose, either an *ola* (burnt offering) or *shelamim* (peace offering).

However, the order of the different sacrifices is not as we would have expected. After the laws pertaining to the *ola* in chapter 1, the text – surprisingly enough – goes on to discuss the *minḥa* (chapter 2). This sacrifice cannot represent an additional instance that falls under the general introduction with which the *parasha* of the sacrifices began, because the introduction specifically refers to animal sacrifices, while the *minḥa* is a sacrifice offered from grain!

This is further substantiated by the fact that the *minḥa* opens with its own, new introduction ("*ki*"):

And when (*ki*) a person offers a *minḥa* sacrifice to God, his offering shall be of fine flour. (2:1)

Without doubt, this introduction is meant to serve as a parallel to the previous one, with which the animal sacrifices began:

When (*ki*) a person from among you brings a sacrifice to God, from the cattle – from the herd and from the flock – shall you bring your sacrifice. (1:2)

Chapter 2, then, starts with its own independent introduction, since the Torah is now going to discuss a meal offering, while the original introduction prepared us for animal sacrifices. Why, then, does the text interrupt its discussion of animal sacrifices and start a new discussion concerning the flour offering, and only thereafter return to continue with another animal sacrifice – the *zevaḥ shelamim*, which complements the *ola*? This is Abarbanel's ninth question on our *parasha*:

Why does the Torah discuss the laws of the *minḥa* in all its varieties prior to the *shelamim*? After all, since the *shelamim* are taken from the cattle or from the herds, we would have thought that they should be commanded prior to the *minḥa*.

I shall follow the lead of Rav David Zvi Hoffmann with regard to this question. Malbim explains that apparently the *minha* is mentioned in close proximity with the *ola* because of the internal connection between them. The defining characteristic of the *ola* is that it is completely burned on the altar. Rav Hoffmann shows that essentially the *minha*, like the *ola*, is offered in its entirety to God, but God decides to give of it to His servants, the *kohanim*. The *kohanim* eating of the sacrifice is another form of being offered to God. We learn this from the law of a special *minha* of which the *kohanim* are forbidden to partake – the meal offering of the *kohen*.

> It is a statute forever to God; it shall be entirely burnt. And every meal offering of the *kohen* shall be entirely burnt; it shall not be eaten. (6:15–16)

If, for whatever reason, the *kohanim* do not eat their portion of the *minha* sacrifice, then the *minha* is offered in its entirety to God, just like the *ola*.

This law is especially interesting when compared with that of another sacrifice in similar circumstances (i.e., where the *kohanim* are prevented from consuming their expected portion), where the sacrifice is not burnt in its entirety (like the *minha* of the *kohen*), but rather the portion usually set aside for the *kohen* is burnt outside of the camp. This is the law of the inner *hatat* sacrifices, which, because their blood is brought into the inner sanctum, are forbidden to be eaten, and the meat, normally eaten by the *kohanim*, is therefore burnt outside of the camp (4:12, 21).

Thus we may conclude that the *minha* is essentially meant to be burnt in its entirety on the altar, even if the *kohanim* usually eat part of it.

In light of this, we can understand another law that appears in the *parasha* of the *minha*. The law regulating the eating of the sacrifices by the *kohanim* or – in the case of the *shelamim* – by the person who brings the sacrifice, always appears only in the second listing of the sacrifices, in *Parashat Tzav*. The *minha* is an exception to this rule, concerning which we are told already in *Parashat Vayikra* that a portion of it is eaten by the *kohanim*. Perhaps the Torah sees fit to explain how it happens that the *kohanim* eat of a sacrifice that is supposed to be offered in its entirety to God. The explanation is formulated as follows:

> And that which remains of the *minha* is for Aaron and his sons; it is a holy of holies of the offerings made by fire to God. (2:3, 10)

Although the *kohanim* eat of the *minha*, it is still to be regarded as having been offered entirely to God, and the *kohanim* are given the privilege of eating "from God's table," as it were.

Indeed, the *minha* is often juxtaposed with the *ola*, with the *shelamim* sometimes presented in contrast. Thus, for example, in the story of the altar built by the children of Reuben, Gad, and the half-tribe of Manasseh: "or to offer a burnt offering or a meal offering upon it, or to offer peace offerings upon it" (Josh. 22:23) – the *ola* and *minha* on the one hand, the *shelamim* on the other.

Because of this connection between the *ola* and *minha*, the text juxtaposes these two sacrifices even though the *minha* does not fall under the first heading, which deals specifically with animal sacrifices.

A similar idea is presented by Abarbanel (2:1):

> The *minha* offerings are mentioned prior to the *shelamim* for two reasons: In order to prioritize the levels of the *ola*… and the *minha* is among them; therefore after mentioning the *ola* from the cattle, which is the most superior, and the *ola* of the flocks which is the next level, and then the *ola* of the birds which is after that, the Torah mentions the *minha which is also an ola* and its level is one lower than that of the *ola* of the birds, since an animal of any type is superior to a meal sacrifice. But the *shelamim* are not an *ola*, and therefore they are mentioned last.

The essential connection between these two sacrifices turns on the intention of the person who offers them. Each involves an attitude of complete sacrifice before the Almighty, a psychological sense of unworthiness to stand before God – an attitude of honor and awe.

The *ola* contains a note of atonement even though it is a free-will offering: "it shall be accepted for him to atone for him" (1:4). This is the impression we gain from the *ola* sacrifices offered by Job for his children: "for Job said, Perhaps my children have sinned, and have cursed God in their hearts" (Job 1:5).

At the same time, there appears to be a fundamental difference between the *ola* and the *minha* (in contrast with Abarbanel's proposition that they are to be considered identical). The hint at the difference between them is to be found in the two introductions. In the case of the *ola*, the Torah begins with the words, "*adam ki yakriv*" (literally, "a person, when he offers"), while the *minha* opens with the words, "*venefesh ki yakriv*" (literally, "a soul, when he offers"). Hazal note this discrepancy:

> For what reason is the [introduction to the] *minha* changed, to say *nefesh*? The Holy One said: Who is it who usually brings a *minha*? A poor person. I will [therefore] consider it as though he sacrifices his soul (*nefesh*) before Me. (Menahot 104b)

The discrepancy in the introduction may also hint at something else. In the context of sacrifices, the term *nefesh* has a clear association:

> For the life (*nefesh*) of the flesh is in the blood, and I have given it to you upon the altar to atone for your souls (*nafshotekhem*), for it is the blood that makes atonement for the soul (*nefesh*). (Lev. 17:11)

"*Nefesh*" expresses the life itself, embodied in the blood – including the blood of the *ola* that is offered upon the altar. We may propose that in the case of those sacrifices whose blood is offered, we cannot speak of a *nefesh* offering the sacrifice, since the *nefesh* (or at least that which symbolizes it) is sacrificed on the altar. However, in the case of the *minha*, where there is no blood – i.e., the *nefesh* is not offered upon the altar – we may say that it is the *nefesh* which offers the sacrifice.

In other words, by the act of sacrificing an animal the worshiper declares that his life, his very existence, belongs to his Maker, and therefore he offers a life upon the altar. By offering a *minha* he is declaring something not about his life but rather about his food and his other vital needs. A person brings his meal to the *Mishkan*, adds oil (a symbol of wealth) and *levona* (a symbol of contentment, according to some of the commentaries) and declares that all of this does not belong to him and he is not worthy of it, and therefore he brings it to its true owner – the Master of the Universe.

This idea also finds expression in the quantity of fine flour that is always required for a *minḥa* offering – a tenth of an *eifa*. This quantity apparently represents a person's food for one day. This may be deduced from the story of the manna, where the Children of Israel are required to take an *omer* per person each day (Ex. 16:16). At the end of that description we read, "And the *omer* is a tenth of an *eifa*" (Ex. 16:36) – teaching us that a person's food for one day is a tenth of an *eifa*. Rashi immediately comments on the connection with the *minḥa*: "A tenth of an *eifa*... and that is the set quantity for *ḥalla* and for *minḥa* offerings" (commentary ibid.). There seems to be a profound connection between the descent of the manna – God providing food for man – and the *minḥa* offering, where man "gives" food upon the altar. In any event, by bringing a *minḥa* a person offers his daily bread to its true owner – God.

In summary, the *minḥa* offering appears immediately after the laws of the *ola* because of the close connection between them – a connection related to the religious declaration that accompanies each of these, in which the person expresses his sense of unworthiness of all the good that God is showering upon him. The religious feeling that is expressed in the *ola* pertains to the person's very existence, namely that he feels that his life is not his own, and he sacrifices a "life" – a "soul" – upon the altar. In contrast – or perhaps as a continuation – the sentiment that finds expression in the *minḥa* pertains to a person's needs – his food and physical welfare. He symbolically brings these to the altar as a declaration that he is unworthy of them, and that God is their true owner.

The Significance of Haktara

Rav Ezra Bick

Parashat Vayikra opens with a concise list of instructions on how to sacrifice the different types of sacrifices – *ola, minḥa, shelamim,* and *ḥatat*. Leaving aside the *minḥa*, which is an offering from the vegetative world, a cursory examination of the animal sacrifices reveals that there are two different climaxes to the sacrificial procedure. Taking the first section in the *parasha* as an indicative example (1:3–9), verse 5, after commanding to slaughter the animal, directs the *kohen* to "sprinkle the blood all around on the altar, which is at the entrance of the Tent of Meeting." The *kohen* then returns to the animal, dissects it, and finally (verse 9) we are told that the *kohen* should burn (*vehiktir*) the animal on the altar as an offering which will be "*rei'aḥ niḥo'aḥ laShem.*"

Bringing a sacrifice has two distinct halakhic goals, *zerikat hadam* (sprinkling the blood), and *hekter eivarim* (burning the flesh).

Halakhically, there is an important difference between the two. Sprinkling the blood is a necessary condition for the fulfillment of the obligation that the sacrifice is representing; in other words, if the blood is not sprinkled, the sacrifice is disqualified and another one must be brought. That is not true for the burning of the flesh on the altar. Specifically, the blood is associated with the concept of *kappara*, expiation.

This is the basis for the idea, advanced by Ramban at the beginning of the *parasha*, as well as many other commentators and philosophers, that the blood of the sacrifice represents the life of him who brings the sacrifice, with the sacrifice vicariously substituting for the person. The Torah's identification of blood with life (*"ki nefesh habasar badam hu"* – "for the life of the flesh is in the blood," Lev. 17:11; also v. 14) supports this idea. It would be easy to conclude, based on the many sections in Tractate Zevaḥim that discuss the importance of sprinkling the blood, that the main goal of sacrifices is the blood, and therefore it is in the ritual of sprinkling the blood that one should find the meaning and purpose of sacrifices.

However, I believe it is fair to say that outside of the framework of Tractate Zevaḥim most of us instinctively think of sacrifices as meat burnt on an altar. For the same reason, it is natural to understand the definition of an altar in the same manner – a structure designed for the burning of sacrifices. Sacrifices described in the Torah outside of the halakhic framework – such as those offered by Noah (Gen. 8:2) and Jacob (46:1) – do not mention sprinkling blood. Strikingly, in our *parasha*, a subtle but nonetheless distinctive emphasis focuses on the burning of the flesh. Whereas the blood is mentioned in the middle of a series of procedures (in verse 5), the burning of the flesh on the altar is left for last, and is itself characterized with the summary phrase *"ola, isheh, rei'aḥ niḥo'aḥ laShem."* It is the burning of the flesh that, apparently, is what gives this particular sacrifice its name – *ola* means that all of the animal is "elevated," i.e., burnt. Being burnt, a *korban* is called *"isheh,"* which Ramban explains means "burnt." And finally, the *korban* is *"rei'aḥ niḥo'aḥ"* – a pleasant fragrance – which of course refers to the burning flesh. More importantly, this phrase, especially its last part, appears to be defining the importance and effect of the sacrifice. While the exact import of the phrase *"rei'aḥ niḥo'aḥ"* is unclear, it definitely implies that the *korban* finds favor in God's eyes, and the fact that the phrase is tied to the burning of the flesh indicates that *hekter eivarim* is the vehicle of achieving that end.

Therefore, I would like to concentrate on that aspect of sacrifices, the burning of parts of the flesh on the altar. The verse reads, "And the *kohen* shall burn it all on the altar." The Hebrew word which is here translated as "burn" is *vehiktir* – וְהִקְטִיר. What does this word actually mean?

The answer to this question seems to me today to be so obvious that I hesitated to write about it. However, when I first realized the correct answer, it changed my understanding of *korbanot*. Since then, I have repeatedly discussed this word with respected scholars, and what I now consider to be the correct interpretation has nearly always surprised them. So I will proceed, and I ask forgiveness from anyone who will find it all simple and obvious.

In all the traditional translations of the Torah into English, both Jewish and non-Jewish, this word was translated as "burn." Practically speaking, that is indeed what the Torah is telling the *kohen* to do – those parts designated for the altar are burnt in fire. The usual word for "burn" in biblical Hebrew, however, is *saraf* (שׂרף), and therefore it is important to understand the specific meaning of the alternative word "*hiktir*" used in this verse – and in every other one describing what is done with the flesh of a sacrifice.

One day, several years ago, I noticed a book about Leviticus in the library and began to read it. On the first page, the book quoted a verse (in English). I generally need to translate the verse into Hebrew in order to recognize it; but, in this particular case, I did not recognize the verse at all. Luckily, there was a reference note, and, after looking it up, I discovered that it was the familiar verse which we are discussing, Leviticus 1:9. The reason why I had not immediately recognized it was because I had never before seen the phrase "turn into smoke" in this context. A quick bit of research led me to the discovery that most of the newer Jewish translations of the Torah translate "*hiktir*" as "turn into smoke," which is the starting point for our discussion.

First, a reverse question. Why does the Torah not write that the *kohen* should *soreif* (burn) the flesh? I think that a short reflection indicates why that would be inappropriate. Meat of a sacrifice that has been "left over" (*notar*) beyond the allotted time is "burnt" – "*vehanotar... yissaref.*" You would never say that *notar* should be *niktar*. The reason is that *lisrof* – to burn – is a negative action – you burn something to get rid of it. Similarly, no one would describe what we do to *ḥametz* before Pesaḥ as *haktara*, precisely because it has no positive aspect. *Lehaktir* is a positive action, and it will often have a participle, as in *lehaktir laShem*. In our minds, *lehaktir* means to sacrifice, or to offer, and of course one does not sacrifice *notar*; one gets rid of it. For the same reason, one does not "burn" sacrifices, since the purpose is not to get rid of the flesh, but to "offer" it to God in some sense. *Haktara* has a positive sense of moving the object forward; *sereifa* has the opposite sense of negating its existence.

So what does the word *haktara* actually mean? The new translations are based on the belief that the root *k-t-r* (ק.ט.ר.) means "smoke." This is true in Aramaic, where smoke is called *kutra*. In modern Hebrew, *kitor* means steam, which is a sort of smoke. In ancient Hebrew, *ketoret* is incense, something burnt in order to make a fragrant smell.

So, I think it is correct to state that the word "*hiktir*" actually means "turn to smoke." It does mean to burn, but in the positive sense of *transformation* by fire and not in the negative sense of *elimination* by fire. There is a result of the burning which is productive – smoke, rather than merely a negative one – destruction.

There is another use of the verb *lehaktir* in the *Mishkan*, and that is in connection with the incense burnt every day. In that framework, we understand why the Torah is interested in turning certain ingredients into smoke. The smoke is the intended result, since it is the smoke which produces the fragrance. But why is this verb used here? Are we in fact interested in the smoke that comes from the burning of the sacrifice?

It appears to me that if sacrificing an animal is characterized as turning the flesh into smoke, the inner meaning of this action is turning the physical into the spiritual. The physics of gases and combustion aside, for the biblical and rabbinic mind, smoke is a symbol of the spiritual. This is clear from the very word used in philosophical Hebrew to indicate the spiritual – "*ruaḥ*," which is the same word as wind. (This reflects the use of the Greek word *pneuma* for the same purpose, and is carried on in the English spirit as well.) In the verse under discussion, this is clearly indicated by the concluding phrase "*rei'aḥ niḥo'aḥ*." *Rei'aḥ* – fragrance – is of course closely related to *ruaḥ* – spirit. Ramban here quotes the statement of the angel who met Manoah telling him that if he is offered meat to eat, he will refuse, but if the goat is sacrificed to God, then he will partake – by joining the flame (smoke) rising in the air. Ramban is comparing eating, which is a physical action and is therefore

inappropriate for the angel (and of course, for God as well), with *rei'aḥ* –
with smelling, which is taken to be a spiritual activity, the enjoyment
of the soul rather than that of the body.[3] Meat is the food of the body;
the smoke, as the vehicle of *rei'aḥ niḥo'aḥ*, is the sustenance of the soul.
In other words, *haktara* is the process by which we convert the ultimate
symbol of the physical, flesh and meat, into the ultimate symbol of the
spiritual, smoke rising towards the heaven.

Expanding this concept a little bit, the significance of this process can be explained as follows. The central problem of the relationship between Man and God is the infinite gap that exists between them,
between the perfect and the decadent, between the absolute and the
relative, between the eternally divine and the temporally mundane. This
problem does not exist in polytheistic paganism, where the gods are part
of nature and freely cavort with humans, but appears to be unbridgeable
in Judaism. One answer is given by God in *Parashat Yitro*, where God
descends and speaks to the Jewish people – and God emphasizes the
revolutionary nature of that occasion when He immediately afterwards
has Moses point out to the Jews that "You have seen that I have spoken
to you *from the heavens*" (Ex. 20:18). Communication, ultimately in both
directions, bridges the gap. The gap, however, remains, and the question is whether real influence can take place. I contend that *korbanot* is
the answer to that question. The *korban* creates an actual metaphysical
link by bridging the gap, by turning the physical into the spiritual, or,
to use the other metaphor in the verse (and naturally I agree it is but a
metaphor), by using our food (meat) to provide a kind of nourishment
(fragrance) for God (*rei'aḥ niḥo'aḥ laShem*).

Since a bridge is by definition bi-directional, it should not come
as a surprise that various sources see the daily sacrifices as the means
whereby sustenance is brought down to the world from God. If the
physical can be transformed into the spiritual, then the spiritual can be
transformed into the physical; in other words, rain can fall from heaven.
But that is already another topic.

---

3. This is the basis for the requirement to smell a sweet fragrance after Shabbat during
   havdala, to accompany the additional soul of Shabbat that is leaving.

I stated at the outset that there are two different foci of a sacrifice, the flesh and the blood. In the opening *parshiyot* of *Parashat Vayikra* – *ola, minha, shelamim* – the sprinkling of the blood is not emphasized, as we saw. In contrast, when the Torah gets to *korban ḥatat*, the sin offering (ch. 4), *zerikat hadam* occupies a much more prominent position. Starting with the first *ḥatat* (the *kohen* who sins), the Torah elaborates on the role of the blood.

> The anointed *kohen* shall take from the blood, and shall bring it to the Tent of Meeting. The *kohen* shall dip his finger in the blood, and he shall sprinkle from the blood seven times before God, in front of the curtain of the sacred. The *kohen* shall place from the blood on the corners of the incense altar before God, which is in the Tent of Meeting, and he shall spill all the [rest of the] blood at the base of the sacrifice-altar, which is at the opening of the Tent of Meeting. (4:5–7).

This is repeated, in various degrees of elaboration, for all the different *hata'ot*. While there is *haktara* of the fats in the case of some of the *hata'ot* as well, this is stated simply at the end, without the usual mention of "*isheh laShem*" or the phrase "*rei'aḥ niḥo'aḥ.*" On the contrary, the Torah goes back to the ultimate purpose of a *korban ḥatat*, which is personal atonement and not the bridging I have described.

> All of its fat shall be burnt (turned into smoke) on the altar, and the *kohen* shall atone for him from his sin, and it shall be forgiven him. (4:26)

As a rule, every mention of *ola, minha,* and *shelamim* includes the phrase "*isheh laShem lerei'aḥ niḥo'aḥ*" in one of its variants, whereas the phrase does not appear for the *ḥatat*. The reason is obvious. *Ḥatat* is *primarily* a sacrifice of personal atonement; the others are *primarily* ones of connecting the upper and lower worlds. The *ḥatat* is *lekhapper*, for atonement; the others are *lerei'aḥ niḥo'aḥ*.

In one case, this is emphasized even more strongly. At the end of the *hata'ot*, describing the individual's sheep-*ḥatat*, the Torah states, "The *kohen* shall burn them on the altar, *in addition to the ishei HaShem*, and the *kohen* shall atone for him from his sin which he sinned" (4:35). The Torah here seems to be explicitly stating that the *ḥatat* is *not* included in the category of *ishei HaShem*. Although burnt, it does not have the status of fire and is not destined to become smoke.

Since the exclusion of the *ḥatat* from *ishei HaShem* and from *rei'aḥ niḥo'aḥ* is so pronounced, the existence of one exception is all the more striking. In the personal goat-*ḥatat*, the Torah concludes, "And he shall burn it all on the altar, as a *rei'aḥ niḥo'aḥ laShem*, and the *kohen* shall atone for him and it shall be forgiven him" (4:31). While yet stressing the forgiveness motif, the Torah in this one exception also includes this *ḥatat* in the category of *rei'aḥ niḥo'aḥ*, in striking contradistinction to the very next section describing the halakhically identical case of the sheep-*ḥatat*. At this time, I have no good explanation for this exception.[4]

---

4. A possible approach could be based on the comments of Netziv to 4:28 and 4:31, where he explains that the goat is psychologically more expiative, leading to a more general atonement of the total personality (based on Sota 32b).

Leaven, Honey, and the Altar of God

Rav Chanoch Waxman

I. WHY NOT?

After opening with the laws concerning the various types of burnt offerings (*ola*), Leviticus turns its attention to the modest meal offering:

> And when a person offers a meal offering (*minḥa*), his offering
> shall be of fine flour; he shall pour oil upon it, lay frankincense
> upon it, and he shall bring it to…the priests. (2:1–2)

Sometimes consisting of raw flour and oil, sometimes baked,
sometimes pan-fried, and sometimes deep fried (2:1–8), the *minḥa* constitutes a way for a person of lesser means to offer something to God
(2:1). Even he who cannot afford cattle, sheep, or birds (see 1:2–17) can
approach the sanctuary, have a portion of his offering burnt on the altar,
and have the remainder consumed by the priests as something "most
holy," *kodesh kodashim* (2:2–3, 8–10).

The Torah closes the laws pertaining to the four standard types
of *minḥa* offerings (2:1–13) with a warning:

> Every meal offering that you offer to God, do not make
> it leavened (*ḥametz*); for no leaven (*se'or*) or honey

(*devash*)[5] may be turned into smoke as an offering by fire to God. You may bring them to God as an offering of first products (*korban reishit*), but they shall not be offered up on the altar for a sweet savor (*rei'ah niho'ah*). (2:11–12)

Given the flow of the text until this point, the prohibition of leaven and fruit-based sweets seems rather striking. Until this point, and indeed throughout the remainder of *Parashat Vayikra*, the Torah details the appropriate objects and methods for the various types of *korbanot*. No other prohibitions are mentioned.

This problem of textual discontinuity possesses a logical and legal dimension as well. Quite simply, one cannot enter the Sanctuary and place anything one pleases on the altar. The Book of Leviticus does not just mandate the bringing of certain objects as offerings, but indeed provides the permission for those very objects as offerings. Here is Abarbanel's formulation of the problem:

> Why was it necessary to state that *se'or* and *devash* cannot be offered? For it is known that it is not permitted to offer anything other than that which God has commanded. For example… regarding birds it was commanded to bring from pigeons and doves, and [consequently it was] wholly unnecessary to prohibit offerings of chickens and ducks. If so… why was it necessary to explicitly prohibit *se'or* and *devash*? (Lev. 1, Question Twelve)

Leaven and honey should be no different than chickens and ducks. Just as the Torah doesn't bother to prohibit the offering of chickens and ducks, so too, the Torah should not bother to prohibit the offering of leaven and honey on the altar.

All of this leads us to the classic and more philosophical formulation of the problem. In general, Jewish exegetes have questioned not so much the textual exceptionality of the prohibition or its logical-legal

---

5. The noun *devash* in the Torah normally refers not to bees' honey but to fruit jelly (usually dates), which is what the Arabic word *dibs* means to this day.

necessity, but rather its very reason for being. Why does the Torah need to prohibit the bringing of leaven and honey as an offering? What is the inner meaning and philosophical rationale of the prohibition?

II. BEYOND THE RATIONAL APPROACH

In his *Guide of the Perplexed*, Rambam suggests that the offering of leaven and honey to the gods constituted part and parcel of pagan cultic practices (III:43). According to Rambam, the Torah prohibited the offering of leaven and honey as part of a programmatic effort to distinguish between idol worship and the worship of God. If so, it is precisely because the offering of leaven and honey constitutes a recognized and consequently "natural" practice that the Torah must explicitly prohibit their offering. If a *minḥa* "normally" involves leaven and sweets, the Torah must dedicate space to defining the parameters of the unique and different *minḥa* appropriate for monotheistic worship.

At first glance, Rambam's approach may be attractive. After all, he resolves the problem of the textual uniqueness of the prohibition and provides a theory that seems to explain the prohibition. However, on closer analysis, Rambam's theory provides very little in the way of satisfying explanation. By assuming that the prohibition constitutes no more than a response to contingent circumstances, to a particular historical moment and practice, Rambam's explanation empties the prohibition of religious significance and meaning. It is no more than a response to dead and buried customs.

Moreover, and more importantly, Rambam's historical explanation fails to deal with all of the text. Although not emphasized until this point, the prohibition of *se'or* and *devash* possesses a flip-side, a partner of positive commands.

In first formulating the prohibition of leaven – *se'or*, the Torah utilizes the term "*ḥametz*." The *minḥa* cannot be "made *ḥametz*" (2:11). Shortly beforehand, the Torah repeatedly emphasized the term "*matza*," the physical and conceptual opposite of "*ḥametz*." The various kinds of baked and cooked meal offerings must be made as *matza* (2:4–5). Similarly, later on in *Parashat Tzav*, in elaborating upon the procedure of the *minḥa* and the consumption of a flour and oil meal offering by the priests, the Torah focuses upon *matza* and *ḥametz*:

And the remainder of it shall be eaten by Aaron and his sons; it shall be eaten as *matza*.... It shall not be baked *ḥametz*. (6:9–10)

The Torah not only prohibits leaven – it seems to mandate *matza*.

Furthermore, the Torah mandates one particular occasion when leaven and honey constitute the appropriate substances. Following on the heels of the first prohibition of *se'or* and *devash*, the Torah states the following:

You may bring them to God as an offering of first products (*korban reishit*). (2:12)

While leaven and honey are prohibited on the altar, they are permitted and even mandated as part of the mysterious and never again mentioned "*korban reishit.*"

All of this should make us realize the inadequacy of Rambam's historical explanation. We need to explain not just the prohibiting of leaven and honey on the altar, but also the mandating of *matza* as appropriate for the *minḥa* procedure. We need to explain not just the unsuitability of leaven and honey for the altar, but also their appropriateness for "*korban reishit.*" Rambam's theory of pagan practices seems to fail these tasks.

III. A SYMBOLIC APPROACH TO *MATZA*

Shifting from a historical to a symbolic-literary approach may help us resolve some of the problems raised above. According to this latter way of thinking, puzzling out the symbolic meanings of *matza*, *ḥametz*, *devash*, and *korban reishit* in the Bible constitutes the key to resolving the story of the meal offering. With this in mind, let us turn our attention back to Exodus, and the entrance of *matza* and *ḥametz* into the collective consciousness of the Children of Israel.

After reporting God's command to place the blood of the Paschal sacrifice upon the doorways, the Torah moves on to the proper procedure for consuming the sacrifice:

They shall eat the meat that night ... with unleavened bread (*matzot*) and with bitter herbs (*merorim*). (12:8)

As Rashi points out, the language of the command to consume bitter herbs harks back to one of the Torah's original descriptions of the suffering of the Children of Israel at the hands of the Egyptians. Back in Exodus 1:14, the Torah stated that the Egyptians "made their lives *bitter* (*vayemareru et ḥayeihem*)." In other words, the consumption of bitter herbs constitutes a reminder of the bitter suffering endured by the Children of Israel at the hands of the Egyptians.

The same is true with the consumption of unleavened bread. In phrasing the prohibition of *ḥametz* and the requirement to eat *matza*, Deuteronomy 16:3 refers to *matza* as "*leḥem oni*," the bread of affliction. This means more than the fact that the actual object of *matza* is low, humble, and afflicted. The stem *a-n-h* (.ה.נ.ע), meaning affliction, constitutes one of the key descriptive terms utilized in the first chapter of Exodus to describe the bondage in Egypt (see Ex. 1:12). Moreover, it is the exact term used by God in the Covenant of the Pieces to inform Abraham of the slavery and suffering of his descendants in a foreign land (Gen. 15:13). In other words, at this point, *matza* symbolizes the lowliness and affliction of the slave. As preparation for redemption, the Children of Israel are required to be fully conscious of the state from which they are being redeemed. *Matza* constitutes one of the tools for cultivating this slavery-awareness.

As we move along in Exodus, the symbol of *matza* undergoes a slow metamorphosis. Shortly after being told to eat *matza* along with the Paschal sacrifice, the Children of Israel are told the following:

> And thus shall you eat it: your loins girded, your shoes on your feet, and your staff in your hand; and you shall eat in haste. (12:11)

The moment of redemption may arrive at any time. The Jewish people must be ready and therefore must eat quickly. In other words, the first consumption of *matza* constitutes not just a reminder of slavery, but an act of preparation for redemption, a transition in the national psychology and historical status of the Jewish people. As such, the first consumption of *matza* also initiates a change in its symbolic meaning. It constitutes not just a symbol of slavery, but also a symbol of preparation for redemption.

In fact, *matza* symbolizes even more. In *Parashat Bo,* immediately after telling Moses to inform the Jewish people regarding the procedure of the Paschal sacrifice, the upcoming smiting of the Egyptian firstborn, the sparing of the Children of Israel and their redemption (12:3–13), God commands a commemorative holiday (12:14–20). The holiday involves eating *matza* for seven days (12:15, 18, 20), where we find the following verse:

> And you shall guard (*ushemartem*) the unleavened bread, for on this day I brought your hosts out of the land of Egypt. (12:17)

The Jewish people are commanded to "guard" their *matza,* ostensibly to prevent it from rising and becoming *ḥametz.* However, this is not the only place the stem *sh-m-r* (.ר.מ.שׁ), meaning guard or watch, appears in the story of the Exodus. Later on, in the closing verse narrating the actual exiting from Egypt, the Torah refers to the night of the Exodus as "a night of watchfulness (*shimmurim*) of God in bringing them out from the land of Egypt" (12:42). Just as God guarded and watched over the Jewish people, protecting them from the destroyer and the death of the firstborn (12:12–13, 23), so too the Jewish people guard and watch over their *matza.* In other words, the watchfulness required for the holiday of unleavened bread commemorates God's protection and His watching over their homes during the crucial moments of redemption. *Matza* symbolizes more than just slavery awareness and redemption preparation. It also symbolizes the moment of redemption.

This brings us to the most prominent reference to *matza* in Exodus. Upon the outbreak of the plague of the firstborn, Pharaoh and the Egyptians, fearing the death of all of Egypt, hurriedly send away the Children of Israel. The people picked up their dough "before it could rise" (12:34), quickly "borrowed" some gold, silver, and other finery from the Egyptians, and set off out of Egypt, journeying from Ramses to Sukkot (12:35–38). At this point, the Torah reports the following:

> And they baked the dough they brought out of Egypt into unleavened cakes, for it was not leavened, for they were driven out of Egypt and they could not delay, nor had they prepared provisions. (12:39)

Matza is the food of the post-redemption journey, eaten after leaving Egypt.

To put all of this together, *matza* symbolizes the various steps of the redemption from Egypt. The Torah adds layer upon layer to the symbolism of *matza*, thereby creating a complex symbol that spans the various stages of the redemptive process. From its beginnings as a symbol of slavery, *matza* accompanies the Jewish people throughout each moment of their leaving Egypt and slowly transforms into a symbol of the moment of redemption and the journey out of Egypt.

IV. A SYMBOLIC APPROACH TO ḤAMETZ

While Exodus provides a rich and developed symbolism for *matza*, such cannot be said for *ḥametz*. Leaven just doesn't play a central role in the story line. At most, we can deduce that leaven constitutes the physical and legal opposite of *matza*. There was no time for the dough to rise before the journey began, and leaven is strictly prohibited during the commemorative holiday (12:34, 39 and 12:15, 19–20). But physical and legal facts do not necessarily impart conceptual content. While logically *ḥametz* should somehow symbolize the opposite of *matza*, we are in the dark as to what might be the symbolic opposite of a redemptive process spanning slavery to journey.

This brings us back to the mysterious *"korban reishit"* mentioned in the *minḥa* narrative (Lev. 2:12), which is the appropriate occasion to bring an offering of *ḥametz*. While the Torah does not explicate what precisely constitutes a *"korban reishit,"* most commentaries correlate it with the one time the Torah explicitly demands an offering of *ḥametz*, namely, the *"minḥa ḥadasha."*

Parashat Emor details various offerings and holidays associated with the grain harvest cycle. At Pesaḥ time, the Jewish people are required to bring the *"omer"* offering, comprised of the first reapings of the grain harvest (Lev. 23:9–11). This act of thanksgiving commences the beginning of the grain harvest and permits consumption of the new harvest's grain (23:14). After counting seven full weeks, the Children of Israel must bring a *"minḥa ḥadasha,"* a new grain offering (23:16). The Torah commands:

From your homes you shall bring two loaves of bread to be a waved offering; each shall be made of two-tenths of a measure of choice flour baked after leavening (*ḥametz tei'afena*); they are first fruits (*bikkurim*) to God. (23:17)

The "breads of first fruits" (*leḥem habikkurim*) are waved before God, sacrifices are brought, and the day is sanctified as a holiday (23:19–21).

This, of course, is the holiday known as Shavuot, a name found only in Deuteronomy 16:9–12 and literally meaning "weeks." According to Deuteronomy, from the time the "sickle falls upon the grain" one counts seven "weeks" (16:9). At this time one celebrates the holiday of "weeks" (*shavuot*) "in accord with all HaShem your God has blessed you" (16:10).

Either way, whether we think of it as the festival of "*minḥa ḥadasha*," the festival of the two breads, or the festival of weeks, Shavuot constitutes a thanksgiving festival celebrating God's bounty.

This brings us back to *ḥametz*. The leavening, rising, and fullness of the breads symbolizes the fullness of the harvest and God's blessing. The richness of the bread symbolizes the richness of the land and homes that God has granted the Children of Israel (see 23:9, 17).

All of this should help explain how "*ḥametz*" comprises the conceptual opposite of *matza*. Whereas unleavened bread symbolizes the redemption process and the beginnings of the Israelites' journey, leavened bread symbolizes arrival, the land, and the end of the journey. *Matza* symbolizes process; *ḥametz* symbolizes fruition and completeness. This literary symbolism dovetails nicely with the physical characteristics of *matza* and *ḥametz*. Whereas *matza* is not yet risen, not yet full, and represents but beginnings, *ḥametz* has risen, has already become full, and represents ends.

Factoring in *devash*, our lone outstanding term, should lend further credence to the parallel between journey-destination and Pesaḥ-Shavuot. As mentioned previously, the term *devash* does not refer to bee honey in the Bible. Rather, it refers to sweet fruits and fruit products, usually dates (see Rashi and Ibn Ezra, 2:11). This is best proven by Deuteronomy 26:1–11, colloquially known as "*parashat bikkurim*," the procedure for offering first fruits.

Upon coming to the land granted by God, one gathers the *"reishit,"* the first "of the fruit of the earth…of the land that HaShem your God has given you" (26:2). Here we have another *"korban reishit"* celebrating the bounty of the land. After the individual's journey to the Sanctuary, arrival in front of the priest and profession that he has arrived in the land promised to the forefathers (26:2–3), the priest places the fruits before the altar (26:4). In the final stage of the procedure, the pilgrim recounts the story of the bondage in Egypt and God's redemption (26:5–8), and concludes:

> And He brought us to this place, and gave us this land, a land flowing with milk and honey. And now, behold, I have brought the first fruits of the land, which You God have given me. (26:9–10)

The point should be clear. Like leaven, honey finds its place in an offering of first fruits. Like *se'or, devash* symbolizes the goodness of the land given by God. Like *ḥametz,* the sweet fruit stuff constitutes the completion of the story of the Exodus, the arrival at the end of the national journey of redemption.

In sum, to put it in Jewish philosophical terminology, while *matza* and Pesaḥ symbolize process and potentiality, *devash, ḥametz,* and Shavuot symbolize realization and actuality. Alternatively, in the language of modern existentialism, while *matza* is about becoming, *se'or* and *devash* are about being.

V. CONCLUSION

To close the circle, let us return to the meal offering and the problems raised earlier: the requirement to bake the *minḥa* as *matza* and the prohibition of offering *se'or* and *devash* upon the altar. Hopefully, the analysis above has demonstrated that leaven and honey are not somehow inherently or metaphysically deficient, insufficient for an offering to God. In fact, I would like to argue that their very fullness constitutes the heart of the matter.

In what might be considered somewhat of a surprise, Leviticus opens with the rules for voluntary *korbanot.* God instructs Moses as to the rules and procedure for "a man of you who brings an offering to God"

(1:2). The story of *korbanot* opens not with obligatory sacrifices, whether individual or communal, but with voluntary offerings, the individual's attempt to connect with God. By no coincidence, in this introductory segment (1:2–3), the stem *k-r-v* (קָרֹב.), meaning offering, approach, coming close, and the like, appears seven times.

In other words, from the very start, the doctrine of *korbanot* propounded by the Torah constitutes a means for approaching God. The sacrifice constitutes not so much God's need, but man's need, the means by which he offers his self to God. In a Copernican turn on the pagan model of sacrifices, the object of the sacrifice becomes not so much the meal of the divine entity, but a representation of the person who offers the sacrifice and a symbolic means to bridge the human-divine chasm (see Ramban 1:9).

But what constitutes the appropriate means of approach to God? Should man represent himself with the symbols of satiated fullness, of destination, complete realization, and full-fledged being? Or perhaps, *se'or* and *devash*, while appropriate for an act of thanksgiving, are wholly inappropriate for an act of penitential approach, for an offering on the altar. In their stead, the Torah mandates *matza*, which symbolizes the redemption process. The Torah demands unleavened bread in all its humble lowliness, potential, and becoming. The poor man's bread constitutes the right means for approaching God. In the words of Psalms 70:6,

> But I am poor and needy; O God, hasten to me!
> You are my help and my rescuer; O God do not delay.

Only the bread of affliction, not leaven nor honey, sends this message.

Parashat Tzav

Between Tzav and Vayikra: Two Aspects of Holiness

Rav Mordechai Sabato

I. SAME SACRIFICES, DIFFERENT ORDER

The first seven chapters of Leviticus deal with the various types of *korbanot* (sacrifices) and their halakhot. This section of the Torah is composed of two subdivisions: chapters 1–5, and chapters 6–7. The Torah deals with the same sacrifices in each section, as demonstrated in the following table:

Chapters 1–5:

> 1 – *ola* (burnt offering)
>
> 2 – *minḥa* (meal offering)
>
> 3 – *shelamim* (peace offering)
>
> 4–5:13 – *ḥatat* (sin offering)
>
> 5:14–26 – *asham* (guilt offering)

Chapters 6–7:

> 6:1–6 – *ola*
>
> 6:7–11 – *minḥa* [6:12–16: the *minḥa* of Aaron and his sons]
>
> 6:17–23 – *ḥatat*

7:1–7 – *asham*
7:11–36 – *shelamim.*

Ramban addresses this apparent redundancy:

> In *Parashat* [*Vayikra*], the Torah states, "Speak to the Children of
> Israel," because there it commanded [the laws] about the *bringing*
> of the sacrifices, and it is Israel who bring them. Here [in *Tzav*] it
> states, "Command Aaron," for it speaks of the *performance* of the
> sacrifices, which is done by the *kohanim.* (commentary to Lev. 6:2)

That the first section is directed towards the nation, whereas the
second addresses the *kohanim*, emerges explicitly from the introduction
of each section, as Ramban notes. But his argument that the first section relates exclusively to the bringing of the sacrifices requires further
analysis, and we will return to this critical point later in our discussion.

From the aforementioned distinction between the two sections – to
whom are the commandments addressed – emerges the obvious difference in sequence between the two sections. Ramban writes,

> The [order of] commandments in *Parashat Vayikra* was the *ola,*
> *minha, shelamim, hatat,* and *asham,* presenting first the voluntary
> sacrifices, and thereafter the mandatory offerings that are required
> of the sinner. But here [in *Tzav*] the Torah explains first the *ola,*
> *minha, hatat,* and *asham* [and only then the *shelamim*], because it
> wishes to deal first with the *kodshei kodashim* [sacrifices of higher
> sanctity] and then with the *kodashim kalim* [sacrifices of lower
> sanctity]. (commentary to 6:18)

In other words, the first section, which addresses those who bring
the sacrifices, can itself be divided into two parts. Chapters 1–3 deal with
the voluntary sacrifices – *ola, minha,* and *shelamim* – while chapters 4–5
deal with the obligatory sacrifices, the *hatat* and *asham.* First the Torah
presents a list of offerings which may be brought voluntarily, and only
then does it command the bringing of mandatory sin offerings in case
of *violation* of Torah laws.

This division within the first five chapters becomes even clearer in light of the fact that no new introduction of "God spoke to Moses" appears until chapter 4, indicating that the first three chapters form a single unit. Chapters 4 and 5, however, constitute a new utterance of God, as they describe the sacrifices required of the sinner, rather than opportunities for voluntary sacrifices. For the same reason, the section dealing with the *asham* also begins with a new introduction. The *ḥatat* and *asham* are not two alternatives to achieving the same end; for some sins a *ḥatat* is mandated, while for others an *asham* is mandated.

The second section of sacrifices in our *parasha*, addressed to the *kohanim* who perform the sacrificial procedure, also features two subdivisions:

1. 6:1–7:10 – *Kodshei kodashim* (*ola, minḥa, ḥatat,* and *asham*). This unit also includes the *minḥa* offering of Aaron and his sons (7:12–16), which is a parenthetical insert, as indicated by the fact that it begins with a new opening of, "God spoke to Moses saying." A new opening follows these verses, thus setting them aside from the overall flow and structure of the *parasha*. Furthermore, while the entire *parasha* speaks in general terms about the various sacrifices, these verses mention a very specific instance of an offering.

2. 7:11–7:36 – *Kodashim kalim* (specifically the *shelamim*). Although the Torah never employs the term *kodashim kalim*, this status emerges from the fact that regarding the other four sacrifices the Torah emphasizes the unique level of sanctity afforded to the *korban*, which requires specific locations for the slaughtering ritual as well as consumption of the meat. With regard to the *shelamim*, we find no mention of a special status of *kedusha*, nor does the Torah insist on specific places for the slaughter or consumption of the sacrificial meat.

Another strong indication of this subdivision appears towards the end of the Torah's treatment of the *asham*. After establishing who among the *kohanim* may partake of the meat of the *asham* (7:6), the Torah summarizes the rights of the *kohanim* regarding all the other sacrifices within the category of *kodshei kodashim* (7:7–10). Thus, a clear division has been drawn between the four *kodesh kodashim* sacrifices and the *kodashim kalim*.

The reason for the alternate division in *Parashat Tzav* is clear – here the Torah speaks to the *kohanim*, who are responsible for properly tending to the sacrifice and following the appropriate procedures. Whether the sacrifice is obligatory or voluntary is of no consequence to them. The difference between *kodshei kodashim* and *kodashim kalim*, however, is critical for the *kohanim*, as the former category demands more rigid guidelines and restrictions.

Earlier, we cited Ramban's contention that in *Parashat Vayikra*, as opposed to *Parashat Tzav*, the Ḥumash deals strictly with the *bringing* of the sacrifice, not the *procedure* of the actual offering. At first glance, this distinction seems inaccurate, as even in *Parashat Vayikra* the Torah specifies the various procedures by which the sacrifices are offered. (The one exception is the *asham*; the reason for this deviation requires a separate discussion.) Given the explicit distinction between the two *parashot* – that *Vayikra* is addressed to the individual who *brings* the sacrifice, whereas *Tzav* speaks to the *kohanim* who *perform* the sacrifice in the *Mishkan/Mikdash* – then the inclusion in *Parashat Vayikra* of laws relating to the actual offering process implies that these laws, too, are relevant to the person bringing the sacrifice. Apparently, these laws reveal the unique character of each sacrifice, and therefore the person bringing the sacrifice must be aware of the precise nature of his sacrifice.

Thus, the distinction between *Parashat Vayikra* and *Parashat Tzav* must be refined. Both include details relating to the performance. However, whereas *Parashat Vayikra* deals exclusively with those details that reflect the unique nature and character of the sacrifice, *Parashat Tzav* instructs the *kohanim* about the specifications related to the *korban*'s level of sanctity (i.e., the locations for slaughtering and eating the sacrifice and the appropriate treatment of the ashes), not those involving the overall nature of the sacrifice.

II. TWO THEMES OF *KORBANOT*

The distinction between these two discussions of the sacrifices – *Parashat Vayikra* and *Parashat Tzav* – may reflect two different perspectives regarding the entire institution of *korbanot*.

Parashat Tzav opens as follows:

> This is the ritual of the burnt offering, the burnt offering itself shall remain where it is burned upon the altar all night until morning, while the fire on the altar is kept going on it. The *kohen* shall dress in linen raiment, with linen breeches next to his body; and he shall take up the ashes to which the fire has reduced the burnt offering on the altar and place them beside the altar. He shall then take off his vestments and put on other vestments, and carry the ashes outside the camp to a clean place. The fire on the altar shall be kept burning, not to go out; every morning the *kohen* shall feed wood to it, lay out the burnt offering on it, and turn into smoke the fat parts of the peace offering. A perpetual fire shall be kept burning on the altar, not to go out. (6:2–6)

These verses relate to two different *ola* sacrifices. The first burns all night on the altar, and the second is arranged on the altar in the morning. These two *ola* sacrifices are the two daily *tamid* sacrifices, prescribed in *Parashat Tetzaveh*:

> Now this is what you shall offer upon the altar: two yearling lambs each day, regularly. You shall offer the one lamb in the morning, and you shall offer the other lamb at twilight … a regular burnt offering throughout the generations, at the entrance of the Tent of Meeting before God. For there I will meet with you, and there I will speak with you, and there I will meet with the Israelites, and it shall be sanctified by My Presence. I will sanctify the Tent of Meeting and the altar, and I will consecrate Aaron and his sons to serve me as *kohanim*. I will abide among the Israelites, and I will be their God. And they shall know that I HaShem am their God, who brought them out from the land of Egypt that I might abide among them; I am HaShem their God. (Ex. 29:38–46)

This section's conclusion, the depiction of the Divine Presence residing among the people, indicates a connection between the *tamid* sacrifice and the presence of the *Shekhina* in the Jewish camp.

In the beginning of *Parashat Tzav*, where the *tamid* appears once again, the constancy of the flame on the altar is emphasized. There are three references to fire in these verses:

1. "While the fire on the altar is kept going on it";
2. "The fire on the altar shall be kept burning, not to go out";
3. "A perpetual fire shall be kept burning on the altar, not to go out."

Apparently, the Torah affords great significance to the constant burning of the flame on the altar.

It seems that *Parashat Tzav* presents a fundamentally different perspective on *korbanot* from that of *Parashat Vayikra*. *Vayikra* offers the individual the opportunity to offer a sacrifice: "When any of you presents an offering of cattle to God." Even the sin offerings come only when circumstances so dictate, but are not a set part of the Temple ritual. Thus, *Parashat Vayikra* presents sacrifices as an opportunity, a privilege granted to the Jew to come before the Almighty and express his feelings through the medium of a *korban*. In contrast, *Parashat Tzav* opens with the constant flame on the altar and the regular daily sacrifice, emphasizing the role of the altar as a means of connecting with the presence of the *Shekhina*. In this way, the Torah teaches that the institution of sacrifices is more than just an opportunity offered to the people; it constitutes an essential part of the *Mishkan*, expressing the constant residence of the *Shekhina* among the Jewish people.[6]

> They shall know that I am HaShem their God, Who brought them out from the land of Egypt that I might abide among them, I am HaShem their God. (Ex. 29:46)

---

6. Herein may lie the theological underpinnings of the well-known dispute between Rambam and Ramban regarding the reason behind the sacrifices, whether they are a corrective response to an existing mode of worship, as Rambam contends (*Guide of the Perplexed* III:32, III:46), or an optimal ritual, as Ramban contends (Lev. 1:9).

Sacrifices: Sinai and Ohel Moed

Rav Yehuda Rock

I. INTRODUCTION

Parashat Tzav's discussion of the sacrifices is not only distinct from *Parashat Vayikra;* it is a unified entity whose various elements are clearly connected. Unlike *Parashat Vayikra,* the units discussing the various sacrifices in these chapters are referred to as *torot* – "teachings."

> This is the *teaching* of the burnt sacrifice.... And this is the *teaching* of the meal offering.... This is the *teaching* of the sin offering.... And this is the *teaching* of the guilt offering.... This is the *teaching* of the peace offering....

In addition, the central laws pertaining to each type of sacrifice here are conveyed through a divine utterance to Moses, which begins with an explicit command to transmit the laws to the *kohanim:* "Command Aaron and his sons, saying..." (6:2); "Speak to Aaron and to his sons, saying..." (6:18).

II. CATEGORIZING THE TWO *PARASHOT*

To Ramban, the command to convey the laws to Aaron and his sons reflects the fundamental difference between the two *parashot.* He states:

In *Parashat* [*Vayikra*], the Torah states, "Speak to the Children of Israel," because there it commanded [the laws] about the bringing of the sacrifices and it is Israel who bring them. Here [in *Tzav*], it states, "Command Aaron," for it speaks of the performance of the sacrifices, which is done by the *kohanim*.

Thus, *Parashat Vayikra* is focused on *bringing* the sacrifices, while *Parashat Tzav* is focused on the *performance* of the sacrifices. To Ramban's view, this explains the difference in the respective recipients of the commands – sacrifices are brought by all of Israel, while the preparation and performance of the sacrifice is the province of the *kohanim*.

This division does not explain all the details of the two *parashot.*[7] I propose to set aside these questions for the meantime, and turn our attention to the conclusion of the teachings of the sacrifices, at the end of chapter 7:

> This is the teaching for the burnt sacrifice, for the meal offering, and for the sin offering, and for the guilt offering, and for the consecration offering (*miluim*), and for the sacrifice of the peace offering; which God commanded Moses at Mount Sinai, on the day He commanded the Children of Israel to offer their sacrifices to God, in the wilderness of Sinai.

These verses conclude the presentation of the laws of sacrifices in *Parashat Tzav*. However, this conclusion gives rise to two main difficulties:

1. The conclusion makes mention of a "consecration offering," but there is no teaching concerning such a sacrifice in the *parasha*. The command describing the "ram of consecration" – a special sacrifice offered on each of the seven days of consecration of the *Mishkan* – is recorded in Exodus 29. Why, then, is it included in the conclusion here?

---

7. See Rav Mordechai Sabato's article above.

2. In the description of the time and place of this *parasha*, there is an obvious contradiction. The first part of verse 38 states that these teachings were given "at Mount Sinai" – i.e., at the time of God's revelation to Moses at Sinai, prior to the construction of the *Mishkan*. The second part of the verse then goes on to say that the teachings were given "in the wilderness of Sinai" – i.e., from the Tent of Meeting, where *Parashat Vayikra* was conveyed, as stated in its first verse.

Ramban addresses the second question and suggests three possible explanations. First, he interprets "as our Rabbis explained it," that all the commandments that appear in the Torah, even those described as having been transmitted from the Tent of Meeting or on the Plains of Moab, were actually given first at Sinai, and God then repeated them later on at those locations. On the basis of this theory, Ramban suggests that the "teachings" in *Parashat Tzav*, along with the laws in *Parashat Vayikra*, were first given at Sinai, and then again in the wilderness of Sinai.

This explanation presents a number of problems. First, this interpretation is not grounded in the literal reading of the text. According to the literal reading of the text, certain commandments were given at Sinai, while others were conveyed later on. Also, if all of the commandments were given at Sinai, why does the Torah choose to note specifically that these laws were first given at Sinai? Finally, if the verse indeed means to indicate that the laws were given twice, the phrase "on the day He commanded" should be preceded by a conjunction.

Ramban's second explanation is "in accordance with the literal text." On this explanation, some of the teachings of the sacrifices listed here ("This is the teaching…") were given at Sinai, while others were given at the Tent of Meeting. The laws of the consecration offering were given at Sinai, as stated explicitly in Exodus 29. The burnt sacrifice and sin offering also appear there, in the context of the sacrifices offered during the days of consecration of the *Mishkan*, and are repeated in our *parasha* (chapter 8). The meal offering, guilt offering, and peace offering appear only in Leviticus, and were transmitted from the Tent of Meeting. In other words, the laws of the sacrifices in the *parashot* of *Vayikra* and *Tzav* were given only from the Tent of Meeting, but verses 37–38 of chapter 7 sum up all of the teachings pertaining to the sacrifices, starting with those conveyed in the context of the days of consecration and continuing to the laws of the sacrifices in *Parashat Tzav*.

The advantage of this explanation is that it also addresses the first question posed above, namely, the fact that the consecration sacrifice is mentioned here. However, there are other difficulties with this explanation. As we have already shown, the expression "the teaching," as well as the order of the sacrifices in verse 37 (aside from the consecration sacrifice), prove that these verses of conclusion pertain only to the teachings of the sacrifices in *Parashat Tzav*, which explicitly contradicts this explanation of Ramban. Similarly, how can the phrase "this teaching," with its specific and focused denotation, refer to laws scattered across chapters between *Tetzaveh* and *Tzav*?

Ramban offers a third possibility:

> It is possible that [the words] "at Mount Sinai" means at this place, in front of Mount Sinai, i.e., in the Tent of Meeting…and therefore the text here reads that "this is the teaching of the burnt sacrifice," and all the sacrifices, which God commanded "at Mount Sinai on the day He commanded him in the wilderness of Sinai," specifying that it was "at Mount Sinai" and "in the wilderness of Sinai," so as to tell us that it was not given on the actual mountain where God told [Moses] the Ten Commandments, nor in the wilderness of Sinai, after they had journeyed away from the mountain, but rather in the wilderness of Sinai while still in front of the mountain…the text is telling us where the Tent of Meeting was at the time.

Namely, the Torah juxtaposes the two terms in order to teach us about the location of the Tent of Meeting, that it is adjacent to Mount Sinai but not on the mountain itself. However, one can object that if the Torah wanted to tell us about where the Tent of Meeting is situated, the most appropriate place to do so would be in the sections dealing with the *Mishkan*, rather than here.

In summary, the questions arising from the "teachings of the sacrifices" in *Parashat Tzav* fall into three main categories:

1. the question of the characterization and definition of the *parasha*, including the difficulty in understanding the considerations guiding the selection of details to be included in or omitted from the various sacrifices;
2. the appearance of the "consecration sacrifice" in this context; and
3. the contradiction between the two parts of verse 38 with regard to the location of the *parasha* in terms of time and place.

III. RAV HOFFMANN'S EXPLANATION

It appears that the best solution to the first two problems was proposed by Rav David Zvi Hoffmann. We shall review the crux of his argument here, and then use this as the basis for solving the third problem.

According to Rav Hoffmann, chapters 6–7 were indeed conveyed to Moses at Mount Sinai, as noted in the first part of 7:38, "at Mount Sinai." These laws were conveyed during Moses' second ascent of the mountain, after the command concerning the *Mishkan*, after the commands concerning the sacrifices to be offered during the days of consecration (Ex. 29), and after the command concerning the daily sacrifice (end of Ex. 29).

To Rav Hoffmann's view, not only was our *parasha* conveyed after Exodus 29, but it also complements that chapter in terms of content, in that our chapter supplies details of the laws of sacrifices that are not known to us from Exodus 29.

Thus, the laws of performing the burnt offering are clear from the verses commanding the ram offered as a burnt offering during the seven days of consecration, "You shall take one ram, and they shall lay hands … and you shall slaughter … and you shall take its blood and sprinkle it upon the altar … and you shall offer the ram wholly upon the altar, it is a burnt offering to God" (Ex. 29:15–18). For this reason, our *parasha* can omit the fundamental laws of performing this sacrifice.

The obligation of the daily sacrifice offered in the afternoon is likewise known from Exodus 29:39–41, and therefore we already know that there is a burnt offering that is burnt upon the altar during the night, such that the "teaching of the burnt sacrifice" can treat as a familiar phenomenon "the burnt sacrifice – which is burned upon the fire on the altar throughout the night."

The meal offering is not mentioned in Exodus 29 at all, and therefore "the teaching of the meal offering" lists all the details of the performance of this sacrifice – the "offering," the fistful offered upon the altar, the offering serving as a sweet savor, and the consumption by the *kohanim* in the courtyard of the Tent of Meeting.

In the command concerning the days of consecration we find the details of the sin offering. However, the sin offering of the days of consecration is distinguished from the sin offerings throughout future generations in that the former is an "external offering" (i.e., its blood is placed only on the altar in the courtyard) whose flesh is burned, while for all future generations a regular, external sin offering may be consumed by the *kohanim*, and only an "internal" sin offering (i.e., an offering whose blood is brought into the Tent of Meeting) is burned. Therefore, the "teaching of the sin offering" in our *parasha* adds these laws concerning the consumption and the burning.

The guilt offering does not appear in Exodus 29, and therefore the "teaching of the guilt offering" in our *parasha* lists all the details of these laws – slaughter, the service involving the blood, the offering of the inner parts, and the consumption by the *kohanim* in the *Mishkan* precincts.

While the offerings of the days of consecration do not mention any peace offerings explicitly, Rav Hoffmann points out that the ram of consecration is offered in a manner similar to a peace offering (aside from the unique aspects of the consecration of the *kohanim*). For this reason, apparently, the "teaching of the peace offering" (7:11–21) only mentions the placing of the blood in passing, while the slaughter, offering of the inner parts as a sweet savor, and the gifts are all omitted; the text here focuses on the loaves that accompany the thanksgiving offering, and the laws of consuming the meat.

Accordingly, the conclusion of the *parasha* relates not only to Leviticus 6–7, but also to the laws of sacrifices set out in Exodus 29. For this reason the conclusion also mentions the consecration sacrifices: "This is the teaching of the burnt sacrifice, of the meal offering and of the sin offering, and of the guilt offering, and of the consecration sacrifices," since these, too, were an independent category worthy of being singled out, even though they were not applicable for future generations.

IV. BACK TO THE CONCLUSION

We have shown that the source of this *parasha* is Sinai, and not the Tent of Meeting. How, then, are we to explain the closing verse, "Which God commanded Moses at Mount Sinai, on the day he commanded the Children of Israel to offer their sacrifices to God, in the wilderness of Sinai"?

In an article in *Megadim* 2, Avraham Shama applies Rav Hoffmann's thesis to answer this question. To his view, the second part of the verse ("on the day he commanded") also refers to the command at Mount Sinai, and focuses on the command of the daily sacrifice at the end of Exodus 29. He posits that "their sacrifices" refers here to the daily sacrifices; "in the wilderness of Sinai" is not the location of the command, but rather the place where the sacrifice is meant to take place – i.e., "on the day when God commanded the Children of Israel to offer the daily sacrifices in the wilderness of Sinai."

This interpretation is problematic in several respects. Firstly, the textual reference to the lamb offered as a daily sacrifice, in Exodus 29, is to a single sacrifice, in the singular (Ex. 29:42): "the daily *burnt offering*." The same is true in the parallel unit in Numbers 28: "This is the offering by fire... the daily burnt offering... the daily burnt offering that is made... an offering by fire to God, and it shall be...." Secondly, the simplest understanding of the term "their sacrifices" would appear to indicate something far broader than just the daily sacrifice. Furthermore, it is stated explicitly in the unit describing the daily sacrifice that the command is "for all your generations"; it is not something that applies only in the wilderness. In addition, the language of the text here is, "on the day he commanded them to the Children of Israel." In the unit discussing the daily sacrifice in Exodus 29 there is no command to the Children of Israel; there is only a command to Moses. While it is clear that the intention is for the command to be relayed to the Children of Israel, this cannot be the meaning of the phrase, "On the day he commanded them to the Children of Israel." Rather, the second part of the verse refers to *Parashat Vayikra* (1:2), where there is indeed a command to Israel ("Speak to the Children of Israel") to offer the various sacrifices; this command was given in the wilderness of Sinai, at the Tent of Meeting.

A structure similar to that of our verses is to be found in Genesis 2:4 – "These are the generations of the heavens and the earth when they were created; on the day HaShem God made earth and heavens." Let us compare them, as follows:

> Genesis:
> These are the generations of the heavens and the earth *when* they were created [*behibbare'am*] on the day HaShem God made earth and heavens.

> Leviticus:
> This is the teaching of the burnt offering, of the meal offering and of the sin offering, and of the guilt offering, and of the consecration sacrifice, and of the sacrifice of the peace offering, which God commanded Moses *at* Mount Sinai [*beHar Sinai*] on the day he commanded the Children of Israel to offer their sacrifices to God in the wilderness of Sinai.

In both cases, there are two expressions describing time or place. The first expression in each case is introduced with a *beit* – ב, meaning at or when ("*when* they were created"; "*at* Mount Sinai"), while the second expression begins with the word "*beyom*" – ביום ("on the day"), followed by a verb in similar conjugation ("*asot*"; "*tzavot*").

But the parallel extends further. The first part of the verse in Genesis ("These … and the earth when they were created") sounds like a conclusion of what has preceded it – the act of Creation. Similarly, in our chapter, the verses are a conclusion of the preceding body of laws.

In contrast, the second part of the verse in Genesis, in terms of style, does not seem to conclude chapter 1, but rather to introduce what follows. Thus, in Genesis, too, we find a sort of combination within the same verse of two descriptions of time that seemingly do not belong together.

A novel interpretation of the verse in Genesis was offered by my revered teacher, Rav Mordechai Breuer. The content and style of the first part of the verse would appear to be suited to serve as a heading for chapter 1 of Genesis. The content and style of the second part of the verse appears suited to stand alone as a heading for what follows it.

In order to unify the messages of the two chapters, the Torah transfers the heading of chapter 1 to the end of the chapter, combining it with the introduction to the chapters that follow.

It would seem that the verses in our chapter may be explained in the same way.

Parashat Tzav really deserves its own heading, meant not only to indicate the subject of the passages that follow, but also to emphasize that what follows represents a deviation from the chronological continuity of the narrative, which now stands at the point after the *Mishkan* has been built, the Divine Presence has descended into it, and God has spoken to Moses (*Parashat Vayikra*), to provide the description of an event that took place many months previously, when Moses was at Mount Sinai. A similar phenomenon is to be found in *Parashat Behar*, where the Torah once again deviates from the chronological continuity in order to go back to a command that was issued at Mount Sinai. There, the Torah notes this transition right at the beginning of *Parashat Behar* (Lev. 25:1): "God spoke to Moses *at Mount Sinai*, saying...." A similar explanation can be offered regarding our verse.

The second part of our verse, in accordance with the model in Genesis, should be read as an introduction to what follows. What follows is God's command to Moses to embark on the procedures related to the days of consecration (which he was commanded in Exodus 29). Were the second part of our verse to stand alone, perhaps the Torah would indeed introduce the word "*vayehi*," so as to read: "And it was (*vayehi*) on the day that He commanded the Children of Israel to offer their sacrifices to God in the wilderness of Sinai, that God spoke to Moses, saying: Take Aaron and his sons...." The meaning of the verse would then be that on the same day that God commanded Moses, in the Tent of Meeting, concerning Israel's sacrifices (*Parashat Vayikra*), He also told him to commence the days of consecration.

That would indeed be a logical formulation, in terms of each *parasha* independently. But the Torah transfers what should logically have been the introduction to the "teachings of the sacrifices" to the end of this body of laws, joining it together with the heading of the next unit – a heading that, chronologically speaking, should have connected the next *parasha* to *Parashat Vayikra*.

Integrating the Torah's presentation of these various commands, we see that the body of laws concerning the sacrifices, conveyed at Sinai, is inserted in between two events: the command of the sacrifices in *Parashat Vayikra*, conveyed from the Tent of Meeting, and the beginning of the service of the days of consecration. The verse that should have connected these two events is brought together with the verse that concludes the "teachings of the sacrifices." What is the significance of this technique?

Let us first try to understand the significance of the "teachings of the sacrifices" in their original context – as the continuation of the unit describing the daily sacrifice, at the end of Exodus 29. The daily sacrifice is described there as an ongoing mechanism for maintaining the conditions for the Divine Presence to rest there. The constant service of the Jewish people at the Tent of Meeting facilitates encounter with God. "The daily burnt sacrifice for your generations at the entrance to the Tent of Meeting before God … and I shall meet there with the Children of Israel … and I shall dwell amongst the Children of Israel, and I shall be their God." The teachings of the sacrifices are meant to expand this system; the function of the *kohanim* in the Sanctuary is to accept the sacrifices of Israel and to prepare them properly, to complement the daily burnt offering and to maintain a full and constant system of divine service in the Sanctuary. Since the emphasis in the *parasha* is not on the ability of the owner of the sacrifice to come close to God and to appease Him, but rather to maintain this system of service in the Sanctuary, the *parasha* is addressed to Aaron and his sons rather than to all of Israel.

Parashat Vayikra, on the other hand, brings the message of how each individual among the Children of Israel has the ability to come close to God and find favor before Him. For this reason, *Parashat Vayikra* lists the voluntary sacrifices before the obligatory ones. A voluntary offering, indicating man's quest for extra closeness to God, is a higher expression of closeness to God than are the obligatory sacrifices, where the distanced sinner seeks atonement that will allow him to close some of the gap that has been created, and to restore his original closeness to God.

Chronologically, the teachings of the sacrifices in *Parashat Tzav* were conveyed at Sinai, long before *Parashat Vayikra* was conveyed. The reason for this is that the maintenance of the system of daily sacrifices and the dwelling of the Divine Presence precede – both logically and chronologically – the possibility of the individual coming before God, to the Sanctuary. But if the Torah had presented this in chronological order, it would seem as though the *kohanim* enjoy preference and greater closeness to God, being more favored by God than the rest of Israel. This is not the Torah's view. While the actual service is performed only by the *kohanim*, and an Israelite is proscribed from participating in it, the Divine Presence is "amongst them," namely among the entire nation of Israel, and is accessible – through the appropriate channels – to everyone. In order to remove any possible misunderstanding of this message, the Torah deliberately postpones the "teachings of the sacrifices," which are entrusted to the *kohanim*, and opens with the inclusive statement, "A person from among you who offers a sacrifice to God ... he shall bring it to the entrance of the Tent of Meeting, for favor before God." Only after this principle has been established does the Torah proceed to detail the "teachings of the sacrifices," so that these, too, should be viewed within the context of "the day when he commanded the Children of Israel to offer their sacrifices to God in the wilderness of Sinai."

The Mystery of the Intertwined Meal Offerings

Rav Elchanan Samet

I. CONTRADICTIONS WITHIN THE *PARASHA*

Among the laws of sacrifices listed in chapters 6–7, directly after the "teaching of the *minḥa* (meal offering)" (6:6–11) and closely connected with it, we find a command concerning a special *minḥa* offering, whose laws appear nowhere else in the Torah:

> And God spoke to Moses, saying: This is the offering of Aaron and his sons, which they shall offer to God on the day of his anointment: a tenth of an *eifa* of fine flour for a permanent meal offering; half of it in the morning and half of it at night.
>
> It shall be made in a pan with oil, you shall bring it when it is well soaked; the baked pieces of the meal offering shall you offer as a sweet savor to God.
>
> And the *kohen* who is anointed in his place, from among his sons, shall also offer it; it is an eternal statute to God, it shall be entirely burnt. (6:12–15)

Who is commanded to bring this obligatory *minḥa* offering, when is it to be brought, and what is the reason for it? The answers to these questions depend, to a great extent, on the interpretation of verse 13. The first words, "This is the offering of Aaron and his sons," implies that *all kohanim* are obligated to bring this sacrifice. But the verse then transitions from plural to singular: "which *they* shall offer to God on the day of *his* anointment." Such transitions are not rare in the Torah; we might interpret it as intending that each one of the *kohanim* should offer this sacrifice "on the day of his anointment" – i.e., on the day on which he is appointed for service.

However, the verse goes on to tell us that this *minḥa* of a "tenth of an *eifa*" is a "permanent (*tamid*) *minḥa*, half of it [to be offered] in the morning, and half of it in the evening." This implies that the sacrifice is in fact a daily one, similar to the daily burnt offering (*olat tamid*) and the incense, both of which are offered twice daily, in the morning and in the evening. The nature of this sacrifice, then, is quite different from what it appeared to be at first. Moreover, the concluding verse of this passage teaches that this *minḥa* applies only to the anointed *kohen* who will succeed Aaron, the *Kohen Gadol* (High Priest); hence, it does not apply to every *kohen*.

II. TWO *MENAḤOT* "IN A SINGLE UTTERANCE"?

The natural place for us to seek an explanation is in the halakha, according to which we could explain the *parasha* as a whole and attempt to solve the contradictions. But this is not the case. In Rambam's *Sefer Avoda*, we find two different instructions. In *Hilkhot Kelei HaMikdash* 5:16, we are told:

> A *kohen* does not begin to serve – nor does a *Kohen Gadol* begin to serve – until he brings his own tenth of an *eifa* and offers it of his own hand, as it is written (6:13), "This is the offering of Aaron and his sons, which they shall offer to God on the day of his anointment."

In *Hilkhot Temidin uMusafin* 3:18, however, Rambam writes:

> The *ḥavitin* (pan-fried meal offerings) of the *Kohen Gadol* – it is a positive mitzva that they be offered daily, half in the morning

with the *tamid* sacrifice of the morning, and half at twilight with the *tamid* sacrifice of twilight. And their kneading and baking supersede the Shabbat and any impurity, like any sacrifice whose time of offering is fixed.

Two different sacrifices, both *minha* offerings brought by an individual, arise from this brief *parasha*. Rambam lists both of them in a single halakha, as the third and fourth out of nine categories of *minha* offered by an individual (*Hilkhot Ma'aseh haKorbanot* 12:4):

The *minha* offered by every *kohen* when he first enters service; he offers it by his own hand, this is called the *minhat hinnukh* (inaugural meal offering). The *minha* offered by the *Kohen Gadol* each day; this is called *havitin*.

Aside from the two different names given to these two types of *minha*, three differences are immediately apparent:

1. Who brings it? The *minhat hinnukh* is brought by all *kohanim*, while the *minhat havitin* is brought only by the *Kohen Gadol*.
2. When is it brought? The *minhat hinnukh* is brought once in the lifetime of each *kohen*; the *havitin* is offered by the *Kohen Gadol* daily.
3. How is it brought? The *minhat hinnukh* consists of a tenth of an *eifa*, all of which is offered together, while the *minhat havitin* is brought "half in the morning and half in the evening."

These discrepancies raise some difficult questions. Is this an example of "God spoke one thing, two I heard" (Ps. 62:12) – namely, are the *minhat hinnukh* and *minhat havitin* both manifestations of the same verse? How can two different sacrifices be based on a single mitzva?

What is the halakhic relationship between these two *minha* offerings, and how can each of them be correlated to the straightforward understanding of the verses? Can both be derived from the text itself? If so – what are these derivations, and what is the significance of this single command implying two such different offerings? And if the text itself teaches us about only one of the *minḥa* offerings, what is the source and status of the other?

We shall review the approaches of various commentators to this *parasha*, and the answers which derive from exegetical approach. We shall also clarify the difficulties which each approach must confront, and finally we shall attempt to propose an approach that both resolves the literal meaning of the text and the teachings of *Ḥazal* as expressed in the *midrashei halakha* and in Rambam.

III. RASHBAM AND IBN EZRA: THE
PARASHA ADDRESSES ONE *MINḤA*

The two great exponents of the straightforward understanding of the text, Rashbam and Ibn Ezra, follow the same path in their explanation: According to both commentators, the expression "Aaron and his sons" refers to Aaron and *all the Kohanim Gedolim* who will succeed him – for all are direct descendants of Aaron. Thus our *parasha* does not mention any sacrifice obligating regular *kohanim*.

But there would still seem to be a contradiction between the definition of the sacrifice that each *Kohen Gadol* is required to bring "on the day of his anointment" – which sounds like a one-time sacrifice – and the definition of this same sacrifice further on in the verse as a "daily *minḥa*." Ibn Ezra explains this:

> "On the day (*beyom*) of his anointment" – Many have proposed that the letter *beit* here (*on* the day) is instead of a *mem* (*miyom*, *from* the day), and that the Torah means that "*from* (starting with) the day of his anointment" he is obligated to bring his *minḥa* offering *daily*.

According to this explanation, the literal text of our *parasha* contains no source for the *minḥat ḥinnukh*; the whole description deals exclusively with the *minḥat ḥavitin* – a daily offering – that applies to Aaron and the *Kohanim Gedolim* who will succeed him.

This explanation gives rise to several questions and difficulties. It in no way reconciles the laws derived by *Ḥazal* from our *parasha* with the text itself. Ibn Ezra fails to address the question of the source of the *minhat hinnukh* discussed by Hazal, while Rashbam suffices with the conclusion that "Hazal derived" the existence of this *minha* – implying that he believes the *minhat hinnukh* to be of rabbinic origin, and that Hazal based it upon the verses of our *parasha* through "*derash*" – exegesis or derivation. But a glance at Hazal's treatment of the matter gives a different impression – the Sifra and the Gemara (Menahot 51b) teaching the law of the *minhat hinnukh* of both the regular *kohen* and the *Kohen Gadol* seem to be learning these laws directly from the text.

The explanation offered by both of these commentators for the words "Aaron and his sons" is difficult to accept, as Malbim writes:

> Wherever the Torah says, "Aaron and his sons," the reference is not to those who will be anointed in his place; rather, it refers to the *Kohen Gadol* who will replace him as well as the regular *kohanim* who will replace his sons.

A second argument against the interpretation of Rashbam and Ibn Ezra appears already in the Sifra and in Menahot (51b):

> "His sons" – this refers to the regular *kohanim*. Does this refer to all the regular *kohanim*, or only to the *Kohanim Gedolim*? When the Torah says [v. 15], "and the anointed *kohen* in his place, from among his sons," the *Kohen Gadol* is already mentioned, so what do we learn from "and his sons"? The regular *kohanim*.

For these reasons, we cannot accept that the Torah does not mention regular *kohanim* here, as Rashbam and Ibn Ezra claim.

IV. RAV HOFFMANN: NEVERTHELESS, THE *PARASHA* REFERS TO ONE *MINHA*

Rav David Zvi Hoffmann addresses our *parasha* in two different places in his commentary, and arrives at the same conclusion as that of Rashbam and Ibn Ezra – according to the literal meaning of the text, our *parasha* deals with the daily *minhat havitin* offered by the *Kohen Gadol*, and has nothing to do with the *minhat hinnukh*. He accepts Ibn Ezra's explanation of the expression *"beyom himasheho"* as meaning *"from* the day of his anointment." But Rav Hoffmann tries to solve the difficulties cited above from the words "the offering of Aaron and his sons," suggesting a different explanation:

> Why is this offering called "the offering of Aaron and his sons" if it is offered only by the *Kohen Gadol*? .... Because the *Kohen Gadol* offers this sacrifice daily not only on behalf of himself, but also on behalf of all the *kohanim*... the *Kohen Gadol* acts here as a sort of agent of all the *kohanim*.

Rav Hoffmann explains the significance of this *minhat tamid* brought daily by the *Kohen Gadol* on behalf of all his fellow *kohanim*:

> Careful scrutiny leads us to the conclusion that the verses in Leviticus 6:12–16 are closely related to the statute that precedes them (*"torat haminha,"* 6:7–11) .... Just prior we are told that God gives all the *minha* offerings to the *kohanim* as an "eternal statute"; this expression can refer only to the statute of "perpetual bread".... Thereafter the instruction is given that starting from the day of *miluim* (inauguration) of Aaron and his sons – the time when God gives them this bread as an "eternal statute" – they are also to separate a contribution to God every day, which represents (according to verse 15) an "eternal statute to God." This contribution is offered by the *Kohen Gadol* on behalf of all the *kohanim*, every day.

What is Rav Hoffmann's view concerning the status of the *minhat hinnukh*?

> We have therefore discovered that according to the simple, literal meaning of the text, the *minhat hinnukh* is not actually mentioned here explicitly... and this being so, we are forced to assume that the mitzva obligating each *kohen* to bring a *minhat hinnukh* is indeed a mitzva given to Moses at Sinai, for although it does not appear here explicitly, it is hinted at. (vol. I, p. 165)

His view here is not essentially different from that of Rashbam, and the difficulties raised against Rashbam's explanation apply to his explanation as well; the treatment of the Sifra and the Talmud (as well as Rambam) concerning the *minhat hinnukh* does not relate to it as a rabbinic law, nor like a "halakha given to Moses at Sinai." Rather, it is treated as a halakha learned directly from the text itself.

Two additional difficulties arise from Rav Hoffmann's explanation:

1. Had the Torah taught, "This is the offering of Aaron and his sons...on the day of his anointment," we could have accepted his innovative explanation. But instead of the three dots here, what the verse actually says is "that *they* shall offer to God." From this use of the plural, the Sifra and the Baraita (Menahot 51b) learn that we must understand this differently than the way proposed by Rav Hoffmann:

> "This is the offering of Aaron and his sons" – Is it possible that Aaron and his sons all offered the same single sacrifice? [Obviously not, for] the verse teaches: "which they shall offer to God" – Aaron on his own, and his sons on their own.

2. Interpreting the words "on the day of his anointment" as though the text had said "*from* the day of his anointment" is itself forced, although examples of this phenomenon do exist in the Torah. But despite the linguistic difficulty, the question that arises here is why the Torah should give any emphasis to the fact that the obligation of the *minhat havitin* applies from the day of the *Kohen Gadol*'s appointment. The very definition of this *minha* as a "*minhat tamid*" brought by the *Kohen Gadol* means, clearly, that it applies daily from the time that he begins to serve.

V. RAV MECKLENBERG'S EXPLANATION

We opened our discussion with two apparent contradictions in the text.

1. Is the Torah discussing a one-time *minhat miluim* – a *minha* brought at the time of every *kohen*'s inauguration, or a daily *minhat tamid*?

2. Does the *minḥa* discussed here apply to "Aaron and his sons" – all the *kohanim* – or only the anointed *Kohen Gadol* who will succeed Aaron?

We then asked how two such different offerings could be learned from a single statement.

In fact, these two difficulties resolve one another. It is the apparent contradictions in the text that serve as the source for the two *minḥa* offerings learned by Ḥazal, and each of these *minḥa* offerings – the *minḥat ḥinnukh* and the *minḥat ḥavitin* – matches one of these aspects. However, this fails to explain the contradiction in the verses. They seem to be speaking about a single *minḥa*, while in fact they command two. How are the verses to be read to reflect this? Our second question likewise remains unanswered – why does the Torah include two different *minḥa* offerings in a single mitzva?

Rav Yaakov Zvi Mecklenberg writes, in his commentary *HaKetav vehaKabbala* on the beginning of our *parasha*:

> "This is the offering of Aaron and his sons" – this offering of Aaron and his sons, offered for the first time on the day of their inauguration (for every *kohen*, whether a *Kohen Gadol* or not, when anointed and inaugurated into his service, must first offer a *minḥa*), *then becomes a daily minḥa*.
>
> Then the Torah explains who it is who is obligated to bring the daily *minḥa*, saying (15), "the *kohen* who is anointed" – for the *Kohen Gadol* alone offers it daily. But a regular *kohen* has no such obligation; it is only when he performs his first service that he must be inaugurated with such a *minḥa*.
>
> Accordingly, the introduction, "This, the offering of Aaron and his sons, which they shall offer to God on the day of his anointment" is the subject, and the object is "a daily *minḥa*." Thus, the literal meaning of the text is clarified in accordance with the understanding of our Sages – that the Torah refers here to both the *minḥa* of each *kohen* as he performs his first service, and to the daily *minḥa* of the *Kohen Gadol*.

And those who explain "This is the offering" without indicating that it refers to something, and "which they shall offer" as the object, have difficulty reconciling "on the day of his anointment" with "a daily *minḥa*," for it is contradictory. Therefore, they have to exchange the *beit* of "*beyom*" to a *mem* – "*miyom*," like Ibn Ezra, or to add the letter *vav* in the word "*minḥa tamid*," like R. Naphtali Wessely.

The advantage of R. Mecklenberg's explanation lies not only in a seamless reading of verse 13, but that according to it, our *parasha* does not describe two different *minḥa* offerings but rather a single one. The text declares that this offering, representing an inaugural offering (*minḥat ḥinnukh*) for Aaron and his sons, will itself also become a daily offering (*minḥat tamid*). This syntactical understanding of verse 13 has far-reaching ramifications – the *parasha* in fact discusses one *minḥa*, which is brought in two ways: as a one-time *minḥat ḥinnukh* brought by Aaron and his sons on the day of his anointment, and as a *minḥat tamid* brought by Aaron's successors – the *Kohanim Gedolim*.

Rav Hoffmann's criticism of this approach arises from his perception (shared by other commentators) that our *parasha* discusses two different *minḥa* offerings. This being the case, Aaron's successors cannot be commanded to continue to offer the *minḥat ḥavitin* so long as it has not yet been stipulated that this mitzva applies to Aaron himself. But according to the explanation of R. Mecklenberg, Aaron's connection with the *minḥat tamid* arises from his explicit obligation to bring this *minḥa* in the form of a *minḥat ḥinnukh*. It is true that at the transitional stage of the verse, in which the *minḥat ḥinnukh* becomes a *minḥat tamid*, we may make the mistake of attributing this *minḥat tamid* also to the other *kohanim* – for they, too, are obligated to bring it in its original form, as a *minḥat ḥinnukh*, like Aaron himself. In order to avoid this confusion, verse 15 comes to limit the scope of those obligated to bring it – only the *kohen* anointed in place of Aaron is to bring it. The meaning of the verse is therefore, "The offering that Aaron and his sons shall offer as a *minḥat ḥinnukh* shall also be a *minḥat tamid*, to be sacrificed half in the morning and the other half in the evening by the *kohen* anointed to serve as Aaron's successor."

vi. "each day they should be as new in your eyes"

What is the significance of the innovation introduced here by R. Mecklenberg, that the two *minḥa* offerings discussed in this *parasha* are actually one and the same? The answer to this question must be given in terms of the reason for this *minḥa*.

The commentators tend to view specifically the *minḥat tamid* as the principal *minḥa* addressed in the *parasha* (so much so that some even omit the *minḥat ḥinnukh* from the *parasha*). This is understandable, as the *minḥat tamid* is indeed important, for it is one of the daily sacrifices offered in the *Mikdash* (related to the *olat tamid*, which is likewise offered in the morning and the evening), and it is brought by the *Kohen Gadol*. Most of the laws in the *parasha* likewise address the *minḥat tamid*. But the reason for this *minḥa* is not generally clarified by the commentaries.

According to R. Mecklenberg's explanation, the reason for the *minḥat tamid* is explained by the Torah by its essential identification with the *minḥat ḥinnukh*. The *minḥat ḥinnukh* serves in our *parasha* only as an assumption (almost known in advance), rather than as a command, and the whole aim of the *parasha* is to direct this well-known *minḥat ḥinnukh* to a new horizon – to turn it into a *minḥat tamid* which the *Kohen Gadol* is obligated to bring each and every day. This teaches us that the obligation of the *Kohen Gadol* to bring this *minḥa* daily is in fact an obligation to renew daily his service in the *Mikdash*! "Each day they should be as new in your eyes" – this is the instruction that our *parasha* gives to the *Kohen Gadol*.

The laws pertaining to the *Kohen Gadol* are different from those pertaining to regular *kohanim* in many spheres, but the theme of all of them is the same: to elevate the service of the *Kohen Gadol* and sanctify it, to preserve its freshness and vitality at all times and in all circumstances. Our *parasha* therefore reveals another sphere in which the *Kohen Gadol* is distinguished from the regular *kohanim*. Both the *Kohen Gadol* and the regular *kohen* are obligated to bring a *minḥat ḥinnukh* on the day they start their service. But for the regular *kohen* it is sufficient that he bring this offering once, and that is the inauguration of his service for the rest of his life. But the *Kohen Gadol* must see himself every day, morning and evening, as someone for whom the divine service is something new, as though today is the first day of his service. Therefore the Torah commands him to bring a *minḥat ḥinnukh* – *tamid*.

Shelamim

Rav Yonatan Grossman

Parashat *Tzav* discusses the details of the various *korbanot*. We shall focus on the timeframe within which the *shelamim* offerings are eaten, and the differentiation between two types of *shelamim*.

The *Rishonim* debate the meaning of the name *shelamim*. Rashi cites two opinions: "that they spread peace in the world," and "that they bring peace to the altar and to the priests and to the owners," meaning that everyone benefits from the consumption of part of the sacrifice (commentary to 3:1).

These two explanations base the word *shelamim* on the word *shalom*, peace. A third possibility for understanding *shelamim* appears in Rashbam (commentary to Lev. 3:1): "The term *shelamim* derives its meaning from 'he vowed and needs to pay (*leshalem*) for his vow' – that is, from the language of payment."

According to Rashbam, the term *shelamim* is derived from the payment of a vow that a person has taken upon himself. According to these two interpretations, the *shelamim* have nothing to do with the absolution of sin. Whether it is related to a type of peace that is found in the world (i.e., God is not angry at the one who brings this sacrifice) or whether it is talking about a sacrifice whose essence depends on a voluntary vow, it is clearly not a sacrifice offered in response to a sin that has contaminated the person bringing the sacrifice. And indeed, when examining the sources where *shelamim* are offered, we see that they do not serve as an absolution, but rather as an expression of happiness and spiritual emotion.

The Book of Deuteronomy expresses this explicitly: "And you shall sacrifice *shelamim* there and eat them, rejoicing before HaShem your God" (27:7). This is also clear from a verse from the beginning of King Saul's reign: "They offered sacrifices of *shelamim* there before God; and Saul and all the men of Israel held a great celebration there" (1 Sam. 11:15) as well as from other sources (Ex. 24, 11 Chr. 29:30–31).

Thus, in contrast to the other sacrifices that are usually brought out of obligation and as an atonement, the *shelamim* are characterized by their association with happiness – public or private – and stem from personal voluntary action. Therefore, there is no binding mitzva for future generations requiring *shelamim*, with one exception – on Shavuot.

In our *parasha*, we find that the Torah differentiates between two different types of *shelamim*: "This is the ritual of the sacrifice of *shelamim* that one may offer to God: If he offers it for a thanksgiving (*toda*) offering.... If the sacrifice he offers is a votive (*neder*) or free-will (*nedava*) offering..." (7:11–12, 16).

The style of introducing the various passages with the phrases, "If... and if..." is common in the laws of sacrifices and it generally refers to two different types that are encompassed within one basic category of sacrifice. Thus, for instance, regarding the *minḥa* we read: "When a person presents an offering of meal to God.... If your offering is a meal offering on a griddle.... If your offering is a meal offering in a pan.... If you bring a meal offering of first fruits to God..." (2:1–14).

There is a general category of sacrifice called the *minḥa*, but there are different ways in which it may be sacrificed and these are specified by the text in the style of "If... and if..."

It follows that there are two types of *shelamim*: thanksgiving (*toda*) offerings and free-will (*nedava*) offerings. There are different laws pertaining to each of these, and our text mainly emphasizes the different times each is eaten.

We shall now carefully examine the basic differences between two classes of offerings. The first are the *"kodshei kodashim"* – sacrifices with a major degree of sanctity which only the priests may eat, and only in a sacred precinct, such as an *ola* or a *minḥa*. The second are the *"kodashim kalim"* (sacrifices with a minor degree of sanctity) which may be eaten by everyone, such as *shelamim* of the free-will or votive kind. Let us outline the major differences between the two categories of sacrifices:

1. *Kodshei Kodashim*
   Slaughtering: In the northern area of the courtyard;
   Place for eating: Only in the Temple courtyard (other than the *ola*, which is not eaten);
   Time for eating: The day it is offered and the following night (the Sages limited the eating until midnight only – "in order to keep man away from sin," but the Torah allows it to be eaten all night).

2. *Kodashim Kalim*
   Slaughtering: Anywhere in the Temple courtyard;
   Place for eating: Anywhere in Jerusalem;
   Time for eating: The day it is offered, the following night, and the entire next day.

What is the significance of the time difference regarding the consumption of the different sacrifices? Why are priests allowed to eat from a *ḥatat* (sin offering) only on the day it is offered and the following night while the owners of *shelamim* are allowed to eat from them until the following day?

In order to understand this, one must consider the two different ways of measuring time – one way is unique to the Temple and the other is in effect for the rest of the world. For the nation, the halakhic day starts at night and continues into the following day. Thus, the Shabbat begins after sunset on the sixth day, and the night is already considered sanctified by the Shabbat. In contrast, Temple time begins in the morning and continues until the end of the following night. Therefore, for example, the offerings that are brought during the day burn until the end of the following night, since it is considered one continuous time unit.

Parashat Vayikra emphasized that the portions of the priests from the *kodshei kodashim* essentially belong on the altar, except that God gives it to them. (In the language of the Talmud, "What they acquire, they have acquired from the divine table.") Therefore, the time within which the priest may eat this offering is integrally associated with the time the altar consumes the sacrifice, since both the priests and the altar share in the consumption. The priests must finish their meal when the altar finishes its meal, and this is at the end of the unit of time within which the sacrifice was slaughtered, meaning the day of slaughtering and the following night (in other words, the Temple day).

In contrast, the meal of the *shelamim*'s owner is not based on God bestowing part of the sacrifice upon him. From the outset the table is set for two – for God and for the owner, two equal partners fully participating in the meal. Therefore, the two time units are joined; first, a Temple day, where the night follows the day, and then the second, a standard day, where the night precedes the day. In effect, the time that results from the combination of these two units of time is two days with the night between them, with the night serving both as the end of the Temple day and the beginning of the standard day.

In light of this, the reason for the different restrictions on the place of consumption also becomes clear. The priests who eat from the divine table must eat in the vicinity of the altar, meaning within the Temple courtyard, while the Israelites, who eat their offerings as men of flesh and blood (but also with participation from God), can eat within the entire holy city.

After identifying the basic differences between the standard *shelamim* and the *kodshei kodashim*, we will look at the second type of *shelamim* – the *toda*, thanksgiving sacrifice:

At first glance, it appears that a *toda* exemplifies a sort of integration between the laws of *kodshei kodashim* and *kodashim kalim*. They may be slaughtered anywhere in the Temple courtyard and eaten throughout the city of Jerusalem (as with all *shelamim*), but may be eaten only during the day and following night, similar to *kodshei kodashim*.

There is another detail regarding the *toda* – that "unleavened cakes with oil mixed in, unleavened wafers spread with oil" (7:12) are brought with the sacrifice. This appears as a law applicable to future generations in only one other instance of an animal sacrifice – the ram that the *nazir* brings as *shelamim* when he purifies himself: "one ram without blemish for *shelamim*; a basket of *unleavened cakes of choice flour with oil mixed in, and unleavened wafers spread with oil*" (Num. 6:14–15).

This comparison was noted by the Sages, who compared the laws of the *nazir* ram to the *toda,* and derived that the ram of the *nazir* could only be eaten during the day and following night, as opposed to the *nedava* (which can be eaten an additional day).

What distinguishes the *toda* and the *shelamim* of the *nazir,* such that they are somewhat related to the *ḥatat*? It seems to me that the answer lies in the basic motivation that causes a person to bring a sacrifice to the Temple.

The *shelamim* are unique in that they are not brought as an atonement for a specific sin, and they are almost never the subject of a divine command to the public or an individual. The *shelamim* are integrally related to the personal generosity a person feels as a servant of God, who desires to bring his animal to God. As such, God invites him to join in the feast and the two of them (together with God's servants – the priests) eat from the sacrifice, as expressed by Rashi: "*They spread peace in the world – that they bring peace to the altar and to the priests and to the owners.*" As such, the two time units combine to become one overlapping permitted time for eating the sacrifice.

In comparison, *kodshei kodashim* are integrally related to atonement, and usually there is an obligation to bring them (note that the free-will *ola* is not eaten at all). For this reason, owners are not "invited" to a feast when they bring these offerings, but stand with a lowered head and request atonement, or aspire for acceptance before God.

There are two sacrifices that do not fit easily into this schema – the *toda* and the *shelamim* of the *nazir.* On the one hand, these two offerings are tied to the inner voluntary motivation of the person who brings them. The one who brings the *toda* wishes to thank God for the kindness He bestowed on him. The *nazir* did not become a *nazir* out of religious obligation. However, these two types of sacrifices are not brought in the same spontaneous manner as a free-will or votive offering is brought. From a spiritual perspective, one who brings a thanksgiving offering is responding to God's actions that bestowed good upon him, and in reaction to this he brings a sacrifice. This is true also for the *nazir*, who is compelled by the Torah to embark on a specific and detailed process of purification in the end, even if the original *nezirut* was voluntary.

Of course I am not coming to denigrate the generous spirit of the two types of people who bring these offerings. However, they are both shrouded in an internal tension regarding their motivation for bringing the offerings, reflected by their laws. On the one hand – they have some of the same laws as a free-will offering, infused with the characteristic of spontaneity; on the other hand, the time for eating them is the same as for *ḥatat* and *asham*, which result from obligation and from religious commandment.

Parashat Shemini

The Eighth Day and Nadav and Avihu's Sin

Rav Yonatan Grossman

P*arashat Shemini* begins: "On the eighth day Moses called Aaron and his sons, and the elders of Israel" (9:1). These people are known to us, in this order, from another, more famous event than the one in question – the covenant established between Israel and God at Sinai. There we read: "Then He said to Moses, 'Come up to God, with Aaron, Nadav and Avihu, and seventy elders of Israel'" (Ex. 24:1; see also 24:9).

The eighth day of the consecration of the *Mishkan* is a direct continuation from the revelation at Mount Sinai. Aaron and his sons (and the elders) were already distinguished at Sinai; likewise, Aaron and two of his sons – Nadav and Avihu – are the central characters of the eighth day.

The festive occasion reaches its pinnacle when God reveals Himself on the altar, and then, suddenly, a terrible tragedy occurs. The two sons of Aaron, Nadav and Avihu, approach the altar and burn the incense, and they die as a result. Consumed by divine fire, the manner of their deaths reinforces the terrible tragedy. Apparently, the same fire that consumed the sacrifices on the altar and represented God's revealed Presence also consumed and killed Nadav and Avihu: "Fire came forth from before God and consumed the burnt offering and the fat parts on the altar…. And fire came forth from God and consumed them; thus they died before God" (Lev. 9:24, 10:2).

To understand the sin of Nadav and Avihu and their subsequent harsh punishment, we have to try to understand the significance of the eighth day.

Rashi offers two explanations for why the sons of Aaron are killed by fire:

> R. Eliezer said: The sons of Aaron died because they made a halakhic ruling in the presence of Moses their teacher.
> R. Yishmael said: They were drunk from wine and in such a state entered the Sanctuary. (Rashi's commentary on 10:2)

According to R. Eliezer, there is no inherent problem with the sons of Aaron offering up the incense. Their sin, however, is that they did it of their own accord, without a specific command from Moses. R. Yishmael also separates their actions from their sin; the burning of the incense did not cause the tragedy, but the violation of another law (whose commandment appears adjacent to the tragic incident) – the prohibition of a priest entering the Sanctuary while under the influence of wine/alcohol – was the cause.

Rashbam cites a different explanation that focuses on the burning of the incense itself. In his opinion, before fire descended from heaven, Aaron's two sons brought their own fire, and this is their sin, since on that day there is a special significance to the sanctification of God's name through the divine fire reaching the altar and consuming the sacrifices that the nation of Israel had brought before God. Rashbam chooses to ignore the subject of the incense which is emphasized in the verse. He focuses instead on the offering of the man-made fire (*eish zara*) which precedes the Godly fire coming down from the heaven.

It is my intention to follow Rashbam. He claims that the reason for the deaths of Aaron's sons lies in their offering up fire. However, in addition I will attempt to explain the reason for the incense emphasized in the verse ("Aaron's sons, Nadav and Avihu, each took his fire pan, put fire in it, and laid incense on it; and they offered it before God" [10:1]).

In order to understand the problem with burning incense on the eighth day, we must first understand the purpose of this day and the special role played by the inauguration of the *Mishkan* and the service of the priests. Moses emphasized the special role of this day already in the beginning of the *parasha*: "And speak to the Israelites, saying: Take a he-goat for a sin offering; a calf and a lamb, yearlings without blemish, for a burnt offering; and an ox and a ram for an offering of well-being to sacrifice before God; and a meal offering with oil mixed in; *for today God will appear to you*" (9:4–5). According to Moses' words, the uniqueness of this day is that God plans to appear before the nation. Subsequently, Moses will again cite this as the reason that so much preparation is invested in the day: "Moses said: 'This is what God has commanded that you do, *that the Glory of God may appear to you*'" (9:6).

Moses emphasizes that on this day, when the *Mishkan* is being inaugurated and the priests are beginning to carry out their work within it, God wishes to appear before the entire nation. The previous time God appeared before all of Israel was when He established His covenant with Israel at Sinai. There it is written: "And they saw the God of Israel ... they beheld God and they ate and drank .... The appearance of the Glory of God appeared in the sight of the Israelites as a consuming fire on the top of the mountain" (Ex. 24:10–17).

This connection is not coincidental, in light of Ramban's opinion that the *Mishkan* itself is a continuation of God's revelation at Mount Sinai. The *Mishkan* essentially represents the desire that the same revelation that occurred on Mount Sinai as a one-time event be perpetuated, through its presence, during all of Israel's years of wandering in the desert:

> And the secret of the *Mishkan* is that the glory that was revealed to all on Mount Sinai will rest on the *Mishkan* in private. About Sinai it is written: "The Glory of God abode on Mount Sinai" (Ex. 24:16), and "HaShem our God has just shown us His glory and His greatness" (Deut. 5:20). Similarly about the *Mishkan* it is written: "The Glory of God filled the *Mishkan*" (Ex. 40:34). The glory that appeared to the nation at Sinai rested continuously amongst them in the *Mishkan*. (Ramban Exodus 25:2)

The *Mishkan* is home to God's spirit which desires to dwell among the nation of Israel: "They shall make me a sanctuary that I may dwell in their midst" (Ex. 25:8). The Divine Presence that descends on Mount Sinai and forms a covenant with the nation does not return to its place in the heavens, but permanently ensconces itself within the People of Israel. As such, the eighth day, when God will rest His Divine Presence on the *Mishkan* and will enter the new home prepared for Him, is a direct perpetuation of the one-time revelation of the Divine Presence at Mount Sinai.

In addition to the parallels made by Ramban between the *Mishkan* and Mount Sinai, I would like to focus on three other items that appear in both events.

The heroes of both events are Moses, Aaron, Nadav, and Avihu (the last two Aaron's sons). On Mount Sinai, Moses receives the Torah and actively forges a covenant between God and Israel. At the same time, Aaron and his sons are distinguished from the rest of the nation and accompany Moses onto the mountain, even though they have no apparent role in the giving of the Torah, since in the future they are the ones who will carry on and allow the Divine Presence to rest in the *Mishkan*. Additionally, public *shelamim* offerings appear in the Torah only three times. The first time is at Mount Sinai with the forging of the covenant: "He designated some young men among the Israelites, and they offered burnt offerings and sacrificed bulls as offerings of well-being to God" (Ex. 24:5). The second time is in our *parasha* on the eighth day of completion: "He slaughtered the ox and the ram, the people's sacrifice of well-being" (9:18); and the third time, it is a commandment for future generations to bring a *shelamim* offering on Shavuot: "and two yearling lambs as a sacrifice of well-being" (23:19).

A link emerges between these three days. On Mount Sinai, the publicly sacrificed *shelamim* offering, symbolizing a joint feast with God, is brought, because a covenant is being forged. This unique event reemerges in two contexts. The first, as Ramban states in his commentary, is the *Mishkan*, a recreation of Sinai. When God rests His Divine Presence on the *Mishkan*, the nation offers up public *shelamim*. Simultaneously, there is a yearly recreation of *Har Sinai* – Shavuot. Therefore, it is the only holiday where public *shelamim* are offered, as Shavuot comes to renew and remind us of the covenant of Sinai.

From the nation's perspective, the eighth day is no less important than the giving of the Torah, which consisted of a direct encounter between God and the nation at Mount Sinai. Then, the nation was privileged to see the glory of God revealed on the mountain. There is no doubt that this was a powerful spiritual experience that left a deep impression on the nation. In our context, when the *Mishkan* is inaugurated and God stands ready to dwell within it, there is a need for another such meeting that will perpetuate the singular and unique contact that took place at Mount Sinai. This is the reason for Moses' focus on God's *appearance*, for this is the purpose of the day itself, "that the Glory of God *may appear to you.*"

With this in mind, we must examine the activities of Nadav and Avihu on this day of divine revelation. In the previous revelation at Mount Sinai, Nadav and Avihu went up together with Moses (up to a certain point) on to the mountain. They distanced themselves from the nation, since they, the priests, were in the future to continue the revelation of Mount Sinai in the *Mishkan*. If we return to the verses that deal with God's appearance at Mount Sinai, we will see that there were two distinct groups that were privileged to see the revelation of the Divine Presence. First the text focuses on the distinguished personalities that went up the mountain: "Then He said to Moses: Come up to God, with Aaron, Nadav and Avihu, and seventy elders of Israel…. Then Moses and Aaron, Nadav and Avihu, and seventy elders of Israel ascended; and they saw the God of Israel…. Yet He did not raise His hand against the leaders of the Israelites; they beheld God" (Ex. 24:1–11).

Until here, the text focuses on the leaders of the nation who began to ascend with Moses. Only a few verses later do we hear that *all of the people* merited seeing the Divine Presence, but at a time when Nadav and Avihu were separated from the nation: "Now the Presence of God appeared in the sight of the Israelites as a consuming fire on top of the mountain" (Ex. 19).

It is certainly plausible that Nadav and Avihu do not know that the entire nation had merited this divine revelation, and they reasoned that only they, as priests, were entitled to such an honor.

The same fire that Israel saw on Mount Sinai ("Now the Presence of God appeared in the sight of the Israelites *as a consuming fire*") comes down on the eighth day onto the altar, and this is the revelation that takes place on the eighth day. The nation again sees the Divine Presence, and the response to this sublime event is dramatic: "And all the people saw, and shouted, and fell on their faces" (9:24).

Nevertheless, at this moment, Nadav and Avihu take up their pans and fill them with incense and offer them up before God. I would like to suggest that whenever there is an act of divine revelation (usually through fire), there is a need for a screen to prevent man from experiencing direct contact with the Presence of God (thus, about Yom Kippur it is written: "In the cloud [of the incense] I will appear over the curtain" [16:13], and many other sources). It appears that here too this was the role of the incense. Nadav and Avihu are worried that there will be direct contact between man and God. If the Divine Presence is being revealed and fire is falling down from the heavens onto the altar, the incense has to be quickly offered up in order to block such a revelation.

The eighth day is a continuation of the revelation at Mount Sinai, but Nadav and Avihu are not aware of the full import of this. They reason that on this day, only the spiritual elite are privileged to divine revelation, while the masses are not entitled to direct contact with God.

However, in fact, on this day, the rules of revealing and screening do not apply. Just as the nation was allowed to see God's Presence at Mount Sinai, so too on the eighth day all the nation is allowed to see the revelation of the Divine Presence. The same fire of God that descends and consumes the sacrifices on the altar continues to consume the priests that are trying to cover up and screen this fire from the nation.

When Moses comes later to explain to Aaron what has happened, he says: "This is what God meant when He said: 'Through those near Me I show Myself holy, and gain glory before all the people'" (10:3). This phrase, "this is what God meant when He said," should be understood in our context. What is it God meant? "Through those near Me I show Myself holy and gain glory before all the people." Granted that through those close to Me, says God, I am made holy. The priests who have the honor of being close to God do indeed make Him holy; however, there is also "and gain glory before all the people." God is also glorified through the people. Throughout the *parasha*, the language of glory signifies the revelation of God, and here too, before all the people (and not only before those who are close to God), the glory of God will be revealed.

Nadav and Avihu come to worship God in the *Mishkan* with an elitist perspective that gives the priests a special status, and does not allow the simple Jew to draw near to the Presence of God. God requests that His Divine Presence be bestowed in a different manner – before the entire nation – the great as well as the small, priests and Israelites together – I will gain glory.

Each Man His Fire Pan: The Deaths of Nadav and Avihu

Rav Chanoch Waxman

I. INTRODUCTION

The deaths of Nadav and Avihu constitute one of the more mysterious events of Leviticus – yet the Torah presents the story in no more than two short verses:

> And Aaron's sons, Nadav and Avihu, each took his fire pan, put fire in it, and laid incense on it; and offered before God a strange fire, which He had not commanded them. And a fire went out from God and consumed them, and they died before God. (10:1–2)

Although the Torah refers to the offering of "a strange fire, which He had not commanded them," the underlying reason for the deaths of Nadav and Avihu, the cause of the violent punishment they suffer, remains obscure, hidden behind the veil of the Torah's brief account.

In contrast to the opacity of the Torah's brief presentation, the Midrash (Leviticus Rabba 20:6) lists no less than twelve distinct explanations for the deaths of Nadav and Avihu. The possibilities entertained include entering the Holy of Holies without being commanded, being drunk at the time of their offering, or having delivered a halakhic ruling in front of their master Moses.

This just sharpens the problem. The plethora of midrashic explanations highlights the lack of clear explanation in the Torah. What exactly constitutes the sin of Nadav and Avihu, and was the "real cause" of their deaths?

II. BETWEEN SINAI AND *SHEMINI*

Let us begin by taking a look at the aftermath of the deaths of Nadav and Avihu. Immediately after reporting their deaths, the Torah presents a strange "conversation" between Moses and Aaron:

> Then Moses said to Aaron, This is what God said: "I will be sanctified in those that come near to Me (*bikerovai ekadeish*), and before all the people I will be glorified (*ekaveid*)." And Aaron was silent. (10:3)

In fact, this "conversation" is not a conversation at all, as Aaron responds with silence. Apparently, Moses' claim that the deaths of Nadav and Avihu somehow conform with God's statement that He will be sanctified and glorified with those that "come near to Him" silences Aaron. Somehow, Moses' statement "explains" the deaths of Nadav and Avihu and perhaps even consoles Aaron. Hence his silence.

But when did God say this? For that matter, what is the connection between God's sanctification and glory through "*kerovai*" (translated as either "those who are close to Me," "that which comes near Me," or even "offerings") and the deaths of Nadav and Avihu?

As Rashi (10:3) points out, Moses' statement probably refers to a key passage located at the end of chapter 29 of Exodus. After delineating the procedure of the *miluim*, the seven-day installation of the priests and dedication of the *Mishkan*, the Torah states:

> This shall be a continuous burnt offering throughout your generations at the door of the Tent of Meeting before God.... And I will meet there with the Children of Israel, and it shall be sanctified

by My glory (*venikdash bikevodi*).... And I will dwell among the Children of Israel. (Ex. 29:42–45)

At the culmination of the *miluim* process and through the initiation of daily sacrifices, God's glory, i.e., Presence, will descend to the *Mishkan* and dwell there. This will sanctify and glorify the *Mishkan* and God in the eyes of the Children of Israel.

This prediction comes to fruition right before the deaths of Nadav and Avihu. Leviticus 9:23–24 details how after the bringing of the final offerings of the eighth day, God's glory appeared to the eyes of all of Israel in order to sanctify and dwell in the *Mishkan*:

> And the glory of God appeared to all the people. And a fire came out from before God and consumed upon the altar the burnt offering... and when the people saw, they cried out and fell upon their faces. (9:23:24)

To put this all together, when Moses tells Aaron that God had said "*bikerovai ekadeish*," when he uses the key terms of "offering/coming close," "glory," and "sanctification," he reminds Aaron that God's Presence is now located in the *Mishkan*. If so, then when Nadav and Avihu offered in the *Mishkan* a non-mandated, strange, and alien offering of incense, they entered into the very Presence of God.

By no accident, the Torah utilizes the phrase "*vayakrivu lifnei HaShem*" to describe the process of their incense offering. Whether we interpret the phrase as referring to no more that the fact that they offered incense to God, or that they themselves ventured into the Holy of Holies, makes not a whit of difference. Either way, they have improperly entered the Presence and compound of God. Consequently, they are consumed.

Also by no accident, they are consumed by fire, the visual image of the glory of God seen by Israel at Sinai. Just as the Israelites saw the glory of God as a "consuming fire" atop the mountain (Ex. 24:17), so too Nadav and Avihu are "consumed" by "fire" (Lev. 10:2).

Finally, it is again no accident that the text utilizes the same phrase for God's "consumption" of the offering upon the altar and the devouring of Nadav and Avihu. In the case of the offering, we are told, "And a fire came out from in front of God and *consumed* the burnt offering" (9:24). So too in the case of Nadav and Avihu, the text states: "And a fire came out from in front of God and *consumed* them" (10:2). On this interpretation, we need not locate a particular moral failing on the part of Nadav and Avihu. In a certain sense they need not have "sinned." Their very act of unwarranted trespass, of non-commanded entry and offering, is the cause of their death. We may even claim that their deaths contain an element or "spark" of holiness. They die "before God" (10:2) and are mourned by all of Israel (10:6).

Netziv (10:1) famously maintains that the "strange fire" (10:1) represented an excess of love of God in their hearts, an overly bold desire to approach God. Although it may be extreme, this interpretation allows us to view Moses' claim to Aaron of "*bikerovai ekadeish*" and the parallel between the consumption of the offering upon the altar and the consumption of Nadav and Avihu as rendering Nadav and Avihu themselves as "offerings" to God. They have unwittingly transformed themselves into actual offerings and been consumed by His Presence.

III. STRUCTURING THE STORY

The mechanistic or unwitting-offering interpretation approach outlined above goes a long way towards explaining the deaths of Nadav and Avihu. Nevertheless, identifying the cause of their deaths is but one of the challenges in reading the Torah's presentation of the tragedy.

As mentioned previously, the text devotes a mere two verses to reporting the core – their deaths (10:1–2). Nevertheless, chapter 10 revolves around the deaths' aftermath. To cite an example already discussed, in the very next verse Moses "explains" the death of Nadav and Avihu to Aaron. Likewise, the chapter includes sections detailing the removal of Nadav and Avihu's bodies from the Sanctuary (10:4–5), forbidding Aaron and his sons from active mourning (10:6–7), and outlining rules for proper priestly conduct (10:9–11).

Finally, the chapter concludes with a dialogue between Moses, Aaron, and the "remaining sons" (10:12–20). The conversation includes Moses' commands regarding the proper disposition of the offerings made that day (10:12–15), his demand for a "missing" sin offering which had been burnt rather than eaten by the priests, his anger at the "remaining sons" for mishandling the offering (10:16–18), and Aaron's reference to the tragedy that had befallen him that day (10:19). All of this can be mapped as follows:

Section #	Topic and link to death	Verses
One	The offering, death, and explanation to Aaron	10:1–3
Two	The removal of the bodies from the Sanctuary	10:4–5
Three	The prohibition of active mourning by the priests, i.e., Aaron and his sons	10:6–7
Four	A code of priestly behavior, including rules for entering the Sanctuary and general priestly responsibilities	10:9–11
Five	The "resumption of the eighth day" – the dialogue referring to the "remaining sons" of Aaron and Aaron's tragedy	10:12–20

Summarizing the chapter in this way leaves us with the expectation of some sort of essential connection between its various parts. While events do unfold in chronological order, something more than mere chronology unites the chapter. We expect to find a thematic connection between the deaths, on the one hand, and the latter sections, such as the "code of priestly behavior" and the "resumption of the eighth day," on the other. If so, what constitutes the guiding concept and organizational principle of the chapter?

At first glance, we may be inclined to make use of the concepts developed above. Until now, we have explained the deaths of Nadav and Avihu as deriving from unwitting trespass upon the Presence of God. In other words, they commit a fateful error in *"hilkhot kodshim,"* the laws of sanctity. Not fully cognizant of the sacred status of the area they enter and the proper conditions for the act of incense offering, they are inevitably consumed.

Likewise, the remainder of the chapter can be viewed as connected to the issue of the status of "sanctity" and the proper mode of relation to sanctified entities, areas, and objects. Both sections two and three – the removal of the bodies from the Sanctuary by others and the prohibition of mourning by the priests – close with the explanatory phrase, "for the anointing oil of God is upon you" (10:7). Because they are priests, they cannot defile themselves by contact with the bodies, participate in public rituals of mourning, or even leave the door of the Tent of Meeting (10:7). They are sanctified entities and must be wary of defiling their status.

Similarly, section five, the "resumption of the eighth day," revolves around the issue of relation to sanctity. In section five, Moses delivers instructions on how to deal with the offerings made that day, and where and how the priests should consume them (10:12–15). His anger at the "remaining sons" stems from their apparent disregard of the details of the laws of "most holy" objects and their careless burning, as opposed to eating, of the sin offering (10:16–18). As Nadav and Avihu disregarded the details of permitted and forbidden, commanded and not commanded, so too the "remaining sons" now apparently disregard the laws of sanctity.

Finally, section four, the "priestly code," also appears to fit this theme. The opening law of the conduct code consists of the rule of sobriety for entering the Sanctuary and the accompanying possibility of death (10:9). After the deaths of Nadav and Avihu upon entering the Sanctuary and the assignment of entering the Sanctuary to remove the bodies to non-priests (10:4), the Torah continues to discourse upon the theme of the proper relation between priests and the act of entering the Sanctuary. One may enter the sacred place only under certain conditions.

Nevertheless, this is not enough. While the motif of sanctity and relation to sanctity may be enough to explain just about everything connected to the deaths of Nadav and Avihu and the structure of chapter 10, it does not explain the inclusion in the priest's code of the function of teaching. While the function of distinguishing between holy and unholy and perhaps clean and unclean requires little explanation, the focus on the general Torah teaching function of the priest seems surprising (10:11). What is the connection between the "laws of sanctity" and the role of the priests as teachers of Israel and teachers of the law?

IV. REDEFINING THE PRIESTHOOD

Rather than reach for the obvious and elaborate upon the status of law as itself a sacred object, the priests as custodians of the sacred, and so on, I would like to return to the "strange fire" of Nadav and Avihu and focus on a hitherto neglected aspect of the story.

The tragedy of Nadav and Avihu's deaths did not occur in a vacuum. The Torah carefully links their deaths with the events reported about the eighth day of *miluim*.

On the simplest level, the impression is that they died almost immediately after the crescendo of the events of the eighth day, the appearance of God's Presence and the consumption of the Children of Israel's offering by the divine fire (9:23–10:2). As pointed out above, the Torah parallels the consumption of the offering and the consumption of Nadav and Avihu by utilizing the exact same language to describe the two events. In both cases, a fire goes out from before God and consumes (9:24, 10:2). Perhaps based upon this parallel, Rashbam maintains that the two events happened simultaneously.

But this is not all. Throughout chapter 9, which recounts the events of the eight day, the Torah makes extensive use of the term "come close/approach/offer," based upon the verb stem *k-r-v* (.ב.ר.ק), and the term "command" (*tz-v-h* – .ה.ו.צ). Consider the following verses:

> And Moses said: This is the thing which God *commanded (tziva)* you to do, and the glory of God shall appear to you. And Moses said to Aaron: *approach (kerav)* the altar and perform your sin offering and burnt offering and make atonement for yourself and for the people, and make the *offering (korban)* of the people and atone for them as God *commanded (tziva)*. And Aaron *approached (vayikrav)* to the altar. (9:6–8)

Altogether, the term "command" appears five times throughout the chapter (9:5, 6, 7, 10, 21). Not including the variation of "*korban,*" the term "approach/offer" appears eight times (9:2, 5, 7, 8, 9, 15, 16, 17). The chapter seems to build up a complex of concepts to foreshadow the deaths of Nadav and Avihu. In what might be thought of as a "reversing parallel," the Torah utilizes the exact same terms to describe the fateful act of Nadav and Avihu.

> They offered/approached/brought close (*vayakrivu*) before God a strange fire, which He had not commanded (*tziva*) them. (10:1)

The essence of Nadav and Avihu's error lies in not apprehending this connection between "command" and "approach." The appearance of God's Presence, atonement, coming close to God, and the like depends on carrying out the precise commands of God. Only by virtue of fulfillment of the exact command can one achieve "closeness" with God.

It is precisely their creativity, their substitution of self and their own version of worship in place of the obedient submission to God's commands, that constitutes their error and the cause of their deaths. In other words, their death results from far more than an unwitting straying into the precincts of God and the automatic result of encounter with the Presence of God. Their death results from a fundamental misconception of what priesthood is about and what it means to serve God.

While this may seem rather striking, the larger context of the overall *miluim* narrative supports this interpretation.

At the beginning of the execution of the *miluim* instructions, Aaron and his sons appear to possess near equal status. Chapter 8 opens with the command to "take Aaron and his sons with him" (8:2). Just as Moses brings Aaron to the door of the Tent of Meeting to wash and dress him, so too he brings the sons of Aaron to the door of the Tent of Meeting to wash and dress them (8:6–13). The sons of Aaron also place their hands on the heads of the various offerings (8:14, 18, 22), have blood placed upon them (8:23–24), participate in the wave offering (8:27), and consume the bread and meat of the *miluim* offerings (8:31). In fact, every mention of Aaron carries with it either a modifier of "and his sons" or a parallel process performed on or by his sons (see 8:2, 6, 13–14, 18, 22, 24, 27, 30–31, 36).

But on the eighth day (the beginning of *Parashat Shemini*), a radical shift ensues. Although the eighth day opens with Moses' calling to "Aaron, his sons, and the elders of Israel" (9:1), the instructions for the procedures of the eighth day are addressed to either Aaron or the Children of Israel (9:2–4). It is Aaron, and Aaron alone, who is told to take various animals and "approach/offer before God" (9:2, 7–8). It is Aaron alone who performs the central rites and offerings of the day (see 9:12, 14–18, 21), and he, along with Moses, who blesses the people (9:22–23). While Aaron plays the key role in causing the descent of the Divine Presence to the *Mishkan*, his sons are reduced to no more than drawers of blood and choppers of meat. They perform no acts of divine service and merely assist Aaron in handling the materials (9:9, 12–13, 18). The main action seems to take place between Aaron, the Divine Presence, and Israel.

All this should shed new light on the subsequent acts of Nadav and Avihu, explicitly identified as "the sons of Aaron," and their taking of "*ish maḥtato*," each man *his* firepan. Their offering "before God" (10:1) constitutes a radical reassertion of the role and significance of the "the sons of Aaron." They too are capable of serving before God. They too are priests, the spiritual elite chosen by God to draw down His Presence amongst the Children of Israel. They choose incense, with its obvious symbolism linking the cloud and the Divine Presence, and seek to come close to God. Once again, the story turns out to be about the self, the spiritual voice, and the revolutionary religion of the sons of Aaron.

v. the "missing" offering

To close the circle, all of this should help provide new perspective on the structure of chapter 10, on the conceptual connection between the deaths of Nadav and Avihu on the one hand and Moses' critique of the "remaining sons" and the "code of priestly conduct" on the other.

As mentioned previously, the core of section five, the "dialogue of the remaining sons" or "the resumption of the eighth day," involves Moses' search for the "missing" sin offering. Moses accuses the remaining priests not just of violating the technicalities of the laws of sanctified objects, but of a fundamental dereliction of duty. If the priests do not consume the sin offering in the appropriate manner, it does not achieve atonement for the People of Israel.

Indeed, the text only mentions a sin offering of a goat at one other point in the narrative. The Children of Israel are commanded to bring as their first joint offering, a "goat for a sin offering," as preface to atonement and the descent of the Divine Presence (9:3–4). In other words, in accusing the priests of mishandling the sin offering, Moses accuses the brothers of Nadav and Avihu of acting not on behalf of the Children of Israel but rather on behalf of themselves, in accordance with their own priorities, interpretation of priesthood, and spiritual agenda. He accuses them of the error of Nadav and Avihu, of serving themselves rather than God and Israel.

This brings us back to the inclusion of the code of priestly conduct and its connection to the deaths of Nadav and Avihu. We no longer need wonder about the inclusion of a code of priestly conduct, consisting of a demand for sobriety, strict concern for the technicalities, distinctions and minutiae of the law, and the teaching of Torah to the People of Israel. After all, priesthood is not about an ecstatic approach to God. It is neither about the individual experience nor about the spiritual and psychic elevation of the priest. Nor is priesthood about the self, the spiritual priorities, desires, and needs of the priest. As the story of Nadav and Avihu aptly demonstrates, it is about careful adherence to the law, about serving the law and the People of Israel. Only through his service of the law and the People of Israel does the priest merit coming before God.

Darosh Darash

Rav Ezra Bick

I. INTRODUCTION

Parashat Shemini contains within it the puzzling episode of the deaths of Nadav and Avihu, Aaron's sons. Yet, despite the lack of clarity concerning their transgression, the basic outline of the story is clear. At the climax of the descent of the Holy Presence onto the *Mishkan*, the two sons of Aaron initiated improper incense, an *eish zara*, within the newly dedicated Tabernacle, which led to their deaths. The general consensus of many commentators is that, whatever the precise nature of the *eish zara*, the story warns against excess unbridled individual initiative in approaching God. The priests are meant to follow the rules that God has set down for approaching Him and serving Him. This undoubtedly lies behind the explicit connection drawn by the Torah between the deaths of Nadav and Avihu and the detailed rules for entering the Sanctuary laid out in *Parashat Aḥarei Mot*.

In the immediate aftermath of their fiery death, we find an incident involving Moses and Aaron that appears to be incomprehensible. The exact nature of the conversation between them is unclear, but what is even more perplexing is the meaning of the entire incident. It is clear that something of the nature of a halakhic dispute is taking place, but we are given no hints what the importance of these halakhot is in the context of the story. Let us first examine the *peshat* level of the incident, as retold in the story, beginning with 10:12.

1. Moses commands *Aaron, Elazar, and Itamar* to eat the remainder of the meal offering (*minḥa*) (12).
2. He adds that they are also to eat parts of the animal sacrifices, though it is not explicit which sacrifices are meant (13–15).
3. Moses investigates and discovers that the sin offering goat (*se'ir haḥatat*) has been burnt. He is incensed and rebukes *Elazar and Itamar* for not eating it (16–18).
4. *Aaron* asks Moses whether it would be acceptable to God had he eaten a sin offering under similar circumstances (19).
5. Moses "hears and it was good in his eyes" (20).

Sections 1–3 tell a clear tale, although we do not actually understand why Moses is so angry. Sections 4–5 are simply a riddle. We understand neither what the subject of the conversation is, nor the nature of Moses' enigmatic reaction. Above all, we do not understand the relation of the incident to the *Mishkan*'s dedication and Nadav and Avihu's deaths.

II. THE HALAKHIC INTERACTION

When examining a story in the Torah, we have a natural tendency to gloss over the halakhic details that may be included in the story, on the assumption that the two distinct areas, the narrative and the halakha, are to be treated separately. In this case, that is impossible, as the very nature of the narrative is based on a halakhic discussion. It is not that some incident occurred in connection with a halakha taught by Moses; rather the incident is precisely the halakha itself, and the debate-discussion that takes place between Moses and Aaron. We therefore must first understand the halakhic issue.

Rashi summarizes for us Ḥazal's explanation (based on Zevaḥim 101). The underlying halakha is that an *onen*, one who has suffered the death of a close relative, is forbidden to eat *kodashim*, sanctified meat. This halakha has not yet been stated; in fact, it is derived from a verse concerning the eating of Ma'aser Sheni by an *onen* that appears only at the far end of the Torah, in *Parashat Ki Tavo* (Deut. 26:14). The Sages assume that both Moses and Aaron were aware of this halakha. Moses tells Aaron that this halakha does not apply to him or his sons at this time, and hence they are to eat the *minḥa* and other portions left over from the sacrifices of the "eighth day." In other words, the command in section 1–2 above is an exception, a temporary suspension of the usual halakha. In fact, the sacrifices are eaten by the sons of Aaron. However, one sacrifice, identified in verse 16 (section 3 above) as a *ḥatat*, a sin offering, is not eaten but is burnt. Moses is upset at this apparent breach of his instruction. However, Aaron argues (in section 4) that the exceptional rule of section 1 is meant to apply only to the special sacrifices that were brought as part of the dedication ceremony of the *Mishkan*. These are not regular sacrifices and therefore it is plausible that special rules apply to them. However, there was also a *korban musaf Rosh Ḥodesh*, an additional sacrifice that was brought at the same time because the "eighth day" was the new moon. Aaron argued that the exception to the prohibition of an *onen* eating from a sacrifice applies only to the exceptional one-time sacrifices (*kodshei sha'a*), but not to a regular permanent sacrifice (*kodshei olam*). The sin offering that was burnt rather than eaten is identified by the Sages as the *musaf Rosh Ḥodesh*, and that explains why Aaron ruled that it should not be eaten by those who were *onen*. Moses accepts this explanation.

Therefore, the subject of the discussion was whether the *kohanim* were supposed to eat all the sacrifices brought on that day, despite being *onenim*, or was one of those offerings, the *ḥatat* of Rosh Ḥodesh, not included in that command and therefore subject to the permanent halakhic rule that meat of a sacrifice may not be eaten by an *onen*.

Does this explain the *parasha*? I do not think so. It explains the details, but only raises more forcefully the question as to the real nature of this dispute. Why is Moses so upset? What is the connection between these arcane halakhic questions and the deaths of Nadav and Avihu, the narrative, the story, which is the real framework of the *parasha*?

III. WHY WAS MOSES ANGRY?

To understand what is really going on here, we must examine more closely the conversation between Moses and the *kohanim*, Aaron and his sons, starting with the command to eat the portions of the sacrifices.

Moses spoke to Aaron, and to Elazar and Itamar his remaining sons: Take the meal offering that remains from the sacrifices of God, and eat it unleavened (*matzot*) beside the altar; for it is holiest of the holy (*kodesh kodashim*).

And you shall eat it in a holy place, for it is your allotment and the allotment of your sons from the sacrifices of God; for thus I am commanded.

And the breast that is waved and the shoulder that is raised shall you eat in a pure location, you, your sons, and your daughters with you, for they have been given as your allotment and the allotment of your sons, from the sacrifices of the peace offerings of the Israelites. (vv. 11–13)

Aside from the actual command to eat the portions of the sacrifice, these verses emphasize two additional points. First, the portions eaten are "your allotment" (*hokkha*) from the sacrifices of God; and secondly, they must be eaten in a "holy place," by the side of the altar.

By contrast, the second point is reemphasized when Moses rebukes them for not eating the *hatat*.

Why have you not eaten the sin offering *in the holy place*, for it is holiest of the holies, and He gave it to you to bear the iniquity of the congregation, to atone for them before God. (v. 17)

Remember that the *hatat* had been burnt, so the crux of the problem was not *where* it had been eaten but the fact that it had not been eaten at all. From the text, it is clear that the eating in the holy place is a crucial detail in the command and the rebuke of Moses.

I think the *parasha* is readily understandable when understood against the backdrop of the tension inherent in the dedication of the *Mishkan*. Several months earlier, the Jews had built the Golden Calf. The Tent of Meeting had been moved out of the camp, and they were effectively banished from God's Presence. For the last few months, they had been building the *Mishkan*, based on God's promise that He would rest His Presence among them when it was completed. All this time, the entire question of the future of the relationship between God and

Israel is in doubt, despite God's promise to Moses. In fact, according to one midrash, a minor moment of tension had taken place at the very completion of the dedication ceremony, when there was seemingly no response from God (see Rashi 9:23). And then, immediately after the fire descended from heaven (9:24), the shocking deaths of Nadav and Avihu! The situation is eerily similar to Moses' descent from Mount Sinai, the two tablets in his arms, only to have the dream dashed – and the tablets smashed – by the Golden Calf. Will the "foreign fire" of Nadav and Avihu prevent the resting of the Holy Presence in the *Mishkan*?

I propose that Moses' anger is a sign of his anxiety. He interprets their not eating the *ḥatat* as a sign that they think that the Sanctuary has not been sanctified; i.e., that the Presence has not come down to dwell in their midst. In other words, the entire massive effort of the last six months has been in vain. In this respect, there is an important difference between the other sacrifices and the *ḥatat Rosh Ḥodesh*. The other sacrifices were part of the dedication ceremony. They were brought *before* the Presence was expected to descend into the Sanctuary. They are not a normal part of the day-to-day operation of the *Mishkan*. The crucial test is not in them, but in the first sacrifice to be brought *after* the completion of the dedication, as part of the regular, post-dedication, ritual of the *Mishkan*, which was the *ḥatat Rosh Ḥodesh*. Moses had specifically instructed them to eat the sacrifices in *the holy place*. The "holy place" was the *Mishkan after* it would achieve its full status; in other words, after the Presence of God would be manifest in it. When he saw that they had not eaten the *ḥatat*, he feared the worst – that they had decided that the *Mishkan* had not been sanctified, and that was the reason that the sacrifice was burnt.

That Moses saw the *ḥatat Rosh Ḥodesh* as the crucial sign of success, rather than the other sacrifices, is indicated by the strikingly unusual verb form of verse 16: "And the sin offering goat, Moses thoroughly investigated (*darosh darash*), and behold, it was burnt." Moses does not find out about the non-eating of the *ḥatat* by chance, having assumed that of course it would be eaten pursuant to his commands. Rather, he initiated a special investigation. The double verb form (*darosh darash*) indicates special emphasis, an investigation on top of an investigation, as it were. Moses, after conveying the command to eat the sacrifices in the holy place, initiated a special, intense, investigation to see what had happened with the *ḥatat*. The reason, I suggest, is precisely that the *ḥatat* was *kodshei olam* and not *kodshei sha'a*; it was a sacrifice belonging to the regular service of the *Mishkan*. Moses desperately wanted to make sure that the erection and dedication of the *Mishkan* had been successful, not in the architectural sense but in its sanctification, in the agreement of God to dwell His Presence therein. It was precisely for the *ḥatat Rosh Ḥodesh* that he was waiting. Imagine his chagrin to find it burnt, discarded. His frustration is expressed as anger – *vayiktzof* indicates *extreme* anger – as he confronts the *kohanim* who have not eaten the sacrifice as he expected.

Darosh darash is also the exact midpoint of the Torah, as measured in words (the gloss in printed editions of the Torah reads, "*darosh* on one side, *darash* on the other"). This moment, while Moses wonders if the entire enterprise is about to go up in smoke (literally, the fire which consumed Nadav and Avihu), is the crossroads, from where the basic story of the Torah will continue in either one direction or the opposite.

Aaron, according to the explanation of Ḥazal, answers that the *ḥatat* was not burned because of a deficiency in the *Mishkan*, but because of the personal status of the *kohanim* as *onenim*. This factor completely reverses the relationship between the dedicatory sacrifices, *kodshei sha'a,* and the regular sacrifices, *kodshei olam*. Precisely because the *ḥatat* is a regular sacrifice, whose eating symbolizes the dwelling of the Holy Presence within Israel, it cannot be eaten by an *onen*. Death, apparently, destroys the ability of a man to commune closely with God. (In the words of my teacher, Rav Yosef B. Soloveitchik, death of a close one impugns the image of God inherent in Man. The possibility of Man being the sanctuary of God is based on his being created in the image of God.) This does not indicate a problem with the *Mishkan*, but with the *kohen*. In fact, not eating the sacrifice by an *onen* might be taken as a sign that the sacrifice does indeed have full sanctity. Hence, not only does Moses accept this answer but it "was good in his eyes," he is reassured and his mood changes from anger and frustration to pleasure. The goal has, in fact, been accomplished.

IV. EATING AND CONSECRATION

It is still not clear why Moses is so upset that Aaron and his sons have not eaten the sacrifice. Even if they did so because they thought that the deaths of Nadav and Avihu had defiled the Sanctuary, or interfered with its dedication, that does not mean that they are correct. It simply means that they had made a mistake. Moses would have to explain their mistake to them, and might even have been upset with them, but he would have no reason to be exceedingly wroth and angry. The fact that Aaron had mistakenly not eaten the *ḥatat* would mean that he had *mistakenly* thought that the *Mishkan* had not achieved its destiny, but it still could be that God's Presence had indeed entered the Sanctuary, as indicated by the descent of the fire from heaven, and the appearance of the "glory of God before the people" (9:23–24).

The answer is that eating the *Rosh Ḥodesh* sacrifice in the holy place is not just a consequence of sanctification of the *Mishkan*, but a cause of it as well. This is clearly indicated by Moses in his rebuke.

> Why have you not eaten the sin offering in the holy place, for it is holiest of the holies, and He gave it to you *to bear the iniquity of the congregation, to atone for them before God.*

Moses is not angry that they have not eaten the sacrifice as an act of transgression on their part, but rather that by not eating it they have damaged Israel by not atoning for them. Moses' statement is the basis for the Sages' conclusion that "the *kohanim* eat and the owners [of the sacrifice] achieve atonement," as indicated by Rashi in his commentary on that verse.

The idea being expressed here is that a sacrifice, brought to God, is eaten, at least in part, by Man. The portion eaten by the *kohanim* is called in these verses "*ḥok*," which I translated above as "allotment." This word usually means law, but in this context it refers to the portion set aside by God from the sacrifice to be shared by the *kohanim*. It implies that the *kohanim* have a portion in the sacrifice, even though by definition the sacrifice belongs to God. This is not merely a gift to the *kohanim after* the fulfillment of the sacrificial ritual, but is an integral part of the ritual itself, for it expresses the idea of God's indwelling among the people. The *kohanim* share a meal on God's table. It is not the giving to God that atones, but the giving back by God that atones, for the atonement is not a result of the sacrifice but of the indwelling. The Holy Presence comes down to the Sanctuary because men eat at the table of God and share the meal.

Therefore, Moses was genuinely worried that the absence of eating for the *ḥatat* would not only indicate that Aaron thought that there was a flaw in the Holy Presence, but that it would itself constitute that flaw. Hence his anger, for the eating was the culmination of the process of God "dwelling in their midst." The inaugural sacrifices were not themselves indicative of this, precisely because they were inaugural, prior to the full sanctification. Moses was crucially interested in the regular sacrifice that would immediately follow the dramatic inauguration, to see if a permanent state of indwelling could be maintained.

Twice in this *parasha*, when Moses addresses the sons of Aaron, he is said to be speaking to Elazar and Itamar "the *remaining* sons of Aaron." There are commentators, at least in the second case (v. 16), where Moses is incensed at them, who interpret this reference as an implied threat – if they are not careful to properly fulfill the ritual, they could meet the fate of their brothers. I find this difficult; after all, there is no reason to think they deliberately chose to act in a "foreign" manner, like Nadav and Avihu. If they had made a halakhic mistake, there is no reason to assume that they faced death. In any event, this reasoning would not apply to the first appearance of the phrase "the remaining sons," which is when Moses innocently tells them to eat the sacrifices.

I think that "remaining" here is an expression of Moses' anxiety. The success of the endeavor of building a *Mishkan* depends on the eating of the *kohanim*, on their sharing the table of God. Of the original four *kohanim* who were sons of Aaron, only two are left. Everything depends on them, and Moses' insistence is magnified by the fact that they are all that is left, that they are the "remnant." It is not a threat, but an exhortation – please do it right, because everything depends on you, and only you.

The idea that lies at the base of Moses' dispute-discussion with Aaron, that God is present in our midst when we literally bring him into our bodies, and that Man and not only the physical building can and must be the seat of God's Presence, is, of course, one which is not limited to the *kohanim* in the *Mishkan* or *Beit HaMikdash*. By extension, it applies to the relationship between God and Israel as a whole.

The Impure and the Pure, That May and May Not Be Eaten

Rav Elchanan Samet

I. STRUCTURING THE CHAPTER AND ITS DIFFICULTIES

In chapter 11, we find a lengthy unit devoted to the laws of the various animals in two different spheres, eating and *tum'a*. On the one hand, there is a long list of forbidden animals and insects, and, on the other hand, the carcasses of some of them render anyone who touches them ritually impure. The chapter begins with a general introduction: "And God spoke to Moses and to Aaron, saying to them, Speak to *Benei Yisrael* saying…" It ends with a conclusion touching both spheres:

> This is the law of the animals and of the birds and of every living creature that moves in the water and of every creature that creeps upon the earth; To make a distinction *between the impure and the pure, between the animal that may be eaten and the animal that you shall not eat.*

The chapter is divided into two equal halves at the point where we find the transition from the subject of eating to the subject of impurity. The first half (1–23) discusses which animals we are permitted to eat and which are forbidden, beginning with the words, "These are the animals that you may eat." The second half (24–47) concerns those animals whose carcasses render one impure, and begins, "And for these you shall be impure."

Each half is comprised of four units, with each unit devoted to a different group of animals with some common characteristic (fish, birds, flying creatures, creeping creatures, etc.), and to the laws pertaining to those animals regarding permissibility to eat them or their characteristic of impurity, as represented in the following table:

Laws of Animals for Food	Laws of Impurity
General introduction (1–2a)	Impurity of the carcass of an animal that does not have signs of *kashrut* (24–28)
Signs of pure animals and a list of four impure animals (2b–8)	Impurity of the carcass of eight creeping creatures and the things that become impure from them (29–38)
Signs of fish that are permitted (9–12)	Impurity of the carcass of an animal that is permissible to eat (39–40)
List of forbidden birds (13–19)	Prohibition of eating any creeping creature (41–45)
Prohibition of flying insects and permissibility of four specific ones (20–23)	General conclusion (46–47)

A cursory examination discloses some inconsistencies. The fourth unit of impurity (41–45) deals with the prohibition of *eating* "every creeping creature that creeps upon the earth." As such, it would seem to belong to A, which deals with which animals can and cannot be eaten, rather than to B, which deals with the laws of impurity.

Similarly, there is in section A an exception to the discussion of the laws of permitted animals, but it is so brief that it is easily overlooked. In the first unit, when the Torah summarizes the prohibition against four animals that bear only one sign of *kashrut*, we are told in verse 8:

You shall not eat of their flesh *and you shall not touch their carcasses*; they are impure for you.

The emphasized words patently belong to the second half, the laws pertaining to impurity. This is not the only problem that arises from a study of the order of the subjects discussed in the two halves, but the dual problem concerning the confusion of subjects is perhaps the most obvious question, and it has great significance for the clarification of our next question.

II. BETWEEN *KASHRUT* AND *TUM'A*

Is there any real connection between the two subjects discussed in our chapter, or are they contained within the same literary unit only because both deal with laws pertaining to animals?

A comparison of the two halves of our chapter reveals that the two categories are not identical; only the first unit of section A, dealing with the large mammals – those that are permissible to eat as well as those that are forbidden – is dealt with in section B. The first unit of B deals with the impurity of the carcasses of those animals that are devoid of signs of *kashrut*, and the third unit deals with the impurity of the carcasses of "the animals that you may eat." In contrast, the three types of animal discussed in the continuation of A – the fish and insects of the sea, birds, and flying creatures – have no parallel law of impurity upon contact, neither for those that are permitted nor for those that are prohibited.

We find a similar phenomenon in relation to the creeping creatures of the earth. This is the largest group of the types of animals that are not to be eaten: "Whatever walks on its belly and whatever walks on four [legs] or whatever has many legs" (v. 42). But only eight of them, listed in verses 29–30, bring impurity upon contact with their carcasses, while all the other thousands of species of creeping creatures are forbidden as food, but do not render one impure after their death.

It is clear that the prohibition of eating does not necessarily cause impurity, while permissibility of a species does not prevent impurity. It is true, however, that no animal that transfers impurity after death can be eaten in that state, for a kosher animal that died by some process other than ritual slaughter is forbidden as food because it is a carcass (*neveila*).

III. BETWEEN *TAMEI* AND *SHEKETZ*

Let us now examine the terms used to describe the status of the animals.

In B, the first three units, dealing with the laws of animals that render one impure after their death, are governed by a single term: "impure" (*tamei* – טמא). This word is repeated there eighteen times, with regard to both the animals themselves ("they are impure for you") and the people or objects that have contact with them ("he shall be impure until the evening").

In A, by contrast, the animals that are forbidden as food are indicated by two different terms: "impure" (*tamei*) and "abomination" (*sheketz* – שקץ). It would seem that these two terms express the same thing – the rejection and loathing of the animal that is forbidden as food. If this is so, the two terms should be interchangeable. Indeed, there are instances in the Torah where something that in our chapter is called "*sheketz*" is elsewhere called "*tamei*." But the use of these two terms in our chapter seems precise and intentional, and attention should be paid to it specifically because the word "*tamei*" appears in two different contexts.

In A the word "*tamei*" appears only in the first unit, where it is repeated five times with reference to four forbidden animals (once for each animal mentioned individually, and a fifth time for the group collectively). No other term is used for forbidden animals in this unit.

But with reference to forbidden fish and other sea creatures, the text uses only the term "*sheketz*" (as a noun or as a verb) four times, with reference to forbidden birds another two times, and with reference to flying insects twice more. The word "*tamei*" does not appear even once in these three units.

Is it coincidental that only the species mentioned in the first unit of A as "impure" (*tamei*) are themselves – or others like them –mentioned in B as "rendering impure" (*metamei*) through contact or transfer, while the species that in the continuation of A are defined as "*sheketz*" are not mentioned at all in B, since they do not render one impure after their death?

The connection between the "impurity" of those species with regard to their consumption and with regard to contact with them is made explicit in verse 8 that summarizes the prohibition of the four impure animals mentioned above: "You shall not *eat* of their flesh nor shall you *touch* their carcasses; *they are impure for you.*" It is clear that the fact that "they are impure for you" has two ramifications – the prohibition of eating their flesh, and the impurity that arises from contact with them. This phrase, "they are impure for you," appearing five times in this unit, also appears in B:

> They are impure for you, anyone who touches them will be rendered impure. They are impure for you, anyone who touches their carcasses will be impure until the evening. (vv. 26–27)

It appears again in verses 28 and 31.

We are forced to conclude that the connection between the two subjects of discussion in our chapter is the opposite of what we suggested above. It is not the prohibition of eating that causes the impurity, but rather the impurity of those species that represents the reason for the prohibition against eating them. The prohibition of eating these species results from the fact that they are *impure by definition* (according to the laws of impurity by contact), and the Torah prohibits the *consumption* of something that is "*tamei*" (even though one is not forbidden to become ritually impure through contact with it).

Thus it seems that the prohibition of eating a carcass may arise from the definition of the carcass as something that is "impure" and therefore as something that is not suitable as food for a "holy nation."

IV. WHY THE *SHEKETZ* IS FORBIDDEN

We find, then, that the prohibition of eating various species of animals can be based on one of two reasons, depending on the essence of those species. Forbidden fish and other sea creatures, the forbidden birds and flying insects are all prohibited because they are defined as "*sheketz*." R. Yosef Bekhor Shor explains as follows:

> It may be compared to a man who tells his servant, "You are around me all the time, so do not defile yourself with loathsome and defiled foods".... A person who is defiled is not worthy of standing before the Holy One.

The term "*sheketz*" indeed expresses loathing and disgust. Ḥazal likewise prohibited other things that they considered abominable:

> Rav Aḥai said, He who waits to ease his bowels violates the prohibition of "You shall not make your souls abominable" (*lo teshaktzu*, Lev. 20:25). Rav Bibi b. Abaye said, He who drinks from the vessel used to draw blood – violates the prohibition of "You shall not make your souls abominable." (Makkot 16b)

In contrast, the large animals that are forbidden as food, such as the camel, the rabbit, the pig, and the horse and other mammals – some of which are kept by man for produce while others live in nature and man hunts them – for these man does not feel disgust and loathing as he does for the "*sheketz*" that is prohibited by the Torah. The reason for the prohibition is explicit in our chapter – "they are *impure* for you."

The phrase that is repeated over and over, "it is impure for you," represents here the reason for the prohibition of eating these animals rather than the definition of the prohibition. The concluding verse may be interpreted: "You shall not eat of their flesh *because* you may not touch their carcasses, for they are impure for you," and it is not proper for you to eat food that renders you impure upon contact with it.

V. "THEY ARE IMPURE TO YOU"

This gives us the key to solving a question that greatly troubled the early commentators. The Torah lists only four prohibited animals. At the beginning of the chapter we are told, "all with split hoofs and that chew the cud among the animals *you shall eat.*" This implies that anything that does not chew the cud or have split feet is forbidden, and a prohibition that derives from a positive command has the status of a positive commandment.

Thus concludes Rambam in his *Hilkhot Ma'akhalot Asurot* (2:1). He continues:

> And regarding the camel, the pig, the rabbit, and the hare we are told, "But this you shall not eat of those that chew the cud or those that have split feet" – this is teaching us a negative command, even though [these animals each] have one of the signs. How much more, in the case of the other impure animals that have neither sign at all, [do we learn] that the prohibition of eating them is

based on a negative command, over and above the positive command that arises from the general rule that "of these you shall eat."

If we look at the unit that opens the second half of the chapter we find that the animals mentioned as rendering impure upon contact or transfer are the following:

> The carcass of any animal that has a split hoof but is not cloven-footed is impure to you; anyone who touches them will become impure. And whatever walks on its paws, of all the animals that walk on four legs, these are impure to you. (26–27)

From the point of view of a categorization of mammals, this unit completes the unit with which the first half began. There we learned about animals that had both signs of *kashrut* (and they correspond to the seven animals listed in Deuteronomy 14:4–5) as well as the four animals that bear only one sign. In the opening unit of B, verse 26 discusses animals that have one imperfect sign – animals that have only a partially split hoof, such that it is not properly divided into two (the horse, the donkey, and their like), while verse 27 deals with the rest of the mammals that have no sign of *kashrut* at all – they walk on paws (the cat, the dog, the bear, the lion, the leopard, the monkey etc.). The combination of both units gives us the complete set of all tall land mammals.

But then we are told explicitly with regard to those animals that bear only one sign of *kashrut* that "they are impure to you" (8), and with regard to those that have one imperfect sign that "they are impure to you" (26), and again with regard to those that have no sign at all, walking as they do on paws, that "they are impure to you" (27). According to what we have said above, this phrase indicates the same thing in each of these three instances – they are impure when dead and they render one impure upon contact with their carcasses. But, again according to what we have said above, this has one additional consequence – all are forbidden as food precisely because they are impure species! If this is so, then there are explicit verses according to which we may prohibit all of these impure animals and include all of them in a single category – "they are impure to you."

VI. THOSE THAT CREEP

Up until this point, we have ignored the "*sheratzim*" (rodents and insects) and the expressions with which the Torah describes the prohibition against their consumption towards the end of our chapter. In this context, we do not find the distinction between "*sheketz*" and "*tamei*" that we encountered in the first half the chapter:

> All the things that swarm upon the earth are an *abomination* (*sheketz*); they shall not be eaten. Anything that crawls on its belly...or anything that has many legs...you shall not eat, for they are an *abomination*. You shall not draw *abomination* upon yourselves through anything that swarms; you shall not make yourselves *impure* therewith (*titam'u*) and thus become *impure* (*venitmetem*)...you shall sanctify yourselves and be holy...you shall not make yourselves *impure* through any swarming thing that moves upon the earth. (41–44)

These verses employ the term "*sheketz*" (abomination) three times, the same number of times as the term "*tamei*" in its various forms appears. Why?

The group of animals classified as "*sheretz*" has the unique characteristic of consisting of some creatures who transmit ritual impurity through contact with their corpses, as well as those that do not. All dead animals ("*beheimot*" and "*ḥayot*") transmit impurity, while all birds and fowl do not. Only the "*sheretz*" group includes both types.

It would thus seem that two different reasons for the prohibition against eating "*sheratzim*" exist. More specifically, there are two underlying reasons for the prohibition against eating the "*sheratzim*" that transmit impurity (29–31), thus accounting for the double expression: "for they are an *abomination*. You shall not draw an *abomination* upon yourselves...you shall not make yourselves impure (*titam'u*) therewith and thus become impure." These creatures contain both the element of "*sheketz*" – which warrants a prohibition against their consumption – and a component of "*tum'a*," which renders one impure upon contact with their carcasses.

One question, however, arises. The subcategory of creatures that transmit impurity is much smaller than its counterpart, the group of "*sheratzim*" that do not. After all, only eight creatures transmit impurity, while all other insects in the world do not. Why, then, does the Torah equate the two components – mentioning both "*tum'a*" and "*sheketz*" three times – when the component of "*tum'a*" applies to only eight out of all the insects on earth!

The answer relates to the underlying reason behind the *tum'a* ascribed to these insects and the designation of specifically these eight species. Certainly, death and subsequent contact with dead creatures causes ritual impurity in principle. But only the death of those creatures that live near and among human beings and which man deems important can transmit *tum'a*. Creatures of "lesser" value or who reside far away from human residence or activity (such as fish and birds) do not generate impurity upon their demise.

The death of the human being generates the most severe form of *tum'a*; a dead body is the strongest source of ritual impurity. Next come the large, land-dwelling mammals, with which man shares the earth (Psalms 104:20–23). Even among the small, "swarming creatures," there exist some significant creatures. They live among or near the human being and have earned their place in his awareness. Man hunts them regularly for their flesh and skin (see Mishna Shabbat 14:1). Given the particular prominence of these eight species, our statistical question regarding the disproportionate attention afforded to them can be answered. In fact, the prohibition against eating "*sheratzim*" was issued primarily regarding these eight, which apparently were more commonly eaten by humans (see Isaiah 66:17).

We can now explain the problem presented earlier – why do verses 41–45, prohibiting the *eating* of "*sheretz*," appear at the end of the second section? This section, as we have seen, includes a compound prohibition, based both on "*sheketz*" and on "*tum'a*." This distinction is only comprehensible after we have learnt that eight species engender *tum'a*, while the other species in this category do not. Therefore, only after concluding the section of *tum'a* does the Torah return to complete the eating prohibition of this category.

One could suggest another reason as well. Our section begins with the words, "This is the animal that you may eat." Unlike the other categories, the "*sheretz*" has no permitted species. Therefore it is not included in the opening of "which you may eat," but is added as an appendix at the end.

Parashat Tazria

The Tum'a Interruption

Rav Menachem Leibtag

I. INTRODUCTION

Parashat Aḥarei Mot begins, "And God spoke to Moses and Aaron after the death of the two sons of Aaron" (16:1). Since *Parashat Aḥarei Mot* opens with God's commandment to Moses and Aaron in the aftermath of the death of Aaron's sons, it would have been more logical for the Torah to include this commandment in *Parashat Shemini* – immediately after the story of their death. Why do the *parashot* of *Tazria* and *Metzora*, detailing numerous laws concerning various types of *tum'a* (spiritual defilement), "interrupt" this logical sequence?

To explain, we shall explore the thematic relationship between the laws of *tum'a* and the story of the death of Nadav and Avinu. Afterwards, we will build an outline that will summarize these laws of *tum'a* that will help us appreciate their detail, and then use it to help us arrive at a more comprehensive understanding of the structure and theme of Leviticus.

II. WHAT DID NADAV AND AVIHU DO WRONG?

The commentators suggest many interpretations of Nadav and Avihu's sin. The reason for this is simple – the Torah only describes *what* they did, but does not explain *why* they were punished. Therefore, each commentator looks for a clue either within the verse or in the neighboring verses in search of that reason. In contrast, we shall focus instead on the more general connection between this incident and the overall structure (and theme) of Leviticus.

Even though the Torah does not tell us specifically why Nadav and Avihu were punished, the verse that describes their sin does provide us with a very general explanation: *"Vayakrivu eish zara, asher lo tziva otam"* – "and they offered a foreign fire that *God had not commanded them"* (see 10:1).

The phrase *"asher lo tziva otam"* should not surprise us, as it appeared – or rather its converse had appeared – numerous times in the *parashot* of *Vayak'hel* and *Pekudei*. *"Ka'asher tziva HaShem et Moshe"* – "As God has commanded Moses," concludes just about every section in *Parashat Pekudei*.

Furthermore, this phrase first appeared at the very introduction of the *Mishkan* unit that began in *Parashat Vayak'hel*:

> And Moses said to the entire congregation of Israel: This is what God has commanded (*zeh hadavar asher tziva HaShem*).

Finally, in Leviticus we find this same phrase twice, when the Torah describes the story of the *Mishkan's* dedication. First, in the seven-day *miluim* ceremony:

> And Moses said to the entire congregation: This (*zeh hadavar*) is what God has commanded to do. (Lev. 8:4–5)

Second, in Moses' opening explanation of the special offerings of the eighth day:

> And Moses said: This (*zeh hadavar*) is what God has commanded that you do [in order] that His glory can appear upon you. (9:6, see also 9:1–5)

Note how Moses declares this statement in front of the entire congregation that has gathered to watch this ceremony, and how the Torah concludes each stage of this special ceremony with this same phrase. Therefore, when the Torah uses a very similar phrase to describe the sin of Nadav and Avihu, we should expect to find a thematic connection between that sin and this phrase. To find that connection, we must consider the reason why the Torah uses this phrase so often in its details of the *Mishkan's* construction.

Recall that Nadav and Avihu's sin took place on the "eighth day." Earlier on that day, Moses gathered the entire nation to explain the precise details of how the offerings would be offered on that day. Why must Moses first explain the details of these procedures to the entire congregation who have gathered to watch? The Torah appears to be sending a very strong message in regard to the *Mishkan*. God demands that man must act precisely in accordance with His command – without changing even a minute detail.

With this background, we can better understand why Nadav and Avihu are punished. On the day of its public dedication, they decide on their own to offer incense. Their fire is considered "*eish zara*" (alien fire) simply because God did *not* command them to offer it. They may have had the purest intentions, but they made one critical mistake – they did not act according to the precise protocol that God had prescribed for that day.

From a thematic perspective, their punishment under these circumstances is quite understandable. Recall the theological dilemma created by the *Mishkan* – the physical representation (or symbol) of a transcendent God. Once a physical object is used to represent God, the danger exists that man may treat that object (and then possibly another object) as a god itself. On the other hand, without a physical representation of any sort, it becomes difficult for man to develop any sort of relationship with God. Therefore, God allows a *Mishkan* – a symbol of His Presence – but at the same time, He must emphasize that He can only be worshiped according to the precise manner "as God had commanded Moses."

Even Aaron had sincere intentions at the incident of *het ha'egel* – the Golden Calf. He wanted to provide *Benei Yisrael* with a physical symbol of God, which they could worship. Despite his good intentions, however, his actions led to disaster. The sin caused the *Shekhina*, God's Glory, present since Mount Sinai, to depart.

Due to Moses' intervention, God allowed the *Shekhina* to return to the *Mishkan* that Israel had built. But when Nadav and Avihu make a mistake similar to Aaron's on the very day of the *Mishkan's* dedication, they must be punished immediately.

Finally, this interpretation helps us understand Moses' statement to Aaron: "This is what God had spoken – I will be sanctified through *those close to Me*" (10:3). At Mount Sinai, both *Benei Yisrael* and the *kohanim* were forewarned:

> And God told Moses: Go down and warn the people that they must not break through [the barrier surrounding] Mount Sinai, lest they gaze at God and perish. The *kohanim* also, who *come near God*, must sanctify themselves lest God punish them. (Ex. 19:21)

As this inaugural ceremony parallels the events of Mount Sinai, God's original warning concerning approaching Mount Sinai, even for the *kohanim*, now applies to the *Mishkan* as well. Therefore, extra caution is necessary, no matter how good one's intentions may be.

In Leviticus, the story of the sin of Nadav and Avihu (chapter 10) introduces an entire set of laws that discuss improper entry into the *Mishkan* (chapters 11–15). Immediately after this tragic event, Leviticus discusses the various laws of *tum'a vetahara*, which regulate who is permitted and who is forbidden to enter the *Mishkan*. Only after the completion of this section discussing who can enter the *Mishkan* does Leviticus return (in chapter 16) to God's command to Aaron concerning how he himself can properly enter the holiest sanctum.

III. THE STRUCTURE OF THE LAWS OF *TUM'A VETAHARA*

We often find ourselves lost in the maze of complicated laws concerning *tum'a* and *tahara* which the Torah details in the *parashot* of *Tazria* and *Metzora*. We shall outline the flow of *parashot* from *Parashat Shemini* through *Metzora* and attempt to explain why they are located specifically in this section of Leviticus. As the following table shows, each of these five chapters deals with a topic related in one form or manner to *tum'a*.

Chapter	Tum'a Caused By:
11	eating or touching dead animals
12	the birth of a child
13–14	tzara'at on a person's skin or garment
14	tzara'at in a house
15	various emissions from the human body

Not only do these *parashot* discuss how one contracts these various types of *tum'a*, they also explain how one can cleanse himself from them and become pure. For the simplest type of *tum'a*, one need only immerse and wait until sundown. For more severe types, one must first wait seven days and then bring a set of special offerings.

This entire unit follows a very logical progression. It begins with the least severe type of *tum'a*, known as *tum'at erev* – one-day *tum'a* (literally, until the evening), and then continues with the more severe type of *tum'a*, known as *tum'at shiva*, seven-day *tum'a*. Within each category, the Torah first explains how one contracts each type of *tum'a*, then it explains the process of purification – *tahara*. The following outline summarizes this structure. Note how each section of the outline concludes with "*zot torat*" – "this is the procedure":

One-day *tum'a* – 11:1–47

1. Person is *tamei* until nightfall – because he ate, touched, or carried the dead carcass of:
    a. forbidden animals and fowl
    b. one of the eight *sheratzim* (swarming creatures)
    c. permitted animals that died without *sheḥita* (ritual slaughter)
    d. other creeping or swarming creatures
    Tahara for the above – immersion (literally, washing one's clothes)
    Concluding verse – *Zot torat habeheima*

Seven-day *Tum'a* – 12:1–15:33

1. *Tum'at yoledet* – a mother who gave birth (12:1–8)
    a. for a boy: 7+33=40

   b. for a girl: 14+66=80
   Tahara – korban ḥatat and *ola*
   Concluding verses – *Zot torat hayoledet*

2. *Tzara'at ha'adam* – a person who contracted *tzara'at*, based on inspection by the *kohen* (13:1–14:32)
   a. on one's body (13:1–46)
   b. on one's garment (13:47–59)
   Tahara –
   a. special sprinkling, then count seven days
   b. special *korban* on eighth day
   Concluding verse – *Zot torat asher bo nega tzara'at*

3. *Tzara'at habayit* – a house that contracted *tzara'at*, based on inspection by the *kohen* (14:33–53)
   a. the stones of the house itself (14:33–45)
   b. secondary *tum'a* (14:46–47) for one who:
      i. enters the house
      ii. sleeps in the house
      iii. eats in the house
   Tahara – a special sprinkling on the house (14:48–53)
   Concluding verse – *Zot hatorah lekhol nega hatzara'at… zot torat hatzara'at*

4. Emissions from the body (chapter 15)
   a. *Tum'at zav* (male) – an abnormal emission of seed
      i. he himself – 7 days (15:1–4)
      ii. secondary *tum'a* – 1 day for one who either touches what the *zav* is sitting on, or sits on an item that the *zav* sat on, and other miscellaneous cases (15:5–12)
   Tahara – waiting 7 days, then washing with *mayim ḥayim* and a special offering on the eighth day (15:13–15)
   b. *Tum'at keri* (male) – a normal emission (15:16–18)
   c. *Tum'at nidda* (female) – a normal flow (15:19–24)
      i. she herself – 7 days

    ii. secondary *tum'a* – one day for a person or items that
       she touches
  d. *Tum'at zava* (female) – an abnormal flow (15:25–30)
    i. she herself and what she sits on – 7 days
    ii. secondary *tum'a* for someone who touches her or
      something which she is sitting on.
  Tahara – waiting 7 days, a special offering on the eighth day
  Concluding verse – *Zot torat hazav*

Our division of the outline into two sections, one-day *tum'a* and seven-day *tum'a*, may appear to be a bit misleading, for we find many cases of one-day *tum'a* in the second section. However, the cases of one-day *tum'a* in the second section are quite different for they are caused by a person who had first become *tamei* for seven days. Therefore, we have defined them as "secondary" *tum'a* in that section.

As we noted, the entire unit contains an important concluding verse:

Vehizartem et Benei Yisrael mitum'atam (And you shall put *Benei Yisrael* on guard against their *tum'a*), *lest they die* through their defilement by defiling My *Mishkan* which is among them. (15:31)

This verse connects the laws of *tum'a* and *tahara* to the laws of the *Mishkan*. *Benei Yisrael* must be careful that should they become *tamei*, they must not enter the *Mishkan*. In fact, the primary consequence for one who has become *tamei* is the prohibition that he cannot enter the *Mikdash* complex. There is no prohibition against becoming *tamei*, rather only a prohibition against entering the *Mishkan* should he be *tamei*.

With this background, we can suggest a common theme for the first sixteen chapters of Leviticus – the ability of *Benei Yisrael* to enter the *Mishkan*, to come closer to God.

The first section of Leviticus, chapters 1–7, explains how and when the individual can bring an offering, and how it is offered by the *kohen*. The next section, chapters 8–10, records the special *Mishkan* dedication ceremony, which prepared *Benei Yisrael* and the *kohanim* for using and working in the *Mishkan*. As this ceremony concluded with the death of Nadav and Avihu for improper entry into the *Mishkan*, Leviticus continues with an entire set of commandments concerning *tum'a* and *tahara*, chapters 11–15, which regulate who can and cannot enter the *Mishkan*. This unit ends with laws of Yom Kippur, which describe the procedure of how the *Kohen Gadol* (High Priest) can enter the most sacred domain of the *Mishkan* – the *Kodesh Kodashim*.

Even though these laws of *tum'a* and *tahara* may have been given to Moses at an earlier or later time, we find that Leviticus prefers thematic continuity over chronological order. First, the book discusses who cannot enter the *Mishkan*. Then it explains who can enter its most sacred domain.

Tum'a: Birth and Death

Rav Avraham Walfish

The laws regarding childbirth and its aftermath appear strange, at least to modern eyes. The joyful and dramatic event is marked by a protracted period of purification, culminating in two sacrificial offerings, including a *ḥatat* (sin offering). The bulk of the *parasha*, concerning the disease *tzara'at*, normally – and inaccurately – translated as "leprosy," will appear yet stranger, an enigmatic amalgamation of (unknown) medical descriptions and purification prescriptions. Here, as in many other problematic Torah passages, we may gain insight into the rationale and significance of our *parasha* by paying close attention, not only to its language, but to its boundaries – its formulae of introduction and closing, its order and structure, and its broader literary context.

Insofar as our *parasha* deals with two topics, childbirth and *tzara'at*, it naturally possesses two introductory formulae and two concluding formulae. If we focus on the closing formulae, we will find a phrase characteristic of the first half of Leviticus: "*Zot torat hayoledet*" (This is the instruction regarding the woman who gives birth – 12:7), "*Zot torat nega hatzara'at*" (This is the instruction regarding the affliction of the *tzara'at* – 13:59). This "*zot torat*" formula appears twelve times between Leviticus 6 and Leviticus 15. Hence we see that the two subjects discussed in our *parasha* are connected with the constellation of topics dealt with in this larger section of Leviticus.

The introductory formulae within our *parasha* indicate that our *parasha* needs to be viewed within a slightly different context. Chapter 13 opens with "God spoke to Moses and to Aaron, saying." The inclusion of Aaron in God's revelation to Moses is characteristic of the majority of passages beginning with Leviticus 11 and culminating in Leviticus 15. In chapter 10 we have an even more impressive phenomenon: "God spoke to *Aaron*, saying" (10:8) – to Aaron alone! Clearly the laws between chapter 10 and chapter 15 have a special connection to Aaron and the priesthood. The overarching theme of this section of Leviticus is *tum'a* and *tahara*, ritual impurity and purity.

This in itself would be enough to explain the special role accorded to Aaron in this section. However, we may arrive at a more profound insight if we pay attention to the way in which this section fits into the larger structure of Leviticus. The special focus on the role of the *kohanim* began already in chapter 6, in the context of the laws of *korbanot* (the offerings). This could explain why the *zot torat* formula begins in chapter 6 and continues through the section of chapters 10–15, linking chapters 6–7 to our section. Yet God's direct address to the *kohanim*, beginning with chapter 10, would indicate that the focus on the *kohanim* in the discussion of *tum'a* is somehow more pressing than the focus on the priestly role regarding the *korbanot*.

The key to understanding this special emphasis on the *kohanim* is in the lengthy narrative passage – unique in Leviticus – which marks the transition from the *korbanot* section to the *tum'a* section. Chapters 8–10 describe the consecration ceremony of the *Mishkan*, climaxing in the dramatically tragic death of Nadav and Avihu. Immediately following their death – and preceding the concluding details of the consecration ceremony – God addresses Aaron for the first time in Leviticus, and warns him not to enter the *Mishkan* after having drunk intoxicating beverages. God commands (10:10–11): "And you shall distinguish between the sacred and the common and between the impure and the pure. And you shall instruct the Israelites all the laws which God spoke to them through Moses."

This command links the laws of *tum'a* with the tragic end of Nadav and Avihu. They failed to distinguish between permissible and impermissible ways of drawing near to God's Presence. Their death conveys a message to all the Israelites, but especially to the *kohanim* resident in the *Mishkan* and entrusted with its sanctity and its service. Approach to God cannot be done in a state of intoxication (literal or figurative), which obliterates boundaries and distinctions, but must be done in full awareness and cognizance of the laws and regulations upon which the very notion of sanctity hinges. Sanctity, *kedusha*, is a Hebrew word whose root means to separate, to set aside. The idea is clearly enunciated at the end of *Parashat Shemini* (11:43–44):

> You shall not defile your souls with any creature that swarms and you shall not make yourselves impure therewith and thus become impure. For I am HaShem your God, and you shall sanctify yourselves (*vehitkadishtem*) and be *holy*, for I am *holy*.

God's holiness resides in His being "Wholly Other," transcendent, separated by an absolute metaphysical gulf from the realm of spatially and temporally conditioned beings. Hence we may approach His Presence only when we learn and practice the divinely ordained laws of separation and division.

The section following the laws of *tum'a vetahara* refers once again to the death of Nadav and Avihu (16:1) and describes the detailed and complex ceremony by means of which Aaron may enter the Holy of Holies. Thus the laws governing *tum'a vetahara* are framed (chapters 10 and 16) by references to the death of Nadav and Avihu, underscoring the connection between these laws of separation and the nobly tragic aspiration of free access to God, represented by these neophyte *kohanim*.

The laws of *tum'a vetahara* open in *Parashat Shemini*, chapter 11, with a discussion of clean and unclean animals. Although we commonly regard chapter 11 as dealing with dietary laws – which it does – the postscript to the chapter indicates clearly that these laws are part of the larger framework of *tum'a vetahara* (11:46–47):

> This is the instruction (*zot torat*) regarding animals and birds and all living creatures swarming in the water and all creatures swarming on the earth. To separate between the impure and the

pure and between the animal which may be eaten and the animal which may not be eaten.

This is further indicated by referring to the forbidden species of animals as "impure." Some animal species are inherently impure, such that they may never be consumed and their carcasses will always defile (11:8, 24–28, 31). Species classified as pure may be consumed, and their carcasses – if ritually slaughtered (see 11:39 and Mishna Ḥullin 2:4, 4:4) – will not defile.

This brings us to the opening of *Parashat Tazria*. Rashi, following R. Simlai in the Midrash (Leviticus Rabba 14:1), explains how the opening of our *parasha* connects with the end of the previous *parasha*: "As man was created after the domestic animals, wild animals, and birds, so his *torah* is explained after the *torah* of domestic animals, wild animals, and birds." This midrash suggests a connection between the laws of *tum'a* and *tahara* and the creation of the world. We may support and underscore this connection by noting the use, in the verse from chapter 11 cited earlier (46), of terms highly reminiscent of the creation account in Genesis 1: "And all living creatures (*nefesh ḥaya*) swarming (*romeset*) in the water and all creatures swarming (*shoretzet*) on the earth." Outside of this passage, the term "*nefesh ḥaya*" appears in the Torah only in the creation account, the root "*romes*" only in the creation account and the uncreation and re-creation of the flood story (and Leviticus 20:25, which repeats our passage), and the root "*shoretz*" appears twice in the Torah outside of our passage, in the creation account and the flood story. By using these terms redolent of the creation story, as well as by preceding the *tum'a* of animals to that of persons, the Torah suggests that *tum'a vetahara* stems from a certain way of relating to creation.

The juxtaposition of human *tum'a* to animal *tum'a* focuses our attention on a fundamental distinction between these two realms, noted by R. David Zvi Hoffmann (vol. I, p. 249): "Animals defile only after their death; as long as they are alive none of them defile. However man, even during his life, finds himself in situations where he may serve as a source of defilement." Herein may lie the explanation for a puzzling omission of the Torah, within our passage. In listing the forms of *tum'a* generated by human beings, in *Parashot Tazria* and *Metzora*, the Torah omits the granddaddy of all *tum'ot* – *tum'at met* (a human corpse), whose laws are outlined in Numbers. Perhaps the reason for this is to emphasize the unique nature of human *tum'a*, which does not make its first appearance at the time of human death.

R. Hoffmann utilizes this idea to explain why the Torah opens the discussion of humanly-generated *tum'a* with the case of childbirth:

> The most severe... is the *tum'a* of *tzara'at*, hence it would appear that the list should begin with this *tum'a*. However, since a human being, immediately upon his emergence into this world, brings *tum'a* to his mother...therefore the Torah thought it proper to begin the order [of *tum'ot*] with that form of *tum'a* which a person causes immediately upon his birth.

This idea, however, seems paradoxical. Normally we understand the idea of *tum'a* as being associated with death. R. Joseph B. Soloveitchik has written trenchantly on this theme (*Halakhic Man*, pp. 30–31):

> Judaism... proclaims that coming into contact with the dead precipitates defilement. Judaism abhors death, organic decay, and dissolution. It bids one to choose life and sanctify it. Authentic Judaism as reflected in halakhic thought sees in death a terrifying contradiction to the whole of religious life. Death negates the entire magnificent experience of halakhic man. "I am free among the dead" (Ps. 88:6) – when a person dies, he is freed from the commandments.

Other forms of *tum'a* also may be seen as death-related, as we have already seen in the case of animal *tum'a*. R. Yehuda Halevi suggests (*Kuzari* 2:60):

> For death is the absolute loss of the body. A limb afflicted with *tzara'at* is similar to the dead, and similarly seed that has been wasted, because it has in it the natural spirit of life, and in it is the potential to join with a drop of blood, from which a man comes to be. Hence the loss of this seed is the antithesis of the property

of life and vital spirit. Because of the subtlety of this loss, people don't feel it palpably.

We may complete his idea as follows: The Torah, by insisting upon (lesser) forms of *tum'a* for any physical process involving loss of a life-force, seeks to sensitize man to these more subtle forms of "death" and to force him to confront its spiritual effects.

R. Yehuda Halevi's explanation of humanly-generated *tum'ot* as expressing the loss or diminishing of a life-force seems to account for all the forms of *tum'a* – except for the one chosen to open the list of human *tum'ot*, childbirth. Here is the coming to fruition of maternal as well as paternal seed, the life-force has been enhanced, not diminished. Why does the Torah here decree *tum'a* upon the joyful mother, indeed a form of *tum'a* whose purification process is lengthier than that of any other *tum'a*?

We might suggest an answer along the lines of R. Yehuda Halevi. Indeed the birth of a child is a joyous event, a celebration of a new life. However, in human reality there is no point of transition which only connotes the attainment of something new without connoting the end of an era, no beginning which does not also mark an end. For the parturient mother, this is particularly dramatic. For nine months the mother felt a new life emerge and grow in her womb, an organic unity was experienced between the mother and the new soul stirring within her body. The emergence of the baby into independent existence in this world, while representing the successful realization of desires and hopes, also marks a separation, a loss from the mother's body of a thrilling vital force. The well-known psychological syndrome known as post-partum depression may be seen as a pathological form of this sense of loss and separation, which normally – as noted by R. Yehuda Halevi – is experienced subtly, or even imperceptibly. However, the Torah recognizes the reality and the importance of this undertone of separation mourning and seeks to sensitize the mother to it by decreeing upon her *tum'a*.

R. Samson Raphael Hirsch suggests a different understanding of the root and nature of *tum'a*. In his view *tum'a* arises from any encounter with

...evidence that Man *must* submit to the power physical of forces.... Man can master, rule, and use even his sensuous body with all its innate forces, urges, and powers, with God-like free self-decision, within the limits of, and for the accomplishment of, the duties set by the laws of morality; all these are Truths which, in the face of human frailty and the powers of the forces of Nature...are to be brought again and again to the minds of living people, so that they remain conscious of their unique position of freedom in the midst of the physical world.

Of course the most dramatic and awesome evidence of the submission of man to physical forces is death, the most dramatic and severe of all the forms of *tum'a*. However, birth is no less a demonstration of the fact of man's bondage to his biology:

The Mother herself, under the fresh impression of her physically completely passively and painfully having to submit to the forces of the physical laws of Nature at the most sublime procedure of her earthly calling, has to re-establish again the consciousness of her own spiritual height.

According to Hirsch we may recognize that there are two sources of *tum'a*, rather than one: death and sexuality. Death and sexuality strip man of his flimsy layer of control, domination, intellectual and spiritual order and render him naked before the forces of biological nature which hold him in thrall. A spiritually naked man may not enter the *Mishkan* or draw close to the Divine Presence, but must observe a period of *tum'a* before re-entering the sphere in which he feels that his spiritual consciousness is firmly in control of his personality.

The Torah's allusions to creation, as well as the juxtaposition of human to animal *tum'a*, may now be understood clearly. The laws of *tum'a vetahara* are a summons to man to reflect upon the relationship of spirit and of animal biology, within his personality. His entry into the presence of God is contingent upon his being a noble, exalted being (R. Soloveitchik, R. Yehuda Halevi), sovereign over his own nature and being (R. Hirsch), capable of freely submitting to the divine call.

However this free and exalted aspect of his being, central as it is to the Torah's anthropology, is not the sum total of human existence. Biological nature consists in an ongoing oscillation between birth and death. Birth and death are bound together in an often mysterious and dialectical rhythm. On occasions which bring home to man how beholden he is to this mysterious rhythm stirring within his body, the Torah bids him to step back, to surrender momentarily to his biological helplessness, to undergo a process of purification designed to refashion that thin buffering layer of spiritual exaltation which raises man above the beasts.

We may further suggest that it is not accidental that the death of Nadav and Avihu serves as catalyst to the topic of *tum'a vetahara*. The death was an enigmatic and numinous event, which added to the joyous celebration of sanctifying the *Mishkan* a note of sobriety and grief. Aaron and his sons are enjoined to continue the celebration, even while the grief over the sudden tragic death is fresh. Nadav and Avihu, in their heedless and unauthorized mode of entry into the Divine Presence, are consumed by the same heavenly fire which consumes the animal sacrifices on the altar, representing that selfsame Divine Presence. The Divine Presence is simultaneously the cause of joy and of grief, as man witnesses simultaneously the attainment of his highest dream and prayer and the shattering of his hopes and his joy. This dialectical and enigmatic enactment of the paradox of man, imprisoned within his space-time and biological urges, drawing near to the transcendent Wholly Other God, casts its shadow over the entire framework of the laws of *tum'a*.

The Torah Prohibitions Concerning Impurity

Rav Yehuda Rock

I. INTRODUCTION

The main laws concerning *tum'a vetahara*, ritual purity and impurity, appear in the *parashot* of *Shemini*, *Tazria*, and *Metzora*, and we encounter a consistent contradiction between the literal reading of these texts and halakha as we know it. From the verses it appears that a person is forbidden to become ritually impure. One who is pure is forbidden to become impure, and one who is impure is obligated to undergo purification. We shall review, in order, the verses that support this assertion:

1. In chapter 5, the Torah lists three sins that require a sacrifice of adjustable value (*korban oleh veyored*, based on economic means). The first and the third are an oath of testimony and an oath of expression, respectively. The second is: "Or if a person touches anything that is impure, or the corpse of an impure animal … and it is hidden from him, such that he is impure and guilty; or if he touches the impurity of man – of any sort of impurity that may defile him – and it is hidden from him, and he comes to know of it, and is guilty" (5:2–3). This would suggest that defilement is a transgression, which, if committed inadvertently, requires a sacrifice of adjustable value.

2. In *Parashat Shemini* we read: "But these you shall not eat…you shall not eat of their flesh, *nor shall you touch their carcass*; they are impure for you" (11:4–8). This tells us explicitly that one is forbidden to touch the carcass of an impure animal, because of its impurity.

3. Throughout the sections that address the various forms of impurity, we find the corresponding laws of purification. The Torah does not describe these actions as a mere precondition for purification; the literal meaning of the text suggests that a person who is rendered ritually impure is obligated to perform these actions and thereby to purify himself. In one place this is explicit (17:15–16): "And he shall wash his clothes and bathe in water, and he shall be impure until the evening, and then he shall be pure. *But if he does not wash [his clothing] and does not bathe, then he shall bear his sin."*

4. At the end of *Parashat Metzora*, after the Torah lists the various types of emissions that render one impure, we read: "You shall separate (*vehizartem*) *Benei Yisrael* from their impurity, so that they do not die in their impurity when they defile My Sanctuary which is in their midst." The word "warn" is derived from the root *n-z-r*, meaning separation. This verse tells us, then, that it is necessary to keep separate from impurity and to maintain purity; one who fails to guard himself against impurity incurs death.

5. In the unit addressing the impurity incurred through contact with a dead body (Num. 19:10–22), we read: "Anyone who touches the dead body of a person who has died, and does not purify himself – he defiles the Sanctuary of God, and that soul shall be cut off from Israel" (v. 13, see also v. 20).

In contrast to all of the above, the Oral Law paints a completely different picture. According to halakha, there is no prohibition related to the state of impurity; there are only prohibitions that apply to a person in that state in the context of the Temple, its sacrifices, and the foods that may be eaten only in its precincts (such as *teruma*). There is, admittedly, an opinion among the *Tanna'im* (that of R. Yossi, which is not accepted as normative halakha) maintaining that "immersion at the proper time represents a commandment." There are laws deduced by Ḥazal requiring a state of purity during pilgrimage to Jerusalem and requiring that even non-sanctified foods be eaten in a state of purity. But these points, even if they are to be considered as binding halakha, are of secondary status, with limited scope, representing at most a positive obligation. They can under no circumstances be regarded as falling under the category of "bearing sin," of negative and positive commandments associated with a punishment of *karet*, as the literal verses suggest.

Halakha interprets the verses as applying to different situations:

1. Concerning the sacrifice of adjustable value, Ḥazal interpret the expression "it is hidden" (*vene'elam*) as an indication that the Torah is talking about impurity related to the Sanctuary and its sacrifices. But these verses make no mention of the Temple or its sacrifices. Ramban comments that the context is obvious, and there is therefore no reason for the Torah to mention it. Rashi suggests that the contact with the Temple and its sacrifices is hinted at in the word "*ve'ashem*" ("and he is guilty"). These opinions notwithstanding, it is difficult to accept the assumption that the Torah leaves such an important point to the reader's understanding.

2. Concerning the prohibition, "nor shall you touch their carcass," Ḥazal offer two interpretations. One (Sifra, *Parashat Shemini* 4:9; *baraita* in Rosh HaShana 16b) focuses this prohibition on the pilgrim festivals (without making clear whether the prohibition is to be considered biblical in origin or not; see Ramban, ad loc.). Clearly, this has no basis in the literal text. A second interpretation (Sifra, ibid., 10) views the contact with a carcass as something "voluntary." It is possible that what the Torah means to convey here is a negative moral consideration, which is not binding (see the first chapter of *Shiurei HaRav Aharon Lichtenstein* on *Teharot*). But this explanation is likewise far removed from the literal meaning of the text, which adopts the imperative case – as in all other prohibitions in the Torah. Rashbam proposes that the text refers to the context of the sacrifices in the Temple; Ramban explains that the Torah is describing the means for maintaining

ritual purity, for one wishing to do so. Only Ibn Ezra adheres to the literal meaning, that the Torah is prohibiting contact with the carcass. This brings us back to the same problem – this conclusion runs counter to halakha.

3. The verses at the end of chapter 17 in *Aḥarei Mot* are also interpreted as referring to the context of the Temple and its sacrifices (Sifra, chapter 11, 14) despite that the verses make no mention of this. Once again, Rashi and Rashbam supply this as missing information, while Ibn Ezra interprets according to the literal meaning, contrary to halakha.

4. *Ḥazal* interpret the injunction, "You shall separate *Benei Yisrael* from their impurity" as referring to separation from their wives close to the time of their menstruation (Nidda 63b). The literal meaning of the text, however, as we have noted, is that a person must separate himself from impurity and maintain a state of purity. Elsewhere, *Ḥazal* deduce from this verse that graves should be marked (Mo'ed Katan 5a). Obviously, this, too, has no basis in the literal text. In Sifra (chapter 9, 7) *Ḥazal* connect the prohibition of "you shall separate" with the death sentence that appears in the continuation of the verse – as the literal reading undoubtedly demands. Accordingly, this *baraita* in Sifra does not interpret the verse as referring to separation in anticipation of a woman's menstruation, nor to the marking of graves, but rather as a prohibition involving the death sentence – apparently, defilement of the Temple and its sacrifices (see Rashi). However, the defilement of the Sanctuary appears here as the reason for the punishment, rather than as a condition in committing the transgression; hence, it would seem that the transgression and the punishment are not mutually dependent.

5. In the Sifrei (Num., *piska* 129) the verses in the unit discussing impurity caused by a dead body are interpreted as applying in the context of defilement of the Sanctuary. Here, too, there is mention of defilement of the Sanctuary, but once again it is as a result, in the wake of the sin, rather than as a condition in committing the sin.

How are we to explain the discrepancy between the literal indications of the Written Law and the normative halakha of the Oral Law? To solve the problem we need to look at another source – the discussion of those removed from the various camps, in *Parashat Naso*.

II. THE SANCTITY OF THE CAMP

> God spoke to Moses, saying: Command *Benei Yisrael*, that they should send out of the camp anyone with *tzara'at*, and anyone who has experienced an issue, and anyone who is impure through contact with the dead; whether male or female you shall send them, to outside of the camp shall you send them, so that they do not defile their camps in whose midst I reside. (Num. 5:1–4)

This represents a source for the law of "removal from the camps" – the prohibition of anyone who is impure approaching the Sanctuary. The "camp" mentioned in the verses is applied, in practice, to the area of Jerusalem and the Temple (Sifrei, Num., *piska* 1; Tosefta Kelim Bava Kama 1:12; Zevaḥim 116b; Rambam, *Hilkhot Biat HaMikdash* chapter 3). However, the Torah does not seem to be directly formulating a law for all future generations; rather, it is narrating an event that took place. Proof of this is to be found in the concluding words: "*Benei Yisrael* did so." The Torah does not conclude every halakhic discussion with these words. What the expression means is that *Benei Yisrael* carried out an instruction that Moses conveyed to them for that particular time. At that time, God commanded that anyone who was ritually impure had to be removed from the camp, and the Torah narrates how *Benei Yisrael* fulfilled this instruction and did so.

Why was it specifically at that time that *Benei Yisrael* were required to remove those who were impure, rather than at some earlier stage? This *parasha* appears after all the arrangement of the camps in the *parashot* of *Bamidbar-Naso*. Rashbam comments on the connection: "After the order of the camps and their encampments had been arranged and established, it was necessary [for God] to mention the removal of the impure from the camps." Ramban concurs: "Once the *Mishkan* had been established, [God] commanded the removal of the impure from the camp, so that the camp would be holy and worthy of having the Divine Presence rest there. This was a commandment that applied both with immediate effect and for all generations."

Rashbam and Ramban view the context of the arrangement of the camp merely as the reason for the law being given here. It seems to me, however, that we may claim that the very existence of the camp, with all of its arrangement and order, necessitates the removal of the impure. The prohibitions of impurity that are recorded in Leviticus, which are related to the sanctity of the camp of Israel as the encampment surrounding the Divine Presence, are dependent upon the actual arrangement of the camps around the *Mishkan*. For this reason it is only now, following the arrangement of the camps, that these prohibitions become applicable.

The same conclusion is supported by the Tosefta (Kelim Bava Kama 1:12): "During the journeys the camps have no status of sanctity, and one is not then punishable for matters of impurity" (see also Rashi on Gittin 60a). In other words, the prohibitions are dependent on the arrangement of the camps; when the camps break up [in order to journey onward], the prohibitions fall away.

Following the entry into the land, *Benei Yisrael* no longer encamped around the *Mishkan*. There is a fundamental halakhic difference between the status of the place of encampment, and the status of the place of Israelite settlement in their land for all generations. The most obvious illustration of this difference concerns the license to eat "meat of desire." In the desert, while *Benei Yisrael* encamped around the *Mishkan*, any consumption of meat required bringing the animal to the *Mishkan* as a sacrifice (Lev. 17, and Ramban on verse 2). Only in preparation for entering the land were they permitted to eat "profane" meat (Deut. 12:15–22).

This, then, would seem to explain the discrepancy between the laws of impurity applicable to the generation of the desert, and the laws for future generations. The unit concerning the removal of the impure from the camp, based on the assumption that prior to the arrangement of the camps there was no such requirement, establishes that the problem of impurity arises only in the context of the encounter with the Sanctuary and its sacrifices. Only in the desert did the structure of the camps define the status of *Benei Yisrael* as existing in a continuous encounter with the Sanctuary. The camp of Israel itself reflected, on a certain level, the sanctity of the Sanctuary.

According to the above explanation, the formulations in Leviticus and Numbers which express an absolute prohibition concerning impurity, and which make mention of the Sanctuary – if at all – only as a reason for a law or for a punishment, refer to the reality of the desert; a reality of the Israelite encampment around the *Mishkan*. Indeed, the sections in Leviticus, which were given at the *Ohel Mo'ed* (Tent of Meeting), make explicit mention of the reality of the encampment; for example, Leviticus 4:12 – "He shall carry the whole ox outside of the camp"; Leviticus 17:3 – "Any man of the house of Israel who slaughters an ox … in the camp, or who slaughters it outside of the camp."

It was clear that the prohibitions were related to and dependent upon the arrangement of the encampment. Hence, when the Torah defines the settlement of *Benei Yisrael* in their land, in Deuteronomy 12, as a settlement of "distance" from the Temple, it thereby establishes that the applicability of the original halakha to the new reality is limited to a situation where an individual enters the Sanctuary in a state of impurity. Expressions such as, "He has defiled God's Sanctuary," are thus transformed from underlying assumptions to necessary conditions for the application of the law.

III. THE SANCTITY OF ISRAEL

The explanation that we developed above provides a good solution to four out of the five examples of impurity that we examined at the beginning of the essay. However, it is of no value with regard to the prohibition of contact with the carcass of an impure animal (example 2, above). As noted, in *Parashat Shemini* we are told (11:4–8): "But these you shall not eat … you shall not eat of their flesh, nor shall you touch their carcass; they are impure for you." The Torah states explicitly that it is forbidden to touch the carcass of an impure animal because of its impurity. Here we cannot claim that the prohibition is dependent on the arrangement of the camps. As we shall see, this prohibition is not dependent on the concept of "sanctity of space" at all.

Chapter 11 in *Parashat Shemini* represents one single speech, devoted entirely to the laws of impurity related to animals, in order of various categories of animals, beasts and cattle, birds, fish, etc. However, the laws pertinent to some categories of animals appear in two separate textual units, with differences in content. Thus, we find the laws of the "creeping things upon the earth" in verses 29–38, and then other laws concerning the "creeping things of the earth" in verses 41–43. In connection with our discussion, with regard to the impurity of impure animals, there are two halakhic units here: verses 2–8, and verses 26–28.

The reason for this is that the text here presents two types of laws; some of the laws appear twice – one appearance of each type of law. One type of law refers to the establishment of impurity as a fact. These laws, obviously, have ramifications for the encounter with the Sanctuary and the sacrifices. Thus, the laws of the impurity of animals that appear in verses 26–28 suffice with the assertion of impurity:

> The carcass of any beast that has a parted hoof but which is not cloven-footed, or which does not chew the cud, is impure to you; anyone who touches them will be defiled. And whatever goes about on paws, of all the beasts that go about on four legs – they are impure to you; anyone who touches them is impure until the evening, and one who bears the carcass of them shall wash his clothes and be impure until the evening; they are impure to you.

The laws of the "creeping things" in verses 29–38 likewise belong to this type of law.

In contrast, other laws establish absolute prohibitions. This category includes the laws of impurity of animals in verses 2–8:

> These are the animals that you may eat, of all the beasts that are upon the earth – all that have parted hoofs and are cloven-footed and chew the cud, among the animals, those you may eat … but these you shall not eat … you shall not eat of their flesh, nor shall you touch their carcass; they are impure for you.

This group of laws includes those addressing the "creeping things of the earth" in verses 41–43: "And every creeping thing that creeps upon the earth is abominable; it shall not be eaten … you shall not eat of them, for they are an abomination." The explanation for the prohibitions of this type appears in the concluding words of this unit, which follow on the laws of the "creeping things" (11:43–47). There, the Torah explains that the prohibitions concerning impurity here arise from the sanctity of Israel – "You shall not make yourselves abominable.... For I am HaShem your God; therefore you shall sanctify yourselves and be holy, for I am holy." Just as the sanctity of the Sanctuary and its sacrifices entails prohibitions of impurity, so likewise the sanctity of Israel. But since these are different types of sanctity, therefore the substance of the prohibitions against impurity are accordingly different. For instance, every type of creeping creature that creeps upon the earth is forbidden as food (sanctity of Israel), but only eight types of creeping creatures represent impurity with regard to the sanctity of the Sanctuary and its sacrifices. Impure animals are likewise included in both categories, and the prohibitions of impure animals also include the prohibition of touching their carcasses.

What we deduce from this is that the prohibition of becoming defiled through touching the carcass of an impure animal – which appears along with the prohibition of eating the carcass of a pure animal (that was not slaughtered according to halakha) – arises as a result of the sanctity of Israel. This being the case, it cannot be dependent on the arrangement of the camps; it must apply for future generations, too – even when *Benei Yisrael* are no longer living in camps around the *Mishkan*.

We must therefore seek some other explanation for why the stated prohibition of touching the carcass of an impure animal is not accepted as halakha. Let us turn our attention to the unit in Deuteronomy that parallels *Parashat Shemini*:

> You are the children of HaShem your God.... You shall not eat any abominable thing. These are the animals which you may eat.... But these you shall not eat...they are impure to you...you shall not eat of their flesh, nor shall you touch their carcass.... You shall not eat any thing that dies of itself; you shall give it to the stranger who is in your gates as food, or sell it to a foreigner. For you are a holy nation unto HaShem your God. (Deut. 14:1–21)

In terms of both language and substance, it is clear that this unit is built on the unit in Leviticus 11. For the purposes of our discussion, too, the prohibitions of impurity are based upon the sanctity of Israel, and here, too, we find the prohibition of contact with the carcass of an impure animal.

Here, however, we find an additional detail concerning the carcass of a pure animal. The Torah explicitly permits giving the carcass to a non-Jew (a *ger toshav*), or selling it to him. This, I think, is the key to solving our problem. If it were forbidden to touch the carcass of a pure animal, it would be impossible to handle it and transfer it to a non-Jew. The practical significance of this would be that a Jew could enjoy no monetary or other benefit from the carcass. Hence there is a practical contradiction between the prohibition of touching the carcass of a pure animal – which would entail the nullification of the monetary value of the carcass, and an actual loss of money to the owner of the carcass – and the license to sell it to a non-Jew, representing the Torah's consideration of this monetary loss, and its recognition of the financial need to handle the corpse. The unit in Leviticus presents only the prohibition of contact with the corpse, while the unit in Deuteronomy (chapter 14) includes both sides of this contradiction. The inclusion of both within the same unit means that there is a difference between the ideal, preferred situation, and the Torah's actual, practical recognition of human needs. The Oral Law confirms that the practical result of the contradiction is that the end of the unit (v. 21) prevails over the first part (v. 8), and the sole prohibition concerns eating, while in terms of normative halakhic practice, there is no prohibition involved in touching or handling the carcass.

IV. SANCTITY AND MERCY

Let us summarize the two main points that we have addressed, and then consider what is common to them. We saw that Leviticus and Numbers, conveyed at the *Ohel Mo'ed*, are formulated on the basis of the reality of the Israelite encampment around the *Mishkan*. This reality involves the "sanctity of space" that applies to the entire camp, and this point has two halakhic ramifications: the first concerns the obligation of bringing any animal that is to be slaughtered for food to the *Ohel Mo'ed* first as a sacrifice (prohibition of "meat of desire"); the other entails certain prohibitions of impurity (or obligation to purify oneself from impurity). Only in Deuteronomy does the Torah announce that the reality in the Land of Israel will be different; it will be a reality of "distance" from the Sanctuary, such that the sanctity of the Divine Presence – insofar as it requires purification of the body and prohibits profane meat – is limited to the Temple precincts. The unit discussing the sanctity of Israel, in *Parashat Shemini*, requires in principle that a person refrain from contact with the carcass of a pure animal; only in Deuteronomy is there an easing of this requirement, based on consideration of monetary loss.

In both cases we observe the Torah's approach with regard to sanctity. On the one hand, it presents – in principle – a high standard of sanctity and purity; only afterwards are some of the requirements eased so as to enable the reasonable existence of Israelite society in their land.

This has dual significance for us. First, we learn about God's mercy. He gives us a Torah of mercy, a Torah that includes the attribute of mercy and seeks normal, reasonable social interaction. Second, we learn the extent of God's desire for us to draw close to Him, the level of sanctity that *Benei Yisrael* are worthy of attaining, and how important it is for their dwelling place to be holy. This conveys a message of aspiration towards purity and sanctity even beyond the formal requirements of the law, even in the domain of that which is "voluntary": "Sanctify yourself [even] with regard to that which is permitted to you."

The Impurity of the Birthing Mother and Her Offering

Rabbanit Sharon Rimon

The *parashot* of *Tazria* and *Metzora* deal with the laws of ritual purity and impurity which *Benei Yisrael* must observe now that the *Mishkan* stands at the center of the camp, such that the Divine Presence rests in their midst. We shall discuss the first category mentioned, the impurity of the birthing mother, and concern ourselves with one question: Why must a mother bring a *sin offering* after giving birth?

The fact that the Torah refers to this sacrifice as a "sin offering" suggests that it is brought as atonement for sin. In *Parashat Vayikra*, the Torah describes the instances where a sin offering must be brought:

> Speak to *Benei Yisrael*, saying: If a soul should unintentionally transgress any of God's commandments concerning that which should not be done, and perform one of them, [or] if the *kohen* who is anointed sins, bringing guilt upon the people, then he shall sacrifice for his sin which he committed a young bullock without blemish, to God as a sin offering. (Lev. 4:2–3)

There is also the general principle stating that "a negative commandment whose deliberate violation is punishable by *karet*, is [atoned for], when committed unintentionally, by means of a sin offering." In other words, a sin offering makes atonement for a sin committed unintentionally, where a person who committed that same sin intentionally would be punishable by *karet*.

What is the sin of the birthing mother?

The commentators offer various opinions on this question. The first answer, offered by Ḥazal and echoed by some of the commentators, is that during childbirth the woman swears that she will no longer have relations with her husband. On account of this "oath" she must bring a sin offering:

> The disciples of R. Shimon b. Yoḥai asked him: Why does the Torah command a woman after childbirth to bring an offering? He answered them: When she crouches to give birth, she determinedly swears that she will no longer have relations with her husband; therefore, the Torah says that she must bring an offering. (Nidda 31b)

Ramban explains as follows:

> Our Sages taught that when a woman crouches to give birth, she determinedly swears: "I shall no longer have relations with my husband." What this means, in essence, is that because her pain drives her to utter this oath, and her oath cannot be honored in any event, since she is obligated to her husband, therefore the Torah seeks to offer her atonement for that passing mood. The thoughts of the blessed God are deep, and His mercy is abundant, in seeking to exonerate His creatures.

Ramban understands the sin as the uttering of an oath that she is unable to fulfill. However, from the Gemara it would seem that the sin lies in the woman's very thought of separating from her husband or avoiding giving birth to any more children.

This raises an obvious question. How can it be known in advance that every woman, during childbirth, will swear that she will no longer have intimate relations with her husband? This certainly represents a possible situation, but surely it is not necessarily and inevitably true! This being the case, why is the commandment not limited to those women who declare such an oath?

Furthermore, even a woman who makes such an oath during childbirth would probably not invoke God's Name, such that her oath has no validity in any case. Why, then, is her utterance regarded in such a severe light – to the extent that it requires a sin offering for atonement?

A different explanation for the obligation is offered by Abarbanel:

> Since there is no one who undergoes pain and suffering in this world without having sinned ... and the birthing mother suffers pain and danger while she is upon the birthing stones; therefore, she would bring a sin offering.

Abarbanel suggests that the sin has nothing to do with what the woman says or does during the birth. Rather, the pain of childbirth itself testifies that she has somehow transgressed, and the sin offering is meant to atone for this sin.

This approach raises several difficulties. Firstly, taken to its logical conclusion, it implies that anyone who undergoes suffering must bring a sin offering for the (unknown) sin that is the cause of his suffering. However, the Torah makes no such demand. Why, then, is the birthing mother singled out in her suffering and required to bring the sacrifice?

Secondly, we may point out that according to the Torah, a person who is saved from danger is obligated to bring an offering of thanksgiving. Hence, it would seem more appropriate that the woman who has emerged safely from childbirth should bring an offering of thanksgiving, not a sin offering! (Today, a woman who has given birth recites the *hagomel* blessing, which expresses the same idea that was represented by the thanksgiving sacrifice.)

A third difficulty with Abarbanel's explanation is that the Torah tells us that the pain of childbirth is not associated with the sin of the particular woman, but rather was decreed for all women at the time of the sin of Adam and Eve.

Indeed, Recanati (commenting on verse 6) asserts that the sin offering is not brought as an atonement for the personal sin of the woman who has given birth, but rather as atonement for the sin of Adam and Eve. The same view is adopted by Rabbeinu Behaye, who writes:

> We might explain that this sacrifice is not offered for her [the woman's] own sin, but rather for her matriarch [Eve], who was the "mother of all living things"...therefore the Torah obligates her to bring a sacrifice to atone for that primal sin.

Each of the three views cited above (the Midrash, Abarbanel, and Rabbeinu Behaye) points in a different direction in tracing the sin that entails the bringing of the sin offering. Yet, a fundamental problem of perception confronts us when attempting to identify with any of these explanations. Quite simply, we do not think about childbirth in terms of "sin"; rather, we perceive it as a positive process. Is it not possible, then, that the sin offering brought by the women after childbirth is not the result of sin, but rather for some other reason?

The Sifra comments on our verse as follows:

> Wherever a sin offering is brought for a sin, the sin offering is mentioned before the burnt offering. Here, since it is not brought for a sin, the burnt offering is mentioned before the sin offering.

According to the Sifra, there are instances in which a sin offering is not brought in the wake of sin, and the offering of the woman after childbirth is one such instance. But if there is no sin, why is a sin offering required at all?

Ramban (commenting on 12:7) suggests that the sin offering is an atonement, of sorts, for the woman's healing and purification:

> "And he shall offer it before God and make atonement for her, and she shall be purified from the issue of her blood" – meaning that she offers an atonement for her soul before God to be purified from the issue of her blood. For a woman during childbirth experiences a sort of soiling, corrupting issue. After she has

completed the days of purification, or during the time that the infant develops as a male or female, she brings an atonement for her soul in order to recover from her issue and to be purified, for the exalted God heals all flesh and performs wonders.

If we examine the portions of *Tazria* and *Metzora* together, we note that the *metzora*, the *zav*, and the *zava* are likewise commanded to bring a burnt offering and a sin offering in order to achieve purification.

And the *kohen* shall offer them – one for a sin offering and the other for a burnt offering, and the *kohen* shall make atonement for him before God owing to his issue. (15:15)

The woman after childbirth is one of the categories of impurity discussed in *Tazria* and *Metzora*, and in each such category we find a sin offering that is brought not because of sin, but rather as part of the process of ritual purification. The woman after childbirth, likewise, undergoes a process of purification, part of which involves bringing the offering.

The concept of *tum'a*, impurity, is abstract and therefore difficult to define. In the material world, there is no impurity. Likewise, in the spiritual world that is completely cut off from the material world, there is no impurity. Impurity is manifest only in the connection between these two worlds. And what is common to all types of impurity is that they are brought about specifically through death. Impurity comes about where there is a separation of material from spirit. It is this parting that the state of impurity signifies.

The process of childbirth is the opposite of death. During birth, a new connection is made between the material world and the spiritual world, and a new life comes into being. Why, then, does this situation cause impurity?

The infant that is born, representing the new connection between material and spirit, is not impure. It is the mother who is rendered impure – not because of the newborn infant, but because of a "death" in a different sense. Firstly, while the infant has begun a new life, the mother has lost a life which, until now, has been contained inside her. Secondly, at the start of the embryo's development, some of the embryonic cells become the placenta, which takes root in the womb and nourishes the fetus during the pregnancy. At birth, the infant – emerging into new life – parts from the placenta. The placenta, which had started off as some of the embryonic cells, and later nourished the developing embryo and fetus and allowed it to grow, leaves the body, and in a certain sense one may say that it is dead.

Thus, the birth of the living infant is accompanied by a certain sort of "death," and this is the source of the birthing mother's impurity.

Nevertheless, the impurity of a birthing mother is different from the other categories of impurity. All of the others are caused by a pathological state, while the impurity of this woman is brought about in a natural, positive, and desirable way, through the creation of new life – which itself is the opposite of impurity.

It is perhaps for this reason that the Torah chooses to address the woman after childbirth first, before the other categories of impurity, as Rav Elchanan Samet explains:[1]

> If the birthing mother were to be listed among the impurities of the *metzora* and the *zav*, or after these, it might somehow imply that birth, too, is an unhealthy and abnormal state. The Torah would not wish to create such an impression, and so the unit on the birthing mother is given before we hear of types of impurity that arise from some pathological condition of the human body. From the fact that the birthing mother appears first, we learn that a person's life cycle is a constant oscillation between impurity and purity, an inevitable pendulum.

Thus, a sin offering is brought not only for sin, but also as part of a process of purification. The woman after childbirth brings a sin offering as part of her process of purification.

A different explanation for the sin offering brought by the birthing mother is offered by Seforno, commenting on verse 8:

---

1. http://www.vbm-torah.org/parsha.60/27tazria.htm.

> "And he shall make atonement for her" – for so long as her impurity flows, her thoughts will all be directed to matters of the vessels of seed and their action, and she will not be worthy…until she brings her atonement and directs herself towards the Sanctuary.

Rav Samson Raphael Hirsch develops this idea further:

> *"Tazria"* – [derived from the word] *zera* (seed) – the primary meaning refers to the seed of a plant…. The term *tazria* is to be found, aside from here, only in Genesis 1:11–12. There it denotes the plant's activity to maintain its species, while here it indicates the activity of the mother to form human seed. Hence, this activity is perceived in the purely bodily sense, as a physiological process. Thus, this very expression expresses the significance of the impurity that is involved here. The lofty and noble deed…is nothing but a purely bodily act. A person is formed, grows, and comes into existence in the same way as a plant… with a lack of freedom…. Now, the mother at this point [the birth] submits…to the physical power of the laws of nature, and this – in the midst of the lofty process that is the essence of her entire purpose in the world. For this reason, she must now refresh the consciousness of her moral destiny. Only when this sensory impression is over will she return to the Sanctuary with the vow of an offering.

According to Rav Hirsch and Seforno, the sin offering atones for submission to the bodily process that is so powerful that it almost leads to forgetting one's lofty spiritual purpose.

But can this situation truly be regarded as a sin?

Seforno and Rav Hirsch do not assert that it is a sin. Rather, they perceive it as a situation that is problematic, not ideal, and therefore the woman must make atonement for it, in order to be worthy of returning to the Sanctuary.

Childbirth is a very powerful process, and also a complex one. On the one hand, it is a process of creation, of forming new life. It is a process in which the mother is God's partner in bringing life into the world. It represents a new connection between body and soul. On the other hand, this process entails a powerful bodily experience, accompanied by great difficulties. The woman is subject to a mighty physical process that takes control of her, as it were, pushing aside the spirit's control over the body.

In addition to this complexity, there is the paradox discussed above. On the one hand, an infant is born, and new life is created; on the other hand, this process involves impurity.

The birth process involves a huge, mighty collision between the material world and the spiritual world. It is no coincidence, it seems, that this collision comes about specifically amidst the process of birth. The creation of man is bound up with the special combination of material body, flesh and blood, and spiritual soul – the image of God. This combination is no simple matter, and it is therefore specifically at childbirth that the two worlds collide with such force. The woman is in the middle of this collision, a partner in this clash.

Perhaps the sin offering is brought for this very collision. During childbirth, the mother is very close to God; at the same time, she is in the throes of a forceful bodily process, and even in a state of impurity. The combination between these two states is out of the woman's control, and hence we cannot speak of any "sin" here. Still, it is a problematic situation, a lack of completion. She is "entering the Sanctuary," as it were, in a state of impurity, and perhaps it is for this reason that she must bring her sin offering.

In light of what we have said above, let us now revisit the commentaries cited above.

The woman experiences most powerfully the physical strain that her body endures, to the extent that she may sometimes become disconnected from the greatness of the process, and feel herself prepared to forego any further pregnancies.

The midrash describing the woman swearing that she will no longer have intimate relations with her husband may be understood as describing a situation in which the woman has experienced her travail so powerfully, and the bodily process has so overtaken her experience, that it is no longer possible for her to perceive the tremendous positive side. She cuts herself off from the grandeur of creating life, and does not wish to repeat the experience. Perhaps the midrash is teaching us that she must bring a sin offering for this situation, in which the body (and its travail) conquers and dominates the spirit.

The suffering in childbirth is the result of the sin of Adam and Eve:

> And to the woman He said: I shall greatly multiply your pain in childbirth; in sorrow shall you bring forth children. (Gen. 3:16)

Were it not for the sin, childbirth would have been simpler and easier.

In light of what we have said above, we may now perhaps understand why the woman's punishment is specifically that "in sorrow shall you bring forth children." The sin of Adam and Eve was the first sin, the first expression of the disparity and incompatibility between the ideal, Godly world and the human reality. It expressed man's inability to live up to divine demands completely. In the wake of this sin, it becomes clear that the creation of man is not a simple matter; there is great complexity in this creation that combines body and soul.

From this point onwards, every birth of a new person is another collision between the material world and the spiritual world. This collision manifests itself in the pain and travail of childbirth.

Perhaps a woman brings a sin offering for the sin of Adam and Eve (as suggested by Recanati and Rabbeinu Beḥaye), in which case its significance is that it comes to atone for the conflict between the material world and the spiritual world – a conflict that arises from man's inherent complexity that is expressed so forcefully specifically at his birth.

We have examined three different explanations as to why a woman who has given birth must bring a sin offering:

1. The sin offering is meant to atone for some sin (either her oath that she will bear no more children, or the sin of Adam and Eve, or some other sin that her travail in childbirth led her to commit).
2. The sin offering is not meant as atonement for sin, but rather represents part of the process of purification. (We explained that the birth process involves a certain "death," and therefore the woman becomes impure.)

3. The sin offering is brought not because of some sin that the woman has committed, but rather because of the necessary and inevitable collision between the spiritual world and the material world – a collision that is inherent to the creation of man. The sin offering atones for the incomplete and imperfect situation in which all mortals exist, and which finds its most powerful expression at the moment of encounter between the body and the soul – at birth.

Parashat Metzora

The One Who Mourns for Himself

Rav Yonatan Grossman

An attempt at understanding the primary laws governing the *metzora* as they emerge from the biblical text will hopefully lead us to a better understanding of the process the *metzora* must undergo and the nature of his purification.

A person who suspects he has contracted *tzara'at* must consult a *kohen*. If the *kohen's* diagnosis confirms his suspicion, then the individual becomes formally categorized as one stricken with this disease. (As the verses indicate, this diagnosis may require a lengthy, complex, multi-stage process before being finalized.) Once the skin condition has been identified as *tzara'at*, the person must leave the camp and live in solitude until the illness has fully healed.

During his period of isolation, the *metzora* bears several obligations:

> As for the person with a leprous infection: his clothes shall be rent, his hair shall be disheveled, he shall cover over his upper lip and he shall call out, "Unclean! Unclean!" All the days that the infection is upon him he shall be unclean, he is unclean; he shall dwell in solitude, his dwelling shall be outside the camp. (13:45–46)

Even a cursory reading of the verses reveals two distinct groups of laws outlined in the text, highlighted by the two headers: "As for the person with a leprous infection"; "All the days that the infection is upon him." The Torah first charges the *metzora* with four personal obligations:

1. to rend his garments;
2. to leave his hair to grow;
3. to cover his mouth;
4. to declare publicly his state of ritual impurity.

The Torah then proceeds to an additional fifth command, which appears as an independent imperative, not as an integral component of the previous group of laws – to live in isolation.

We must, therefore, understand wherein lies the significance of these special laws relevant to the *metzora* and why the Torah divides them into two distinct categories.

The first three commandments appear several other times in Tanach, in the context of the laws regarding mourning. For example, after the death of Aaron's two sons, Moses turns to Aaron and his remaining sons and instructs them, "Do not dishevel your hair and do not rend your clothes, lest you die and anger strike the entire community. But your kinsmen, all the house of Israel, shall bewail the burning that God has wrought" (10:6). Moses must specifically order Aaron and his sons not to let their hair grow and not to rend their clothes in response to their recent loss. Were it not for this special command, they would have observed these measures of mourning. Moses emphasizes that instead of Aaron and his sons observing these practices, the rest of the nation will "bewail the burning." This contrast clearly suggests that letting one's hair grow and tearing one's garments constitute standard methods of expressing grief over the loss of a close relative.

We learn this not only from this specific episode, but also from the Torah's formulation of the general prohibition against a *Kohen Gadol*'s observance of mourning for a relative: "The *kohen* who is exalted above his fellow, on whose head the anointing oil has been poured and who has been ordained to wear the vestments, shall not dishevel his hair or rend his garments" (21:8). The *Kohen Gadol*, on whose head the anointing oil was poured, is ordered not to let his hair grow; the one who dons the special priestly garments may not tear his clothing. Here, too, the context refers to a prohibition against observing mourning practices for a deceased family member.

We also find the *metzora's* third obligation – covering his mouth – in similar contexts. An explicit reference to this practice appears in Ezekiel. God forewarns the prophet of the imminent death of his wife ("the delight of your eyes") and forbids him to mourn for her. In this context, Ezekiel mentions the practices observed by mourners from which he must abstain. These practices include the covering of the mourner's mouth:

> O mortal, I am about to take away the delight of your eyes from you through pestilence; but you shall not lament or weep or let your tears flow.
>
> Moan softly, observe no mourning for the dead. Put on your turban and put your sandals on your feet; do not cover over your upper lip, and do not eat the bread of comforters. (Ez. 24:16–17)

Ḥazal derived the laws of mourning from these verses. Everything from which God ordered Ezekiel to abstain, a regular mourner must observe. As stated, these observances include the covering of the mouth, implying that it, too, constitutes a practice of mourners. Indeed, Rashi (on 13:45) comments on the *metzora's* requirement of covering his mouth, "like a mourner."

It thus emerges that a *metzora* must observe the practices of mourning. If so, we can readily understand the fourth obligation – to proclaim his state of impurity, as mourners, who have recently buried a relative, are ritually impure.

This raises the obvious question: For whom does this leper mourn? Even if this skin disease generates a special form of ritual impurity, how did issues of mourning creep into the laws governing the *metzora*, even if no one around him has died?

It appears that Ḥazal themselves sought to solve this mystery for us when they formulated an equally mysterious proverb: "A *metzora* is considered dead" (see Rashi, Num. 12:12, based on the Sifrei). Ḥazal apparently understood that the laws of mourning that found their way into the world of the *metzora* represent the *metzora*'s mourning for himself! He himself has "died," and he must therefore observe the practices of mourners.

In order to understand this phenomenon, of one "burying" oneself and "mourning" for oneself, we must remind ourselves of the physiological phenomena that took place on the *metzora*'s skin and prompted the *kohen* to declare him impure. The Torah presents two primary criteria:

1. The discoloration's color: it must be white in order to attain the status of *tzara'at* that generates impurity.
2. The appearance: it must appear deeper than the person's skin.

(In instances of uncertainty, the *kohen* isolates the person for a period of time and examines him again later. In these cases, the growth and expansion of the eruption also indicate impurity.)

However, most *Rishonim* do not view these as two distinct criteria. Rather, one determines the existence of the other. Rashi, for example, writes (13:3), "Deeper than the skin of his body – every white spot is deep, just as the sunlight appears deeper than the shade" (see also Ramban there). In other words, the white discoloration must affect the appearance of the infection, such that it appears more shallow than the skin.

Thus, the color white emerges as the critical determinant within the system of leprous infections. It alone determines whether the given discoloration signifies *tzara'at*, which generates ritual impurity, or a standard skin disorder unrelated to *tzara'at*. As we would expect, much of Tractate Nega'im (the tractate dealing with the laws of *tzara'at*) deals with the various shades of white in order to clarify which shades render the individual a *metzora* and which do not.

Why does the Torah focus specifically on the color white? Stated otherwise, is there some particular reason why this special disease, which yields far-reaching spiritual and social ramifications, surfaces on the body specifically in this color?

It seems to me that one verse in our *parasha* alludes to this issue: "But if the live flesh [referring to undiscolored skin] again turns white" (13:16). The text here contrasts "live" – or healthy – skin with "white" skin; white signifies the polar opposite of life. It stands to reason that the color white relates fundamentally to the concept of death. In a certain sense, if only symbolically, the individual's body begins to die. He suddenly notices that "life" – the normal reddish hue, which relates to blood and life – has begun to leave his skin, replaced by a dead, white coloring. The skin of his body appears to him like the skin of a corpse. Obviously, we are dealing here with symbolic allusions, but it seems that this disease serves to hint to the individual that God's anger has been aroused against him. In this sense, the significance of this illness exists exclusively on the level of symbolism and subtle allusion.

However, this symbolism finds expression in real-life, concrete terms, upon which the final of the *metzora's* obligations is focused: "He shall dwell in solitude – his dwelling shall be outside the camp." The *metzora* must leave his place of residence and relocate outside the camp. The halakha emphasizes that he must exit all three camps and live in isolation (as opposed to a "*zav*," for example – see Sifra, Nega'im 14).

It seems to me that this last requirement is more than just another law relevant to the *metzora*; it constitutes the very essence of his "death." It stands to reason that the significance of his death lies specifically in the sphere of social activity. The *metzora* must detach himself from communal life, in which the *Shekhina* resides, and through this very detachment he "dies." The individual's existence outside the camp, meaning, outside the general, public partnership of the community, is the functional equivalent of detachment from life, detachment from the life of the nation within which the *Shekhina* resides.

This commandment appears separate from the rest, for it, as mentioned, constitutes the essence of *tzara'at*, whereas the other requirements reflect the result of this detachment. Elsewhere (VBM *Parashat Tazria*, 5759), I analyzed the sins for which we find *tzara'at* as a punishment in Tanach, and discovered that they all involve communal, social wrongs. We will not repeat that discussion, but we must mention Hazal's claim that *tzara'at* served as a punishment for *lashon hara* (gossip). The *metzora's* penalty thus becomes readily understandable.

One who harmed another by casting aspersions on his social standing is now banished from society, considered dead. (Compare with Rashi, 13:46 – "Whoever publicly *whitens* the face of another is considered as having shed blood.") His punishment thus directly parallels the crime.

In light of this, I would like to address the *metzora*'s purification process and consider how the *metzora* makes his way back into society. This process consists of three stages:

1. Return to the camp – by bringing two birds;
2. Return to his tent (i.e., to his wife) – after seven days of residence in the camp;
3. Return to the *Mishkan* – on the eighth day, when he brings special sacrifices.

I would like to focus specifically on the first stage, by which the individual reenters communal life, when he returns to the camp. After the *kohen* visits the *metzora* outside the camp and sees that the illness has in fact healed, he institutes a series of procedures (14:1–7):

A. The *kohen* shall order two clean, *live birds*, cedar wood, crimson stuff, and hyssop.
B. The *kohen* shall order *one of the birds slaughtered* in an earthen vessel over *live* [i.e., fresh] *water*.
C. He shall take the *live bird*, along with the cedar wood, the crimson stuff, and the hyssop...
C1. ...and dip them together with the *live bird*...
B1. ...in the blood of the *slaughtered bird* over the *live water*.
A1. He shall then sprinkle it seven times on him who is to be cleansed of the *tzara'at* and cleanse him; and he shall set the *live bird* free in the open field.

Notice that the verses outline this process in chiastic structure, which can be very easily discerned through the repeated use of the term "*ḥayim*" ("live") in reference to both the water and the bird.

The outer frame of this segment (A-A1) mentions live birds, one of which the *kohen* ultimately, at the end of the process, sets free "in the open field." In B, the *kohen* slaughters a bird over "live water," and in B1 we learn what the *kohen* does with this blood-stained water (dip the live bird therein). The centerpiece of the process, itself doubled (C-C1), describes the dipping of the live bird (with additional elements).

Wherein lies the significance of this ritual? As this procedure does not occur anywhere near an altar and nothing is brought as an offering, it clearly does not fit into the normal framework of sacrifices. Why, then, does the *kohen* slaughter a bird over fresh water, dip a live bird in its blood and then send it away?

It seems to me as no coincidence that *"ḥayim"* (life) emerges as the most prominent term in this unit. This ceremony marks the transition from death to life, or the rebirth of the *metzora* who seeks reentry into the camp. There is room to assess each of the items dipped into the water (the cedar wood, the crimson stuff, and the hyssop), but we do not have space in this context to develop this issue. I would, however, like to emphasize two important points.

First, this list also appears elsewhere, as part of the purification process of one who had come in contact with a dead body (as described in *Parashat Ḥukkat*). Secondly, the "crimson stuff" colors the fresh water red, and the *kohen* later adds the bird's blood into the colored water. From this redness the bird bursts forth and flies freely. I believe that the color red assumes so prominent a role in this ceremony because it represents the antithesis of the white coloration that had surfaced on the *metzora's* skin. If the white color signifies the whiteness of death, then redness relates to blood, or to life, as we know from the Scriptural association: "Blood is life."

The live bird, which flies away from the red solution, represents the individual returning to life, his rejoining society and life with the *Shekhina*.

Immediately following this ceremony, the verse commands the cured *metzora* to turn himself, as it were, into a small child:

> The one to be cleansed shall wash his clothes, *shave off all his hair*, and bathe in water; then he shall be clean. After that he may enter the camp. (14:8)

We are familiar with immersion in water as a form of purification, but why must the *metzora* shave his hair? Apparently, this ritual expresses rebirth, symbolizing a brand new entry into the world and a desire to live. The departure from the immersion waters without a single hair on the body very much brings to mind childbirth. The *metzora* must indeed be seen as reborn, in the sense of a "dead" person coming back to life.

The Person, the Garment, and the House

Rav Amnon Bazak

I. INTRODUCTION

The structure of the section in the Torah devoted to leprous sores, which begins in *Parashat Tazria* and concludes in *Parashat Metzora*, gives rise to an obvious question concerning the order of the topics addressed. The following is a summary of the structure of the discussion as a whole:

1. 13:1–46 – sores on human flesh (this section is further divided according to the different types of sores; we shall not discuss this breakdown);
2. 13:47–59 – leprosy on clothing;
3. 14:1–32 – the procedure for ritual purification of a leper from his sores;
4. 14:33–53 – leprosy on a house;
5. 14:54–57 – summary.

The obvious question concerns the placement of the subject of leprosy on clothing, which creates a break in the middle of the discussion of bodily leprosy. Why does this section not appear after the end of that discussion, as does the matter of leprosy on a house? Abarbanel, commenting on the beginning of our *parasha*, formulates the question (the eleventh in his list) as follows:

Why does the Torah command [us] concerning leprosy of clothing in this place, after mentioning the various types of human leprosy, but before stipulating the way in which this leper, discussed as the first subject, is to be purified? It would seem more appropriate for the Torah to complete the laws pertaining to human leprosy and purification, and only then to discuss leprosy on clothing, and then leprosy on houses; why is the order jumbled?

The question is further reinforced if we review the progression of the verses. At the end of the section dealing with human leprosy, the Torah describes the behavior required of a person who has been pronounced ritually impure:

> The *tzarua* in whom the plague exists – his clothes shall be torn, and the hair of his head left long, and he shall place a covering over his upper lip, and shall cry, "Impure, impure."
> All the days that the plague is within him, he shall be impure; he is impure, he shall dwell alone; *outside the camp* shall be his habitation. (Lev. 13:45–6)

The direct continuation of these verses is to be found at the beginning of chapter 14, where we read:

> This shall be the teaching concerning the leper on the day of his purification, when he is brought to the *kohen*. The *kohen* shall go *outside of the camp*, and the *kohen* shall look, and behold – if the plague of *tzara'at* is healed from the *tzarua*.

Only in the concluding verses of the section regarding bodily leprosy do we find the expressions "*tzarua*" ("leprous") and "*maḥaneh*" ("camp"); this serves to highlight the linguistic connection between these verses and the introductory verses to chapter 14, dealing with leper's purification.

Moreover, the section addressing leprosy on clothing concludes with the words, "This is the teaching concerning the plague of *tzara'at* in a garment of wool or of linen; either in the warp or in the woof, or in any [garment] made of skins, to declare it pure or to declare it impure" (13:59). This, in fact, concludes the subject altogether. But when it comes to leprosy on human flesh, a parallel verse appears only at the end of the entire discussion of the human disease, in chapter 14, verse 32: "This is the teaching concerning one in whom the disease of *tzara'at* exists."

In light of these linguistic aspects of the text, our question becomes even more insistent: Why are the verses that deal with leprosy on clothing – seemingly an independent unit – inserted in the middle of this discussion?

II. THE LEPER AND HIS GARMENTS

In Abarbanel's view, this juxtaposition emphasizes the connection between a person and his clothing. The laws of leprosy emphasize two aspects that relate not only to the person who contracts ritual impurity, but also to his clothing:

First, the verses tell us twice that if, by the end of the second week, the plague has not spread, the person is regarded as ritually pure, but he must nonetheless wash his clothing:

> The *kohen* shall look at him again on the seventh day, and behold, if the plague is dimmer, and the plague has not spread in the skin, then the *kohen* shall declare him pure – it is [merely] a scab – *and he shall wash his clothes* and be pure. (v. 6)

> The *kohen* shall look at the patch on the seventh day, and behold, if the patch has not spread in the skin, and it does not appear to be deeper than the skin, then the *kohen* shall declare him pure, *and he shall wash his clothes* and be pure. (v. 34)

When the leper is declared impure, this has implications for his clothes, as well:

> The leper, in whom the plague exists – *his clothes shall be torn,* and his hair left long, and he shall cover his upper lip, and shall call out, "Impure, impure." (v. 45)

Hence, a clear connection exists between the state of a person's ritual purity, and the state of his clothing. Partial impurity of a person requires washing his clothes, while complete impurity requires that they be torn. Needless to say, no such connection exists between a person and his house. We may therefore now answer our question. The laws of leprosy in clothing are discussed in the middle of the laws of bodily leprosy to express this connection between a person and his clothing.

It should be noted that the connection between a person and his clothing finds expression not only in the procedures associated with ritual purity and impurity, but also in procedures associated with consecration. There are clear parallels between the purification of a leper from his impurity and the consecration of Aaron and his sons as *kohanim*, as described in *Parashat Tetzaveh* and *Parashat Tzav*. Inter alia, we may point to the following parallel:

> You shall slaughter the ram and take of its blood and paint it on the tip of the right ear of Aaron and of his sons, and upon the thumb of their right hands, and upon the big toe of their right foot. (Ex. 29:20)

> The *kohen* shall take of the blood of the guilt offering and the *kohen* shall paint it on the right ear of the person to be purified, and upon the thumb of his right hand, and upon the big toe of his right foot. (Lev. 14:14)

In the procedure for the *kohanim's* consecration, the sanctification of their clothing assumes a prominent role:

> You shall take of the blood that is upon the altar, and of the anointing oil, and you shall sprinkle it upon Aaron and upon his clothes, and upon his sons and upon his sons' clothes, with him, *and he shall be sanctified, and his clothes, and his sons and his sons' clothes, with him.* (Ex. 29:21)

The priestly garments, too, require special sanctification – but this sanctification is performed alongside, and as part of, the sanctification of the *kohanim*. When the *kohanim* are sanctified, their clothes become sanctified along with them – just as when a person becomes impure, his clothes require washing.

III. THE LEPER AND HIS HOUSE

Thus far we have adopted one approach to answering our question, following Abarbanel, based on a perspective viewing clothing as an extension of the individual. However, there is another factor which would emphasize the comparison between leprosy *of the house* and leprosy of the person.

In chapter 13, the Torah describes the laws of *"tzara'at,"* and in this respect the chapter includes bodily leprosy and leprosy of clothing. However, chapter 14 – *Parashat Metzora* – does not discuss the laws of impurity, but rather addresses the process of purification. This process exists only where a leper is purified from his bodily leprosy, or when a house is purified from its plague; it does not exist in the context of leprosy of clothing.

The purification processes for a person and for a house bear considerable resemblance to one another:

Purification of person:

The *kohen* shall command to be taken for the person to be purified two live, clean birds, and cedar wood, and scarlet, and hyssop. The *kohen* shall [then] command that one of the birds be slaughtered in an earthen vessel, over running water. Then he shall take the living bird, and the cedar wood, and the scarlet, and the hyssop, and he shall immerse them – as well as the live bird – in the blood of the bird that was slaughtered over the running water. Then he shall sprinkle over the person to be purified of leprosy, seven times, *and declare him purified,* and then send off the live bird into the open field. (vv. 4–10)

Purification of the house:

He shall take to cleanse the house two birds, and cedar wood, and scarlet, and hyssop. He shall slaughter one of the birds in an earthen vessel, over running water. Then he shall take the cedar wood and the hyssop and the scarlet, and the live bird, and immerse them in the blood of the bird that was slaughtered, and in the running water, and he shall sprinkle the house seven times. And he shall cleanse the house with the blood of the bird and with the running water, and with the live bird, and with the cedar wood, and with the hyssop, and with the scarlet. Then he shall send off the live bird out of the city, to the fields, *and make atonement* for the house *and it shall be purified.* (vv. 49–53)

Without embarking on a discussion of the significance of this process of purification, it is clear that the two procedures parallel one another. However, one important difference stands out – while the house is purified and atoned for by means of the birds, the cedar, the hyssop, and the scarlet, for the leper himself these means are only part of the purification, but they are not part of the atonement. The process of atonement is concluded only by means of the sacrifices and the placing of the blood and the oil upon the leper:

The remnant of the oil that is in the *kohen's* hand shall he place upon the head of the person to be purified, and the *kohen shall make atonement for him* before God. And the *kohen* shall offer the sin offering *and atone* for the person to be atoned from his impurity, and thereafter he shall slaughter the burnt offering. And the *kohen* shall offer the burnt offering and the meal offering upon the altar, and the *kohen* shall *make atonement for him, and he shall be purified.* (vv. 18–20)

This difference seemingly stems from the fact that the atonement for the leper is performed after he has been proclaimed impure, as explained in chapter 13, thus demanding a more complex process. As regards the house, by contrast, the process is necessary only in the case where, after the second week, the "plague is healed," and has not spread. In any event, what is common to the person and the house is that both require atonement – a process that does not exist at all, in any form, with regard to clothing. Thus, the division of the textual sections (and the chapters) evolves naturally from the difference between the laws of impurity and the process of atonement; for this reason, the leprosy of clothing belongs only to *Tazria*, not to *Metzora*.

This division appears to accord a unique status to the house, in that it, too, like a person, requires atonement when it becomes defiled. Wherein lies the significance of this requirement?

IV. "AND HE SHALL ATONE FOR HIMSELF AND FOR HIS HOUSEHOLD"

This is not the only instance where we encounter the concept of "atonement" in connection with a house (*"bayit"* – house, or household). Two chapters later, in the Torah's description of the *Kohen Gadol's* service on Yom Kippur, this phenomenon appears once again:

> Thus shall Aaron come to the *kodesh*: with a young bull as a sin offering, and a ram as a burnt offering... and Aaron shall offer up the bull of the sin offering, which is for himself, and *make atonement* for himself and for *his house*... and Aaron shall offer the bull of the sin offering which is for himself, and he shall *make atonement for himself and for his house*, and shall slaughter the bull of the sin offering which is for himself.

As we know, the Sages interpret the repeated mention of the atonement for the house in two senses: the first refers to the family of the *Kohen Gadol*; the second refers to the *kohanim*:

> He would approach the bull, while the bull stood between the vestibule and the altar, its head facing south and its face westwards; the *kohen* would stand on the eastern side, facing westwards. He would rest both his hands upon it and recite his confession, and this is what he would say: "Please, O God, I have sinned and trespassed and done wrong before you, *I and my household.*" (Mishna Yoma 3:8)

> Then he would approach the second bull, and rest both his hands upon it, and recite his confession, and this is what he would say: "Please, O God, I have sinned and trespassed and done wrong

before you, I and *my household and the children of Aaron, your holy people.*" (ibid., 4:2)

But the very fact that the Torah refers to the *kohen's* relatives as his "house" (*"bayit"*) proves the connection between the concept of a physical house and those who live within it.

It emerges, then, that when a person's house is struck with plague, this is an expression of impurity towards that which represents its inhabitants as a collective whole. This is not the impurity of a specific individual, and therefore no individual is required to bring a sacrifice for it. However, there is impurity attached to a person's home, to the place where his family resides; this requires a process of purification and atonement.

V. AND I SHALL BRING THE PLAGUE OF LEPROSY

We may now move onto an additional difference between leprosy of clothing and leprosy of the house. The *parasha* concerning leprosy of clothing opens with the words, "The garment *in which the plague of leprosy exists*, in a garment of wool or in a garment of linen." The *parasha* concerning the leprosy of a house, on the other hand, opens in an entirely different style:

> When you come into the land of Canaan which I give you as a possession, *and I bring the plague of leprosy* to a house in the land of your possession. (14:34)

From the difference between these two formulations it appears that leprosy of clothing is a natural process, while leprosy of a house is a deliberate divine act, apparently a form of punishment.

When it comes to leprosy of human flesh, the Torah does not hint at a determined divine act, but rather speaks in natural terms ("If a person should have, in the skin of his flesh, a swelling, a scab, or a bright spot"; "If a person shall have the plague of leprosy"; etc.). Nevertheless, human leprosy also appears to be a punishment, for two principal reasons. First, the process is a particularly harsh one, involving the leper's isolation from human company. In the world of biblical concepts of reward and punishment, such a process cannot occur without reason. Second, in most cases where we encounter in Tanach a person stricken with leprosy, the disease followed a sin. This idea also seems to underlie God's message to David via Nathan's vision: "I shall be a Father to him, and he shall be a son to Me – that when he sins I shall reproach him with a human staff and with mortal plagues" (II Sam. 7:14). The Sages offer various opinions as to which sorts of sins bring plagues upon a person.

It would seem, therefore, that leprosy on clothing – concerning which there is no mention of any process of atonement – is indeed fundamentally different from leprous sores on human flesh or on houses. Leprosy in a person expresses a problem in that person; leprosy on a house indicates a general problem concerning the nature of the house and its inhabitants. Therefore, both these types of leprosy require a process of atonement. Leprosy on clothing, on the other hand, is part of nature. These sores have their own laws – like other types of impurity – but they have no element of atonement, since they do not come about as a punishment.

The Meaning of the Tzara'at Laws

Rav Elchanan Samet

P*arashot Tazria-Metzora* constitute a single literary unit addressing
one topic: the laws of *tum'a* and *tahara*. These laws began at the end of
Parashat Shemini, where the Torah discusses the status of the carcasses
of various creatures which transmit *tum'a* through contact. In these
parashot, however, the Torah discusses *tum'a* that originates from a living human being. Under various circumstances in a person's life, he
can contract different forms of *tum'a*, each requiring its own process of
tahara, purification.

These *parashot* deal with three main categories: the *tum'a* of a
childbearing woman and her *tahara* process, the *tum'a* of the *metzora*
(leper) and his *tahara* process, and *tum'a* resulting from bodily emissions (seminal and menstrual).

I. WHAT IS *TZARA'AT*?

What is the reason behind *tzara'at*? Before we discuss this question,
we must first address a more basic question: What is *tzara'at*? Rambam
notes the fundamental problem in the inclusion of different phenomena
under the shared title of "*tzara'at*":

> *Tzara'at* is a shared name that includes many matters that do not resemble one another. For the whitening of human skin is called *tzara'at*, the loss of some hair of the head or beard is called *tzara'at*, and the discoloration of garments or houses is called *tzara'at*. (*Hilkhot Tum'at Tzara'at* 16:10)

It appears that Rambam saw even bodily *tzara'at* not as a single phenomenon, but as a shared name for different phenomena.

Researchers have tried to identify the bodily *tzara'at* described in chapter 13 with various diseases familiar to us nowadays, but have not succeeded in pointing to a disorder that parallels in all its features the *tzara'at* described by the Torah. It appears that *tzara'at* was a skin disorder (though even on this point we find a lack of unanimity among the scholars). Since no skin disorder known to us nowadays corresponds precisely with the Torah's description, it seems reasonable to assume that the illness of which the Torah speaks has since disappeared from the world.

The claim of a change in nature to explain inconsistencies and contradictions between the natural world familiar to us and the descriptions of the natural world in ancient sources – in the Torah and in our oral tradition – ought to be employed as rarely as possible. Nevertheless, with regard to illness in the ancient world and our times, this is not the case. Various illnesses have changed form over the course of many generations, and others have entirely or almost entirely disappeared. On the other hand, new diseases have appeared which the ancients never knew. It should not surprise us, therefore, if the *tzara'at* described by the Torah no longer exists.

If this is the case, then we cannot pose any definitive theory as to the nature of this illness, given the fact that the Torah deals not with the essence of *tzara'at*, but rather with its diagnosis. It is therefore difficult to speculate as to why the Torah singled out *tzara'at* from among all other disorders as a source of a stringent form of *tum'a* that falls upon the patient, to the point where he must leave all three camps and sit alone like a mourner outside the camp. Nevertheless, we cannot exempt ourselves from attempting to explain what we can, based on what we know of *tzara'at* from the Tanach itself and even from other sources.

II. PREVENTATIVE MEDICINE?

Various commentators assumed that *tzara'at* was a dangerous, contagious disease, and on this basis they explained the laws of *tum'a* and isolation associated with *tzara'at* as a means to protect society from infection. We will not elaborate on this position, but merely point out that many commentators adopted it.

The problem with this assumption is that it has absolutely no support from the text where we find mention of *tzara'at*. Nowhere do we read in Tanach of a person dying from *tzara'at* or even of the possibility of such an occurrence.

Particularly enlightening is the story of Naaman in II Kings (chapter 5). The story begins by describing him as "commander of the army of the king of Aram…a great warrior, a *metzora*." Despite his *tzara'at*, he functions as an active military commander, who fights and travels with his entourage over vast distances, and his master, the king of Aram, "leans on his arm" during religious ceremonies (ibid., v. 18). Still, his illness causes him distress and he tries to have it cured. It thus seems that Naaman saw his *tzara'at* as a nuisance, or perhaps an aesthetic-social defect, but it did not disrupt his day-to-day functioning. Nor do we find any indication of a concern that his disease would spread; in fact, the king of Aram would lean on the arm of his commander the *metzora*, without any fear of the effects of this physical contact.

The cessation of Uzziah's functioning as king of Judah as a result of his *tzara'at*, and his taking residence in isolated quarters from that point until his death (II Kings 15:5; II Chr. 26:19–21), are due not to medical reasons, but rather to religious reasons – the mitzva forbidding a *metzora* from living in his home and town.

Similarly, the four *metzora'im* who resided outside the city of Shomron (II Kings 7:3–4) thereby fulfilled the Torah's command that the *metzora* shall leave the camp. In the Land of Israel, this requirement translates into the *metzora's* departure outside walled cities. They do, indeed, fear for their lives – not because of their illness, but rather because of the famine and the army of Aram. They, too, are described as perfectly functional (ibid., vv. 8–10), and even make a point of hiding gold and silver for safekeeping for the future.

Opposing the approach of viewing the isolation of *metzora'im* as "preventative medicine," later commentators advanced different claims. Shadal (R. Shmuel David Luzzato) claims:

> Many thought that the shunning of the *metzora* is because of the illness which is transmitted through contact. It appears to me that if the Torah feared the spreading of the illness, there are other contagious illnesses for which the Torah prescribed no [precautionary] measures – and how did it not command anything concerning these plagues?

III. ḤAZAL'S VIEW: PUNISHMENT

Throughout the Talmud and Midrashim, *Ḥazal* view *tzara'at* as a punishment for various transgressions involving interpersonal misconduct, particularly the sin of *lashon hara* (slander/gossip):

> R. Yossi b. Zimra said: Whoever speaks *lashon hara* – *tzara'at* infections come upon him.
> Reish Lakish said: "This shall be the ritual for a *metzora*" – this shall be the ritual for the *motzi shem ra*.
> R. Shmuel b. Naḥmani said in the name of R. Yoḥanan: *Tzara'at* comes on account of seven things: (1) *lashon hara*; (2) murder; (3) false oaths; (4) immorality; (5) arrogance; (6) theft; (7) stinginess. (Arakhin 16a)

The final passage continues by citing Scriptural proofs for each sin mentioned. Indeed, several events in Tanach prove that *tzara'at* served as a divine punishment for various forms of wrongdoing. Miriam is stricken with *tzara'at* for speaking against Moses (Num. 12); Geiḥazi is punished for his greed and false oath to Elisha (II Kings 5); Uzziah is punished with *tzara'at* for offering incense in the Temple in defiance of the *kohanim* (II Chr. 26:16–21).

Ḥazal's outlook on *tzara'at* as a punishment parallels their perspective on other forms of disaster that befall an individual or community as a punishment for a certain transgression or several transgressions. This outlook, then, does not answer the question: What is the reason behind the laws of *tum'a* of a *metzora*? As Rav David Zvi Hoffmann notes:

> In truth, if every affliction serves as a punishment for a sin, then why should the affliction of *tzara'at* not also come as a punishment for certain sins? However, just as, on the other hand, there are extraordinary cases where tragedies befall people without any possible way of seeing them as the result of sins, so too... instances of *tzara'at* can occur in extraordinary fashion.... Moreover, it is difficult to understand why specifically *tzara'at* generates *tum'a*, whereas other diseases, which also generally come as a punishment for sins, do not generate *tum'a*. (vol. I, p. 220)

Thus, *Ḥazal's* view of *tzara'at* – a disease like any other – as a punishment for certain sins does not explain the reason for the *tum'a* of *tzara'at*. However, Rambam and later writers (Ramban, Seforno to 13:47) explain that the *tzara'at* of houses and clothing are not natural disasters, but rather deviations from the natural order, an overt miracle intended as a signal to the individual. According to this approach, we cannot isolate the question regarding *tum'at tzara'at* from the question concerning its very nature. One answer resolves both issues: the very appearance of *tzara'at* and all its regulations serves as a warning to a person to repent. Rambam writes:

> This discoloration mentioned with regard to clothing and homes, which the Torah called *"tzara'at,"* a name that it shares [with the physical disease *"tzara'at"*], is not a natural phenomenon; rather, it was a sign and wonder in Israel in order to warn them against *lashon hara*, evil speech. One who spoke *lashon hara* – the walls of his home became discolored. If he repented – the home became pure. If he continued... his skin becomes discolored and he contracts *tzara'at*, and he is separated and publicly isolated, until he no longer engages in the sinful speech of frivolity and *lashon hara*.
>
> The Torah warns against all this and says (Deut. 24:8–9), "In cases of skin affection, be most careful.... Remember what

HaShem your God did to Miriam on the journey." (*Hilkhot Tum'at Tzara'at* 16:10)

A partial source for this description of the gradual progression of calamities that befalls the person is found in the Midrash (Leviticus Rabba 17:4). However, neither this midrash nor other sources dealing with the *tzara'at* of the home and garment provide any basis for Rambam's view of these phenomena as supernatural, "a sign and wonder in Israel." It appears that Hazal made no distinction between bodily *tzara'at* and that which affected houses and clothing. All these forms of *tzara'at* are seen as natural calamities which serve to reprimand the individual for the sin of *lashon hara* and other violations concerning interpersonal conduct.

Therefore, the sources in Hazal relevant to our question are specifically those which explain the laws of *tum'a* and the *tahara* (purification) process prescribed, rather than the disease itself. Sure enough, several passages in Hazal explain the *tum'a* and *tahara* of a *metzora*, too, within the context of the sinner's punishment and process of *teshuva*:

> Why is the *metzora* different, that the Torah states, "He shall dwell in isolation; outside the camp shall be his residence"? He caused a separation between husband and wife, between a man and his fellow [Rashi: for *tzara'at* comes on account of *lashon hara*], and the Torah therefore writes, "He shall dwell in isolation."
>
> Why is the *metzora* different, that the Torah states that he must bring two birds for his purification? The Almighty says: He committed an act of *"patit"* (chatter), and so the Torah says that he must bring a sacrifice of a *"patit"* [Rashi: because birds chirp at all times]. (Arakhin 16b)

Two points must be made concerning Hazal's approach to *tzara'at* and its laws. First, throughout the *tzara'at* section, the text of the Torah makes no mention of the ethical background to the arrival of *tzara'at* or its cure. We find not even an allusion to any sin preceding the onset of *tzara'at*, nor do we read of any instruction that the *metzora* pray or repent during his period of isolation outside the camp. The Torah never hinges the cure from *tzara'at* on the patient's conduct or awareness. Second, we cannot isolate the laws of *tzara'at* from all other laws of *tum'a* in the Torah. We need a general explanation for all these laws – those in *Parashot Tazria-Metzora*, those in *Parashat Shemini* (the *tum'a* of animal carcasses), and those in *Parashat Ḥukkat* (the *tum'a* of a deceased human being). Only on the basis of their common denominator can we proceed to explain the laws of the *metzora* – even those unique to this form of *tum'a*. As such, the ethical reason *Ḥazal* give for *tzara'at* does not provide an explanation for the vast majority of other *tum'ot* (with the exception, perhaps, of the *tum'a* of *"zavim,"* who might indeed have contracted an illness as punishment). After all, one who touches the carcass of a rodent or the remains of a human being has committed no sin; likewise, a menstruating woman is not a sinner. Why, then, did the Torah decree a status of *tum'a* upon them?

IV. RAV HOFFMANN: EDUCATIONAL SYMBOLS

In his commentary to Leviticus (vol. I, pp. 219–223), Rav David Zvi Hoffmann attempts to explain the reason behind all forms of *tum'a* as an integrated group. He makes a slight but critical change in *Ḥazal*'s view:

> *Tzara'at* does not generate *tum'a* because it results from the sin [for this is not always the case; other illnesses also result from various sins but do not generate *tum'a*]. Rather, *tzara'at* generates *tum'a* because the outward appearance of the disease is the symbolic image of the sinner. (p. 220)

In other words, *tzara'at* and the laws of *tum'a* related to it are not a punishment, but rather a symbolic system. *Tzara'at* serves as a symbol of a certain type of wrongdoing. The *tum'a* is intended to establish the appropriate attitude towards these sins, whereas the *tahara* process symbolizes the process of ridding oneself of these spiritual ills.

Through this slight deviation, Rav Hoffmann transforms *tzara'at* and its laws from an ethical expression of reward and punishment to an educational, symbolic system expressing the proper attitude towards sin and repentance. This allows him to expand upon this theory and apply it to all types of *tum'a*:

In general, every *tum'a* symbolizes sin. By distancing themselves from the symbol of sin and carefully ensuring its distance from the Temple and everything sacred, Israel remembers at all times its ultimate destiny. The observance of the laws of *tahara* brings one to purity of thought and action.

Rav Hoffmann applies this symbolic outlook to other forms of *tum'a*:

When we consider the phenomena that serve as a source of *tum'a*, we find three categories of *tum'a*: the *tum'a* resulting from the death of human beings and animals – human corpses, animal carcasses; *tum'ot* resulting from bodily emissions, which we may perhaps refer to as "sexual *tum'ot*" – *ba'al keri, zav, zava* (various forms of emissions), menstruation, and the childbearing woman; and the *tum'ot* of *nega'im* (i.e., forms of *tzara'at*).

All the *temei'im* (impure people) must leave certain regions. The first category of *temei'im* leave only the Temple grounds, meaning, the "camp of the *Shekhina*." Those in the second group leave even the second camp, meaning, the camp of the Levites "who are near God." Those in the third category are expelled even from the camp of Israel, meaning, from the camp of the nation of God.

If we also recall that the sin that causes the *Shekhina's* departure from among Israel is also referred to by the connotation "*tum'a*," and that the annual atonement ritual on Yom Kippur serves to atone for the Temple, which "dwells among the impurities (*tum'ot*) of *Benei Israel*" (Lev. 16:16), it will become clear to us that the various types of *tum'a* symbolize the various sins, which God despises to a lesser or greater extent, and that they must remain at a distance from the sacred territory.

Therefore, the three types of *tum'a* reflect three categories of transgressions: transgressions against God; transgressions against the individual himself; and transgressions against one's fellow or against society.

With regard to the first category of sins and *tum'ot*... a person is meant to serve God, to cling to Him, to love Him and obey His word. The punishment for betraying God is death.... One who touches a corpse may not enter the camp of God that exists eternally, for he has become a symbol of the betrayal of God....

With regard to the second category of sins and *tum'ot*... *Am Yisrael*... is obligated to be a "sacred nation"...distant and apart from sensual desires and striving towards elevation.... We may view the *tum'ot* of the second category as symbols reminding us of the opposite of this sanctity.... One who descended to this level [of a life of desires and frivolity] must stay away not only from the camp of the *Shekhina*, but also from the camp of "those near to God," who yearn to resemble Him.

Finally, regarding the third category of sins, which *tzara'at* parallels...the *tzara'at* infection symbolizes transgressions between man and his fellow.... [*Tzara'at*] serves as an example of those sins which appear on the surface of the country that has been stricken with them and which gradually destroy its entire social structure.... The person afflicted must therefore distance himself from societal life and dwell in isolation outside the camp.... *Nega'im* on a garment or home allude to and symbolize the corruption of one's character and the illegality of his possessions, requiring their removal from societal life.

Later, Rav Hoffmann explains the details of the *tahara* laws on the basis of this symbolic system. The shortcoming of this approach, however, is that this explanation does not flow at all from the verses anywhere throughout the Torah's discussion of *tum'a* and *tahara*. Not only are the details of his approach not to be found, but in addition, and primarily, the basic precept upon which his entire explanations stands – the perspective of these laws as part of a symbolic system – has no basis in the text. According to Rav Hoffmann, the laws of *tum'a* and the process of purification all constitute symbols within a single system. But what objective indication can we bring to this far-reaching approach?

Rav Hoffmann sensed this problem and tried to base his explanation on the comparison frequently made in Tanach between sin and *tum'a*:

We find clear proof to the fact that *tum'a* is but a symbol of sin from the use made by the prophets while speaking of the purification from sin of the same expressions employed by the Torah to express purification from *tum'a*: "Wash yourselves clean" (Is. 1:16); "I will sprinkle clean water upon you, and you shall be clean from all your impurities" (Ez. 36:25); "Purge me with hyssop until I am pure" (Ps. 51:9). These expressions prove as clearly as possible that the prophets viewed *tum'a* as symbolic of sin, and purification from *tum'a* as symbolic of purification from sin.

I believe this proof is far from convincing. The verses cited by Rav Hoffmann do not compare *tum'a* to sin (as Rav Hoffmann does), but rather compare sin to *tum'a*. For those living in the biblical period, *tum'a* was not an abstract, theoretical concept difficult to comprehend, as it has become for modern commentators. Situations of *tum'a* and purification played an important role in day-to-day life. By contrast, sin and its contaminating effect on the person, and the need to repent, were less clear to the people of the time. The prophets and poets of Tanach therefore likened the abstract, ethical-religious world of sin and repentance to the more tangible world of *tum'a* and *tahara*.

V. RAV YEHUDA HALEVI: DEATH AS THE SOURCE OF *TUM'A*

We find an attempt at a general approach to all forms of *tum'a* already in the *Kuzari* of Rav Yehuda Halevi (2:58–62). The rabbi who is talking to the king of the Khazars prides himself on God's closeness to, and constant providence over, Israel, as expressed, among other ways, through the appearance of *tzara'at* infections on their homes and bodies. The king then asks the rabbi for more convincing proof "which brings the matter closer to the mind." The rabbi replies:

> I have already told you that our intellects are not comparable to that of the Divinity, and it is proper not to make any attempt to find a reason for these lofty concepts or anything similar to them. But after I ask for forgiveness and disclaim that this is surely the reason, I will say that *tzara'at* and abnormal discharges are related to the spiritual impurity related to death. Death is the absolute

spiritual deficiency, and a limb afflicted with *tzara'at* is like a corpse in this respect.

Similarly, an abnormal discharge also represents death, in that the discharged material had a certain life-force, which gave it the ability to become an embryo that would eventually develop into a human being. The loss of this material, then, is in opposition to the property of life and the spirit of life.

Because this spiritual deficiency is very ethereal, it can be detected only by people with refined spirits and significant souls, who strive to attach themselves to Divinity.... Most of us feel different when we come close to the dead or to a cemetery, and our spirits become confused for a while when we enter a house where a dead person has been. Only one whose nature is coarse will not be able to detect any of this.

Rav Yehuda Halevi thus transforms the *tum'a* resulting from death into the central hinge around which all forms of *tum'a* revolve, to one extent or other. All situations which bring about *tum'a* somehow resemble death, and *tum'a* itself constitutes the halakhic manifestation of the impression made upon man by this encounter with death. The corpse and carcass bring *tum'a* upon the living person who encounters them, and this *tum'a* expresses the confusion and change experienced by a person as a result of this encounter. Bodily emissions and *tzara'at* are all forms of "partial death" – in large or small measure – within a person's body, and they therefore result in a partial encounter with death itself, expressed through *tum'a*.

Two forms of *tum'a* in the Torah appear to negate Rav Yehuda Halevi's theory: that of the childbearing woman, and the *tum'a* brought on by normal sexual relations (15:18). Both these contexts involve specifically the creation of new life – the direct opposite of the phenomenon which, according to Rav Yehuda Halevi, is responsible for the onset of *tum'a* in general. It is clear that the two *tum'ot* just mentioned also lie along the axis between life and death. Apparently, only that which somehow connects to life and death generates *tum'a*; the corpse and half-corpse on the one hand, and the woman's blood and man's seed, on the other.

Perhaps the answer to this question is that, though indeed the processes of conception and childbirth create new life, nevertheless, the creators of this new life – the father who fertilizes the egg and the mother who gestates the child – are emptied of some of their life-force during the respective events of insemination and birth. This loss of life-force constitutes a form of partial death, which gives rise to a new, different life.

This is particularly evident in the case of childbirth. For nine months, new life develops within the mother, and now, at the moment of birth, she loses it. The baby begins an independent life, while the mother loses a life that had been part of her. Therefore, the mother becomes *tamei* as a result of childbirth, whereas the child, who has now received new, independent life, is *tahor*.

Tzara'at of the House

Rabbanit Sharon Rimon

Tzara'at of the house is one of three types of plagues mentioned in *Tazria-Metzora*. There are plagues of the body (various types of which are listed in *Parashat Tazria*), plagues on clothing, and plagues of the house.

Despite the similarities, the plagues of the house are unique:

- The plagues that affect the person or his clothing are covered in *Parashat Tazria*, and then *Parashat Metzora* begins with a discussion of the process of ritual purification for a person who is a *metzora* (i.e., someone struck with *tzara'at*). Only afterwards does the Torah introduce the plagues that affect houses. In other words, plagues of houses are separated, in the text, from the other sorts of plagues.
- Concerning all other plagues, we read: "*if there be* in the skin of a person's flesh"; "*if there be* the plague of *tzara'at* in a person"; "*if there be a plague* in a man or woman"; "*if there be* upon the garment." When it comes to *tzara'at* of the house, the Torah introduces the law in a unique fashion: "*and I place* the plague of *tzara'at*."

- Only in relation to *tzara'at* of the house is mention made of coming to the land: "*When you come to the land of Canaan…* and I place the plague of *tzara'at* upon *a house in the land* of your possession." In the process of purification of the *metzora*, the Torah addresses the situation in *the desert*. We are told, "outside of *the camp*"; "he shall dwell outside of *his tent*"; "before God at *the entrance to the Ohel Mo'ed*." In the process of purification of the house, we read about a "house" rather than a "tent," and "outside of the city" instead of "outside of the camp."

The portion describing plagues upon houses is introduced with the words, "When you come to the land of Canaan." This indicates that house *tzara'at* – in contrast to other types of plagues – occurs only in the Land of Israel. (Some commentaries claim that Ramban maintains that all of the plagues occur only in the Land of Israel, but this is a minority view.) It may be for this reason that *tzara'at* of houses is treated separately and differently from that of the body and of garments. The Torah begins with a discussion of *tzara'at* of the body and of garments, both of which were relevant already in the desert, and then goes on to describe the process of purification of the *metzora*. Only afterwards is mention made of *tzara'at* that affects the house, since it is not yet relevant, but may appear only in the future, when the nation enters the land. Why does *tzara'at* of houses occur only in the Land of Israel?

By studying the continuation of the *parasha*, with its description of the purification process involved in *tzara'at* of the house, the Sages deduced that the house must be one that is built from stones, wood, and earth, not a tent:

> "And I place the plague of *tzara'at* upon a house in the land of your possession" – this refers to a house that is made of stones, wood, and earth, which are able to contract ritual impurity. Is it possible that a type of house that is not made of stones, wood, and earth could contract impurity? [It is not;] for this reason it is written, "He shall break apart the house, with its stones, its wood, and all the earth of the house." Thus, we learn from the description of its ultimate fate that a house cannot be struck with

this ritual impurity unless it is built of stones, wood, and earth. (Sifra, *Baraita DeRabbi Yishmael* 1:1)

If the plague appears only in a house of stone, then it is clear that it was not relevant in the reality of the tents in which *Benei Yisrael* dwelled in the desert. In other words, *tzara'at* of the house appears only after the entry into the land, because there were no permanent houses in the desert. According to this view, there is no fundamental connection between the plague upon houses and the Land of Israel specifically.

Admittedly, this answer solves some of the questions posed above, but gives rise to two new difficulties. First, why does *tzara'at* affect specifically a house of stone and not a tent? Second, the Torah could have said, "If there be a plague of *tzara'at* upon a house" – and it would have been clear that there were no houses in the desert, and hence that the plague would not appear there. However, the *parasha* makes explicit note of the entry into the land, and the fact that God gave the land to Israel. The first verse sounds like the herald of some auspicious declaration or promise. After the words, "When you come to the land of Canaan which I give to you as a possession," we expect some stately continuation, and are disappointed at the "promise" that follows: "And I place the plague of *tzara'at* upon a house of your possession." In the context of this structure and style, the expression "and I place" (*venatati*) has the effect of conveying the sense of something positive that is going to happen.

Second, in all the other types of *tzara'at*, as noted, the introduction is formulated in conditional terms. By *tzara'at* of the house, the Torah proclaims that it will definitely happen. Why does the introduction to the discussion of *tzara'at* of the house appear to convey the sense of good news, i.e., that it is a positive phenomenon?

Taking his cue from the Midrash (Deuteronomy Rabba 17:6), Rashi explains:

"And I shall place a plague of *tzara'at*" – this is good news for them, that the plagues would come upon them, for the Emorites had hidden gold coins in the walls of their houses throughout the forty years that Israel were in the desert. By means of the plague, the house would be dismantled, and they would be found.

The Midrash and Rashi understand from the introduction to this *parasha* that the plague upon the house carries a special, positive message related to the entry into the land; they explain the law of the plague upon the houses as a positive promise. The plague leads to the house being demolished, and this in turn provides the opportunity to discover the hidden treasure.

But this raises a difficulty. A plague is not a positive phenomenon. It involves ritual impurity; it causes the house to be taken apart. This is not what we would regard as a positive process, and were it not for the festive introduction, we would never dream of suggesting that "this is good news for them"; in fact – quite the opposite.

Ḥazal explain that all of the plagues come as a result of sin, of a certain corruption:

> R. Shmuel b. Naḥmani said in the name of R. Yoḥanan: Plagues come [as punishment] for seven things: *lashon hara* (slander), bloodshed, a false vow, sexual immorality, vulgarity of spirit, theft, and stinginess. (Arakhin 16a)

(In Leviticus Rabba 17:3 there is a list of ten transgressions, while Yalkut Shimoni Zechariah 572 lists eleven.)

All plagues come as punishment for sin, or as warning concerning a situation that needs correcting. Plagues upon houses are no exception to this rule.

For which sin is a plague upon the house sent as a punishment? The Midrash provides a graphic description of the character trait that requires correction:

> It is written, "The produce of his house will disappear, they shall flow away in the day of His anger" (Job 20:28), they will flow away and be found. When? On the day that the Holy One arouses His anger against that person. How does this come about?

A person says to his neighbor, "Lend me a measure of wheat." The neighbor replies: "I have none." "Then a measure of barley?" "I have none." A woman says to her neighbor: "Lend me a sifter." She replies, "I have none." "Lend me a sieve?" She replies, "I have none."

What does the Holy One do? He brings a plague on the house, and when the man is forced to take out all of his belongings, everyone sees and they say, "Didn't he say that he had nothing? Look how much wheat he has! How much barley! How many dates there are here!" (Leviticus Rabba 17)

According to this midrash, *tzara'at* comes upon a house because of miserliness. Now miserliness is not a sin. A person has the right to do as he pleases with his own property. There is no obligation to lend to others. But miserliness is a negative character trait that must be corrected. From this point of view, *tzara'at* of the house is not really a punishment, but rather a catalyst for change, causing the person to mend his ways. Through the experience of *tzara'at* upon his house, he comes to understand that it is not proper that he hoard his property to himself; he must also share with others.

If *tzara'at* of the house is not meant to be "good news," however, but rather a signal to the person to mend his ways, how are we to explain the special introduction to this subject? The *Keli Yakar* describes how the introduction addresses the mistake of the miserly person, who is struck with *tzara'at* upon his house:

It seems to me in this regard that the main reason is because of miserliness, as our Sages deduced from the verse, "And he to whom the house belongs shall come" to mean "He who made his house belong only to himself, and did not share of it with others," for *it is for this reason that God gave him for a possession a house full of all kinds of goodness – in order to test him and see whether he would also share of his house with others,* "For the silver and gold is Mine, says God" (Haggai 2:8).... Therefore it is written, "When you come to the land of Canaan which I give to you as a possession" – for it is not by their sword that they inherit the land, nor did their arm deliver them, but rather the right hand of God that is uplifted, to give them the portion of the nations. There is no room for the miserly to say, "My strength and the power of my hand have achieved all this valor for me," for it is God who gives you strength and possession.

The *Keli Yakar* suggests that a person who understands that God has given him the land as a possession is conscious of the fact that the land really belongs to God; he himself has merely received a gift from God, and therefore he does not treat his property as belonging only to himself. He knows that he must share with others the good that God has granted him.

In contrast, a person who treats his house as "a house of your possession" feels that his house belongs solely to himself, and therefore is not interested in giving of his own possession to others. This is the person's mistake – the property and the house are not his; they are a gift from God. If his sense of ownership of his property expands to the point where he is not prepared to give any of it to others, then "I shall place the plague of *tzara'at* upon the house of your possession." The plague will come, reminding him that the house is not really his own possession, but rather something granted to him by God.

The plague that appears on his house is not regular mold, and it cannot be treated in natural ways. It is a special plague sent by God. This plague is meant to remind the person who the true Owner of the house is. Only if the person mends his ways will his house be healed. The removal of the objects from the house teaches the person that his property is not entirely in his own possession. If this step does not have the effect of causing him to repent, and the plague attacks his house once again, then it is dismantled. Taking the house apart is a more drastic step; it teaches him that this type of house is not worthy of being inhabited. Only when a person recognizes the true Houseowner, is his house worthy of being lived in.

Now we understand why *tzara'at* appears specifically on a house of stone. The reason would appear to be that in this type of house there is a greater chance of a person having a sense of absolute ownership and forgetting that the house was given to him as a possession by God, as the Torah describes:

> Guard yourself lest you forget HaShem your God…lest you eat and be satisfied, *and build good houses, and dwell in them.* And your cattle and sheep multiply, and you have much silver and gold, and all that you have is abundant. And your heart becomes haughty, and you forget HaShem your God. (Deut. 8:11–14)

Rashi's explanation (following the Midrash), according to which the Torah is giving good news about finding treasure, is surprising because a plague is not something positive; why would God choose to reveal the place of the treasure by means of a plague? Perhaps we may connect Rashi's interpretation with that of the *Keli Yakar*. Finding the treasure is the end of the process. The person has erred in having forgotten that his house actually belongs to God. By means of the *tzara'at* and the process of purification of the house, the person undergoes a significant process of inner change. The dismantling of one's house is a significant psychological experience; everything that the person has is broken up. The thing that was so secure in his eyes, and over which he felt such secure ownership, is taken apart. When he is left with nothing of his own, he understands that the true Owner of the house is God.

Another idea is to be found in Midrash Tanḥuma:

> "If there be in the skin of a person's flesh" (Lev. 13) – the Holy One does not wish to harm this person. What does He do? First He gives him warning, and only afterwards does He strike him, as it is written (ch. 14), "And I place a plague of *tzara'at* upon a house in the land of your possession." First he strikes the house. If the person repents – fine; if not – He strikes his clothes, as it is written (ch. 13), "If there be the plague of *tzara'at* upon a garment." If he repents – fine; if not, it comes upon his body, as it is written, "If there be in the skin of a person's flesh." (*Tazria, siman* 10)

According to this midrash, the plague upon the house is the initial warning, with the aim of avoiding the need to strike the person himself with a plague. According to this understanding, the good news here is that God does not immediately strike the person himself, but first warns him by placing a plague upon his house.

Why then does the Torah not begin with house *tzara'at*? The Midrash answers that God told them the *parasha* about *tzara'at* in the desert, where they did not yet have houses: "The Holy One said: Because you do not have houses, I am starting [the discussion] with your bodies, but after you enter the land, will start with your houses" (Midrash Tadsheh 17).

This good news is unique to the Land of Israel; only there does the plague appear upon the house before it strikes the person himself. Why specifically in the Land of Israel does God first strike the houses, rather than sending a punishment directly to the person's body? Why is there no warning to a person in the desert, in the form of a plague upon his tent, before his body is struck with *tzara'at*?

Ibn Ezra explains as follows:

> The reason why the Torah says, "When you come to the land of Canaan," is because this [discussion] applies exclusively in the land, *because of the unique greatness of the land*, for the Sanctuary is in their midst, with God's glory within the Sanctuary. (Lev. 14:34)

Because of the unique character of the Land of Israel, plagues may occur on the houses in the land. The Land of Israel possesses a unique degree of holiness, and therefore it does not tolerate sin. It is for this reason that the land "expels" from its midst the nations that have been sinful:

> Do not defile yourselves with all of these, for with all of these the nations which I drive out from before you, were defiled. And the land became defiled, so I visit its iniquity upon it, *and the land expels its inhabitants*. But you yourselves shall observe My statutes and My judgments, and you shall not do any of these abominations – neither the native born among you nor the stranger who dwells in your midst … that the land not expel you when you defile it as it expelled the nation that was before you. (Lev. 18:24–28)

This special land does not tolerate spiritual and moral corruption; it expels such phenomena from its midst. If there are houses that suffer some spiritual defect, the land will not tolerate it, and therefore the plague will appear upon them.

But we may add a further stage, on the basis of the principles that we have discussed thus far. Plagues appear upon a house when a person is miserly and is not prepared to share what he has with others. Such a person lives with a misguided consciousness concerning his home. The house is given to him by God; he fails to understand this and believes that the house is his own possession. The land – God's land – is unable to bear such a house, which denies its ownership by God, as it were. Therefore it is specifically in the Land of Israel that plagues appear upon such a house.

What is the good news about these plagues? The good news is that the land is of such unique sanctity that even its houses are affected by plagues as a result of a defective spiritual state.

And there is more: a person whose character traits are flawed and corrupted – even if has not violated any explicit prohibition – receives divine signals to change his ways. Thus, the plague leads to the maintenance of the high spiritual level that is needed specifically in the Land of Israel.

It is the lofty level of the Land of Israel that causes *tzara'at*; this brings about a correction of a person's traits, thereby leading us to a higher and more worthy spiritual level.

Parashat Aḥarei Mot

Yom Kippur and the Eighth Day

Rav Yoel Bin-Nun

I. BETWEEN THE EIGHTH DAY AND YOM KIPPUR

The Torah connects the description of the seven days of consecration of the *Mishkan* and the account of the following "eighth day" with the unit detailing the service of the *Kohen Gadol* in the *Kodesh Kodashim* on Yom Kippur.

As described in chapter 9, the eighth day, the revelation of the Divine Presence to the congregation of *Benei Yisrael* in the *Mishkan* in the midst of the camp, unquestionably provides the culmination of the preceding seven days of consecration. Nevertheless, in contrast to the seven days – concerning which Moses is commanded prior to the establishment of the *Mishkan* – the description of the eighth day is recorded after its establishment. Similarly, the command concerning the consecration that appears in Exodus and is then repeated in Leviticus likewise does not include the eighth day.

The unit concerning the eighth day ends with the deaths of Nadav and Avihu, the prohibition of entering the Sanctuary in an inebriated state, and the goat for the sin offering, which is burned (Lev. 10). However, it is clear that the same subject is then resumed in the description of the service performed in the *Kodesh Kodashim* and the Yom Kippur service for all generations:

> God spoke to Moses *after the deaths of Aaron's two sons, when they came near before God and they died*. And God said to Moses: Speak to Aaron your brother, that he should not come at all times into the Sanctuary, within the veil that is before the covering upon the Ark, so that he will not die, for I shall appear in a cloud above the covering. Thus shall Aaron come into the Sanctuary. (Lev. 16:1–3)

In other words, the description of the proper manner of entry into the Sanctuary is a result and continuation of Nadav and Avihu's improper entry into the Sanctuary. Here the Torah sets forth how the entry into the place of the cloud is to be carried out for the purposes of purifying the Sanctuary as well as *Benei Yisrael*, who visit there.

This unit on the service in the *Kodesh Kodashim* – the Yom Kippur service for all generations – follows the same model as the commandment of circumcision (Gen. 17) and the Pesaḥ sacrifice in Egypt (Ex. 12): first comes the commandment to Abraham/Moses/Aaron for that specific time, and it is then expanded for all generations (Gen. 17:9–14; Ex. 12:14–20; Lev. 16:29–end).

The Vilna Gaon claims that Aaron could enter the *Kodesh Kodashim* whenever he wanted to, not only on Yom Kippur – subject, of course, to the procedure prescribed in the text: "*Thus* shall Aaron come into the Sanctuary" (16:3). On the other hand, in later generations, the *Kohen Gadol* could only enter the *Kodesh Kodashim* on Yom Kippur – as stated explicitly at the end of the chapter (v. 29 onwards).

This resolves a number of difficulties arising from the unit on Yom Kippur. The Midrash teaches:

> "That he should not come at all times" – R. Yehuda b. R. Shimon said: Moses suffered great sorrow over this matter. He said, Woe to me; perhaps Aaron, my brother, has been rejected from [God's] Presence…a "time" can last an hour…a "time" can last a day…a "time" can last a year…a "time" can last forever.
>
> The Holy One, blessed be He, said to Moses: It is not as you think…. Rather, at any time that he wishes to enter, he may enter, only he must enter in accordance with this procedure. (Leviticus Rabba 21)

It is possible that this *parasha* was connected to Yom Kippur even then, in the wilderness. Rashi asserts that Aaron put it into practice on the following Yom Kippur; Rashbam similarly concludes that from this point onwards, Aaron would enter the *Kodesh Kodashim* only on Yom Kippur. This may be because this was the day when, as the Torah suggests (Deut. 9:9–11, 17–18, 25; 10:1–5; Ex. 34:1–4, 27–28), the second tablets were received; according to *Ḥazal*, the day when the nation was forgiven for the sin of the Golden Calf and the Torah was restored to them. Thus, as part of the special command issued to them here, in the wilderness, they were also commanded concerning Yom Kippur for all future generations – paralleling the model of Pesaḥ in Egypt.

On the other hand, it is possible that "after the deaths of Aaron's two sons" is meant literally – immediately after their deaths (in the month of Nisan). The conclusion, "And he [Aaron] did as Moses had commanded," may accordingly mean that Aaron did all of this immediately, in the first month, and only later on did this *parasha* come to apply to Yom Kippur. This closing formula, "And he did as Moses had commanded," is commonly employed to indicate an activity prescribed for a specific time; it is quite inappropriate in the context of an activity that is to be continued for all generations. Thus, the plain meaning of the text would seem to be that at this stage there was no connection between the "eighth day" and Yom Kippur.

Either way, it is clear that *Parashat Aḥarei Mot* represents the conclusion of the commandment concerning the *Mishkan* and the process of bringing the Divine Presence to rest in the midst of the camp. This connection between the *parashot* and its significance requires thorough study.[2]

---

2. The connection between the literary unit concerning the "eighth day" and the Yom Kippur service finds halakhic expression. The beginning of Mishna Yoma states that for the seven days preceding Yom Kippur, the *Kohen Gadol* is separated from his wife and moves to a Temple chamber. In other words, Yom Kippur is approached like an "eighth day" that follows seven "days of consecration," during which time the *Kohen Gadol* is separated and prepared for the atonement service that he will perform. According to *Ḥazal*, during these days the *Kohen Gadol* would rehearse his Yom Kippur service: "Throughout the seven days he sprinkles the blood and offers the incense and prepares the lamps and offers the head and the hind leg" (Yoma 14a).

   Indeed, in the Gemara, this connection between the biblical "eighth day" and the historical Yom Kippur seems quite self-evident. The Gemara derives the law of

II. SACRIFICES – SIMILARITIES AND DIFFERENCES

A connection between the eighth day and the service in the *Kodesh Kodashim* is also clearly discernible from the nature of the service itself. In both cases, Aaron offers the same sacrifice – an ox as a sin offering and a ram as a burnt offering (9:2; 16:3). (The "eighth day" is the only place in the Torah where the offering is specified as a "calf" – *egel*. This hints strongly at the purpose of atonement, both for Aaron and the nation, for the sin of the Golden Calf.) In both cases the nation brings a goat that is sacrificed as a sin offering. In both cases the nation brings a burnt offering; on the eighth day, it is "a calf and a lamb, both of the first year" (9:3), while on Yom Kippur, the calf is omitted and there is only a ram as a burnt offering (16:5). Only the peace offering and the meal offering, which are mentioned on the eighth day, do not appear on Yom Kippur; the reason being that this is the day of forgiveness and atonement, a day of affliction of the soul, such that there can be no sacrifice that is eaten.

A comparison with the sacrifices of the days of consecration is similarly enlightening. There, too, we find an ox as a sin offering and a ram as a burnt offering (exactly like Aaron's offerings on the eighth day and on Yom Kippur). Likewise there is a peace offering – the ram of consecration (in addition to the ram of the burnt offering), which is eaten together with the unleavened loaves at the entrance of the Tent of Meeting on each of the seven days. Thus, during the seven days of consecration, the *kohanim* brought a sin offering, a burnt offering, and peace offerings – but the nation brought no sacrifice. On the eighth day, Aaron brought a sin offering and a burnt offering, and the nation matched these with their own offerings. The peace offering, an offering representing joy and celebration, is brought on the eighth day by the nation, since the essential purpose of this day is the revelation of the Divine Presence to the nation (outside, in front of the entrance to the

---

separating the *kohen* for the seven days preceding Yom Kippur from the "seven days of consecration": "From where do we deduce this? R. Manyumi b. Ḥilkiah said in the name of R. Maḥsiah b. Idi, in the name of R. Yoḥanan: It is written, 'As he has done on this day, so God has commanded to do, to make atonement for you' (Lev. 8:34). 'To do' – this refers to activities pertaining to the heifer; 'to make atonement for you' – this refers to the activities pertaining to Yom Kippur" (Yoma 2a; 3b; 4a).

Tent of Meeting), and not only to Moses (inside the Tent of Meeting). The *kohanim*, on the other hand, having already completed their training and practice, no longer need to partake of the peace offerings. On Yom Kippur, too, Aaron's sacrifice comes to atone for him and his household, and to prepare him for sacrifice as on the eighth day. It is matched by the sacrifice of the nation – but this time without the peace offering, since on this day there is no joy associated with the eating of sacrifices.

However, herein lies also the essential difference between the days of consecration and the eighth day on the one hand, and Yom Kippur on the other. The sacrifice of the ox as a sin offering on the days of consecration and on the eighth day is described in detail (Ex. 29:10–14; Lev. 8:14–17; Lev. 9:8–11), and it involves only the external sacrificial altar. Despite this, it is followed by burning outside of the camp: "He burned the flesh and the skin with fire outside of the camp" (9:11). As Rashi notes, this is the only instance in which a sin offering is burned even though it was offered on the external altar without having its blood brought inside the Sanctuary.

In contrast, all other sin offerings that are burned have their blood brought into the Sanctuary, where the anointed *kohen* sprinkles it. This applies to both the ox as sin offering of the anointed *kohen*, and to the sin offering of the congregation (Lev. 4:5–7; 10:16–18) – where the *kohen* sprinkles upon the *parokhet* (veil) and upon the inner (incense) altar. On Yom Kippur, too, the *kohen* sprinkles – this time in the *Kodesh Kodashim*, on and in front of the covering of the Ark, and then upon the inner altar.

The uniqueness of Yom Kippur lies in the fact that only on this day is there a service that is performed within the *Kodesh Kodashim*, including the offering of incense and the sprinkling of blood (Lev. 16:12–19; Mishna Zevaḥim 5:1–2).

In contrast, on the eighth day the situation is reversed – this was the day when Aaron offered sacrifices for the first time and commenced his priesthood; nevertheless, his special service on this day involves no "inner" service, and even the sacrifice that should have its blood sprinkled inside the Sanctuary – his ox as sin offering – is not brought inside, but rather burned, at God's command, *as though it had been brought inside*!

While the reasons may differ, the reality is nevertheless identical – on the eighth day, there was no priestly service inside the *Mishkan*, and certainly not inside the *Kodesh Kodashim*, just as there had not been during the seven days of consecration.

In contrast, on Yom Kippur both the blood of the ox and the blood of the goat are brought into the Sanctuary: "And he shall slaughter the goat for the sin offering that is for the nation … and do with its blood as he did with the blood of the ox, and sprinkle it upon the covering (*kapporet*) and before the covering" (16:15), and both are burned together (16:27).

In other words, the ox for the sin offering, on the eighth day, is altogether "external," yet it is burned (at God's command, deviating from the usual procedure). On Yom Kippur, on the other hand, its blood is brought into the *Kodesh Kodashim* (similarly unique – in the opposite manner), in contrast to the usual ox of the anointed *kohen*, whose blood is always brought into the Sanctuary but only as far as the *parokhet*.

We may summarize the above as follows:

- The ox of the days of consecration and of the eighth day – external, but burned;
- Ox of the anointed *kohen* – blood sprinkled upon the *parokhet* and upon the golden (incense) altar;
- Ox of Yom Kippur – blood sprinkled between the staves of the Ark, upon the *parokhet*, and upon the golden altar.

The goat for a sin offering offered by the nation, on the eighth day, is similarly "external," and theoretically should have been eaten (but was burned instead, because of the deaths of Nadav and Avihu). On Yom Kippur, however, the blood of the goat is brought into the *Kodesh Kodashim* and it is burned. Obviously, no sacrifice that is usually eaten is brought on Yom Kippur.

Most importantly, though, the contrast finds expression in the incense. Throughout the year there is a commandment to offer incense before God in the Sanctuary, and to bring "regular fire" (from the external, sacrificial altar). On the eighth day, however, incense is not brought into the Sanctuary and regular fire is considered "strange fire" (10:1); for this reason Nadav and Avihu are punished. On Yom Kippur, however, incense is brought not only into the Sanctuary, but into the *Kodesh Kodashim*.

It is clear, then, that the relationship between the eighth day and Yom Kippur is an inverse parallel. The similarity merely serves as background to the stark contrast. The eighth day and Yom Kippur are two opposite poles in the single system of divine revelation to *Benei Yisrael*. The usual situation, in this system, is one of sanctified service with its pinnacle in the Sanctuary (*heikhal*); it does not reach as far as the *Kodesh Kodashim* (*dvir*). Two exceptions contrast with this usual situation – the eighth day, when the sanctified service involves only the *external* altar, at the entrance to the Tent of Meeting, outside the *heikhal*, and Yom Kippur, where the situation is reversed, and the most sanctified service is performed not in the *heikhal* but on the other side of the *parokhet*, in the *Kodesh Kodashim*.

The three distinct situations comprising this system may be presented in tabular form, as follows:

	Eighth Day	**Regular Situation**	**Service of *Kodesh Kodashim* (and for future generations, Yom Kippur)**
Line dividing man's actions from God's revelation	At the entrance to the *Ohel Mo'ed*	At the *parokhet*	At the *Aron*, facing the *keruvim*
Fire from heaven	Purpose of service on this day	None	None
Regular fire	Forbidden (Rashbam 10:1) – it burned Nadav and Avihu	Mitzva – for the inner (incense) altar in the Sanctuary	Mitzva – *with the incense for the Kodesh Kodashim*
Entrance to Sanctuary or *Kodesh Kodashim*	No entrance for any service, but for prayer	Entry for service	Entry to *Kodesh Kodashim*
Service	Only on external altar	On external altar and internal altar, not in *Kodesh Kodashim*	Also in *Kodesh Kodashim*

	Eighth Day	Regular Situation	Service of Kodesh Kodashim (and for future generations, Yom Kippur)
Sin offering of anointed *kohen*	External, but burned like an "internal" sin offering. Blood placed on horns of external altar.	Internal, but only in the Sanctuary. Blood sprinkled on the *parokhet* and on the inner altar. Also placed on horns of the inner altar.	Internal – in *Kodesh Kodashim.* Blood sprinkled upon the *parokhet,* and upon the inner altar. Also placed on horns of inner altar.
Sin offering of the congregation	External, and burned – debate as to whether the burning was proper.	Internal – for unintentional transgression of one of the commandments. External, regular – for unintentional transgression of all the commandments (= sin offering of idolatry, Num. 15).	Internal (as in regular service throughout the year)

The significance of the contrast between these different situations will become clear if we explore the meaning of the "Sanctuary" ("*Kodesh*") and of the "*Kodesh Kodashim*," and the meaning of the *parokhet* that separates them (Ex. 26:33). We are used to viewing this separation as a matter of ascending levels of holiness in one direction – from the outside inwards. There is a courtyard and there is the Sanctuary, and within the Sanctuary itself there is the "*Kodesh*" and there is an inner place that is even more holy (Mishna Kelim 1:6–9).

It is not difficult to prove that this representation is not accurate. This arrangement places all the levels of holiness on a single continuum, a single common scale. Upon closer inspection, however, we find not one continuum, but rather two; two areas that are fundamentally different from one another and which are orientated in two opposite directions.

One area includes the courtyard and the *"Kodesh"* – the *Ohel Mo'ed* outside of the *parokhet*. In describing the Menora, the table for showbread, and the incense altar, the Torah emphasizes over and over that these vessels are placed "outside of the *parokhet*" (Ex. 27:21; 26:35; 30:6–8; 40:22–26). In the *"Kodesh,"* man arranges the showbread continually upon the table before God, prepares the light that burns continually in the Menora, and offers the continuous incense upon the inner altar. The fire here is regular fire, from the external altar, from earth to the heavens.

The *Kodesh Kodashim* represents the opposite. It is the place of the Divine Presence, the place where God's Kingship is revealed in the midst of Israel and the world; it is the place of divine communication with Moses "from above the covering, from between the two *keruvim*" (Ex. 25:22; Num. 7:89). Since the essence of God cannot be perceived at all, the *Kodesh Kodashim* contains nothing but the support for God's "Throne": the "Ark of the Covenant of HaShem, the footstool of our God" (1 Chr. 28:2), with *keruvim* on either side, and containing the tablets, with a *sefer Torah* "alongside the Ark of the Covenant of HaShem" (Deut. 31:26).

The cloud and the Divine Glory that rest upon the Tent of Meeting and within it are the revelation of God's word to man, and their root and essence are to be found in the *Kodesh Kodashim*. Therefore, no man may enter there except on Yom Kippur. For the same reason, man cannot perform any sacrificial service or prayer there, nor can regular fire be brought in. Rather, everything in the *Kodesh Kodashim* is "from the top down," "from heaven to earth," like Creation itself, where man was not present at all – "for I appear in the cloud above the covering [of the Ark]" (16:2, and Rashi).

From the *Kodesh Kodashim* God speaks to man, while in the *"Kodesh"* man stands before God. "And the *parokhet* will separate for you between the Kodesh and the *Kodesh Kodashim*" (Ex. 26:33) – a sharp division between two spheres which together form a complete Temple, a complete world, unified – but with clear distinctions.

This distinction and this clarification provide us with the key to understanding the significance of the difference between the eighth day and Yom Kippur. The eighth day is the day of God's appearance above the Tent of Meeting as a whole – i.e., above the *Kodesh*, too, and not only the *Kodesh Kodashim*. In this unique instance, the entire Tent of Meeting serves as the place of abode for the King, for HaShem God of Israel, on the day when He appeared to the nation, thereby expressing the special nature and quality which usually applies only to the *Kodesh Kodashim*, as applying to the *Mishkan* as a whole.

Thus on this day entry is forbidden not only to the *Kodesh Kodashim, but even to the Kodesh*. Therefore no mention is made on this day of inner service, and even that which should seemingly have been offered inside – the calf as sin offering – is offered outside, and is nevertheless burned like an "internal" sin offering.

Moreover, even the fire on the external altar comes from on High. On this day, incense cannot be brought with the coals of a regular fire, since this would be considered a "strange fire" even in the *Kodesh*. Even on the external altar, the fire is a fire that has emerged "from before God"; there is no room for regular fire; this is certainly so inside the *Kodesh*.

Only Moses and Aaron come into the Tent of Meeting. Before the fire emerges from before God, they enter into the cloud – yet this is not an entry for the purposes of sacrificial service, but rather for the purposes of bringing a blessing: "And they emerged and they blessed the people" (9:23).

In light of the above, the literal reading of the text suggests that the sin of Nadav and Avihu is their very entry into the forbidden divine area in the *Mishkan*, which made it, in its entirety, like the *Kodesh Kodashim* and therefore forbidden to enter. This was an attempt to blend the two spheres, to blur the full significance of the divine revelation, to which man could not be party.

All the other disqualifications that the various commentaries attribute to Nadav and Avihu, and which are hinted at in the text (such as, for instance, the prohibition against performing the priestly service in a state of inebriation), should be understood as factors in or results of the blurring of the division between the mortal sphere and the divine.

The terrible tragedy of the eighth day, and the weeping of the entire congregation over the fire that God sent, leaves in its wake a difficult question – is it possible to draw near to God without losing one's life? At this point, following the sin and God's justice as meted out to the sons of Aaron, there is a feeling that there must be a way of coming before the King and asking for forgiveness and mercy!

This question is not formulated explicitly in Leviticus, but it is voiced in similar circumstances in Numbers. Here, the two hundred and fifty princes of the congregation – men of standing, but not *kohanim*, who offered censers of incense before God – were all burned with a fire that emerged from God when His glory was revealed to the congregation at the entrance to the Tent of Meeting, just like what happened on the eighth day (Num. 16:16–19, 35; 17:1–5). Likewise, the congregation, which complained the next day about the deaths of these princes of the congregation, was struck with a plague when God's glory appeared in the Tent of Meeting, and this plague was halted when the incense was brought out by Aaron. At that time, the question was starkly expressed:

> *Benei Yisrael* said to Moses, saying: Behold, we perish, we are done for, we are all done for. Anyone who approaches, who approaches God's Sanctuary, dies; shall we perish altogether? (Num. 17:27–28)

It is to this question – "how can we approach the Sanctuary without loss of life?" – that the unit on Yom Kippur responds: "Thus shall Aaron come into the Sanctuary." It is possible to atone and to purify. It is possible to approach – not only the *Kodesh*, but even the *Kodesh Kodashim*!

However, the eighth day is fundamentally different from Yom Kippur. On the eighth day, the Divine Presence is revealed before the eyes of the entire congregation, outside. On Yom Kippur, the Divine Presence is hidden, withdrawing, as it were, in the *Kodesh Kodashim* itself, in order for man to be able to enter. In the unit on Yom Kippur

(Lev. 16) there is no revelation or even any expression of revelation. What Yom Kippur offers is not only the possibility of entering and making atonement, but the vital need to do so, owing to the impurities and transgressions that have adhered even to the inside of the Sanctuary: "And he shall make atonement for the *Kodesh*, from the impurities of *Benei Yisrael* and from their transgressions, for all of their sins, and so shall he do for the Tent of Meeting, which dwells with them in the midst of their impurity" (16:16). If these are not atoned for, the Divine Presence may not be able to remain in their midst.

It turns out, then, that the nature of man's entry into the *Kodesh* changes during Yom Kippur itself, and progresses one stage further inward. The incense altar, which always faces the Ark and the covering, "before the *parokhet* which is by the Testimony," but which is placed "in front of the covering (*kapporet*) which is upon the Ark of Testimony" (Ex. 30:6) – i.e., separated by the partition – is imported to the *Kodesh Kodashim* by means of the censer and the burning coals. Likewise, the ox as the sin offering of the anointed *kohen*, whose blood is usually sprinkled "seven times before God, towards the *parokhet* of the Sanctuary" (Lev. 4:6), likewise has its blood sprinkled inside, after the covering is itself covered with the cloud of incense (which replaces the covering of the *parokhet*!). This sprinkling is "upon the covering eastward, and before the covering" (Lev. 16:14).

The inner altar must likewise have atonement made for it once a year with the blood of the sin offering of Yom Kippur (Ex. 30:9–10). That which is performed throughout the year on the external altar – placing the blood upon the horns of the altar (Lev. 4:30; Mishna Zevaḥim 5:3) – is manifested on Yom Kippur on the inner altar. At the same time, the essence of what the inner altar represents throughout the year – the offering of the incense – is manifested on Yom Kippur in the *Kodesh Kodashim*.

If the *Kohen Gadol* emerges safely from this "encounter" with the Divine Presence, it is clear to the entire nation that their sins have been forgiven, and the Divine Presence will continue to dwell in their midst, as in the beginning, with the usual division, represented by the *parokhet*.

The Yom Kippur service, then, is a complement to the eighth day. This is the answer to the question of how *Am Yisrael* can live while the *Shekhina* is in our midst and anyone who approaches will die; how we can live with the manifest attribute of justice, or how we can exist in close proximity to the Sanctuary of the King, where any slight deviation brings a fierce divine fire. The purifying atonement of Yom Kippur is the answer; it is the *tikkun* that makes it possible to live.

III. STRUCTURE AND ORDER OF THE SERVICE IN THE *KODESH KODASHIM* (LEV. 16)

On the basis of the absolute contrast, discussed above, between the service of the eighth day and the service in the *Kodesh Kodashim* (which is the service for Yom Kippur, for all future generations) we are able to examine very closely the service of the *Kodesh Kodashim*, and find the solution to the internal difficulties that it raises.

First, a distinction should be drawn between most of the unit – which is conveyed as a commandment for that generation, applying specifically to Aaron "at all times," and the commandment for future generations – which is conveyed only at the end of the chapter, and which applies to Yom Kippur only: "This shall be for you as an eternal statute, to atone for *Benei Yisrael* for all of their transgressions, once in the year" (Lev. 16:34).

We shall divide our analysis of the details of this unit into two parts: A clarification of the main purpose of Aaron's entry into the *Kodesh Kodashim* (as opposed to objectives that are merely secondary), and resolution of the repetitions and difficulties in the verses.

A close examination of the unit on the service in the *Kodesh Kodashim* (Lev. 16), with the questions and difficulties that arise from it, has already been undertaken by my rabbi and teacher, Rav Mordechai Breuer, in his excellent work, *Pirkei Mo'adot* (Jerusalem, 5746, vol. 2, p. 503ff.), and he adopts a dual fundamental position:

1. There is a similarity between the service of the eighth day and the service of the *Kodesh Kodashim* (limited to that generation, and to Aaron alone). Therefore, every sacrifice that is mentioned in chapter 16 has an aspect to it that is similar to the sacrifices of Aaron and the congregation on the eighth day – i.e., external sacrifices that are burned. It is only the additional aspect that

appears in Leviticus 16 – the atonement for the Sanctuary, the *kohanim*, and the nation (which has, as its source, the purpose of the Yom Kippur service for future generations) – that causes the sin offering of Aaron and the congregation, in chapter 16, to be an internal sacrifice. This is also the source of the repetition in the *parasha*.

2. The entry into the *Kodesh Kodashim* is not, in essence, for the purpose of performing sacrificial service there, but rather for the purpose of prayer and prostration – like on the eighth day. It is only the accompanying addition of the need for atonement for the Sanctuary, for the *kohanim*, and for the nation – with its source, as mentioned, in Yom Kippur for future generations – that causes each instance of entry there to entail a sacrificial service, too.

Rav Breuer's approach assumes particular clarity in verse 23: "Aaron shall come into the Tent of Meeting," paralleling the verse concerning the eighth day (9:23), "And Moses and Aaron came into the Tent of Meeting, and they emerged, and they blessed the people." The entry is for the purpose of prayer and prostration.

However, I cannot accept these fundamental assumptions of Rav Breuer in analyzing the unit, since we have shown above that the service of the *Kodesh Kodashim* does indeed resemble the service of the eighth day – but in an *inverse* parallel!

Therefore, the alternative explanation proposed below adopts the opposite assumption regarding these two issues. In other words,

1. There is an absolute contrast between the service of the eighth day, which takes place entirely in the courtyard, and the service of the *Kodesh Kodashim*, which is carried out mainly inside. The service of the *Kodesh Kodashim* (Lev. 16) expresses phenomena which are the direct opposite of those of the eighth day (Lev. 9).

2. The entire purpose of entry into the *Kodesh*, in chapter 16 – even the entry that is unique to Aaron "at all times" – is to perform the internal service of atonement and purification, in keeping with whatever need may arise, for the Sanctuary itself, for the *kohanim*,

or for the entire congregation. This is a contrast to the nature of the entry on the eighth day.

In general, entry for the sole purpose of encountering the *Shekhina* or to hear God's word is a role that belongs, almost entirely, to Moses. Aaron, on the other hand, is a sort of *sheliaḥ tzibbur* for atonement and purification – including for needs that may crop up, as for example during the episode of the plague following the sin of Korah, as explained above.

Based on these assumptions, and based also on the assumption that there were different possibilities for the need for atonement and purification, let us consider the structure and order of the unit and try thereby to resolve the repetitions and difficulties to which it gives rise.

Our unit presents a number of difficulties, and we shall present them briefly:

1. For what reason does the text create an intrusion in the form of the commandment concerning the garments (v. 4), in between Aaron's sacrifice (v. 3) and the sacrifice of the nation (v. 5)?

2. Why does the verse repeat itself – "And Aaron shall sacrifice the ox for the sin offering which is his, and shall make atonement for himself and for his household" (vv. 6 and 11), and what sacrifice is referred to in verse 6? No slaughter is mentioned there, unlike verse 11, which does mention slaughtering the sacrifice.

3. A similar question may be asked concerning the goat for the sin offering. First we read, in verse 9, "And he shall prepare it as a sin offering" – seemingly, referring to the act of sacrificing it (as opposed to the "goat for Azazel," which "is presented, alive, before God"). However, we then read in verse 15, "*And he shall slaughter the goat for the sin offering of the nation.*" Has this sacrifice not already been slaughtered and offered? (Here, Ḥazal interpret the words "*he shall prepare it as a sin offering*" in verse 9 as merely setting aside the animal as a sacrifice "to God as a sin offering." This, however, is not the plain meaning of the verse.)

4. The location and meaning of verses 23–24: For what purpose will Aaron enter the Tent of Meeting? Is it really for the sole purpose

of removing his holy garments? (*Ḥazal* explain that this is meant to allude to the removal of the incense shovel, and that "the entire *parasha* follows the chronological order, except for this verse" [Yoma 71a].)

It is simple enough to explain this *parasha* and to resolve the difficulties if we keep in mind that there are different instances of Aaron entering the *Kodesh Kodashim* for the purposes of atonement. Thus, the *parasha* adopts a complex approach to address these various instances. This is the key to understanding the repetitions and the difficulties enumerated above.

As noted above, the commandment to Aaron is different from the commandment for future generations, insofar as Aaron is entitled to enter the *Kodesh Kodashim* "at all times" (not necessarily on Yom Kippur), and this fact establishes two or three reasons for entering in order to make atonement and to purify:

1. for the needs of Aaron himself (and for "his household" – his wife, his family);
2. for the needs of his brethren, the *kohanim* serving in the Sanctuary, and for the Sanctuary itself and its vessels;
3. for the needs of all of the congregation of Israel.

This, of course, implies the assumption that the entry "at all times" does not mean "whenever he so wishes" (in the words of the midrash quoted above), but rather, "whenever he needs to do so" – i.e., whenever there arises, during the wanderings in the wilderness, the need to make atonement for the Sanctuary, for the *kohanim*, or for the nation.

The complexity of the *parasha* and its repetitions, according to this approach, arise from the fact that it is not the same situation that is being discussed each time; rather, the repetition gives expression to the various instances in which a need would arise for Aaron to enter.

Below are schematic presentations of different possible views of the chapter and its structure. Let us first consider the simpler possibility – that the *parasha* is a dual one, built on two axes. One voice speaks about Aaron's atonement *"for himself and for his household"* (and includes his atonement for the Sanctuary); the other speaks about Aaron's atonement *"for himself and for the entire congregation of Israel."* These two voices are expressed alternately in the verses, so as to emphasize the mutual connection between them, despite their differences. However, each can also be read independently, like a single voice within an ensemble. From the point of view of halakha, the right-hand column is dependent upon the left, and only the left column can truly stand alone.

The structure of the *parasha*, based on the assumption that it addresses two different instances, may be presented thus:

INTRODUCTION: VERSE 1

Aaron's atonement for himself and for his household	Aaron's atonement for himself and for all of the congregation of Israel
Verses 2–4	Verse 5
Verse 6	Verses 7–10
Verses 11–14	Verses 15–22
Conclusion to both atonements: verses 23–25	
	Verse 26
	Verses 27–28
Commandment for future generations: verses 29–34	

This shows how it is possible to read about Aaron's entry in order to atone "for himself and for his household" as a single continuum within the structure, such that there is no break in his actions caused by the goats for the nation; they are simply in the right-hand column, pertaining to the atonement for the nation. Therefore, verse 4 does not represent any sort of interruption between the sacrifices, since it is part of Aaron's atonement for himself and for his household. It is also important to note that Aaron wears special garments only for the atonement of himself and his household. Accordingly, the repetitious language of verses 6 and 11 could be interpreted as a technique for getting back to the original topic. Since the goats in verses 7–10 interrupt the discussion, the Torah repeats in verse 11 what was already said in verse 6, to indicate a return to the original topic. Since the Torah now returns to Aaron's sacrifice, and to the first column, it could continue by going to detail the procedure for the slaughter, and then move on to discuss the incense that makes it possible to sprinkle some of the blood of the ox towards the covering (*kapporet*) in the *Kodesh Kodashim*. This tells us that the sacrifice in verse 6 and that in verse 11 are one and the same, and just as in the details of a burnt offering or a sin offering the Torah first speaks about the sacrifice and only afterwards mentions the slaughter of the animal (Lev. 1:3–5; 4:3–4, etc.), so likewise verse 15 goes back to the conclusion of verse 9, following the lengthy break for the atonement of Aaron and his household.

However, the unit also offers the possibility of a more complex reading, involving three, four, or perhaps even seven instances of entry into the *Kodesh*, for the purpose of atonement, which may arise "at any time." Based on this view, the unit reveals itself as comprising a number of columns, a multiplicity of voices harmonizing together, each representing a different instance of atonement. Some verses are common to a few columns – i.e., to a few voices in this choir. The opening and concluding verses are common to all of the instances.

1. The dual introduction: Verse 1 refers to the entire unit, while verse 2 introduces Aaron's atonement for himself and for his household.
2. Verse 11 repeats verse 6 following the interruption, but on the basis of the conclusion it is possible to interpret "his household" as referring to his close, personal family in verse 6, and to the wider fraternity of *kohanim* in verse 11. (It must be borne in mind that Aaron's family includes all of the *kohahim*.)
3. The language at the beginning of verse 16, the end of verse 17, and in verse 20, sounding in each case like a conclusion, is understood on the basis of the structure of the unit as conclusions for each of the various instances of atonement performed by Aaron in the *Kodesh Kodashim*.

Each of the possible approaches that we have presented here leads to the same conclusion – that the entire unit is written in order, except for verses 23–25, which serve as a conclusion to all the types of atonement.

Aaron's entry into the Tent of Meeting, in these verses, is indeed understood as his emerging from the *Kodesh Kodashim* into the Tent of

Meeting, and not according to the order (as Rav Breuer concludes; see p. 546 onwards). However, the reason for this is not simply a change of order, but rather that these verses may also be read after verse 14 – i.e., after the atonement for the *Kodesh* and for the *kohanim*, in which case the *Kohen Gadol* would unquestionably be coming from the *Kodesh Kodashim* into the Tent of Meeting. Only when he enters after atoning for *Am Yisrael* in general does his entry not follow the order.

This is what led Ḥazal to discuss at such length the place of this verse within the order of the Yom Kippur service, preceding it with the services that are performed outside, wearing the golden garments (of which no mention is made in the text), and this is the major point of debate in the talmudic discussions (Yoma 70) concerning the order of the service. Convincing proof of the complex structure described above (and particularly in the latter approach) is to be found in the conclusion of the unit (vv. 32–33). In setting down the commandment for future generations, these verses detail all the instances of atonement, for on Yom Kippur all are obligatory. In the commandment for future generations, the atonement for himself includes also the atonement for his family, while the atonement for the *kohanim* is mentioned separately. Here we also see that the wearing of the holy garments, in verse 4, is a special, emphasized element of the atonement for himself and his family, as demonstrated in the schematic presentations above; it is only by virtue of and following this atonement that all the other categories of atonement can follow.

The Death of Aaron's Sons, and the Priestly Service on Yom Kippur

Rav Yair Kahn

God spoke to Moses after the death of Aaron's two sons, when they came close before God and died. And God said to Moses: Speak to Aaron, your brother, that he should not come at any time to the *Kodesh* that is inside the *parokhet* (partition), before the covering which is upon the Ark, so that he will not die, for I shall appear upon the covering in a cloud. [But] thus shall Aaron come to the *Kodesh*, with a bull for a sin offering, and a ram as a burnt offering. (Lev. 16:1–3)

By means of this introduction, the Torah draws a substantive connection between the commandment concerning the priestly service on Yom Kippur and the death of Aaron's sons. This connection is certainly meant to convey a certain message, and in this essay we shall examine several of its aspects, with the aim of reaching a deeper understanding of the significance of Yom Kippur and its service.

I. "THAT HE SHOULD NOT COME AT
ANY TIME TO THE *KODESH*"

On the simplest level, the Torah mentions the death of Aaron's sons in its introduction to the Yom Kippur service because this entire command came about as a reaction to the death of Nadav and Avihu when they came close before God, to "offer before God a strange fire, which He had not commanded." Aaron, then, is warned not to enter the *Kodesh* at any time, except within a cloud of incense, as part of the Yom Kippur service. But if the whole section regarding the Yom Kippur service is indeed a response to, and a means of rectification for, the sin of Aaron's sons, we must ask why this *parasha* is not recorded immediately after their death (10:2). A number of different issues are discussed between the death of Nadav and Avihu and the Yom Kippur service: laws of *kashrut*, ritual impurity associated with childbirth, and the impurity arising from *tzara'at* (leprous infections) and from *zivut* (bodily discharges). Why are these matters inserted here, forming what appears to be a separation between the death of Aaron's sons and the *parasha* of *Aharei Mot*, which was transmitted in its wake?

Let us begin by examining the *parasha* that immediately follows the story of the death of Nadav and Avihu, the list of forbidden foods. In order to understand the nature of this *parasha*, we must contrast it with the parallel section in Deuteronomy (chapter 14). The latter consists of a virtually word-for-word repetition of the animals specified in *Parashat Shemini*. It includes the signs of kosher animals and kosher fish, and even repeats the detailed list of kosher birds. But then we find a discrepancy between the two *parashot*. Whereas the section in Deuteronomy ends at this point, after enumerating the various kosher and non-kosher animals, the parallel section in Leviticus continues with the laws concerning the impurity of carcasses and of people who partake of their meat, and the prohibition against eating *sheratzim* (creeping creatures):

> From these shall you be impure; anyone who touches their carcass shall be impure until the evening, and whoever carries any part of their carcass shall wash his clothes and be impure until the evening: [the carcass of] any beast with a parted hoof but which is not cloven-hoofed and does not chew the cud – these

are impure for you; anyone who touches them shall be impure.....
Do not make yourself abominable with any creeping thing that
creeps, nor shall you make yourself impure with them, such that
you will be defiled by them. (Lev. 11:24–43)

Thus, the comparison between these two *parashot* reveals that the
section devoted to forbidden foods in Leviticus is fundamentally a section dealing with the concept of impurity, and is therefore related to the
other *parashot* that address this subject. Hence, we are left with only one
subject wedged between the death of Aaron's sons and the Yom Kippur
service – the subject of ritual impurity – and we must therefore understand the relationship between the *parashot* discussing ritual impurity
and the death of Nadav and Avihu.

II. PERETZ UZA

A solution to our question is hinted at in the story of *"Peretz Uza"*
("the breach of Uza"), which the Sages selected as the *haftara* to *Parashat Shemini*. At first glance, the tragedy of Uza's death appears to have
resulted from a very specific, isolated error. If this were the whole story,
however, there would be no need for David to implement any proce-
dural changes when attempting to bring the Ark to Jerusalem a second
time, other than warning the bearers of the Ark not to touch it. But as
the narrative in Samuel reveals, there were indeed significant differences
between the two attempts. When the Ark was taken the first time from
the house of Avinadav, we are told:

> They bore it from the house of Avinadav, which was in Giv'a,
> with the Ark of God, and Aḥyo went before the Ark. And David
> and all of Israel *played* before God on all types of [instruments
> made of] cypress wood, and on lyres and on lutes and timbrels
> and on rattles and cymbals. (11 Sam. 6:4–5)

These verses describe an atmosphere of festivity and celebration,
bordering on frivolity, as expressed in the word *"mesaḥakim"* ("played").
This word is not usually used in relation to musical instruments, but
rather parallels the other meaning of the English word – lightheartedness.

The second attempt to bring the Ark to Jerusalem occurred three months later, when the Ark was taken from the house of Oved Edom. There it is written:

> David went and took up the Ark of God from the house of Oved Edom to the city of David with joy. And when those bearing the *Aron* of God took six steps, he offered an ox and a fatling. (ibid., 12–13)

Although the text again mentions joy, the atmosphere is unquestionably more cautious and serious. After every six paces, an ox and a fatling are offered, and David and all of Israel are not "playing before God," but rather bringing up the *Aron* "with shouting and with the sound of the shofar."

We may conclude, then, that David understood that God's punishment of Uza did not result from a one-time, isolated failure – the fact that Uza made the mistake of putting forth his hand towards the Ark. David understood that there had been a broader problem with the entire atmosphere in which they had tried to move the Ark. Carried away with the festive feeling of "playing before God," they had lost sight of the command to transport the Ark in a somber and cautious manner, as commanded by the Torah: "The service of the Sanctuary is upon them; they shall bear it on their shoulders" (Num. 7:9).

Indeed, in the parallel account in Chronicles, we discover several details omitted from the narrative in Samuel:

> David called Zadok and Evyatar, the *kohanim*, and the *levi'im*, and Uriel, Asaiah and Joel, Shemaiah and Eliel and Amminadav. And he said to them: You are the heads of the households of the *levi'im*; sanctify yourselves and your brethren that you may bring up the Ark of HaShem God of Israel to the place which I have prepared for it. For it was because you did not do this the first time that God burst forth among us, for we did not seek Him in proper fashion. (1 Chr. 15)

Before the tragedy of Uza, there was an eruption of spiritual emotion. After the return of the Ark from the Philistines, it became possible once again to come close to God and to take shelter in the Divine Presence. The people presumptuously imagined that man, created in the image of God, described as "You have made him [only] a little less than God" (Ps. 8:6), can access the Divine Presence via a short and straight path. Swept away by unbridled intoxication of religious feeling, they believed that a person who is full of love of God could cleave to the *Shekhina*, as it were. They did not appreciate that "HaShem your God is a consuming fire" (Deut. 4:24), and the distance between the Creator and mortal man is infinite. Moses himself, who spoke with God "face to face, as a man speaks to his fellow," was told, "No man can see Me and live" (Ex. 33:20).

This explains the teaching of Rabba:

> For what reason was David punished? Because he called words of Torah "songs" (*zemirot*), as it is written: "Your statutes are songs for me in my dwelling." The Holy One said to him: Words of Torah, concerning which it is written, "If you close your eyes from it, it is gone" – you call them "songs"? I shall therefore cause you to stumble regarding a matter which is known even to young children, as it is written, "To the children of Kehat He did not give [wagons], for the service of the Sanctuary [is upon them, they shall bear it on their shoulders]" – and he [David] brought it on a wagon. (Sota 35a)

The episode of Uza taught David that God is to be served with fear and awe; the joy experienced before Him must be accompanied by trembling. King David learned that lesson well: "And David feared God on that day" (11 Sam. 6:9).

III. NADAV AND AVIHU

The commentators present many different explanations concerning the sin of Aaron's sons, but most agree on a fundamental concept when it comes to the root of the sin – religious presumptuousness. According to the view of Rebbi, God issued a warning, "Also the *kohanim* who come to approach God shall sanctify themselves, lest God break forth among them" (Ex. 19:22), specifically to prevent the ascent of

Nadav and Avihu to Mount Sinai. The Sages (Leviticus Rabba 20:10) describe Nadav and Avihu as arrogantly ruling on halakha in front of their teacher. They were prominent members of the religious aristocracy, who at a young age were already ranked among the elders of Israel who merited to ascend and see, as it were, the God of Israel. According to the Targum Yerushalmi, it is with reference to them that the Torah says, "They beheld God, and they ate and drank" (Ex. 24:11); in other words, as Rashi explains, "They gazed at Him with a coarse heart, while eating and drinking." In the view of Nadav and Avihu, man has a natural right to participate in an encounter with God, and out of thirst for God, they charged into the *Mishkan* without any prior divine command.

Netziv beautifully interprets the "foreign fire" brought by Nadav and Avihu as a reference to the fire of love for God:

> They entered out of a fiery enthusiasm of love of God. The Torah says that although the love of God is precious in God's eyes, it should not be expressed in this way, which He had not commanded. Therefore, it is said concerning them, "I shall be sanctified among those close to Me" – because they yearned to enjoy the splendor of the Divine Presence.

In other words, they fulfilled what we are told in Psalms (Ps. 55:15): "We walked to God's house with excitement." But they were punished because they lost sight of the warning of Kohelet (Eccl. 4:7): "Guard your feet when you enter the house of God."

The laws governing the manner in which one is to approach the *Mikdash* serve as an expression of the infinite distance separating man and his Creator. Human worthiness is insufficient to behold God and serve Him. In order to serve in the *Mikdash*, a divine command is necessary to allow what is otherwise absurd. One who wishes to approach the *Mikdash* must fulfill a list of conditions in order to obtain the divine license required to enter God's house, which is granted only through compliance with the laws of the Torah. According to Ḥazal, Nadav and Avihu ignored these conditions (whether we adopt the view that they entered in a state of intoxication or the view that they entered without the priestly garments), and for this they were punished.

In light of the above, we can now reexamine the sequence of the *parashot* at the beginning of Leviticus. The *sefer* opens with God inviting Moses to enter the *Mishkan*. It continues with a discussion of the sacrifices, and of man's ability to offer them before God. Following the discussion of the sacrifices, the Torah describes the seven days of inauguration, culminating with the divine encounter of the eighth day. Thus, from the beginning up until the revelation of the *Shekhina* on the eighth day, the Torah addresses only one aspect of religious experience – the possibility of a man-God encounter. At the very moment of climax, when fire emerges from before God and consumes whatever is upon the altar before the eyes of the nation, there is a sudden disruption – Aaron's sons enter the *Kodesh* with no divine command, and they are immediately consumed. In the blink of an eye, everything changes. It becomes clear that there are laws and conditions describing the possibility of human service in the *Mikdash*. Israel learns that man's encounter with the divine cannot be taken for granted.

In this context, the *parashot* relating to the various types of ritual impurity emphasize the other aspect of religious experience and teach us about the infinite abyss that separates man and God. Impurity is an inseparable part of a human's reality. It accompanies his birth, as well as his death; it is bound up with his eating and his marital relations. Mortal man, mired in impurity, cannot come before God without the laws of purification that God Himself commands. Without fulfillment of the purifying divine command, mortals cannot approach the King: "You shall separate *Benei Yisrael* from their impurity, that they shall not die in their impurity, when they defile My dwelling that is among them" (Lev. 15:31).

IV. YOM KIPPUR

Here we come to the *parasha* describing the Yom Kippur service, in which the Torah warns Aaron not to come to the *Kodesh* at any time, except within a cloud of incense as part of the Yom Kippur service. Concerning the significance of the incense, attention should be paid to the fascinating insight of Seforno at the end of *Parashat Tetzaveh* (Ex. 30:1), where he explains why the command to build an incense altar is not mentioned together with the other vessels of the *Mishkan*:

This altar is not mentioned together with the rest of the vessels, in *Parashat Teruma*, for its intention was not to allow God to dwell among us, as was the idea behind the rest of the vessels, as God says – "And I shall dwell in their midst; in accordance with all that I show you, the form of the *Mishkan* and the form of all its vessels." Nor was its intention to bring down a vision of God's glory into the house – as was the intention of the sacrifices – as He says, "I shall meet there with *Benei Yisrael*," and as Moses testifies, when he says: "This is the matter that God commanded you to do, that the glory of God may appear before you." [Rather,] the point of this altar was to give honor to the blessed God after He came to accept with favor the service of His people in the sacrifices offered morning and evening, to welcome Him, as it were, with an offering of incense, in the spirit of "Give honor to God's name; bring an offering and come before Him."

According to our approach, the *Mishkan* and its vessels are the means of restoring the *Shekhina* within Israel. But the golden altar, upon which the incense is offered, symbolizes the abyss that separates the *Shekhina* from *Am Yisrael*. Only after the command to build the *Mishkan* and its vessels do we find the command concerning the golden altar, as though to declare, "God's honor is to hide a matter" (Prov. 25:2). It is only by means of the screen of smoke created by the burning incense that God appears above the covering of the Ark.

Thus, there are two aspects to religious experience. On the one hand, there is the thirsting of the soul for the living God. On the other hand, there is the awareness that "no man shall see Me and live." Only after we have absorbed the message of the *parashot* concerning impurity, only after we have internalized the mistake of Aaron's sons, only once we have understood the two aspects of religious experience, is it possible to return to the instructions concerning the entry into the *Kodesh*, behind the *parokhet*: "By this shall Aaron come to the *Kodesh*." Once it has become clear that one cannot come into the *Kodesh* whenever one chooses, the Torah can then inform us that God will nevertheless appear above the covering – but only by means of the cloud of incense.

V. "FOR ON THIS DAY GOD WILL APPEAR BEFORE YOU"

But it seems that there is yet another connection between the death of Aaron's sons and the Yom Kippur service. Yom Kippur is the day when God delivered to Moses the second set of tablets, when *Benei Yisrael* achieved atonement for the sin of the Golden Calf. But this, it appears, was not the end of the process of atonement for the sin. Immediately after Yom Kippur, *Benei Yisrael* are commanded to construct the *Mishkan*. The Torah (Ex. 35:20–29) describes the enthusiasm that greeted the campaign for donations towards the building project – to the extent that they brought even more materials than were needed (36:5–7). Apparently, this enthusiasm arose not only from the thirst for the Divine Presence, but also from feelings of guilt for having fashioned the Golden Calf. *Benei Yisrael* had previously removed their gold earrings in order to fashion the calf; in contributing towards the *Mishkan* they were given an opportunity to offer their jewelry for the sake of the *Mishkan* and its vessels. Therefore, the very engagement in the *Mishkan* was part of the process of the nation's repentance for the sin of the Golden Calf, as *Ḥazal* explain:

> When they made the calf, God told Moses: "Now leave Me alone." He said to Him: Test them, [to see] whether they will make the *Mishkan*. What is written with regard to that failure? "Remove the gold rings." And what did they bring? Rings. And when they made the *Mishkan*, they made the same contribution. And that which is written, "All who were generous of spirit brought nose-rings and earrings, rings and bracelets" – they sinned by means of earrings, and by earrings He was appeased. The divine spirit moved Hosea to declare, "Instead of them being told, You are not My nation, they will be told, You are the children of the living God." Moses said to God, You wrote: "If a man steals an ox or a sheep, and he slaughters it or sells it, he shall pay five oxen for that ox." Behold, they have brought to God nose-rings and earrings, rings and bracelets. (Exodus Rabba 48:5)

The eighth day of the *Mishkan*'s inauguration – the conclusion of the consecration process – is therefore also a day of atonement for the sin of the Golden Calf. *Am Yisrael* had toiled for months to build the *Mishkan*, with the aim of once again meriting a divine revelation reminiscent of that at Sinai. And indeed, following seven days of inauguration, on the eighth day, God promises, "On this day God will appear to you" (Lev. 9:4). With great anticipation, *Benei Yisrael* approach and stand around the *Mishkan*, awaiting word of their expiation. The tension mounts continuously, until the fire emerges from before God: "And God's glory appeared to all the nation, and a fire emerged from before God and consumed [that which was] upon the altar – the burnt offering and the fats" (Lev. 9:23–24).

The eighth day therefore marks the end of a lengthy process that began with Moses' bringing the second Tablets of Testimony that he received at Sinai, and concludes with the *Shekhina's* descent onto the *Mishkan* – a process reflecting a profound religious drama within the collective spirit of *Benei Yisrael*. But this drama plays itself out with special intensity within the recesses of one person's soul – Aaron. Aaron played a central role in the sin of the Golden Calf, and there can be no doubt that a powerful sense of guilt lurked within him. Here, Aaron is called upon to sanctify himself and serve during the days of inauguration, to atone for the sin of the calf. Aaron, who took part in the transgression, who "exposed them, so that they were an object of derision to those who oppose them" (Ex. 32:25), is the one chosen to serve as *Kohen Gadol*, in order that God's glory can once again appear before *Am Yisrael*.

Ḥazal sense Aaron's psychological tension, and explain the verse, "Moses said to Aaron: Approach the altar, and offer your sin offering and your burnt offering" (Lev. 9:7), as an expression of a lack of religious confidence, as a result of his part in the creation of the Golden Calf:

> To what may this be compared? To a mortal king who got married. His wife was shy in his presence, so her sister came to her and said: For what reason did you agree to this? In order to serve the king! Be confident, and come to serve the king! Thus Moses told Aaron: Aaron, my brother, for what reason were you selected to be the *Kohen Gadol*? Only so that you may serve before the Holy One, blessed be He. Be confident and come to perform your service! (Sifra, *Parashat Shemini, Mekhilta DeMiluim*, 1)

Moreover, the Sages explain:

> Some say that Aaron perceived the altar as having the form of an ox, and he was afraid of it. Moses said to him, My brother, that of which you are fearful – be confident and approach it! For this reason it is written, "Approach the altar."

However, we find that even after Aaron finishes offering all the sacrifices and blesses the nation, the *Shekhina* does not immediately descend to the nation. The *Shekhina* appears only when Moses joins him:

> Aaron lifted his hands to the nation and blessed them. And he descended from offering the sin offering and the burnt offering and the peace offerings, and Moses and Aaron came to the *Ohel Mo'ed*, and they came out and blessed the nation, and God's glory appeared to all the nation. (Lev. 9:22–23)

Ḥazal point out that Aaron felt that the *Shekhina* was not appearing because of his role in the sin of the Golden Calf:

> "And Moses and Aaron came to the *Ohel Mo'ed*" – When Aaron saw that all the sacrifices had already been offered, and all the actions had already been performed, but the *Shekhina* was not descending to Israel, Aaron stood and was troubled. He said, I know that God is angry with me; it is because of me that the *Shekhina* has not come down to Israel. This is what my brother Moses did to me – I went forth and I was embarrassed, for the *Shekhina* did not descend to Israel! Moses immediately entered with him, and they asked for divine mercy, and the *Shekhina* descended to Israel. Therefore it is written, "Moses and Aaron came to the *Ohel Mo'ed*." (Sifra, *Shemini, Mekhilta DeMiluim*, 1)

Ultimately, after Moses joined Aaron, the *Shekhina* descended upon Israel. But immediately thereafter, Nadav and Avihu were consumed by fire. According to one view in the Midrash, Aaron's sons died as punishment for their father's role in the debacle of the Golden Calf:

At first, a decree was pronounced against him, as it is written, "God was exceedingly angry at Aaron, [and decided] to destroy him." R. Yehoshua of Sakhnin said in the name of R. Levi: The term "destruction" (*hashmada*) is never used except to mean the annihilation of one's children, as it is written, "I shall destroy his fruit above and his roots below." Because Moses prayed for him, he was spared from half the decree – two died and two remained. This is as it is written, "Take Aaron and his sons with him." (Leviticus Rabba 10:5)

Even if we do not adopt this midrash, we cannot ignore the possibility that Aaron blamed himself for the death of his sons. Indeed, the phrase, "Aaron was silent" (10:3), is interpreted not only as an expression of mourning, but also as a justification and acceptance of God's judgment and punishment, as part of Aaron's remorse for the sin of the Golden Calf. Admittedly, the Torah does not elaborate at any length on Aaron's penitence, or how he overcame his part in the Golden Calf, in order to be worthy once again of serving God as the *Kohen Gadol*. But in these two words – "*vayidom Aharon*" – the Torah offers us a glimpse into the drama that was playing out in his soul. These two words testify, like two reliable witnesses, to one of the most inspirational examples of *teshuva*.

Thus, on the eighth day, Aaron's struggle with his sin reached new heights and new depths. However, we find that it was only *after* the eighth day that Aaron was permitted to enter the *Kodesh HaKodashim*. The sacrifices of the eighth day, despite their similarity to the sacrifices of Yom Kippur, were offered outside, in the *Mishkan*'s courtyard. Only after the death of his two sons is Aaron told, "With this shall Aaron come to the *Kodesh*, with an ox as a sin offering."

In order to enter the *Kodesh HaKodashim*, Aaron must first offer the sacrifices that atone for the sin of the Golden Calf. The order of the Yom Kippur service includes two central sacrifices, whose blood is sprinkled inside the *heikhal*, an ox brought as the *Kohen Gadol*'s sin offering, and the goat that serves as the nation's sin offering. It would seem that at their root, these sacrifices are meant to atone for the sin of the Golden Calf. The nation's sin offering is entirely burnt; the only other sacrificial goat that is burnt in its entirety is the sin offering brought when the nation transgresses with regard to idolatry (Num. 15:22–26). In contrast to the goat, which comes as a public sin offering, the *Kohen Gadol's* ox is the sin offering of an individual. And the only other individual sacrifice that is entirely burnt is the sin offering brought by the *Kohen Gadol* when he commits an inadvertent violation (Lev. 4:3–12). Regarding the process of sacrificing and sprinkling the blood, too, we find a great deal of similarity between the sin offerings of Yom Kippur, on the one hand, and the nation's sin offering for idolatry and the ox brought by the *Kohen Gadol*, on the other. It would seem, therefore, that these sacrifices are offered in order to atone for the sin of worshiping the Golden Calf. In order to enter the *Kodesh HaKodashim* on behalf of the nation of Israel, Aaron must bring atonement for his own part in the calf, as well as for the sin of the nation. For this reason, he is commanded to offer a goat as a sin offering for the nation's inadvertent violation of idolatry, and, to atone for his own part in the sin, he brings an ox as the *Kohen Gadol's* sin offering.

VI. "IT SHALL BE FOR YOU AN ETERNAL STATUTE, IN THE SEVENTH MONTH, ON THE TENTH OF THE MONTH"

Yom Kipppur, then, is a day of atonement for the sin of the Golden Calf – not only because the second set of tablets were given on this day, but also because Yom Kippur was chosen as the day on which Aaron – or whoever would succeed him as *Kohen Gadol* – must offer an ox and goat as a sin offering, and sprinkle their blood in the *heikhal*, like the *Kohen Gadol's* sin offering, and the goat offered to atone for the sin of idolatry. It is with these that the *Kohen Gadol* approaches the *Kodesh HaKodashim*.

Concerning the connection between the *Kohen Gadol's* entry on Yom Kippur and the sin of the calf, we learn in Tractate Rosh HaShana: "For what reason does the *Kohen Gadol* not enter the *Kodesh HaKodashim* in his golden garments, to perform the service? Because a prosecutor cannot become an advocate" (26a). This gemara teaches that Aaron's role in the sin of the Golden Calf forms the background to the *Kohen Gadol's* entry into the *Kodesh HaKodashim*. The *Kohen Gadol* enters the holiest place wearing only the simple priestly garments made of linen, showing that he is completely clean of this sin.

In light of the above, Yom Kippur is found at both ends of the process of atonement for the sin of the Golden Calf, with the eighth day of the inauguration placed in between. On the one hand, Yom Kippur is the day when the second tablets were given to Israel. On this day, in the first year following the Exodus from Egypt, Israel were granted the opportunity to atone for the Golden Calf by means of building the *Mishkan*. On the eighth day, at the conclusion of this process of construction and preparation, the *Shekhina* once again descended to the nation. But from Aaron's point of view, the eighth day was a day for grappling with his part in the sin. This grappling reached its climax with the death of his two sons, and his silent reaction – "Aaron was silent." This reaction – an expression of the depth of his repentance, and his acceptance of divine justice – led to his ability to atone for the sin of the calf, for himself and for his household and for all of the congregation of Israel, and to the license to enter the *Kodesh HaKodashim*. This entry takes place every year on Yom Kippur, when Israel seek atonement for all their sins before God.

VII. "THE PLACE WHERE PENITENTS STAND"

It thus emerges that Nadav and Avihu, who were not part of the sin of the Golden Calf, died when they tried to approach God. Aaron's sons believed that they deserved to behold God. In their arrogance, they entered the *Kodesh* without consulting with their teacher. They failed to understand that a mortal man – even the most righteous and the most holy – does not have the right to demand to behold God. The license to enter the holiest of places is awarded specifically to Aaron, who did play a role in the sin of the Golden Calf, and who lived with a sense of failure and missed opportunity. His sin gave him no rest. He felt, in a most profound way, that he had no right to behold God's countenance. He knew that his calling to enter the holiest place, the most intimate meeting with God, was granted not by right, but rather by God's mercy and compassion, after he himself had sinned and then repented.

Ḥazal teach: "The place where penitents stand – even the completely righteous cannot stand there" (Berakhot 34b). The completely righteous, who have never tasted sin, do not recognize the weaknesses and limitations of human reality; therefore, they cannot occupy that special place before God that is reserved for the penitent. The latter has experienced, firsthand, the impurity that surrounds human reality; he knows that his calling to stand before God comes only as a result of divine mercy and compassion.

The *Kodesh HaKodashim* is open not to Nadav and Avihu, but rather to Aaron (or the *Kohen Gadol* who will succeed him), dressed only in the simple, linen priestly garments so as not to recall the Golden Calf. Even today, in the absence of our Temple, we do not come before God by virtue of our righteousness, but rather by virtue of His immense compassion. With a profound sense of regret we declare, "Like the destitute and downtrodden we knock on Your door." We give stark expression to the limitations of human existence:

> After all, the valiant ones are all like nothing before You,
> and people of fame – as though they had never existed,
> and the wise – as without knowledge,
> and the discerning – as without intelligence.
> For most of their actions are worthless,
> and the days of their lives are vanity before You,
> and man has no advantage over the animals, for all is vanity.

In complete submission we pray and entreat the Holy One Himself, as it were, to cleanse us, as the *mikveh* purifies the impure, and that the promise be fulfilled: "For on that day He shall give you atonement, to cleanse you of all your sins; you shall be purified *before God*" (Lev. 16:30).

The White Garments of Yom Kippur

Rav Yonatan Grossman

With the conclusion of the unit dealing with ritual impurity (ch. 11–15), Leviticus now proceeds to the next topic, the purity of the *Mishkan*. After having discussed the many forms of ritual impurity that endanger the *Shekhina*'s residence within the Israelite camp, the Torah now addresses the solution to this problem – the process of the *Mishkan*'s purification, conducted once annually, on Yom Kippur.

I would like to try to identify the function of the special "*bigdei lavan*," the white, linen garments donned by the *Kohen Gadol* on this special day, referred to by the verse as "*bigdei habad*" – "linen clothing." Why must the *kohen* change out of his standard clothing? Does this change mark a heightened spiritual quality or a lower status?

Ramban, quoting Leviticus Rabba, appears to have paved the way for many others, by viewing the donning of these garments as indicative of an additional quality assumed by the *Kohen Gadol* during the Yom Kippur service:

> Like the service in the upper spheres – so is the service in the lower spheres. Just as in the service of the upper spheres, one individual wears white [see Ezekiel 9:3, Daniel 10:5], the same

occurs in the service in the lower spheres – "He shall be dressed in a sacral linen tunic."

According to Ramban, these vestments are to afford the *Kohen Gadol* the appearance of an angel. On this day, when the *kohen* purifies the *Mishkan* and the entirety of *Benei Yisrael* becomes cleansed from its wrongdoing, the *Kohen Gadol* assumes this unique quality.

If however this is the case, then we would expect to find a similar basis for other instances of the *kohen's* wearing *bigdei habad*. Yet, a review of the other contexts in which the *kohen* wears these garments demonstrates just the opposite, a lowering of the *kohen's* stature.

The Torah makes explicit mention of *bigdei habad* in two other instances. The first concerns the *Terumat HaDeshen*, the removal of the ashes from the altar:

> The *kohen* shall dress in *linen apparel*, and he shall wear *linen trousers on his skin*, and he shall take up the ashes to which the fire has reduced the burnt offering on the altar and place them beside the altar. (Lev. 6:3)

A clear parallel exists between this verse and that describing the *kohen's* garb on Yom Kippur: "He shall be dressed in a *sacral linen tunic, and linen trousers shall be on his skin.*" This parallel can only mean that the *kohen's* changing from his traditional vestments on these two occasions serves the same function in both. Why does the *kohen* wear special clothing for removing the ashes from the altar? *Ḥazal* (Sifra 82:1; Yoma 23b) understood that the verse in fact does not require that the *kohen* change his clothing, but rather teaches that his garments must fit his size. However, the clear textual association drawn to the Yom Kippur service indicates that the *kohen* did, in fact, perform this particular service in special linen garments.

I suggest that the verses describe two stages of the removal of the ashes from the altar to outside the camp. In the first stage, the *kohen* lifts the ashes from altar. As this ritual involves direct contact with the altar, the *kohen* must wear the *bigdei habad*. After this stage concludes with the *kohen's* placing the ashes "next to the altar," the verse then proceeds to the second stage, the removal of ashes from the altar's side to an area outside the camp. The *kohen* no longer works at the altar itself, and may therefore wear other clothing. According to Ramban, he may even don ordinary, laymen's clothing; he need not wear priestly vestments at all. (By contrast, Rashi, following Ḥazal in Yoma 23b, maintains that the *kohen* wears garments of lower quality but that are nevertheless special priestly vestments.) Once the *kohen* takes the ashes outside the camp, the second and last stage of the ashes' trip reaches its conclusion. According to the simple reading of the text, this procedure must be performed each morning.

In summary, the ashes' removal is solely the technical necessity of removing the remaining ashes from atop the altar. During the first stage of this process the *kohen* comes in direct contact with the altar, and may therefore not wear ordinary clothing during the execution of this task. However, since this activity is not inherently part of the sacred *avoda* (service), but rather merely the removal of ashes, the *kohen* does not wear the standard priestly garments. Instead, he dons the *bigdei habad*. It thus emerges from this commandment that these linen garments reflect not the *kohen*'s attainment of an additional level, but on the contrary, the lower status of the activity at hand – preparing the altar for future rituals.

The second context in which we encounter a command concerning *bigdei bad* does not involve a special or specific event; rather, one of the priestly garments – the *kohanim*'s trousers. The Torah states:

> You shall make for them *linen trousers* to cover their nakedness; they shall extend from the hips to the thighs. They shall be worn by Aaron and his sons when they enter the Tent of Meeting or when they approach the altar to officiate in the sanctuary, so that they do not incur punishment and die. It shall be a law for all time for him and for his offspring to come. (Ex. 28:42)

How should we understand the significance of the linen in the *kohanim*'s trousers? In order to arrive at a clearer understanding of this issue, we must address a broader topic – the general role of the trousers and their relationship to the other priestly vestments. Chapter 28 in Exodus, which describes the various garments, opens with a general command listing the vestments to be prepared for the *kohanim*:

> These are the vestments they are to make: a breastpiece, an *ephod*, a robe, a checkered tunic, a headdress, and a sash. They shall make those sacral vestments for your brother Aaron and his sons, for priestly service to Me. (Ex. 28:4)

The Torah then proceeds one-by-one down this list, outlining the details of the fashioning of each garment. Surprisingly, however, this brief introductory survey of the garments omits two of them: the head-plate (*tzitz*) and the trousers! The issue of the head-plate does not concern us right now, and we should note that the Torah does devote three verses to describing its fashioning later in this chapter (36–38). The trousers, by contrast, are absent not only from the introductory verse, but even from the detailed list presented thereafter.

This presentation concludes in verse 41: "Put these on your brother Aaron and on his sons, as well; anoint them, ordain them, and consecrate them to serve Me as *kohanim*." This concluding verse strongly resembles the introduction – "They shall make those sacral vestments for your brother Aaron and his sons, for priestly service to Me," thus forming a clear, self-contained, literary framework of the priestly garments. Only after the Torah completes this presentation does it mention the trousers: "You shall make for them linen trousers."

Why did the Torah delay this commandment until after the conclusion of this section dealing with the *kohanim*'s garments? Why do the trousers appear as a mere afterthought of sorts? The answer lies in the verse's characterization of this garment's particular role. Whereas the other vestments serve to reflect "glory and adornment" (Ex. 28:2), as well as to "sanctify [Aaron] to serve Me as *kohen*" (28:3), the trousers' role is "to cover their nakedness…. They shall be worn by Aaron and his sons when they enter the Tent of Meeting or when they approach the altar to officiate in the sanctuary, so that they do not incur punishment and die" (28:43). The trousers clearly do not reflect glory and adornment, nor do they involve the sanctification or consecration of the *kohen* as an attendant of the Almighty. They merely fill the technical role of "covering their nakedness."

Here, too, it would seem, the verse refers to the trousers as "*bigdei bad*" specifically on account of their lesser importance compared with the other vestments.

Returning to the Yom Kippur service, I believe that we must view the *bigdei habad* in a similar vein. The *kohen* does not acquire an elevated stature through these garments; to the contrary, he detaches himself entirely from his priestly vestments and wears clothing of a stature lower than that of his regular priestly garments. Similarly, at the outset of the *parasha*, the Torah lists four garments worn by the *Kohen Gadol* during the Yom Kippur service, whereas a *Kohen Gadol* generally wears eight special vestments. The Sages have pointed out that from here we see that the *Kohen Gadol* officiates on Yom Kippur as a *kohen hedyot*, a regular *kohen*, who wears only four priestly garments (see Rashi, 16:4).

If at first glance a lowering of the *Kohen Gadol*'s stature on Yom Kippur seems surprising, at second glance it becomes understandable and even compelling. Rav Yoel Bin-Nun has elaborated on the relationship between Yom Kippur and the initial consecration of the *Mishkan*, the *miluim*. This relationship is manifest in four ways:

1. The Torah presents the Yom Kippur service after its description of the eighth and final day of the *miluim* and emphasizes this association in the opening verse of our *parasha*: "God spoke to Moses after the death of Aaron's two sons [which occurred on the final day of the *miluim*]" (16:1).

2. Both Yom Kippur and the eighth day of the *miluim* feature two distinct systems of offerings: those of the *kohanim* and those of *Am Yisrael*.

3. A strong textual parallel between the two contexts also underscores this association. On the eighth day of the consecration, Moses tells Aaron, "Approach the altar and sacrifice your sin offering and your burnt offering, *and atone for you and for the nation*; and sacrifice the people's offering and atone for them, as God had commanded" (Lev. 9:7). Compare this verse with the following expressions found in the Torah's description of the Yom

Kippur service: "Aaron shall sacrifice the bull of his sin offering *and atone for himself and for his household…*. He shall atone for himself and for his household *and the entire congregation of Israel*" (Lev. 16:6, 11, 17).

4. On both the eighth day of the *miluim* and Yom Kippur, the *Shekhina* descends. In the former case, the entire nation earned this revelation, which occurred on the outer altar, whereas on Yom Kippur the *Shekhina* is revealed only to the *Kohen Gadol*, in the innermost sanctuary.

It would seem that the basic relationship drawn by the Torah between these two events points to one's functioning as the continuation of the other. On Yom Kippur, the *kohen* purifies the *Mishkan* and altar from the impurities generated throughout the year, effectively restoring the *Mishkan* to its earliest beginnings, before the surfacing of any impurity. In effect, the *Mishkan* on Yom Kippur returns to the status it had on the eighth day of its initial consecration, when the *Shekhina* first entered its "home," so to speak. We could formulate this idea in allegorical terms: Yom Kippur marks the renewed "birthday" of the *Mishkan*, the point at which it returns to its original state, thus allowing the *Shekhina* to dwell in a home clean of spiritual impurities. On this day, the *Mishkan* is thoroughly cleansed from the "defects" it accumulated over the course of the year as a result of *Benei Yisrael's* impurity.

This comparison, however, involves more than just the cleansing of the *Mishkan*. Just as the *Mishkan's* initial consecration involved an additional stage beyond the anointing of the *Mishkan's* vessels with oil (preparing them for the *Shekhina*), so must we anticipate a parallel feature on Yom Kippur. This addition is the *kohanim's* donning of their priestly garments. The Torah emphasizes this component of the original consecration of the *Mishkan*:

Moses brought Aaron and his sons forward and washed them with water. He put the tunic on him, girded him with the sash, clothed him with the robe, and put the *ephod* on him, girding him with the decorated band with which he tied it to him. He put the breastpiece on him, and put into the breastpiece the

Urim VeTummim. And he set the headdress on his head; and on the headdress, in front, he put the gold frontlet, the holy diadem – as God had commanded Moses. (Lev. 8:6–9)

The importance of this ceremony, the dressing of the *kohanim*, cannot be overlooked. As an integral part of the *Mishkan*, they, like the vessels therein, required formal consecration through the sprinkling of blood and oil (as described there in chapter 8) as well as through dressing them in their special vestments. As we have seen, these garments serve, among other purposes, as "glory and adornment"; they prepare the *kohanim* for their service in the *Mishkan*. As such, the donning of the special clothing earns its place as part of the *miluim*, the general process of preparation for the *Shekhina's* descent onto the *Mishkan*.

What about Yom Kippur? Are the *kohanim* dressed anew in the priestly garments then, too? Do they, too, undergo renewed purification on this "birthday" of the *Mishkan*? Undoubtedly, the Torah strongly emphasizes the *kohanim's* atonement as an individual community on Yom Kippur, not merely as part of *Am Yisrael*; the special sacrifices of the *Kohen Gadol* serve this very purpose. Beyond that, however, even the *kohanim's* donning of their priestly garments undergoes a renewal on this day, just as during the original consecration.

It seems that the white garments of the *Kohen Gadol*, the *bigdei habad*, serve precisely this function. As we have seen, when serving with these garments, the *kohen* descends from his normal stature, reflected by his usual clothing. Hence, the verse must emphasize that "they are sacred garments" (16:4) because this is not at all self-evident. These garments allow the *Kohen Gadol* to serve in the *Mishkan* despite their falling short of the stature of his usual vestments. However, these garments serve but one purpose – to define the *kohen* as returning to his "pre-garment" state. He wears these *bigdei habad* only so that he can change into his normal priestly garments later that day, assuming his renewed appointment for service in the *Mishkan*.

As we saw earlier regarding the *Terumat HaDeshen*, the *kohen* wears the *bigdei habad* in instances where he must officiate in the *Mishkan* without his usual, unique stature as a *kohen*. Whereas when dusting off the altar this results from a lower-level activity, on Yom Kippur this involves the return of the *kohen* – together with the *Mishkan* – to its prior state, before his original consecration.

If so, then we must identify the precise point during the Yom Kippur service at which the *kohen* changes back into his year-round garments. It seems to me that the Torah refers to this clothing change immediately following the sending of the scapegoat (*se'ir la'azazel*):

> Aaron shall go into the Tent of Meeting, take off the linen vestments that he put on when he entered the Shrine, and leave them there. He shall bathe his body in water in the holy precinct and put on his vestments. (16:23)

At this point, when the entire service has been completed, the *kohen* receives permission to once again wear "his vestments," his usual priestly garments. (This follows the majority view held by Ḥazal and most commentators; Ibn Ezra disagrees.) The formulation of this verse seems to stress the contrast between the two changes of clothing: "[He shall] take off the linen vestments *that he put on when he entered the Shrine*." Why must the Torah reiterate the *kohen*'s having worn these linen garments when performing the service in the Sanctuary? We would have expected the verse to state more simply that he changes his clothing, and we would have naturally associated this reference with the clothing he currently wears, the same clothing worn during the service – the *bigdei habad*. Can someone change out of garments other than those he currently wears?

Apparently, the verse wishes to highlight the contrast between the two types of clothing of which it speaks: "the linen vestments that he put on when he entered the Shrine" on the one hand, and "*his* vestments" on the other. The first refers to garments with no inherent connection to the person wearing them; they are worn only for a specific purpose and function. These garments are not those of the *Kohen Gadol*, but rather those worn when he enters the Sanctuary for the Yom Kippur service. The second change of clothing, by contrast, refers to "*his* vestments," the garments of the *Kohen Gadol*, his special clothing worn regularly as he attends to his responsibilities in the *Mishkan*.

It is worth noting that the term "*begadav*," "his vestments," appears in two additional instances in the Yom Kippur section in our *parasha*, both in reference to one's normal clothing. (See verse 26 regarding the clothing of the one commissioned to send away the goat, and verse 28 in reference to the one who burns the sin offerings.)

The *kohen* must immerse himself prior to receiving and wearing his priestly vestments. Together with the *Mishkan* that has now been purified and the entire nation whose sins have now been forgiven, the *kohen* is granted permission to conduct the sacred service of his Creator for an additional year.

Blood Prohibitions in Sefer Vayikra

Rav Tamir Granot

I. THE REPETITION OF THE PROHIBITION

The prohibition against eating blood is mentioned several times in Leviticus. At the end of the introduction to peace offerings, the Torah summarizes: "It shall be an eternal statute for your generations throughout your dwelling places, that you shall not eat any fat nor any blood" (3:17). The section on peace offerings in *Parashat Tzav* concludes similarly: "The fat of an animal that died of itself...you shall not eat of it.... Nor shall you eat any blood throughout your dwelling places, of either bird or beast. Anyone who eats any blood – that soul shall be cut off from its people" (7:24–27). Finally, in our *parasha*, discussing the law of animals that are slaughtered outside the *Mishkan* (and which must be brought to the *Mishkan* for the *kohen* to sprinkle their blood and offer their fat), the Torah continues:

> Any person from the house of Israel, or of the strangers that reside in their midst, who eats any blood – I shall set My countenance against the person who eats the blood, and I shall cut the person off from amongst his people. For the life of the flesh is in the blood, and I have given it to you upon the altar, to make atonement for your souls, for it is the blood that makes

atonement for the soul. Therefore I have said to *Benei Yisrael*: No one of you shall eat blood, nor shall the stranger who dwells in your midst eat blood. And any person from *Benei Yisrael* or of the strangers who dwell in their midst who hunts venison of an animal or bird that may be eaten – he shall pour out its blood and cover it with dust. For the life of all flesh is in its blood, and I said to *Benei Yisrael*: You shall not eat the blood of any flesh, for the life of all flesh is its blood; anyone who eats it shall be cut off. (17:10–14)

These multiple repetitions give rise to some difficulties. First, why does the prohibition need to be repeated three times in three different places? Furthermore, close examination reveals that in chapter 17, the prohibition of blood is actually mentioned twice, first in the context of the definition of *karet* as the punishment for eating blood, and then again as part of the reason for the commandment of covering the blood.

Additionally, in chapter 3 and chapter 7, the prohibition of eating blood is mentioned along with the prohibition of eating forbidden fat – signifying some connection between them. But there is no mention of this connection in chapter 17, where the prohibition of blood is mentioned alone.

Finally, the prohibition of blood is always mentioned in connection with the offering of sacrifices. In fact, there is a verse that makes explicit mention of the connection: "I have given it to you upon the altar to make atonement for your souls" (17:11). Why is this mentioned specifically in connection with the peace offering? Chapter 17 begins with the prohibition against slaughtering animals purely for the sake of satiating one's appetite; the animal must be brought as a sacrifice. This necessarily implies a peace offering – since the peace offering is the only type of sacrifice that is eaten by the person who brings it.

To all of the above we must add the fourth and fifth appearances of this command, in Deuteronomy, where this prohibition appears twice in the same chapter:

You may slaughter and eat meat to your heart's desire, according to the blessing of HaShem your God which He grants you, throughout your gates; the pure and the impure may eat of it, as they do of the deer and the gazelle. Only the blood you shall not eat; you shall pour it upon the earth like water.... When HaShem your God expands your borders, as He has spoken to you, and you say: I shall eat meat, for your soul will desire to eat meat.... Only be sure not to eat of the blood, for the blood is the life, and you may not eat the life together with the flesh. You shall not eat it; you shall pour it upon the earth like water. You shall not eat it, in order that it may be well with you and with your children after you forever. (Deut. 12:15–28)

The repetition is not unusual; after all, many commandments are reiterated in Deuteronomy. But the presentation here appears exaggerated in two respects. First, the prohibition is repeated twice within the same *parasha*, in two different contexts. Second, the same command is repeated and emphasized over and over, with words of persuasion and encouragement – "Only be strong," followed by a reason, followed by a promise, "In order that it be well with you."

The importance of the prohibition against eating blood in the Torah's eyes is clear. We need to understand why it is of such crucial importance.

II. ESTABLISHING THE PRIMARY COMMAND

When a command or story appears more than once, it may be that one instance is primary while the others are secondary. In some cases the various sources parallel one another and are of equal status, but this does not seem to be the case in this instance. Let us undertake a systematic review of each instance where the prohibition appears and their special style:

Location of the Prohibition	Nature of the Prohibition
Leviticus 3 – peace offering, directed to *Benei Yisrael*.	A plain, brief command concerning forbidden fats and blood in general.
Leviticus 7 – peace offering, directed to the *kohanim*.	A detailed command concerning forbidden fats and blood, and the punishment "that soul shall be cut off."

Location of the Prohibition	Nature of the Prohibition
Leviticus 17 – animals that are slaughtered outside the *Mishkan*.	Only the punishment of *karet* is mentioned, with no command, and the formulation is, "Any person…and also the stranger," with the punishment formulated as "I shall set My face." The prohibition is given in the past tense, with dual reasons given: "For the life of the flesh is in the blood," and "I have given it to you upon the altar."
Deuteronomy 12 (a) – Obligation of sacrificing burnt offerings only in the place that God will choose, but license to slaughter for consumption in any place.	The prohibition is laconic in style and formulated as a limitation. The meat is permissible; only the blood is forbidden. The command to pour it on the earth appears identical to the prohibition against eating it.
Deuteronomy 12 (b) – If the place is far away, meat may be eaten anywhere, but sanctified meat must be brought to the altar.	There is a lengthy presentation of the prohibition which here, too, appears as a limitation on the license to eat: meat – yes; blood – no. An explanation is given: "for the blood is the life," with two repetitions and reinforcement of the prohibition, along with a promise of good reward.

We shall focus on Leviticus alone – even though some of our conclusions will be relevant to Deuteronomy as well.

Seemingly, the place where the prohibition is set out in detail and in an orderly fashion is the principal source; this would lead us to conclude that chapter 7 represents the primary source of this prohibition. It includes all the elements of a full command: (1) the commandment; (2) its conditions; (3) the punishment for transgressing it.

The fact that this is not the first mention of the prohibition should not mislead us. It must be remembered that, chronologically speaking, chapter 7 preceded chapter 3, for it was given at Sinai as part of the command concerning the inauguration of the *Mishkan*. As we read at its conclusion: "which God commanded Moses at Mount Sinai on the day He commanded *Benei Yisrael* to offer their sacrifices to God in the wilderness of Sinai" (Lev. 7:38), before the construction of the *Mishkan*.

Support for this view would seem to be found in chapter 17. According to its introduction, this chapter is addressed to both the *kohanim* and *Benei Yisrael*. "Speak to Aaron and to his sons, and to all of *Benei Yisrael*." Here the prohibition of blood is treated as a subject that is already known: "Therefore I *have said* to *Benei Yisrael*, no one of you shall eat blood." In other words, it would seem that the appearance of the prohibition in chapter 17 is a repeat of chapter 7 and of chapter 3.

Despite this, I posit that the primary exposition of the command is in chapter 17, rather than chapter 7, for the following reason. Chapter 17, too, includes all of the elements of a command that we mentioned above – the command itself, its conditions, and the punishment, but here we are also given a reason (actually, a dual reason, as noted above), which occupies a central place in this *parasha*. The lack of any reason for the prohibition, in chapters 3 and 7, demands some explanation, for it would seem logical that the reason for a command should appear in the first (chronological) instance of its appearance. According to what we have said above, this would point to chapter 7. Its absence there would appear to indicate that it could not have yet been uttered because the prohibition within the context of the sections about the sacrifices is not in its initial, original place. Therefore it cannot be fully explained; only in chapter 17 can it be treated thoroughly. Further on we shall address this hypothesis in greater detail.

We may summarize as follows: Chronologically speaking, chapter 7 does indeed precede chapter 17, and therefore the appearance of the prohibition against blood in chapter 7 came first and chapter 17 treats it as a law that is already familiar. However, in terms of the prohibition itself, chapter 17 is primary and chapter 7 comes afterwards, but since the general subject of chapter 17 (animals slaughtered outside the *Mishkan*) must come after chapters 3 and 7 (the *Mishkan* and the sacrifices), the prohibition of blood that it includes is also mentioned later chronologically, and it refers to a preceding command. But it is actually chapter 17 that forms the basis of the prohibition.

This helps us to understand the various *parshiyot*, their repetitions, and the differences between them.

III. REASON FOR THE PROHIBITION

Let us examine chapter 17 in its entirety, subdividing it into four sections:

1. Any person (of Israel) ... who slaughters an animal for the purposes of eating its meat, not at the entrance to the *Ohel Mo'ed* (the altar) as a sacrifice – his slaughter is considered as bloodshed, and his punishment is *karet*. The reason for the prohibition and the punishment is so that animals meant for eating will be brought to the *Ohel Mo'ed* for the blood to be sprinkled upon the altar, rather than simply being spilled, and that will lead to an additional result – that *Benei Yisrael* will no longer offer sacrifices to the wild spirits after whom they go astray (vv. 3–7).

2. Anyone (Israelite or stranger) who offers a burnt offering or sacrifice *not* at the *Ohel Mo'ed* is punishable by *karet*. Here the Torah speaks of slaughter for the purposes of sacrifice, not just for eating. There is no mention that this person is considered as having spilled blood. It should also be noted that the first part is addressed to "the house of Israel," while the second – dealing specifically with sacrifice – applies also to the stranger who dwells in their midst (vv. 8–9).

3. Anyone (Israelite or stranger) who eats blood – God will set His face against him and cut him off from amongst his people (vv. 10–12).

4. Anyone (Israelite or stranger) who hunts a beast or bird must pour out its blood and cover it with dust, so that his soul will not be cut off. As an addendum, the final verses here also mention the impurity of an animal that died naturally (without *sheḥita*), which attaches itself to anyone who eats of its meat. This impurity has already been mentioned previously, in chapter 11, and its repetition here also demands some explanation (vv. 13–16).

We offer the following preliminary explanation. The first unit appears to prohibit any slaughter of an animal that may be offered as a sacrifice, without bringing it as a sacrifice. Such slaughter, which is not for the sake of heaven, is a deed comparable to bloodshed, and the expression "spilling of blood" is meant here in both senses. The blood is spilled, rather than sprinkled (on the altar, as it should be), physically. At the same time, the deed is similar to the shedding of human blood ("One who *spills* the blood of man shall have his blood spilled by man" [Gen. 9:6]).

The second unit forbids the offering of any sacrifice outside of the Sanctuary precincts. In other words, not only is it forbidden to kill a *beheima* (an animal that would be fit to offer as a sacrifice), but even ritual slaughter of an animal "for the sake of heaven" – i.e., with the purpose of offering as a sacrifice – is forbidden elsewhere than the *Mishkan*. Here the aim is to centralize divine worship in one place, not only to prevent profane slaughter. In this unit we are not told that the person who performs the slaughter is comparable to one who sheds blood – since ultimately he is acting for the sake of heaven. Likewise there is no mention of any suspicion that the slaughter is meant for the evil spirits – for, once again, the intention is to serve God. But the punishment for this person, too, is *karet*. The reason for the Torah wanting to centralize worship in the *Mishkan* is not given explicit expression, but there may also be internal, religious aspects to it (the Divine Presence is revealed only in the *Mikdash*), and a distancing from idolatrous practices – even without the fear that *Benei Yisrael* would actually worship evil spirits.

The third unit forbids the eating of blood. Not only is the eating of the flesh itself forbidden, but also eating the blood of the flesh. Two reasons are given here for the prohibition:

1. "For the life of the flesh is in the blood" – i.e., one is not to eat the "life" of the animal.
2. "I have given it to you upon the altar" – i.e., the blood plays a critically important role in divine worship; it makes atonement, by means of being sprinkled upon the altar with every sacrifice that is brought. What this means is that the blood always belongs to God – like the forbidden fats, which are always required to be offered upon the altar. Therefore they may not simply be consumed.

Admittedly, these two reasons are interconnected. Why is the blood chosen to be offered upon the altar? Because it is the life, and the life must be offered upon the altar. In other words, the fundamental reason is that the blood equals the life. The second reason – the fact that the blood effects atonement – is itself a result of the first.

Nevertheless, each reason is sufficient in its own right to prohibit the eating of blood.

The fat may not be eaten even though it is not the life of the animal, because it is always offered upon the altar. In other words, it is God's portion. Even if the blood were not the life, it would be forbidden to eat it because, like the fats, it is always offered upon the altar.

On the other hand, even if the blood were not offered upon the altar at all, it would be forbidden to eat because it is the life of the animal, and the life cannot be eaten along with the flesh. In other words, even where there is license to eat flesh, it must be eaten without its vitality – that which makes it fully alive. Plants have no blood. Therefore their life is not cut off when a portion is removed from them, or even when they are cut down to their roots. If an animal is wounded, even if only in one spot, its life force – its blood – leaves it. Taking blood, according to the laws of Shabbat, is equivalent to taking a life (see Tosafot on Shabbat 75a). Eating the meat without the blood makes the eating permissible, for it is not the life that is being consumed but rather something that is dead – just the meat.

The difference between the two reasons has several practical ramifications. The most important of these is, "Any person … who hunts venison of a wild animal or bird that may be eaten" – i.e., there are animals that are not offered upon the altar, and these from the outset are not prohibited as profane food (unlike the animals that may be offered, which were discussed in chapter 3). May the blood of these kinds of animals be eaten? If the blood is forbidden only because it should be offered upon the altar, there is no basis for the prohibition here, for the blood of an animal or bird that is hunted for venison is not brought for sprinkling on the altar. Indeed, the Torah teaches:

> Any person from *Benei Yisrael* or of the strangers who dwell in their midst who hunts venison of an animal or bird that may be eaten – he shall pour out its blood and cover it with dust. *For the life of all flesh is in its blood, and I said to Benei Yisrael: You shall not*

eat the blood of any flesh, for the life of all flesh is its blood; anyone who eats it shall be cut off.

Here the reason of offering upon the altar is indeed omitted, and only the fact that the "blood is the life" is mentioned; since the blood is the life, it must not be eaten – just like the blood of animals that may be offered. In the case of animals that may be offered there is a further reason – the blood is sprinkled upon the altar and it brings atonement.

This understanding serves to clarify a further halakhic point. According to halakha, the law of covering the blood applies only to a *ḥaya* (an animal not fit to be brought as a sacrifice), not to a *beheima* (an animal that may be brought as a sacrifice). Why is the blood of a *ḥaya* – which must be covered – different than that of a *beheima*? The answer becomes clear from what we have said above. Each of the two categories has its own law with regard to blood:

> *Beheima*: "The *kohen* shall sprinkle the blood upon God's altar at the entrance to the Tent of Meeting" (17:6).

> *Ḥaya*: "He shall pour out its blood and cover it with dust."

The blood of the *beheima* is not covered for the simple reason that it is offered on the altar; this is its exalted destiny. The blood of the *ḥaya*, which does not make atonement, must be poured out (as opposed to being eaten or being offered upon the altar), and then covered in order that the blood will not be exposed, representing, as it were, the cry of the animal.

This also appears to be the reason for the dual mention of the prohibition of eating blood in this chapter. In the third unit it is mentioned in connection with *beheimot*, and there its principal reason is the fact that the blood is offered upon the altar. In the fourth unit it is mentioned in relation to *ḥayot*, and there the reason given for the prohibition is that the blood is the life. The assumption that the crux of the innovation in the law of the *ḥaya* is the obligation to pour out the blood (even though no divine service is performed with it) rather than the commandment of covering it, explains the reason for this. If the new teaching that the Torah was giving here was that the blood must be covered, we would not understand how the prohibition against eating blood explains the obligation of covering it. But if the emphasis is, "He shall pour out its blood," the matter is clear. Even in the case of a *ḥaya*, with no ritual context, the blood must be poured out. Why? Because God says: When I forbade the eating of blood, it concerned the blood of all flesh – not only the blood of an animal fit for sacrifice. Why? "Because the life of all flesh is its blood." Note: "of *all* flesh" – *all* animals; not only the flesh of a *beheima*. Although a *beheima* is offered as a sacrifice while a *ḥaya* is not, in both cases the blood is the life of the flesh.

This understanding also arises from the discrepancy of the wording in the two cases. The first unit tells us, "Every person who slaughters" – in other words, we are speaking of *beheimot*, domesticated animals raised as livestock (oxen, sheep, and goats). Therefore a person who wants to kill them must slaughter them – and their blood obviously pours out. But *ḥayot*, which usually go about freely and are not under human control, are hunted in all kinds of ways; they are not necessarily killed by means of ritual slaughter. Hence, their blood is not necessarily poured out. What the Torah is telling us here is that they must not be eaten unless their blood is indeed first poured out. I believe that this command should be regarded as a substantial basis for the obligation to slaughter all kinds of animals, not only those that may be brought as sacrifices. By means of slaughter (severing the aorta) the blood is poured out on the ground and the animal does not suffer any further pain, as it does in many other forms of death.

In light of our conclusions thus far, let us have another look at the structure of the chapter as a whole. We now discover that it is chiastic in form.

A. Unit 1 – Prohibition of eating *beheimot* of profane slaughter; the blood is to be offered. Spilling of blood – the blood is accounted to the person who does this.

B. Unit 2 – Prohibition of sacrifice to God (anywhere other than the place that God will choose) – *beheimot*.

B1. Unit 3 – Prohibition of eating the blood of an animal that is sacrificed – *beheimot*.

A1. Unit 4 – Prohibition of eating blood – profane slaughter.

Comparing units A and A1: The chapter begins and ends with profane slaughter. The slaughter of a *beheima* within a profane framework is forbidden outright; the way of making it permissible is to bring it as a sacrifice and sprinkle the blood upon the altar – in unit 1. The slaughter of a *haya* is permissible, and hence the way to go about it is to pour out the blood and cover it – in unit 4. The expression "spilling of blood" serves to connect these two units. Where there is no license to slaughter, the spilling of blood represents a serious transgression – both in the case of a person and in the case of an animal. Where there is license to kill, the spilling of blood and its covering are the condition for license to eat.

Comparing units B and B1: We noted above that unit 3 discusses the prohibition of blood in the case of *beheimot*, which are animals that may be brought as sacrifices. This was our conclusion from the previous section. Since the reason for the prohibition is that the blood is placed upon the altar, the Torah cannot be talking here about a prohibition against the blood of a *haya*, since it cannot be offered. The connection here to unit 2 is direct and obvious. In B the Torah is speaking of slaughter that is meant for the purposes of divine service, but it is not performed at the Tent of Meeting. Slaughter that is performed anywhere other than the designated place is punishable by *karet*. In unit B1 the Torah is speaking of slaughter for the sake of heaven, in the proper place, but the blood is eaten. Here, too, the punishment is *karet*. We have already noted that the crux of the reason for the prohibition here is the fact that the blood serves a function related to divine service; the blood is offered. The statement, "The blood is the life," explains the fact that the blood is offered, not the actual prohibition against eating blood. What the Torah means, then, is the following: The moment that the slaughter of the *beheima* is permitted, by means of offering it as a sacrifice, the eating of its blood is not problematic in and of itself. Even though the blood is the life, the slaughter of the animal for a higher purpose justifies the taking of its life. The eating of blood is prohibited here only because the blood should be sprinkled – thereby completing the act of sacrifice; eating the blood is sacrilegious.

In summary, the prohibitions in units 2 and 3 are related to divine worship, while the prohibitions in units 1 and 4 are related specifically to profane slaughter.

It should also be noted that the additional command concerning the impurity associated with eating an animal that dies of natural causes should be viewed in a similar context. The Torah permits the eating of a *beheima* by means of slaughtering. A person who eats a *beheima* or *ḥaya* that was slaughtered does not become impure. Why is impurity brought about specifically by an animal that died of natural causes?

It would seem that the reason is not only that slaughter is a permissible way of killing, but rather that slaughter causes the blood to leave the animal's body. An animal that is slaughtered, whose blood leaves its body, does not convey impurity because it contains no trace of the life, the vitality, that it used to possess. It is like an inanimate object. An animal that died of natural causes, although dead, still contains the essence of its vitality – the blood. Therefore, consumption of its meat involves impurity – because blood always causes impurity when its departure involves loss of life (as in the case of childbirth, menstruation, *zava*, etc.). The same applies here. Therefore the matter of impurity is added on here, even though in terms of essential subject matter it seems far removed from the actual prohibition against eating blood.

IV. FORBIDDEN FATS AND BLOOD

Now we can understand the additional prohibitions in the first two appearances. The most striking fact is the appearance of the blood prohibition there in conjunction with the prohibition concerning the fat. In chapter 17 there is no mention at all of the prohibition of fat. This fact hints to the significance of the appearance of the prohibition in the chapters devoted to the sacrifices. It appears there only in the context of divine worship. Just as the fat is forbidden because it is offered upon the altar, and only for that reason, so the blood is forbidden for the same reason. This is undoubtedly also the reason for the prohibition being mentioned specifically in the context of the peace offering – since the other parts of this sacrifice are eaten by the owner or by the *kohanim*, with only the fat and the blood being offered upon the altar. In other words, if the prohibition were to be mentioned in the context of the burnt offering or the sin offering, we could not have understood its logic, for there all the flesh is consumed by the altar, or by the *kohanim* as part of their priestly privilege. Only in the case of the peace offering does the unique status of the fats and the blood come to light; they are offered not because of the special nature of the sacrifice, but because of their own status, and therefore the law is identical in the case of every sacrifice.

This is also the reason for the focus of the prohibition in chapter 7 being turned to birds and *beheimot*: "You shall not eat any blood throughout your dwelling places, neither of bird nor of *beheima*." The *ḥaya* is not included here, because from the perspective of divine worship there is no reason for the blood of a *ḥaya* to be prohibited. Chapter 17 introduces the moral reason: "For the blood is the life." Therefore it is only in chapter 17 that blood of a *ḥaya*, too, is prohibited.

Indeed, the fat is also prohibited only in the case of an ox, sheep, or goat, all of which may be offered as sacrifices, but not in the case of a *ḥaya* – like the blood.

Why the repetition between *Parashat Vayikra* and *Parashat Tzav*? *Parashat Vayikra* includes the entire system of sacrifices, and it is addressed to all of Israel. Therefore the laws that it contains are related primarily to the perspective of the person who brings the sacrifice. *Parashat Tzav* is addressed to the *kohanim*. It, too, includes commands concerning all of the sacrifices, which here are called "*torot*" ("teachings") and which emphasize mainly the perspective of the *kohen* – i.e., his tasks, the parts of the sacrifice that may be eaten, the elements of service that are performed after the actual sacrifice (the ashes, etc.). It seems that the Torah wants to command the prohibition of blood both from the perspective of the Israelite, who brings his sacrifice, and from the perspective of the *kohen*, who performs the sacrificial service. The prohibition in both cases concerns divine worship, but – as noted above – it is possible that the "worship prohibition" itself arises from two different points.

The use of blood in the sacrificial service has a negative aspect and a positive aspect. On the one hand, it negates the pagan sacrificial feast, which appears to have included also the consumption of the blood. The offering of the blood upon the altar represents a rejection of this manner of worship. On the other hand, the positive aspect is that since the blood is the life of the animal, it has the power of atonement.

From the perspective of the Israelite who brings his sacrifice, it is clear that he cannot eat the blood, for the blood atones for his sin by being sprinkled on the altar. But the same would not necessarily hold true concerning the *kohen*. Consumption of the blood by the *kohanim* could have been considered – like the consumption of the meat itself – a gift from God: partaking of food from God's own table, as it were. Therefore it is necessary that the prohibition against blood appear again in the section dealing with instructions to the *kohanim*, in order to negate the notion that eating the blood could be considered a legitimate form of worship.

V. CONCLUSION

We posited that the section prohibiting blood, in chapter 17, is the major exposition of this law, even though chronologically it comes after both chapter 3 and chapter 7. We shall now follow the logic of this argument in light of what we have said thus far. In chapter 17 the Torah introduces the fundamental reason for the prohibition of eating blood: "For the blood is the life." This reason prohibits the eating of blood on the basis of a moral norm. The other sections – chapter 3 and chapter 7, where the prohibition is associated with and arises from the sacrificial service – are related to the matter of divine worship, i.e., the fact that the blood has a role to play upon the altar. Since this reason is secondary, the command that arises from it likewise does not occupy a central place.

But, we may ask, why does the Torah not state the main reason earlier – in chapter 7? Why does it wait until chapter 17 to teach us that the blood is the life? It seems that the answer is simple, and it may be explained in light of the major innovation of chapter 17.

Chapter 17 is the first chapter in Leviticus that does not discuss instructions for service in the *Mishkan*, but rather talks about life outside of it. In this chapter, the Torah regulates the relationship between divine worship in the Sanctuary and everyday life outside of it. It is in this context that the prohibition arises against profane slaughter taking place away from the Tent of Meeting. It turns out that only divine worship gives license to slaughter a *beheima* and then to eat it. The slaughter of a *beheima* purely to satisfy one's desire for meat is considered a form of bloodshed. This norm returns *Benei Yisrael*, in a certain respect, to the situation that existed prior to the Flood. At that time it was forbidden for people to eat meat; animal life was considered almost equivalent to human life. However, the sacrifice of burnt offerings was practiced and acceptable to God even then. Both Abel and Noah (prior to the license to eat meat) brought burnt offerings, and they were accepted by God.

The prohibition against eating meat other than in the sacrificial context represents a sort of return to this ideal situation. Animal life is also valuable and purposeful – as it was prior to the Flood – and therefore killing an animal is considered as bloodshed. "It shall be considered blood for that person; he has spilled blood." When an animal is brought as a sacrifice to God, its slaughter is justified, and hence there is license to eat it. But the crux of the significance of the offering is in the placing of the animal's life force – its blood – upon the altar. Thus, on the theoretical level, the reason for offering a sacrifice – according to its significance in the Torah, which places the act of sprinkling the blood upon the altar in the center – arises from the view of the animal as possessing a life force, a *nefesh*, and therefore it is possible to atone for one *nefesh* (the person) by offering a different *nefesh* (the animal). The importance of the blood, as an expression of the essence of organic vitality, finds expression in the prohibition against eating it – even in the case of those animals that cannot be brought as sacrifices. Even where it is permissible to eat meat solely to satiate a desire for it, the "life" may not be eaten. This, then, is the reason why the principle that "the blood is the life" is located specifically in chapter 17. Only a departure from the discussion of the *Mikdash* and its internal laws reveals to us that offering the blood on the altar is not only an act of worship, but also the "license" to slaughter *beheimot*, for otherwise they would be forbidden as food because of their inherent status, the importance of their lives. This understanding places our relationship towards animals, and towards their blood, on a moral and ideal plane, giving rise to the principle that "the blood is the life." The use of blood as appeasement, for atonement, is the result of this principle. It is for this reason that the Torah does not provide this as the reason for the prohibition of eating blood within the "worship" contexts where it previously appeared (chapters 3 and 7), until the basis of its importance could be established, in chapter 17.

Parashat Kedoshim

The Holy Constitution

Rav Ezra Bick

Chapter 18 of Leviticus has a dramatic opening, which sets it off from the previous section in a far more distinct manner than the usual *"Vayedabber HaShem el Moshe leimor."*

> God spoke to Moses, saying: Speak unto the Children of Israel, and say to them: I am HaShem their God. (Lev. 18:1–2)

The following section details the laws of incest and other forbidden sexual relations. However, before discussing the actual details, the Torah introduces these laws with a caveat.

> After the actions of the land of Egypt, where you dwelled – you shall not follow; and after the actions of the land of Canaan, to where I am bringing you – you shall not follow, and in their laws you shall not walk. Follow My edicts and observe My laws to walk in them, I am HaShem your God.
>
> And you shall observe my laws and edicts which a man shall do and live by them, I am HaShem. (3–5).

The implication of the contrast between not following the laws of Egypt and Canaan and following My laws is that the following section defines a particular set of laws which are in some sense constitutive – they define the social and legal differences between Jewish society, based on God's laws, and the two idolatrous societies which form a framework – past and future – of the Jewish experience in the desert year.

The Torah details a long list of sexual offenses (6–23). At the end, it concludes with the consequences of violating the "constitution" of Jewish society.

> Do not defile yourselves with any of these [practices], for the nations whom I am expelling before you defiled themselves with all these.
>
> And the land was defiled, and I visited its iniquity on it, and the land ejected its inhabitants.
>
> But you shall observe my laws and edicts, and not do any of these abominations, neither a citizen nor a stranger who dwells in your midst.
>
> For all of these abominations were done by the people who preceded you in the land, and the land was defiled.
>
> Let not the land eject you when you defile it, as it ejected the nation that preceded you. For anyone who does any of these abominations, and the performing souls shall be cut off from their people.
>
> And you shall observe My observance, not doing these abominable laws which were done before you, and not be defiled by them, I am HaShem. (24–30)

This gives the appearance of being the closing bookmark of the section that began at the beginning of the chapter, an impression strengthened by the fact that *Parashat Aḥarei Mot* ends at that point (even though in most years the Torah reading continues with *Parashat Kedoshim*).

In fact, if we continue to read *Parashat Kedoshim*, we discover that the "constitution" is not over. It begins with a command to speak and a short introduction – "You shall be holy, for I, HaShem your God, am holy" (19:2).

This is followed by a list of positive commandments of various and sundry kinds, and a great deal of the traditional commentary on *Kedoshim* is devoted to trying to identify which mitzvot are included in the general category of "be holy." Many of the following verses conclude with the phrase "I am HaShem" or "I am HaShem your God," a phrase which appeared in the introduction to the "constitution" of *Aḥarei Mot* and at its apparent conclusion. But what is even more impressive is the continued mention of the actual introduction at various stages of the list in *Kedoshim*.

> You shall observe all My laws and all My edicts, and do them, *I am HaShem.* (19:36)

> You shall observe My laws and do them, *I am HaShem who sanctifies you.* (20:8)

This is followed by a list of prohibited sexual relations, parallel to the list in *Aḥarei Mot*, and then:

> You shall observe all My laws and all My edicts, and do them, and the land to which I am bringing you to settle in it shall not eject you. And you shall not go in the laws of the nations which I am expelling before you, for all these they did and I despised them.
> And I said to you: You shall inherit their land, and I shall give it to you, a land flowing with milk and honey, I am HaShem your God *who has separated you from the nations…. You shall be holy unto Me, for I HaShem am holy, and I have separated you from the nations to be Mine.* (20:22–26)

It is clear that these verses parallel the opening section of the "constitution" of *Aḥarei Mot*, and conclude with the theme that concluded that section – the danger of being expelled from the land because of the disregard of the laws of God. There is one prominent addition in *Kedoshim* not present in the parallel verses before – not surprisingly, it is the element of *kedusha*, holiness.

Taking all of this structure into account, I think the meaning of the double portion is clear. The overall structure is a set of laws which are the social norms of God's people, based on God's laws and edicts (*ḥukkim umishpatim*), which are contrasted with the social norms of the societies in the surroundings. The entire section is divided into two – the first part is negative, and is almost completely based on sexual deviations – that which you must avoid. The second section, named and characterized by the word "*kedusha*," details the positive aspect of Jewish, God-based society. God has "separated you from the nations" (20:26) that you should be His, His people, and that aspect, the positive side, is constitutive of sanctity, *kedusha*.

This explains why the overwhelming majority of *Parashat Kedoshim*'s laws contain a pronounced social aspect. The traditional exegesis examined these laws solely through the prism of *kedusha*, which formed the basis of many rabbinic sermons claiming that the core meaning of *kedusha* is found in the social realm. But once we realize that the concept of *kedusha* being espoused in this *parasha* is part of the social contract between God and His people, and only arises after the larger framework of distinguishing between the perverted and corrupt ways of the nations and their laws and the laws and edicts which will constitute the national and social character of the Jewish nation, the emphasis on specifically social norms is much more understandable. It is correct that forming an ethical community is constitutive of *kedusha*, but that should not be taken to mean that there are no other aspects of *kedusha*, as they belong to the individual spiritual side of *kedusha*. This *parasha* is dealing with social *kedusha*, the sanctity that distinguishes society as a whole and which connects God's people to the Land of Israel and protects them from the "ejecting" referred to in the verses. In that context, we may conclude that the distinguishing mark of the holy community is its commitment to social justice, love, ethics, and – once again – sexual purity.

As we have seen, the structure of this social constitution is twofold, divided between the two *parashot*. *Aḥarei Mot* contains the negative prohibitions of *arayot* (sexual transgressions), and *Kedoshim* contains the positive social practices which are meant to characterize Jewish society. The Torah uses two different words to define these two subsections. In the conclusion of *Aḥarei Mot*, the Torah repeatedly refers to the concept of *tum'a*, defilement. In *Kedoshim*, both in the opening and the conclusion, the Torah refers to *kedusha*, holiness (as well as *havdala*, separation).

In the first case, the Torah warns us not to defile ourselves "with all these [sexual transgressions]," adding that they lead to the defilement of the land which will lead to ejection from the land, as indeed is happening to the nations of Canaan.

Tum'a is a difficult concept in Leviticus. It is divided into two. There is what we may call halakhic *tum'a*, which is a specific halakhic state requiring a purification ceremony (immersion in a *mikveh* and sometimes more, as discussed in Seder Teharot). But the Torah also applies the term *tum'a* to a wide range of activities, without applying the laws of *tum'a* from the first category. This includes prohibited foodstuffs (in fact, forbidden animals are regularly called *beheimot temei'ot* in the Torah), and certain specific sexual transgressions (adultery and bestiality [18:20, 23]) as well as the entire list of sexual transgressions generally (18:24–27; 30). This relationship is a subject of extensive debate and discussion in the commentators. In our section, I think the relationship is clear. The inclusion of these transgressions under the rubric of *tum'a* is specifically tied to the consequence of expulsion from the land, not as a punishment but as a natural result. The land itself will eject you. This is a clear parallel to the basic consequence of halakhic *tum'a*, which is exclusion from the sacred precincts. Defiled people are sent out of the *Mikdash*, with different degrees of *tum'a* resulting in different degrees of expulsion. Our *parasha* states that moral *tum'a* also leads to expulsion from the sacred precincts, though here the result is not legal but natural, or rather divine-natural. The Land of Israel is being implicitly defined as a sacred precinct. The basic parallelism is that of a contradiction between *tum'a*, in whatever form, and the sacred.

The concept of *kedusha* envelopes *Parashat Kedoshim*. *Kedusha* and *tahara* (purity – the opposite state of *tum'a*) are not identical, but they are linked in that one presupposes the other. Only the pure are allowed to come into contact with *kedusha*. *Tum'a* is what one needs to avoid; *kedusha* is that to which one is meant to aspire. Hence, we may conclude: *Parashat Aḥarei Mot* details the actions which must be avoided in order to remain undefiled and capable of relating to God, and God's land. *Parashat Kedoshim* details the actions which must be pursued in order to reach the state of positively being like God, holy as He is holy, so as to be properly considered God's people, God's nation.

Concluding verses in *Kedoshim* appear not once at the very end, but three times.

1. At the end of the list of (mostly) social and ethical practices, the Torah states: "You shall observe all My laws and all My edicts, and do them, I am HaShem (19:36)."

2. This is followed by a separate section concerning the prohibition of the *Molekh*, which is followed by the conclusion: "You shall sanctify yourselves and be sacred, for I am HaShem your God (20:7)."

3. Finally, a list of sexual transgressions with their appropriate punishment, and the conclusion:

> You shall observe all My laws and all My edicts, and do them, and the land to which I am bringing you to settle in it shall not eject you. And you shall not go in the laws of the nations which I am expelling before you, for all these they did and I despised them.
>
> And I said to you: You shall inherit their land, and I shall give it to you, a land flowing with milk and honey, I am HaShem your God who has separated you from the nations…. You shall be holy unto Me, for I HaShem am holy, and I have separated you from the nations to be Mine. (20:22–26)

The last, without using the term *tum'a*, reiterates the concept of the connection between these practices and dwelling in the land, as well as the contrast with the practices of the other nations. Hence, I believe that this final conclusion is the parallel to the original opening verses in *Parashat Aḥarei Mot*, and hence the entire double section is the social constitution. The previous concluding verse was based on *kedusha*, and hence should be seen as the parallel to the opening verse of *Parashat Kedoshim*. In other words, the total structure consists of two parts, *Aḥarei Mot* with its concentration on sexual transgressions and the consequence of *tum'a* and the subsequent ejection and expulsion, and *Kedoshim*, with its concentration on social ethics, under the title of *kedusha* and the consequence of being holy. The two sections together are unified with the phrase "You shall observe all My laws and all My edicts," contrasted with the laws of the other nations.

However, the section of sexual transgressions in *Parashat Kedoshim* is in neither subsection, but rather appended to the end and included only in the overall structure, even meriting its own introduction: "You shall observe My laws and do them, I am HaShem who sanctifies you" (20:8). This verse comes after the concluding verse of sanctity (20:7), and while obliquely referring to God's sanctity as the basis for the instructions, does not directly enjoin it. It half belongs to the sanctity section, and half does not.

The topic of sexual transgression was the entirety of the *Aḥarei Mot* section, and shouldn't be repeated here at all. The repetition in *Parashat Kedoshim* is explained halakhically by the necessity to list the punishments. Legally, Jewish law requires an explicit injunction and a separate statement of punishment for every crime. However, this does not explain the placement of this section of punishments in *Kedoshim*.

I think the answer must be that sexual immorality belongs to the negative section of *tum'a*. It defiles the individual in such a way that invalidates him from being a resident of the sacred land. *Parashat Kedoshim* speaks of society's reaction to sexual immorality. The Torah does not suggest that executing adulterers will confer sanctity on the executioner (hence it is not found within the bookends of "Be holy"), but it is saying that the sanctity of the community requires that as a society it fight against such practices. As a social unit, and as a collorary of the formation of a social unit, there must be policing and punishment of certain areas of individual behavior, not merely because crime should be punished, but because these particular crimes impugn the sanctity of society as a whole. For modern Jews, raised on liberal theories of law and society, this may be a difficult idea to accept. However, the Torah is clearly stating that in the context of God's society, of God's people who have been separated from the nations to be His people, society must extirpate certain activities which defile society, undermine its defining quality, and threaten its legitimacy in the sacred land.

A Stumbling Block Before the Blind: The Metaphoric Approach

Rav Elchanan Samet

I. FOUR INTERPRETATIONS OF THE PROHIBITION

> You shall not curse the deaf, and you shall not place a stumbling block before the blind. You shall fear your God; I am HaShem. (Lev. 19:14)

These two prohibitions, of cursing the deaf and leading the blind to stumble, both involve the protection of those vulnerable due to physical disability. Indeed, these two crimes are linked by the single admonition towards the end of the verse: "You shall fear your God." Nevertheless, we will devote our discussion entirely to the second prohibition, addressing the first half of the verse only insofar as it affects our understanding of the second.

We present here the four interpretations that have been offered to this verse, in the sequence of their deviation from the simple, straightforward meaning, from closest to furthest:

1. "Blind" refers to an individual who cannot see, and "stumbling block" denotes a physical object, such as a stone or beam, that

physically endangers the unsuspecting blind person as he walks. This is the interpretation of the *Kuttim*, who rejected the Oral Law's extrapolation of biblical verses. (See Nidda 57a, Ḥullin 3a.)

The prohibition according to this approach involves taking unfair advantage of the handicap of another. The earlier prohibition against cursing the deaf would presumably be explained in a similar manner.

2. "Blind" here means anyone, even without any handicap, who does not see the stumbling block placed before him. With respect to this specific danger, he may be considered figuratively "blind." "Stumbling block" refers to a physical trap lying innocuously in one's path, such as a pit with an indiscernible covering.

In other words, this approach maintains virtually the same interpretation of the term "stumbling block," and only minimally expands the definition of the word "blind," to include a person with operative vision but who cannot see the stumbling block before him. The prohibition thus comes to forbid taking unfair advantage of not only the handicapped, but anyone in a situation where they cannot detect a given threat to their well-being. Similarly, the ban against cursing the deaf would include not only the deaf, but anyone incapable, for whatever reason, of responding to the slur.

This appears to be the approach of Targum Onkelos, who translates "deaf" and "blind" in our verse as "one who does not hear" and "one who does not see," while elsewhere he invokes the Aramaic terms for "deaf" and "blind" in his translation of these words (see Exodus 4:11; Leviticus 21:18; Deuteronomy 15:21, 27:18 and 28:29). Onkelos here translates the word "*mikhshol*" (stumbling block), which appears nowhere else in the Torah, as "*takala*," meaning something upon which people stumble.

3. "Blind" here refers to one lacking certain information or a proper understanding regarding a given situation, and "stumbling block" means misleading counsel given to that individual. This approach interprets both "blind" and "stumbling block" figuratively, as referring to intellectual "blindness" and a mistake resulting in some form of loss in one area or another.

This is the approach taken by the Sifra in its comments on our verse. The Sifra provides three examples of such a "stumbling block": telling a *kohen* that a prospective spouse is permissible for him, when in fact she is forbidden to him (such as a divorcee, etc.); advising one to leave on his trip at a time when he is exposed to certain dangers, such as thieves early in the morning and sunstroke at midday; advising one to sell his field and purchase a donkey instead, only to be able to personally purchase the field. (Rashi interprets the verse likewise, citing as an example the third instance mentioned in the Sifra.) Rambam (negative commandment 299, *Hilkhot Rotzei'aḥ* 12:14) and *Ḥinnukh* (232) adopt this view, as well.

In order to appreciate the significance of the prohibition according to this approach, let us carefully examine the motives of the misleading counsel in each of the three cases introduced by the Sifra. In the first case, the violator is apparently trying to help the woman. While his concern for her well-being is laudable, this interest does not justify misleading the *kohen*. In the third instance, the advisor deceives the victim for his own personal gain. This prohibition thus outlaws misleading others for either one's own interests or those of a third party.

In the second case, however, no motive seems to have prompted the deceit. No one benefits from the victim's miscalculated departure. Why, then, did the advisor set this trap? Apparently, this prohibition involves misguiding one for the sheer joy of watching another fail. If so, then this approach bears some similarity to the second interpretation, and the relationship between this prohibition and the earlier one concerning the deaf becomes clear.

4. The most surprising interpretation of the verse appears in a twice-repeated *baraita* in the Talmud (Pesaḥim 22b, Avoda Zara 6b) and occupies a substantial portion of halakhic literature to this very day. One may not assist one in committing a sin or cause him to sin. The examples presented in the *baraita* are giving wine to a *nazir* and offering meat taken from a live animal to a gentile.

The figurative meaning of "stumbling block" according to this interpretation resembles its meaning according to the previous approach. The meaning of "blind," however, is far from clear. Both the culprit and victim know full well what's at stake, no one is misled. How, then, does this approach understand the word "blind" in the verse?

Rambam addresses this issue in several places in his works, and explains that the one assisted in his sinning is considered blind because his desire "obscured his vision," and "he does not see the truthful path." (See negative commandment 299 and *Hilkhot Rotzeiaḥ* 12:12–14.) According to his interpretation, "blind" here refers not to visual impairment (as in the first two approaches) nor to a misunderstanding of a given situation (as in the third approach). Rather, it connotes "moral blindness," suffered by one whose drives and inclinations lure him off the proper path. Needless to say, this approach steers quite a distance from the straightforward interpretation of the verse.

In any event, the significance of the prohibition according to this approach is clear. One may not assist another in committing a sin, even if he offers his help out of camaraderie, good manners, or any other noble motive.

II. THE HALAKHIC STATUS OF THE FOUR INTERPRETATIONS

The issue of the halakhic status of these approaches essentially translates into a different question: Which of these four interpretations of the verse do *Ḥazal* view as correct?

All the sources in *Ḥazal* indicate that they viewed the figurative interpretation, that one may not lead one to "stumble" in the metaphoric sense, as binding on the biblical level (*mide'oraita*). Clearly, they approached this interpretation as a primary explanation of the verse and rejected the position of the *Kuttim* who limited the verse's implication to placing a *physical* stumbling block before a blind person. However, as some *Aharonim* indicate, this does not preclude the possibility that *Ḥazal* viewed all four approaches as primary interpretations of the verse. Both Rav Meir Simcha of Dvinsk (*Meshekh Ḥokhma*) and Rav Barukh Epstein (*Torah Temima*) are of the opinion that the prohibition includes all four interpretations mentioned above. *Ḥazal* disagreed with the *Kuttim* only regarding their rejection of the figurative approach;

they conceded, however, that the literal approach is legally relevant. The *Minḥat Ḥinnukh* likewise raises such a possibility.

However, the omission of any mention of such a prohibition – the placement of a physical obstacle before the blind – in halakhic literature from *Ḥazal* onward casts serious doubts on such a possibility. Furthermore, if indeed *Ḥazal* accepted the literal interpretation as legally binding, it is hard to imagine that the figurative approach would likewise apply on a biblical level. In the presence of the literal interpretation, we must relegate the figurative meaning to the lower level of *derash*.

It would seem, therefore, that *Ḥazal* outright rejected the literal interpretation of the verse upheld by the *Kuttim*. They did not merely add an additional level of interpretation; they believed that the figurative approach to the verse is the only plausible explanation of the prohibition. Indeed, this is the view of a wide array of commentators and halakhic authorities, some of whom we will encounter in the course of our discussion.

Two obvious questions emerge from this conclusion. First and foremost, as Rav Yerucham Perlow (in his work on Rav Sa'adia Gaon's *Sefer HaMitzvot*, p. 107) asks, why did *Ḥazal* reject the straightforward interpretation? To this we may add, why and how did *Ḥazal* choose a metaphoric interpretation of the prohibition? This second question raises a more general, fundamental issue – may we approach mitzvot metaphorically?

III. METAPHORIC INTERPRETATION OF THE MITZVOT: THE RULE AND THE EXCEPTIONS

A *baraita* entitled *"Baraita DeLamed-Bet Middot"* enumerates thirty-two literary guidelines employed by *Ḥazal* in their exegesis of biblical verses. The twenty-sixth principle establishes that while parables and metaphors are employed in the Nevi'im and Ketuvim, "regarding the words of the Torah and mitzva you may not interpret them as allegories." The *baraita* then proceeds to provide three exceptions, instances where R. Yishmael explained a mitzva figuratively.

Is there any rational explanation behind the exceptions to this rule? Could we perhaps determine the basis for *Ḥazal*'s interpreting them figuratively? How does their interpretation of our verse accommodate this principle?

IV. TWO TYPES OF METAPHOR

In his dictionary of literary terms, Professor Yosef Eban distinguishes between two types of metaphor. The first type features two words or groups of words, one of which maintains its original, literal meaning, while the second receives an entirely new meaning through its association with the other word or words. For example, we may describe an inspiring, soul-stirring speech as "breaking down the walls of indifference among the audience," meaning that it significantly transformed their emotional or mental mindset. The expression "breaking the walls" has been borrowed from its natural habitat – a battle waged against a besieged city – and infused with an entirely new meaning through its introduction into the context of a persuasive lecture.

The second group of metaphors, by contrast, consists of a word or group of words that loses its literal meaning without any textual association with a foreign context. Rather, purely external circumstances change the meaning of the words(s) and advise the listener to reinterpret the word(s) accordingly. For example, someone recently relieved of some financial or personal crisis might say, "I have finally arrived at safe shores." While a stranger might conclude from this remark that the individual has just returned from a stormy voyage at sea, those familiar with his situation know that he had been on dry land, only caught in a mire of tension and anxiety.

With this background, let us proceed to examine the instances where R. Yishmael approaches a mitzva with a figurative interpretation. We begin with the second example, the case of a thief who breaks into a home (Ex. 22:2). The Torah states, "If the sun shone upon him [the thief], he [the homeowner] is held accountable [if he kills the thief in alleged self-defense]." Rather than interpreting "the sun shone upon him" literally, R. Yishmael understands this phrase as referring to a case where the intruder clearly intends no harm to the homeowner. It would seem that this metaphor belongs to the first category. As the *baraita* notes, the sun shines not only upon the thief, but upon the whole world. Thus, the association of the sun's shining with the specific expression, "upon him," forces us to consider an allegorical interpretation of the sun's shining. We may conclude, then, that the Torah itself requires that we approach this verse as an allegory.

The other two examples in the *baraita*, however, are of the second type of metaphor. The Torah addresses a situation where the victim of a beating recovers from the blow: "If he then gets up and walks outdoors upon his staff, the assailant shall go unpunished" (Ex. 21:19). The *baraita* observes that "staff" cannot be understood literally, for we are dealing with a case where the victim has been completely cured, thus relieving the aggressor of punishment. Therefore, "his staff" here means his body, and the verse thus refers to a healthy individual capable of walking independently. Nothing in the verse itself compels us to adopt a figurative interpretation. Rather, the legal consideration of acquitting the attacker only upon the victim's complete recovery leads us to a metaphoric reading. (I shall not address the third instance, the investigation of a bride whose husband accuses her of a premarital affair [Deut. 22:17], where the compelling reason for the figurative reading is unclear.)

To which of these two categories would we place our verse – the prohibition against placing a "stumbling block" before "the blind"?

V. THREE ATTEMPTS TO PROVE THE METAPHORIC INTERPRETATION

Several attempts have been made throughout the ages to identify a textual basis within the verse for Ḥazal's rejection of the literal meaning. Rav Yerucham Perlow cites the various suggestions and subjects them to his rigorous critique. We will generally follow in his footsteps.

The first approach is that of Rav Eliyahu Mizrachi, who authored a classic work on Rashi's commentary:

> It seems to me that the reason why they interpreted in this way [in the Sifra] is because we cannot say that "blind" here implies the straightforward meaning, since "blind" must resemble "deaf" [in the first half of the verse]. Just as "deaf" does not refer specifically to the deaf, so does "blind" not refer specifically to the blind.

However, if this was the sole concern, then Ḥazal should have interpreted the verse according to the second approach listed above, that "blind" here refers to anyone who cannot see a given obstacle placed in his path. There would be no need to steer even further from the simple meaning and arrive at the allegorical interpretation of the third and fourth approaches.

Maharal of Prague, in his commentary on Rashi entitled *Gur Aryeh*, identifies the source of the allegorical interpretation in the conclusion of the verse: "You shall fear your God." He writes:

> "You shall fear your God" is stated only with regard to something given over to one's heart [i.e., a sin not discernible from the outside, thus requiring genuine fear of God to refrain therefrom – see Rashi on our verse]. This instance [placing a physical obstacle before the blind], however, is not given over to one's heart, for at times the blind person will discover who placed the stumbling block before him, or others will see, or he will be recognized by his voice, etc.

The obvious problem with this interpretation is that according to the literal approach to the verse, this prohibition clearly refers to a situation where one would hurt a helpless person in such a way that he would never be discovered. In a situation where the blind victim or anyone else could identify the perpetrator, no one would attempt the prank, and there is no need for the prohibition. Thus, given that we are dealing with a situation where the perpetrator would never be discovered, there is no context more suitable than this one for the admonition, "You shall fear your God."

A third suggestion was posed by Rav Aharon Ibn Ḥayim, in his commentary on the Sifra, *Korban Aharon*. He notes that the verse describes the "placing" of the stumbling block with the word "*titen*," which generally means, "to give," rather than the Hebrew word for "to place," "*tasim*." He argues:

> One who places an obstacle for another to stumble upon will not be called "giving." What or to whom is he giving? He would rather be called "placing," and the verse should have therefore stated, "Do not *place (tasim)* a stumbling block before the blind." On account of this, *Ḥazal* were compelled to interpret the verse in a manner that would accommodate [the use of the verb] "giving," that he gives someone this stumbling block, meaning the advice that he gives.

However, as Rav Perlow already notes, in biblical Hebrew the verb form "*netina*" is often used in reference to placing, particularly when followed by the word *"lifnei"* (before), such as in Exodus 30:36 and Leviticus 5:11.

Thus, none of the three attempts satisfactorily provides a textual basis for the rejection of the literal meaning of the verse.

VI. ESTABLISHING ḤAZAL'S METAPHORIC INTERPRETATION IN THREE STAGES

We must therefore look for an external factor – outside the text – that led Ḥazal to their figurative approach to the verse. Since external considerations are generally less compelling than internal, textual ones, it would be worthwhile to look for some textual support for the allegorical interpretation. If we can establish biblical precedents for the metaphoric usage of the terms "blind" and "stumbling block" and verify the widespread usage of their allegorical meaning, we can increase the likelihood of their figurative meaning in our context. Our third and final step will then be to explain why the Torah selected metaphor as the means by which to present this specific prohibition.

As we explained at the outset of our presentation, the literal approach to the verse yields a prohibition against taking unfair advantage of the handicapped. It forbids one from causing harm to a helpless individual by capitalizing on his handicap such that he cannot guard himself or identify the antagonist. Such a warning would be directed to an audience with an inclination towards such sadistic tendencies, generally young children who relish the opportunity to watch others fail. However, the Torah prohibits only those crimes against others that people are led to commit by reasonable motives. One might steal out of desperate poverty or desire for a higher economic standard; a person may kill out of uncontrolled vengeance. The Torah warns against following through on these motives.

Placing a stone before the blind, however, involves sadism for its own sake. Ḥazal presumed that the Torah would have no need to address such conduct with an explicit prohibition, as this behavior falls far short of the basic moral standards of the audience towards whom the Torah directs itself. They therefore interpreted the prohibition as outlawing the deception of others for personal gain or as assisting sinners, even when prompted to do so by understandable social interests. In these instances, where the potential violator may have reasonable interests or concerns at stake, the Torah must explicate a prohibition.

We now proceed to the second step, our search for similar usage of "blind" and "stumbling block" throughout Tanach. The word "*iver*" (the word for "blind" in our verse) appears twenty-six times in Tanach, and an additional five times in the verb form. In at least ten of these instances it is used metaphorically, mostly in Isaiah. Particularly noteworthy is one example appearing twice in the Torah, where bribes are said to "blind (*ye'aver*) the eyes of the wise." This figurative usage of the term fits beautifully with Rambam's aforementioned explanation of "blind" in our verse. Regarding the second term, "*mikhshol*" (stumbling block), in each of its fourteen appearances in Tanach, together with the two instances of the related term, "*makhshela*," it emerges as a metaphor. In fact, half of these metaphors involve spiritual "stumbling blocks," i.e., sins. Thus, Ḥazal's figurative approach to the verse implies no irregular usage of biblical terms.

In conclusion, we turn our attention to the issue of why the Torah invokes metaphoric usage in its presentation of this prohibition, rather than employing straightforward terminology suitable for legal code. One answer may lie in the fact that this verse includes two distinct prohibitions, offering misleading advice and assisting sinners. Rambam (*Sefer HaMitzvot*, Shoresh 9) cites this verse as an example of a *lav shebeklalot*, a negative commandment that subsumes multiple prohibitions. Rambam writes that we must consider all the various prohibitions included within one verse as just one of the 365 negative commandments of the Torah. As such, the Torah needed to present these two prohibitions – against misleading counsel and assistance in sin – in a form that would include both under a single category. Were the Torah to have articulated these prohibitions in a straightforward manner, it would have had to separate them into two negative commandments.

Alternatively, the use of metaphor generates an association between the present context and the one from where the metaphor is borrowed. The Torah sharpens our awareness of the severity of these crimes – offering unsound advice and helping to facilitate a Torah violation – through the image of the placement of an obstacle before the unsuspecting, helpless, blind person. With this metaphor, the Torah teaches us that there exist various levels of "blindness," and one who leads one to stumble in the figurative sense is considered to have placed an actual stumbling block before a blind person.

Orla and Reishit

Rabbanit Sharon Rimon

> And when you come to the land and plant every type of fruit
> tree, then you shall consider their fruit as *orla* (literally, "uncir-
> cumcised"); for three years it shall be *orla* for you; it shall not
> be eaten. And in the fourth year all of its fruit shall be holy as
> thanksgiving to God.
>
> And in the fifth year you shall eat its fruit, that it may yield
> for you its increase; I am HaShem your God. (Lev. 19:23–25)

These verses contain two commandments: the prohibition of *orla* – i.e.,
the use of the fruit that grows on a tree for its first three years, and the
commandment of *neta revai* – the obligation to bring the fruit of the
fourth year to Jerusalem and eat it.

These two commandments are related to one another; following
the three years during which the fruit is forbidden, in the fourth year
the fruit has special sanctity. Let us take a closer look at the first verse
cited above, dealing with the prohibition of *orla*.

I. ORLA, BIKKURIM, AND ARELIM

At first glance, the prohibition of *orla* resembles the commandment of
bikkurim (the first fruits). Both involve first fruits, and in both cases we

are forbidden to eat these first fruits. Similarly, the Torah introduces both commandments with the formula, "When you come to the land":

> And it shall be, when you come to the land that HaShem your God gives you as an inheritance, and you take possession of it and dwell in it, then you shall take of the first of all the fruit of the earth … and you shall place it in a basket, and you shall go to the place which HaShem your God will choose. (Deut. 26:1–2)

However, there is a clear difference between the two commands. In the case of *bikkurim*, the first fruits are consecrated to God, and are brought to the Sanctuary with joy and thanksgiving. When it comes to *orla*, on the other hand, the fruits are not dedicated to God; moreover, the Torah stresses their negative status: "It shall not be eaten."

More importantly, the appellation by which the Torah refers to *orla* is surprising. They are referred to as "uncircumcised" (*arelim*), and this term is repeated three times in a single verse: "*va'araltem orlato … arelim.*"

The term *arel* in Tanach carries a negative connotation. The first appearance of this word is in God's covenant with Abraham:

> This is My covenant which you shall observe between Me and you, and your descendants after you; every male among you shall be circumcised. And you shall circumcise the flesh of your *orla* [referring to the foreskin], and it shall be a sign of the covenant between Me and you.
>
> And an uncircumcised (*arel*) male, who does not circumcise the flesh of his *orla* – that soul shall be cut off from his people; he has violated My covenant. (17:10–11, 14)

The primary meaning of the term *orla* in the Torah is a reference to the foreskin, which must be removed. This is certainly not a positive connotation. An uncircumcised male is an "*arel*," similarly not a positive title.

There are places where the term appears in other contexts:

- "*Arel sefatayim*" (of uncircumcised lips): "Moses spoke before God saying, 'But *Benei Yisrael* have not listened to me; how, then, will Pharaoh listen to me, since I am of uncircumcised lips?'" (Ex. 6:12)

- *"Arel lev"* (of uncircumcised heart): "Circumcise yourselves to God and remove the foreskins of your hearts." (Jer. 4:4)
- *"Arel ozen"* (of uncircumcised ears): "Behold, their ears are uncircumcised; they cannot listen." (Jer. 6:10)

In the above three expressions, the state of being "uncircumcised" clearly indicates a negative situation. It would appear that in these contexts the word *orla* is borrowed from its original sense, such that it connotes some deficiency or blemish that must be repaired or removed.

Rashi explains the word *orla* in each of these cases as indicating "impermeable," sealed (on Exodus 6:12), while Ibn Ezra holds that it connotes "heaviness" (ibid.). Thus, *orla* is a word that indicates some sort of deficiency or blemish. Its appearance in connection with fruit is unusual and unclear.

Finally, in many different places the Torah commands us *"limol et ha'orla,"* meaning, to remove the foreskin, to correct the deficiency. Here, in contrast, we read, *"va'araltem orlato,"* and the meaning appears to be the opposite of circumcision. The verb, from the same root stem as *orla*, seems to commanding us to *cause* the fruit to be *arel*.

What is the meaning of *orla* with regard to fruits? And what is man's place and role in this *orla*?

II. PROHIBITION OF BENEFIT

Rashi, commenting on *Parshat Kedoshim*, states:

> "It shall be uncircumcised for you" – you shall *seal up its sealing*; it should be sealed and barred against having any benefit from it. (Lev. 19:23)

According to Rashi, here too the word may be understood to mean "sealing." What is means is that the fruit must be barred from eating; it is prohibited to enjoy any benefit from it.

This explanation suggests that there is no problem inherent in the fruit itself. The command pertains to man; he is commanded to turn the fruit into *orla*, to "seal" it from himself, so that he will not derive any benefit from it.

In other words, this is a regular prohibition against deriving benefit. The question is, why does the Torah use the expression *orla* specifically in connection with this prohibition? After all, there are many things concerning which we are forbidden to derive benefit, yet none of them adopt such language.

Ibn Ezra (commenting on Leviticus 19:23) provides the following explanation for the use of the term *orla* in connection with the fruit:

> And the reason for [the Torah stating] "*va'araltem orlato*" is that that fruit is considered like *orla*, which is detrimental and not beneficial, like "uncircumcised lips" and "uncircumcised ears" and "foreskin flesh." And the reason for [the specific formulation] "*va'araltem*" is so that it will be considered in your eyes as something that is *orla*."

To Ibn Ezra's view, *orla* (the foreskin) is removed because it is flesh that is superfluous, not beneficial. Likewise, the fruit that grows during the first three years of a tree's growth should be considered as an *orla* – i.e., as devoid of benefit and even as detrimental.

Why is the fruit prohibited during the first three years?

III. UNRIPENESS

Ramban (on Leviticus 19:23) maintains that the fruit of the first three years of a tree's growth are like unripe fruit that is detrimental to one's health:

> And it is a further truth that the fruit [that grows] at the beginning of a tree's planting have excess moisture which is harmful for the body and is not good for eating, like a fish that has no scales (above, 19:9). The foods that are prohibited in the Torah are also bad for the body.

Accordingly, it is clear why the fruits are called *orla*. They are harmful, and therefore they should be removed and not used. However, we are left with the question of why the Torah adopts the peculiar expression, *"va'araltem orlato."* What is man's active role in rendering the fruit *orla*?

At the beginning of his explanation, Ramban provides a different explanation for the prohibition of *orla*. He suggests that the crux of the commandment is the *neta revai* (the produce of the fourth year), whereby the "real" first fruit, as it were, is brought to the Sanctuary. The prohibition of *orla* is merely the preface to the commandment of *neta revai*. It is necessary to wait for three years, until the fruits are of a quality that renders them worthy of being brought before God. Until they are brought, the fruits are prohibited

IV. ACCELERATING THE RIPENING

A completely different reason for the prohibition of *orla* is proposed by Rambam:

> The ancient pagans also … performed many acts of sorcery. They wanted this to be readied by each person, such that when he planted a fruit tree, he would scatter some rotten remains of that same fruit, and then the tree would grow quickly and produce fruit within a shorter time than usual. They maintained that this was a wondrous matter, belonging to the realm of sorcery, to accelerate the bearing of fruit. And we have already explained and stated that the Torah keeps distant from all of those acts of sorcery. Therefore the Torah forbids all that the fruit trees produce for three years from the time of their planting, such that there is no need to accelerate their growth…. By the end of three years, most fruit trees in *Eretz Yisrael* produce fruit on their own, and they have no need for that act of sorcery. (*Guide of the Perplexed* III:37)

According to Rambam, like many other prohibitions in the Torah, the prohibition of *orla* is meant to distance *Benei Yisrael* from the customs of the pagan nations. Since the pagans would perform certain actions to accelerate the fruit-bearing process, and then sacrifice the fruit to their pagan gods, God forbade us to eat the first fruits of the tree in order that we would not come to adopt these magical tricks, nor be mistaken into believing that idolatry could accelerate the ripening of the fruit.

We may utilize Rambam's explanation to explore a different aspect of the prohibition. Perhaps the very attempt on man's part to accelerate the production of fruit is a negative phenomenon. While God has given man the right to "improve" the world through technological advances, there are still areas in which the Torah limits us and forbids certain actions, even though they appear to us to further the aims of perfecting the world. One example is the prohibition of *kilayim* – the cross-fertilization of different species. While we might imagine that a certain procedure of crossbreeding would improve the livestock or agricultural produce involved, God tells us that such procedures are improper.

The same would appear to apply to *orla*. Left to grow naturally, a tree does not generally produce plentiful, high-quality fruit during its first three years. Perhaps man may become capable of performing some sort of procedure that would cause fruit to appear earlier, and perhaps this would appear to him as an improvement and enhancement, but the Torah tells us that this would not be proper. Therefore, the fruit of the first three years should not be consumed.

This leads us to formulate our question in a different way: Why does the Torah not simply and explicitly state that it is forbidden to accelerate or enhance the development of the fruit? From the language of the Torah it seems that the fruit that grows in a natural manner is "uncircumcised"; i.e., it is somehow deficient or blemished.

V. "*REISHIT*" – A HOLY NUCLEUS, OR A POLLUTED SHELL?

We started our discussion by drawing a comparison between *orla* and *bikkurim* – two commandments that concern first fruits. There are a number of other commandments that address a *reishit* (beginning, first manifestation), and in every instance *Benei Yisrael* are required to give of this *reishit* to God:

- The firstborn: "Sanctify unto Me every firstborn who opens the womb of *Benei Yisrael*, whether of man or of livestock, it is Mine." (Ex. 13:2)
- *Bikkurim*: "And now, behold, I have brought the first of the fruit of the land which God has given me – and he shall place it before HaShem your God." (Deut. 26:10)
- *Teruma* (the tithe): "The first of your grain, your wine, and your oil, and the first of the fleece of your flock shall you give to him." (Deut. 18:4)
- *Ḥalla*: "You shall offer up a cake of the first of your dough as a gift." (Num. 15:20)
- *Omer* and the prohibition of *ḥadash*: "When you come to the land which I give to you, and you reap its harvest, then you shall bring an *omer* of the first of your harvest to the *kohen*." (Lev. 23:10)

The commandments of *bikkurim*, *teruma*, *ḥalla*, and the *omer* require that the "first" be given to God. When it comes to *orla*, in contrast, we reject the "first" and label it as somehow unworthy. Only afterwards do we take the fruits of the fourth year – which are no longer *reishit* – and sanctify them, "Sanctified for praise to God."

Against the backdrop of the other commandments of *reishit*, the use of the term *orla* with reference to these first fruits is most puzzling.

Apparently, the Torah is teaching us the proper attitude towards these first fruits. The fruits that grow during the first three years are not *bikkurim* – the sumptuous fruits that we have awaited. Rather, they are *orla* – superfluous, even harmful. The Torah specifically employs the term *orla* to indicate the parallel between these fruits and a bodily *orla*. Just as a bodily *orla* (foreskin) represents an imperfect situation, and its removal is the correction – i.e., man is created incomplete, and he must perform a certain action in order to bring his body to completion and perfection – so the first fruits are imperfect; they are *orla*.

Thus, the Torah provides two different views of *reishit*. On the one hand, there are many commandments which express the special sanctity of the "first." The first is dedicated to God – not only out of thanksgiving, and as a declaration that all belongs to God, but also because the *reishit* itself is actually closer to its divine source; it has a greater level of purity, and therefore greater sanctity, and is worthy of being given to God. (This is particularly manifest in the status of the firstborn. The firstborn is automatically consecrated to God; there is no need to consecrate him.)

At the same time, the prohibition of *orla* expresses the fact that the *reishit* is actually deficient or blemished. What is the meaning of these two opposing ideas?

Anything that is formed in this world has its source in the connection between the upper world and our earthly reality. The commandments that reflect the sanctity of the *reishit* express the fact that everything in our world has its source in God, and the *reishit* is closest to the source. It reflects the beginning of the connection between the upper world and our reality. However, although everything in our world comes from God, our earthly reality is not complete and perfect; it is not Godly. The divine world cannot appear in its completion in our world. Our material world uses divine powers in a lowly, material manner. During the process of formation, these powers are covered over with a "shell"; they are sealed with an *orla*. Therefore, it is specifically the first appearance in the world that is covered with this covering, which must be removed in order to attain the more perfect and complete essence.

Man's first appearance in the world is incomplete; it is covered with an *orla* which must be removed. Similarly, the first fruits that a tree produces are not complete. They are not *bikkurim*, but rather *orla*. They are sealed with an outer covering, as it were, and are therefore forbidden.

Fruits that are *orla* are the first appearance of the produce of a tree, and this appearance is not complete. This is the shell, which must be avoided, removed. Only afterwards may one make use of the sumptuous fruits that grow later.

This idea is also expressed in the physical dimension – these first fruits are sparse and not of good quality. The root of this phenomenon, however, is to be found in the spiritual dimension. Nothing in our world is complete and perfect; everything is a mixture of good and bad. And it is specifically the first appearance that bears an outer shell, and external aspect of evil, which must be removed.

VI. "*VA'ARALTEM ORLATO*"

In contrast to the *orla* of the body, which must be removed, the Torah commands us, concerning the fruit, "*va'araltem orlato.*" This means that man must actively establish that these first fruits be *orla*. Even if such fruit have grown and appeared, even if they appear to be of good quality, and even if they are not harmful, man must recognize them as *orla*. He must declare them to be such.

Perhaps the significance of this commandment is that man must discern that the reality of our world is not holy in its natural state. We must first recognize the reality and the presence of an outer shell which is not Godly at all, but rather a blemish.

The next stage is to remove these coverings; to discard the blemished fruit. Only after this stage are we able to arrive at the chosen *reishit*, which is closer to its divine source. This *reishit* is dedicated to God: "And in the fourth year all of its fruit shall be sanctified for praise to God" (v. 24).

The commandment of *neta revai* resembles the commandments of *bikkurim* and *teruma* in its emphasis on the divine aspect of reality, finding its strongest expression in the *reishit* – but only after the blemishes and "shells" of that *reishit* have been removed.

The final stage is the possibility of man making use of these fruits in this world for his own benefit, in a proper and blessed manner: "And in *the fifth year* you shall eat its fruit, that it may yield for you its increase" (v. 25).

The Dual Prohibitions of Forbidden Unions

Rav Amnon Bazak

I. INTRODUCTION

Chapter 20 of Leviticus deals with the various prohibited sexual relations. The obvious question that arises is that it appears to repeat the laws we learned just two chapters earlier, in chapter 18. Let us begin by comparing the two chapters:

Leviticus *18*	Leviticus *20*
(1) God spoke to Moses, saying: (2) Speak to *Benei Yisrael* and say to them, I am HaShem your God. (3) You shall not act in the manner of the land of Egypt, where you dwelled; nor shall you act in the manner of the land of Canaan, to where I am bringing you, nor shall you walk in their ways. (4) [Rather] you shall perform My judgments, and observe My statutes, to walk in them – I am HaShem your God. (6) None of you shall approach anyone that is close of kin to him, to uncover nakedness – I am HaShem. (7) You	(7) You shall sanctify yourselves and be holy, for I am HaShem your God. (8) You shall observe My statutes and fulfill them; I am HaShem who sanctifies you. (9) Any person who curses his father or his mother shall surely be put to death; he has cursed his father or his mother; his blood shall be upon him. (10) And anyone who commits adultery with another man's wife – who commits adultery with his neighbor's wife – shall surely be put to death; the adulterer and the adulteress. (11) If any person lies with

Leviticus *18*	Leviticus *20*
shall not uncover the nakedness of your father or the nakedness of your mother. (17) You shall not uncover the nakedness of a woman and her daughter. (18) Nor shall you marry a woman and her sister, as her rival, and uncover her nakedness, during the former's lifetime. (19) Nor shall you come close to a woman in the impurity of her menstruation, to uncover her nakedness. (20) Nor shall you lie with your neighbor's wife, to defile yourself with her. (22) You shall not lie with a male in the manner of a woman; it is an abomination. (23) Nor shall you lie with any animal to defile yourself with it; nor shall a woman stand before an animal to lie before it; it is perversion. (27) For all of these abominations were committed by the people of the land who were before you, and the land was defiled. (28) So that the land will not expel you when you defile it, as it expelled the nation that came before you. (29) For anyone who does any of these abominations – the people who perform them shall be cut off from their nation. (30) And you shall observe My ordinance, so as not to act in any of the ways of abomination that were practiced before you, and that you shall not defile yourselves in them; I am HaShem your God.	his father's wife…. (14) If a person takes a wife and her mother, this is lewdness; they shall be burnt with fire, both he and they, that there be no lewdness among you. (18) A person who lies with a menstrual woman and uncovers her nakedness, he has uncovered her fountain and she has uncovered the fountain of her blood; both shall be cut off among their people. (22) You shall observe all of My statutes and all of My judgments and do them, that the land to which I bring you, to dwell there, not expel you. (23) You shall not walk in the ways of the nation which I cast out before you, for they did all of this, and I abhorred them. (24) I have said to you, "You shall inherit their land, and I shall give it to you, to inherit it – a land flowing with milk and honey"; I am HaShem your God who has distinguished you from the nations. (25) You shall therefore distinguish between clean animals and unclean, between unclean birds and clean, and you shall not make your souls abominable with animal or bird or anything that creeps upon the ground, which I have separated for you as unclean. (26) You shall be holy unto Me, for I, God, am holy, and I have separated you from the nations to be Mine.

Both chapters are built upon a similar structure, consisting of introductory verses (18:1–5; 20:7–8), then a list of the forbidden relations (18:6–23; 20:9–29), followed by verses of conclusion (18:24–30; 20:22–26). There is, however, a striking difference between the two sections: chapter 18 is formulated as a series of warnings or negative commands

("You shall not uncover"; "you shall not come close"; etc.), while in chapter 20 the text refers to punishments ("he shall surely be put to death"; "they shall be childless"; etc.). Obviously, this difference cannot be sufficient reason to repeat this list in two separate chapters; the text could have simply stated each prohibition together with its punishment, all in one section. For what reason, then, does the Torah devote two separate chapters to the same subject?

II. IMPURITY AND PURITY, THE PROFANE AND THE SANCTIFIED

The explanation for this repetition seems to suggest a more fundamental difference between the two chapters. Following the death of Nadav and Avihu, Aaron and his remaining sons were commanded, "to distinguish between the sanctified and the profane, and between the impure and the pure; and to teach *Benei Yisrael* all of the statutes concerning which God has spoken to you by the hand of Moses" (Lev. 10:10–11). Following this, we find a series of sections that present these laws, beginning with the *parshiyot* dealing with ritual impurity and purity – the impure and pure animals, and the impurity related to animals (chapter 11); the ritual impurity of a woman who gives birth and the process for her purification (chapter 12); the impurity of *tzara'at* and its purification (chapters 13–14); the impurities associated with *zav, zava,* and menstruation (chapter 15); the purification of the *Mikdash* from the impurities of *Benei Yisrael* (chapter 16); and the conclusion of this unit – the impurity of the land, resulting from forbidden sexual relations, in chapter 18.[3] Hence, chapter 18 teaches us that the crux of the sin of forbidden sexual relations lies in the fact that it defiles the land. In verses 20–30 of this chapter, the root *t-m-a* (.א.מ.ט – impure) appears nine times, and at the conclusion

---

3. Chapter 17 appears, at first glance, unconnected to matters of purity and impurity, except for the final two verses (15–16), which discuss the impurity of a person who eats meat from a carcass (i.e., an animal that died in some manner other than ritual slaughter). In fact, this chapter seems to be an appendix to chapter 15 – the service of the *Kohen Gadol* on Yom Kippur – since it talks about the importance of an animal's blood as a means of atonement, the most extreme manifestation of which occurs in the atonement ritual described in chapter 15.

of the chapter, we are told explicitly that the concept of *tum'a* underlies these prohibitions:

> For all of these abominations were committed by the people of the land who came before you, *and the land was defiled.* So that the land shall not expel you *when you defile it,* as it expelled the nation that came before you. (vv. 27–28)

Eretz Yisrael is "pure," and it therefore cannot bear sins of sexual immorality. Transgression of these prohibitions thus leads directly to exile from the land.

In contrast, chapters 19–23 comprise a unit devoted to the distinction between the sanctified (*kodesh*) and the profane (*ḥol*); accordingly, our *parasha*, which opens this unit, begins with the command, "Be holy" ("*Kedoshim tiheyu*"). Chapter 19 presents the guidelines by which we achieve sanctity; chapter 21 deals with the sanctity of the *kohanim*, chapter 22 with the required protection of sacred items, and chapter 23 with the sanctity of the festivals. Thus, the discussion of sexual immorality included within this section – chapter 20 – accordingly addresses the subject not from the perspective of the land's impurity caused by such conduct, but rather from the perspective of the obligation to be holy. Indeed, this section begins: "You *shall sanctify yourselves and be holy,* for I am HaShem your God. You shall observe My statutes and perform them, I am God *who sanctifies you.*" The root *t-m-a* appears nowhere in the unit on sexual relations in chapter 20; instead, we find the root *k-d-sh* (קד.ש. – sanctify) appearing seven times. This latter root, needless to say, does not appear in chapter 18.

What is the difference between these two systems – impurity and purity, sanctity and profanity? The answer is simple. The natural state of all matter is pure, but profane. This situation can be changed in one of two ways: in the negative direction, it may be caused to become impure, or – in the positive direction – it may be sanctified. What the chapters on impurity actually require of a person is to avoid causing things that are pure to become impure. And should impurity indeed occur, these chapters present instructions for restoring the situation to a state of purity. In the chapters on sanctity, the situation is different.

Sanctity must be created, rather than merely preserved. Therefore, the laws of sanctity represent the way in which sanctity can be achieved; without them, sanctity will not come about at all.[4]

Eretz Yisrael is both pure and holy. *Benei Yisrael* are required to refrain from infringing upon its purity, on the one hand, and also, on the other, to express its sanctity. Transgression of the laws of forbidden sexual unions causes the land to become defiled, as described in chapter 18, but it also blemishes the land's sanctity, as we understand from chapter 20. This difference becomes especially apparent when we contrast the two parallel verses which describe the influence of these forbidden unions on the land. In chapter 18 we are told, "That the land shall not expel you *when you defile it*, as it expelled the nation that came before you" (v. 28), in accordance with the theme of this chapter. In chapter 20, however, we read, "That the land to which I bring you, to dwell there, shall not expel you" (v. 22). The defilement of the land is not mentioned in chapter 20; instead, the text mentions the unique stature of the land as the one to which God brings *Benei Yisrael*; herein lies the source of its sanctity.

This distinction also accounts for the discrepancy in the respective descriptions of the expulsion of the Canaanite nations. In chapter 18, the Torah emphasizes, once again, the aspect of impurity: "You shall

---

4. The distinction between the two systems finds special expression in the questions which the prophet Haggai is commanded to ask the *kohanim*:

On the twenty-fourth [day] of the ninth [month] in the second year of [the reign of] Darius, God's word came to Haggai the prophet, saying: So says the Lord of Hosts: Ask a teaching of the *kohanim*, saying, "If a man carries consecrated meat in the skirt of his garment, and the skirt touches bread, or pottage, or wine, or oil, or any other food – does it become holy?" They said, "No." Haggai said, "If a person who is impure because of contact with a dead body touches any of these things, does it become impure?" The *kohanim* answered and said, "It does become impure." Then Haggai answered and said, "Such is this nation; such is this nation before Me, says God, and such is all the work of their hands. That which they offer there is impure." (Hag. 2:10–14)

Impurity is created by contact, but contact is not sufficient to create sanctity. In this way, apparently, Haggai seeks to emphasize the effort that must be invested in order to achieve sanctity – as opposed to the danger of impurity, which can arise without any effort, even through unintentional contact.

not defile yourselves with all of these, for the nations which I cast out before you *were defiled* in them. So the land *was defiled*, and I visit its sin upon it, and the land expels its inhabitants" (vv. 24–25). In chapter 20, the concept of impurity is altogether absent: "Nor shall you walk in the ways of the nation which I cast out before you, for they did all of this, and I abhorred them" (v. 23).

This difference is also manifest – albeit in more limited fashion – in the details of the laws of forbidden unions. For example, concerning the prohibition of a menstrual woman, the formulation in chapter 18 emphasizes – expectedly – the aspect of impurity: "Nor shall you come close to a woman in *the impurity* of her menstruation, to uncover her nakedness" (v. 19). Chapter 20, meanwhile, focuses on a different element: "A person who lies with a menstrual woman and uncovers her nakedness, he has uncovered her fountain and she has uncovered the fountain of her blood; both shall be cut off among their people" (v. 18). We find a similar distinction with regard to the prohibition of "*eishet ish*" (adultery). In chapter 18, the Torah states: "Nor shall you lie with your neighbor's wife, *to defile yourself* with her" (v. 20), while chapter 20 teaches, "And anyone who commits adultery with another man's wife – who commits adultery with his neighbor's wife – shall surely be put to death; the adulterer and the adulteress." Likewise, chapter 18 formulates the prohibition of bestiality by emphasizing the element of impurity: "You shall not lie with any animal *to defile yourself with it*." Chapter 20, expectedly, makes no mention of this theme at all: "A woman who comes close to any animal, to lie down before it, you shall slay the woman and the animal; they shall surely die, their blood is upon them" (v. 16).

III. SEQUENCE OF PROHIBITED UNIONS

The division that we have proposed helps us understand yet another conspicuous difference between the two chapters, the sequence by which the respective lists of forbidden unions are arranged. In chapter 18, where the Torah focuses upon the aspect of impurity and defilement, the forbidden unions are arranged according to the degree of familial closeness, with the understanding that the closer the familial relationship between the two parties, the greater the impurity that results from their union. The following outline demonstrates this arrangement:

1. Verses 7–11: the closest of direct family relations: father, mother, father's wife, sister, son's daughter, daughter of father's wife;

2. Verses 12–14: the parents' siblings: father's sister, mother's sister, father's brother's wife (aunt);

3. Verses 15–16: wives of close relatives: daughter-in-law, brother's wife;

4. Verses 17–18: the wife's close female relatives: a woman and her daughter, a woman and her sister;

5. Verses 19–20: women with no family connection: a menstrual woman, another man's wife;

6. Verses 21– : other abominations: *Molekh*, homosexuality, bestiality.

In chapter 20, by contrast, the emphasis is on the severity of the sin. Sanctity flows from the Source of sanctity – from God – and the blemishing of sanctity is determined in accordance with the severity of the prohibition in the eyes of Torah. The severity of these prohibitions is not necessarily determined according to the measure of familial closeness; other parameters are involved, as well. Thus, the list in *Parashat Kedoshim*, which proceeds according to degree of severity, is arranged as follows:

1. Verses 10–15: prohibitions punishable by death: another man's wife, one's father's wife, his daughter-in-law; homosexual relations, a woman and her mother, bestiality;

2. Verses 17–18: prohibitions punishable by "*karet*" (being "cut off" from one's people): one's sister, a menstrual woman;

3. Verses 19–21: prohibitions with special punishments: the sister of one's father or mother – "they shall bear their sin"; uncle's wife – "they shall bear their sin, they shall die childless"; and brother's wife – "they shall be childless."

When considering these different sequences of presentation, an interesting difference emerges between the two *parashot* with regard to the prohibition of "*eishet ish.*" In chapter 18, the Torah places this prohibition near the end of the list (vv. 19–20), and hence the aspect of impurity here is less obvious, since it does not involve sanguinity, like the other prohibitions. This prohibition arises from a legal relationship, rather than from a natural, family relationship. For this reason, perhaps, specifically with regard to this law (as in the prohibition of a menstrual woman, which likewise does not arise from biological closeness, but rather from a temporary situation) the Torah must explicitly note that here, too, there is an aspect of "impurity," which is not mentioned in the previous prohibitions. By contrast, in chapter 20, the prohibition of *eishet ish* heads the list, because of its unique severity, as evidenced by this prohibition's inclusion in the Ten Commandments ("You shall not commit adultery").

Hence, observance of the laws of forbidden sexual relations involves two different aspects: refraining from defiling the land, and preserving its holiness.

Parashat Emor

Ḥametz and Matza: Between Pesaḥ and Shavuot

Rav Yoel Bin-Nun

I. INTRODUCTION – BETWEEN ḤAMETZ AND MATZA.

While Pesaḥ and Shavuot are linked by the counting of the *Omer*, they differ radically in their relationship to *ḥametz* and *matza* – on Pesaḥ *ḥametz* is forbidden and *matza* is compulsory, while the central sacrifice on Shavuot consists of two loaves of *ḥametz*. How are we to understand this? To properly explain of the significance of *ḥametz* and *matza*, and demonstrate that these are all details of a complete, unified system, we must analyze the various sources that appear throughout the Torah.

What is the essential, unifying concept behind *ḥametz* and *matza*? Leaven, *ḥametz* (and also honey, the jam of sweet fruits), represents the completed product of the farmer's work. Both *ḥametz* bread and the ripe, sweet fruits express the fulfillment of the successful process. They therefore also symbolize wealth and success, the abundant divine blessing of a person who has seen the realization of that which he had visualized at the start, and which he actively pursued.

In contrast, *matza* represents a station in mid-process, before the end result is achieved. It represents a deficiency that is waiting for completion. Similarly, salt (which must accompany every meal offering [2:13]) also expresses a raw, primal substance unprocessed by human hands; it is entirely a gift from God.

We may expand this idea somewhat and propose that *matza* – both practically and symbolically – is "poor man's bread"; it is the bread of someone who lacks the ability and resources to bring the material process to its completion in the form of a full, leavened loaf. *Ḥametz* – the leavening that allows the dough to rise and form a rounded cake – is the symbol of the wealthy person of means and power.

II. ḤAMETZ AND MATZA IN THE OFFERINGS

This understanding of the symbolism of *ḥametz* and of *matza* is the key to understanding all of the various contexts in which they occur in the Torah. Let us list them briefly:

- The Pesaḥ sacrifice: *Ḥametz* is prohibited, while there is a mitzva to eat *matza*.
- The Festival of *Matzot*: *Ḥametz* consumption is prohibited and punishable by *karet*, while *matza* is ubiquitous. Here, the context of the prohibition for all future generations is anchored in the *matza* baked during the Exodus from Egypt (Ex. 12:39).
- The *omer* offering and the two loaves: The *omer* offering of non-*ḥametz* barley brought on "the day after the Sabbath" (Lev. 23:15–16), meaning, according to Ḥazal, on the second day of the Festival of *Matzot*, is followed by a fifty-day count until the offering of the two loaves on the *bikkurim* holiday, where *ḥametz* is mandated (Lev. 23:17).
- *Minḥa* (the meal offering): All meal offerings sacrificed on the altar are *matza* and not *ḥametz* (Lev. 2:11–12).
- *Korban toda* (thanksgiving offering): This offering includes three types of *matzot* along with one type of *ḥametz* (Lev. 7:12–13).
- *Korban hamiluim* (consecration offering): Like the offering of thanksgiving, there are three types of *matza* involved (Ex. 29:2, also Lev. 8:26), as indicated in the Mishna (Menaḥot 7:2). However, unlike the thanksgiving offering, there is no *ḥametz* in this offering.

- *Nazir*: "On the day that his nazirite vow is fulfilled," the *nazir* brings a burnt offering, a sin offering, and a peace offering. Along with the peace offering he brings two types of *matzot* (Num. 6:15), and the Mishna (Menaḥot 7:2) points to the fact that these are two of the three types offered in the thanksgiving offering.

- *Minḥat ḥinnukh* (meal offering of inauguration): This meal offering was brought by every *kohen* on the day of his inauguration into the service of the Sanctuary, and by the *Kohen Gadol* upon assuming this position. Like the "consecration offering," the inaugural offering also involves only *matza*, with no *ḥametz* (Lev. 6:12–16).

- The prohibition of bringing *ḥametz* on the altar: "For you shall not burn any leaven nor any honey in an offering to God" (Lev. 2:11). Therefore, even the offering of the two *ḥametz* loaves on Shavuot are brought to the altar and are waved before God, but are not offered upon the altar itself. The same applies to the first fruits of "honey" – i.e., the honey of the sweet fruits.

III. THE ROLE OF ḤAMETZ AND MATZA IN PERSONAL OFFERINGS

Like prayer, the offering that a person brings upon the altar is an expression of Man standing before God, filled with a sense of his own lowliness and insignificance, with a corresponding sense of how beholden to and dependent he is on God (see 1 Chr. 29:10–15). A person cannot stand before the altar with a pride that declares his independence, as in the verse, "My strength and the might of my hand have achieved all of this valor" (Deut. 8:17). A sacrifice offered with such a feeling would be an act of impudence, of pride and arrogance – one of the most serious transgressions in man's relationship with God.

For this reason, "You shall not burn any leaven, nor any honey" – the symbols of wealth and the sense of satiety – "in an offering to God" (2:11). Even the first fruits (*bikkurim*) that are brought to the Temple with a ceremonial declaration (Deut. 26:2), which serves to inculcate recognition of God's role in one's success, are not offered upon the altar, since they are not offered like "the prayer of a poor man when he is faint, who pours out his case before God" (Ps. 102:1).

Not coincidentially, rabbinic tradition identifies leaven with the evil inclination (*yetzer hara*). A person who is blessed with an abundance of physical health and material assets – even if rooted in *Eretz Yisrael* – may fall into a false sense of might and independence, and forget God, "who gives you the strength to perform valor" (Deut. 8:17–18). This corresponds to the *yetzer hara* that tempts a person, especially on settling in *Eretz Yisrael* (see Deut. 8, and the song of *Ha'azinu*, Deut. 32).

Therefore a person is obligated to remember his humble beginnings – his servitude, his wandering in the wilderness, and the manna of the Exodus – specifically at the hour of his great prosperity in *Eretz Yisrael*:

> You shall remember all of the way that HaShem your God has led you for these forty years in the wilderness … in order to make it known to you that man does not live by bread alone, but man lives by all that emerges from God's mouth. (Deut. 8:2–3)

This is also the significance of the *bikkurim* recitation, reminding the bearer of his forefathers' affliction and wandering specifically at the time of celebrating his successful and abundant harvest and the bringing of the first fruits.

IV. SACRIFICE OF THANKSGIVING

An offering of thanksgiving is brought by a person who faced some danger or predicament and was delivered from it. Therefore, when he is saved, it is indeed proper that his offering include both *ḥametz* loaves and *matzot*. The *matzot* symbolize the trouble that he was in, the bitter cry that he uttered, and the process of redemption from that predicament. The *ḥametz* represents the completion of his deliverance and his current state of tranquility; it is an expression of reaching the end of this particular road, the attainment of peace and satisfaction.

V. CONSECRATION OFFERING AND MEAL OFFERING OF INAUGURATION

This sacrifice is offered by the *kohanim* as they commence their service. This auspicious occasion signifies the *beginning* of a period that continues for as long as the *kohen* serves in his capacity. Therefore it is appropriate that the offering include only *matza* without *ḥametz*.

VI. SACRIFICE OF THE *NAZIR*

Analyzing the *nazir's* sacrifice in accordance with the principle set forth above sheds new light on the nazirite status. Nazirite abstention is not an end in itself, but rather a period of preparation for a more elevated and perfected life afterwards. The entire experience is orientated towards the future: "*Thereafter* the *nazir* may drink wine" (Num. 6:20). In other words, the *nazir* returns to normalcy on a higher level, with improved spiritual protection against deviation and attraction to wine. He is now able to drink wine in a state of moral purity.

For this reason, "on the day that his period of separation is fulfilled," the *nazir* offers only *matzot*, without *ḥametz*. The conclusion of his nazirite abstention is not an objective or achievement; rather, it is the beginning of a more perfected and noble way of life. His great mission of living a better life actually begins only when the nazirite abstention ends. There is no justification for an indulgent celebration with loaves of *ḥametz* when his vow ends. Rather, he behaves like a *kohen* who is entering his service. He offers two of the *matzot* that are included in the consecration offering.

VII. THE *MATZA* OF THE PESAḤ OFFERING
AND THE FESTIVAL OF *MATZOT*

We can now apply this principle to the *matza* that characterizes Pesaḥ. Concerning the Pesaḥ sacrifice the Torah speaks of "the bread of affliction," not only because of the haste with which it was baked, but also because those who left Egypt were indeed oppressed refugees, setting out on a long journey through the wilderness (Deut. 16:3).

On Pesaḥ eve, *Benei Yisrael* were still in Egypt; they were still Pharaoh's slaves until midnight. Under such conditions, there is no place – either at that time or on Pesaḥ eve for all later generations – for *ḥametz*. At midnight, God struck all the firstborn of the land of Egypt, and redeemed His nation from its imprisonment. Generations of spiritual and physical subjugation were brought to a sudden end with the long-awaited fulfillment of the promised redemption. Seemingly, the nation should now have been able to lounge about like free people, setting a festive banquet table and singing praise and thanks in a relaxed atmosphere, with rich bread. But it suddenly becomes clear just how far the redemption is from being complete:

> And the Egyptians pressed upon the people, to send them out of the land in haste ... and the people took their dough before it was leavened – their kneading troughs bound up in their clothes upon their shoulders. (Ex. 12:33–34)

The people embark on a long, arduous journey "in the great and terrible wilderness of snakes and scorpions and thirst, where there is no water" (Deut. 8:15). Before they have a moment to relax and enjoy their freedom, filling their lungs with the clear air of freedom, they are already gasping in their hasty flight to a land of arid desolation.

Apparently, redemption is a prolonged, difficult process requiring endurance and a patient capacity for discomfort; the ability to achieve the desired level of prosperity and comfort is not yet in their hands. "*Ḥametz*" lies beyond the horizon for them. When *Benei Yisrael* leave Egypt, all that they have is their *matza* – the bread of affliction (Ex. 12:39).

Their ongoing sustenance as fleeing refugees continues to be provided not by their own efforts, but rather as a kindness from Above: "They asked and He brought quails, and He satisfied them with bread from the heavens. He opened the rock and water gushed forth; it ran in dry places like a river" (Ps. 105:40–41).

For this reason, *ḥametz* is strictly forbidden for all generations specifically on the days following the anniversary of the Exodus from Egypt. The *matza* that is eaten for the seven days of the "Festival of *Matzot*" expresses the true redemption – with all of its trials and tribulations; an ongoing redemption comprising many stages.[5] The prohibition of *ḥametz* highlights the absence of an instantaneous complete redemption

---

5. We see from here the importance of thanking God for the beginning of the redemption – even though it does not yet include either Torah or Shabbat, neither the Land of Israel nor a Temple, while, at the same time, appreciating that the beginning of the redemption is not the same as its completion.

– emphasizing that the *ḥametz* of Shavuot is not within reach immediately after the Pesaḥ. The danger of expecting "instant *ḥametz*" (i.e., that things should immediately become easier, more comfortable, perfect), which is quite understandable and natural to a redeemed nation, explains the severity of the prohibition that distances us from it (the need to remove it from the house, and the "*karet*" punishment for eating it during the holiday of *matzot*).

This tortuous path that starts with freedom from subjugation, ultimately leading to the hoped-for peace and tranquility of *Eretz Yisrael* at the end of the journey, finds expression in the counting of fifty days from the beginning of the harvest (Deut. 16:9), from the day when the *omer* offering is brought, until the festival of the harvest – which is the day of the first fruits, on the day following the end of the seventh week.

VIII. SHAVUOT'S TWO LOAVES OF ḤAMETZ AND THE ENTRY INTO THE LAND

The day of the *bikkurim* represents the conclusion of the process, the attainment of its real and metaphoric fruits. This conclusion is expressed on two levels. The first, a veiled allusion, leads from the Exodus to Sinai and the giving of the Torah. The second, open and explicit, expresses permanent habitation in *Eretz Yisrael*. Both levels come together and connect with the day of *bikkurim*.

The entry into the land and the permanent habitation in it are mentioned explicitly on this day:

> Until the day after the seventh week you shall count fifty days, and you shall offer a new meal offering to God. *From your habitations* you shall wave two loaves of two tenth measures; they shall be of fine flour, they shall be baked as *ḥametz*, they are first fruits to God. (Lev. 23:9–17)

The Festival of Shavuot, which is also the harvest festival and the festival of *bikkurim*, is therefore an agricultural celebration in all of these senses. It is the beginning of the wheat harvest in the Land of Israel, and thus it is the day of bringing the two loaves of *ḥametz* – the climax of the beginning of the harvest, which began with the *omer* offering.

The first aspect – the conclusion of the process that began with the Exodus from Egypt, and which reached its climax at the giving of the Torah – is likewise connected, albeit indirectly, with the day of *bikkurim*. While the connection is not explicitly indicated in the text, it nevertheless arises from the structure of the text and from the broad parallel between the giving of the Torah and the giving of the land. I shall elaborate on this point because of its fundamental importance, arising from the rabbinic identification of Shavuot with the time of the giving of the Torah.

The time when *Benei Yisrael* gathered in order to receive the Torah is mentioned in the Torah: "In the third month from *Benei Yisrael's* Exodus from Egypt, on that day they came to the wilderness of Sinai … and Israel encamped there before the mountain" (Ex. 19:1–2). This refers to the first day of the third month (Sivan) of the first year of the Exodus. Even one who claims that the actual date in the third month is missing would have to admit that the giving of the Torah clearly took place close to the fiftieth day, with the commemoration being based on the fifty-day count alone.

An exact parallel to this is to be found in the original plan for the desired arrival of *Benei Yisrael* in Kadesh Barnea, the southern gateway to the land of Israel, in anticipation of the conquest. The original plan for the journey seems to have been aimed at the same date as the arrival on site for the giving of the Torah, one year later – in other words, Rosh Ḥodesh Sivan in the second year. *Benei Yisrael* left Sinai on the twentieth day of the second month (Num. 10:11–13), and the Torah describes the journey from there to Kadesh Barnea as an eleven-day journey (Deut. 1:2).

Taken together, these two sources indicate that *Benei Yisrael* were supposed to reach Kadesh Barnea on Rosh Ḥodesh Sivan in the second year – exactly a year after arriving at Mount Sinai. Furthermore, each journey is presented as a direct continuation of Pesaḥ. In the case of the giving of the Torah, the connection is manifest; after all, *Benei Yisrael*, as well as the Egyptians, had been told in advance that the objective of the journey was to serve God in the wilderness on their way from Egypt, "This shall be the sign for you that I have sent you: when you take the people from Egypt, you shall serve God upon this mountain" (Ex. 3:12).

Like the Exodus from Egypt, the journey to Israel, in the second month of the second year, comes as a continuation of the Pesaḥ commemorated in the wilderness (Num. 9:1–14). These two periods share much in common, and this is reflected in various commentaries.

The description of God's giving of the land, like His giving of the Torah, appears not in the Torah itself, but in Joshua, owing to the various travails along the way. Some of the early troubles caused a delay of a month (Num. 11:19–20), such that *Benei Yisrael* arrived at Kadesh Barnea after the intended time of the wheat harvest, during the "time of the first of the grapes" (Num. 13:20). Thus it was their arrival at the peak of summer, in their exhausted and weakened state, that led to God's decree for weeping for all generations.[6]

While the covenant of the Plains of Moab is presented as a parallel to the covenant of Horeb (compare Deuteronomy 4–5 with 27–28), the occasion that is most reminiscent of the gathering at Sinai is recorded in Joshua, in the conquest of Jericho. The beginning of this process parallels the Exodus from Egypt – the parting of the Jordan unquestionably parallels the splitting of the Red Sea – in terms of the nature of the event, its description, and its psychological effect on all the surrounding kings (compare Joshua 5:1 to Exodus 15:15–16). Indeed, the parallel is given explicit expression in Psalms 114: "The [Red] sea saw it and fled; the Jordan was turned back," with both events introduced with, "When Israel came out of Egypt."

The circumcision in Gilgal is likewise an integral part of the exodus from the wilderness, which is somewhat like a renewed Exodus from Egypt, being defined as the point of severance from Egypt and all that it symbolized:

---

6. Physical and spiritual fatigue go hand in hand. With the desert sun burning overhead, the people want to remain at the oasis of Kadesh Barnea. The initiative to send spies may be interpreted as an attempt to postpone the journey. The punishment – "measure for measure" – is that the people miss the most opportune time for a speedy, surprise campaign of conquest, and wait in the wilderness for an entire generation. This, it seems, is what motivated Ḥazal in their formulation of the fundamental connection between mourning and the months of Tamuz and Av: "The Holy One, blessed be He, said: You wept for nothing; I will establish a weeping for all generations" (Ta'anit 29a, and Yerushalmi, ad loc.).

And God said to Joshua: This day I have rolled the reproach of Egypt from upon you. (Josh. 5:9)

For all the people who left [Egypt] had been circumcised, while all those who were born in the wilderness, *on the way from leaving Egypt*, had not been circumcised. (5:5)

The parallel between the entry into the land with the Exodus from Egypt holds the key to the meaning of the "reproach of Egypt" referred to in the verse cited above,[7] and also hints to the circumcision that preceded the Exodus from Egypt, which had been only indirectly referred to in the Torah.

Finally, the Pesaḥ offering observed by *Benei Yisrael* on the plains of Jericho is a fundamentally necessary precondition to the conquest. Just as there is a Pesaḥ sacrifice in anticipation of the Exodus from Egypt, there is a Pesaḥ sacrifice in anticipation of the conquest of the land.

The conclusion that arises from the above analysis is that the Exodus from Egypt represents the point of departure for a dual process. Its goal is, on the one hand, the giving of the Torah, and, on the other hand, the giving of the land – which is the clearly stated objective of the Exodus in many sources (see, for example, Leviticus 25:38). Since the giving of the land was not achieved by the generation that left Egypt, the renewed effort to reach the land in the time of Joshua starts off with the splitting of the Jordan, a mass circumcision, and the Pesaḥ in Gilgal – a replay of sorts of the Exodus from Egypt.

This parallel between the giving of the Torah and the giving of the land is clearly borne out in Joshua:

---

7. The difficulty lies in the phrase, "the reproach of Egypt." It seems that the proper explanation is based on the documented assumption that the Egyptians practiced circumcision, and scorned *Benei Yisrael* for failing to observe it – based on their understanding of the covenant of circumcision as fundamentally bound up with *Eretz Yisrael*. Thus, the "reproach" – the foreskin – was removed from them for the first time in a mass circumcision prior to leaving Egypt, and then at the second mass circumcision in preparation for the conquest of the land (Josh. 5:2) – thereby emerging completely from both slavery and their status as "uncircumcised." The "reproach of Egypt" was removed from them and they merited the land of their inheritance.

- Mount Horeb (Sinai) and Jericho are both defined as "hallowed ground," where an angel of God appears to the prophet, God's emissary. In the case of Moses, this happens at the burning bush, at the mountain of God at Horeb (Ex. 3:1–5). In the case of Joshua, this happens at Jericho (Josh. 5:13–15).
- In the description of God's appearance before *Benei Yisrael*, before the giving of the Torah, the shofar blast announces God's revelation (Ex. 19:16). The shofar is, of course, a central element in the fall of Jericho.
- Both at Sinai and in Joshua, a six-day waiting period is followed by a climatic seventh day. In Joshua, *Benei Yisrael* circle the city daily for six days, and on the seventh day, they circle seven rounds, shofars blowing. The content and style of these verses clearly parallel the experience at Sinai, including the preliminary six days followed by a definitive seventh day:

> God's glory rested upon Mount Sinai, and the cloud covered it for six days, and He called to Moses on the seventh day out of the midst of the cloud. (Ex. 24:16)

It is also interesting to note that according to the prevailing view in the midrashim, the seventh day on both occasions – the Revelation at Sinai and the gathering at Jericho – took place on Shabbat. (This is the opinion of R. Yossi in the Gemara [Ta'anit 28b; Yoma 4b; Shabbat 86b]. The Yerushalmi asserts that "Joshua's conquest of Jericho took place on Shabbat.")

The intrinsic reason for this parallel lies in the fact that at Jericho, as at Sinai, there was a revelation and descent of the Divine Presence; an occasion of God's judgment – of Israel, on the one hand, and of the land of Canaan and its inhabitants, on the other, ascertaining that the "sin of the Emorites" is complete (see Gen. 15:16). The "Ark of God, Master of all the earth" (Josh. 3:13) which goes around the city, and the sounding of the "*shofarot* of ram's horns before the Ark of God" (6:13), proclaim that "the supreme, awesome God, King over all the earth…sits upon the throne of His holiness" (Ps. 47:3, 10), and that this represents "a judgment of the God of Jacob" (ibid., 81:5). Therefore, at that moment, "It is holy ground!"

This may shed light on the verse: "Jericho was tightly shut up before *Benei Yisrael*; none emerging and none entering" (Josh. 6:1). The inaccessibility is not only a technical problem arising from the barred gates. *Benei Yisrael* may not enter because a place where the Divine Presence appears is out of bounds to them, just as Moses is commanded to set bounds around the mountain and sanctify it, "Lest they break through to God to gaze and many of them perish" (Ex. 19:21).

IX. CONCLUSION

We have found that the day of *bikkurim*, fifty days after the Pesaḥ sacrifice, expresses the conclusion and ultimate purpose of both the Exodus from Egypt and the beginning of the *omer* that is harvested in the land – both regarding the giving of the Torah and the giving of the land, and that these two themes are interwoven in the Torah itself as in the tradition of *Ḥazal*.

Therefore, the essential uniqueness of this day lies in the commandment of the two loaves, which are specifically *ḥametz*, with no *matza* at all – as a sign that the ultimate purpose of the Exodus from Egypt has been achieved. It is now proper and appropriate to set a festive table, to celebrate in tranquility, in the land of our inheritance, the completion of the Exodus and the completion of the counting of the harvest, and to bring a meal offering of *ḥametz*, first fruits to God, as a special communal sacrifice, from the Land of Israel.

Between the Sacred and the Profane:
The Unique Nature of Sukkot

Rav Mordechai Breuer

I. REASONS FOR THE FESTIVAL

The theme of the Festival of Sukkot is explained in many places in the Torah. In Exodus it is called *"Ḥag HaAsif"* – the Festival of Ingathering (23:16; 34:22). In addition, it is stated that the festival is celebrated "when you have gathered in your labors out of the field" (23:16). Similar wording is found in Leviticus (23:39) and in Deuteronomy (16:13) as well. We see from this that Sukkot is an agricultural festival, on which Israel expresses its gratitude to God for blessing the land and its produce.

This theme of Sukkot also finds expression in the festival's unique mitzvot. The commandment to rejoice is mentioned three times in connection with Sukkot (Lev. 23:40; Deut. 16:14, 15), whereas with respect to Shavuot it appears only once (Deut. 16:11), and is not mentioned at all regarding Pesaḥ. Gathering in the year's produce is indeed cause for rejoicing. For this reason, rejoicing begins on Shavuot, when the grain harvest comes to a close. We have all the more reason to rejoice on Sukkot, which marks the end of the ingathering of all of the year's produce. *Ḥazal* said: "The time of rejoicing extends from the Festival of Shavuot to the Festival of Sukkot" (Pesahim 36b); and the Festival of Sukkot itself is called "our time of rejoicing."

The commandment to take the four species that is recorded in Leviticus (23:40) seems to be connected as well to the agricultural element of Sukkot. Abarbanel states this explicitly in his commentary: "The four species of the *lulav* were taken in order to bring them joy and to thank God for the ingathering of the produce."

Another theme of Sukkot seems to find expression in the unique commandment to dwell in a *sukka*. This mitzva is accompanied by a reason: "That your generations may know that I made the Children of Israel dwell in booths, when I brought them out of the land of Egypt" (Lev. 23:43). Sukkot is not only an agricultural holiday, but also a holiday with historical significance. It reminds Israel of the kindness that God performed for them in the wilderness after having taken them out of Egypt.

These two meanings of Sukkot are expressed in the two names that were given to the holiday, for it is called both "*Hag HaAsif*" and "*Hag HaSukkot*" (the Festival of Booths). As *Hag HaAsif*, it has agricultural meaning, and as *Hag HaSukkot*, it has historical significance. These two aspects of the holiday are connected in various ways to the festivals that precede them. *Hag HaAsif* is a direct continuation of Shavuot, also known as "*Hag HaKatzir*" (the Festival of the Harvest). *Hag HaSukkot* is a direct continuation of *Hag HaMatzot* (the Festival of *Matzot*), for on *Hag HaMatzot* the People of Israel remember the unleavened bread they ate when they left Egypt, and on *Hag HaSukkot* they remember the booths in which they lived in the wilderness following the Exodus from Egypt.

The date that the Torah chooses for Sukkot can be explained in similar fashion. Sukkot is celebrated "when you have gathered in your labors out of the field" (Ex. 23:16), and also "on the fifteenth day of the seventh month" (Lev. 23:34). Both of these times are consistent with the agricultural significance of the festival. It is fitting that the Festival of Ingathering should fall in mid-Tishrei, at the end of the summer. In contrast, the time for gathering in the produce is irrelevant to the booths in which Israel dwelt in the wilderness. However, if we consider Sukkot a historical continuation of Pesah, which we celebrate on the *fifteenth day of the first month* (Nisan), then it is perfectly fitting to remember the booths of the wilderness on *the fifteenth day of the seventh month*.

This clear parallel between Pesaḥ and Sukkot exists because the whole purpose of the Exodus from Egypt – to bestow nationhood and identity as God's chosen people upon the enslaved Israelites – was only truly achieved and perfected in the wilderness. While we certainly celebrate the physical exodus of the People of Israel from Egypt, it was only in the wilderness that they merited the Shabbat, the revelation at Mount Sinai. and the giving of the Torah. Because of this, we celebrate Pesaḥ and Sukkot as two complementary festivals, as each contributed significantly to the birth of *Am Yisrael*.

II. SUKKOT AND AGRICULTURE

This dichotomy that we established between the agricultural aspect of Sukkot and the historical aspect of Sukkot does not adequately account for all the passages in the Torah that deal with Sukkot. It can be applied to the passage in Exodus, for there the holiday is called "*Ḥag HaAsif*," and it is observed "when you have gathered in your labors out of the field" (23:16). It can also be applied to the passage in Leviticus, where it says that the festival is observed "on the fifteenth day of the seventh month, when you have gathered in the fruit of the land" (23:39). The wording here is consistent with both the agricultural and historical significance of the festival. Accordingly, the Torah goes on to list all the special mitzvot of the festival: the mitzva regarding the four species and that of rejoicing (40), which express the agricultural meaning of the festival, and the mitzva to dwell in a *sukka* (42), which expresses its historical meaning. However, if we look at the passage in Deuteronomy that discusses Sukkot, we see that the name of the festival and the time of the festival do not match according to our explanation. The festival is called "*Ḥag HaSukkot*" (16:13), but instead of a historical reference to the fifteenth day, as we might expect, we find that the time of the festival is "when you have gathered in your corn and your wine." Moreover, the commandment to rejoice, which we established as a distinctly agricultural element, is also present (14–15). It is therefore difficult to understand why, in this context, the festival is called *Ḥag HaSukkot*, which expresses only the festival's historical meaning.

It was apparently for this reason that Rashbam reinterpreted the mitzva of *sukka*. In his opinion, this mitzva is also connected exclusively to the agricultural aspect of Sukkot. He writes:

You shall observe the Festival of Sukkot, after you have gathered in your corn and your wine, after you have gathered in the produce of the land and your houses are filled with all goods, corn, wine, and oil, that you may remember that I made the Children of Israel dwell in booths for forty years in the wilderness, without settlement or inheritance, and from that you will offer thanksgiving to Him who gave you an inheritance and houses filled with all goods. And you shall not say in your heart, "My power and the might of my hand have gotten me this wealth." And therefore they leave their houses filled with all goods at the time of ingathering and dwell in *sukkot* as a reminder that they did not have an inheritance in the wilderness or houses in which to dwell. And for this reason, the Holy One, blessed be He, established the Festival of Sukkot at the time of the ingathering of the corn and wine, so that your hearts not become lifted up because of your houses that are filled with all goods, lest you say, our hands have gotten us this wealth. (Rashbam, Leviticus 23:43)

According to Rashbam, the agricultural aspect of Sukkot is not limited to the mitzva of the four species and the mitzva of rejoicing. In fact, even the mitzva of *sukka*, which we assumed was strictly historical in nature, seems to carry agricultural importance as well: We thank God for providing us with "all goods, corn, wine, and oil," while recalling for contrast our sojourn in the wilderness when we lacked these things. Rashbam's idea – that agricultural celebration characterizes every facet of the Festival of Sukkot – requires further analysis.

III. THE EXODUS AND THE WILDERNESS

There are two adjacent passages in Deuteronomy that recount, respectively, the Exodus from Egypt and the period of the wilderness: the final ten verses of chapter 7 and the first eighteen verses of chapter 8. The first passage commands the People of Israel to remember the Exodus: "You shall well remember what HaShem your God did to Pharaoh, and to all Egypt" (7:18); whereas the second passage commands the people to remember "all the way which HaShem your God led you these forty years in the wilderness" (8:2). The two different objects of remembrance correspond to the different subjects of the two passages. The first passage is directed at the People of Israel as they stand poised to conquer the land. The Torah is concerned that Israel will say in their hearts: "These nations are more than I; how can I dispossess them?" (7:17). The Torah therefore answers that they should remember all of God's deeds – "the great trials which your eyes saw" (7:19) – at the time of the Exodus, so as to prepare them to wage war against the kings of Canaan. Not only do both events place Israel against kings of the nations – Pharaoh of Egypt and the thirty-one kings in the land of Canaan – but both share a common theme. When Israel was subjugated to Egypt, the very existence of the nation was in peril, and Israel could only be saved by God's miraculous intervention. The same was true at the time of the conquest of the land. Every war is liable to end in defeat, and defeat endangers the very existence of the people. All the more so in a war waged against a multitude of nations, which surpassed Israel in both power and numbers. For this reason, Israel was commanded to remember the Exodus from Egypt at the time of the war over the land of Canaan – to remind them that the same "mighty hand" that took them out of the land of their servitude would guide them in their conquest of the land of their inheritance.

It is surely appropriate for those who are preparing to conquer the land of Canaan (the subjects of the first passage) to recall the Exodus from Egypt. But for those who are already living in the land (the subjects of the second passage), this is not so. For this latter group, there is no longer any struggle between them and the other nations; Israel's existence is not in danger. Therefore, there is no need for miraculous intervention. Israel dwells in peace and security – each man under his grapevine and under his fig tree. The land yields its produce in a natural manner, as is the way of the world. Furthermore, this land "is a good land, a land of water courses, of fountains and depths that spring out of valleys and hills; this is a land of wheat, and barley, and vines, and fig trees, and pomegranates; a land of olive oil and honey" (8:7). But it is precisely for this reason that the spiritual existence of the people is threatened, for Israel is liable to think that they no longer need God's help to ensure their continued existence in the land. With their power and the might of their hand they bring forth their bread from the land, and increase their herds and flocks, their silver and their gold; and "they no longer remember that it is God who gives them the power to get this wealth." They trust only in themselves and their resourcefulness to continue their success in the land.

It is, therefore, not enough to remember the Exodus in order to be saved from this dangerous way of thinking. At the Exodus, God's hand was made known only by way of a one-time miracle of redemption from the hand of the enemy, but God's power to ensure sustenance, day after day and year after year, had not yet been revealed. For this reason, the People of Israel are now commanded to remember primarily the period of the wilderness. During the period of the wilderness, Israel learned that even their daily bread depended on that which "proceeded from the mouth of God" (8:3). God not only redeems Israel from the one-time danger of destruction, but also sustains the whole world with goodness, and gives food to all creatures. This faith is the primary lesson of the period of the wilderness, and Israel is bound to preserve it, when they dwell in their land generation after generation. Israel is charged to view their existence in the Land of Israel as a continuation of their journey in the wilderness; even when they are supported by the land in a natural manner, they should see themselves as eating manna coming down from heaven. This faith is not easily acquired. It is easy to see God's hand in a one-time act of salvation; it is much more difficult to see His hand in day-to-day natural existence. The blessing recited over redemption breaches forth from the heart spontaneously; the Grace after Meals requires training that is only acquired with great faith.

This relationship between redemption and sustenance finds clear expression in the following midrash:

> Rabbi Elazar says: "Redemption is compared to sustenance and sustenance is compared to redemption. As it is stated: 'And He has delivered us from our enemies,' and this is immediately followed by: 'Who gives bread to all flesh' (Ps. 136:24–25). Just as

redemption involves miracles, so too sustenance involves miracles; just as sustenance is every day, so too redemption is every day." (Genesis Rabba 20:22)

Scripture equates redemption with sustenance. A person is saved from danger each and every day simply by receiving sustenance every day and continuing to thrive. Indeed, daily sustenance is a divine miracle, no less than one-time redemption.

It seems that the complementary themes of redemption and sustenance find expression in the two great holidays that open and close our cycle of biblical festivals. Pesaḥ expresses the miracle of one-time redemption, as the *matzot* that we eat proclaim that God is Israel's redeemer. In contrast, Sukkot expresses the miracle of day-to-day sustenance, as the *sukkot* in which we dwell inform the nature of our continuing existence in the Land of Israel. A person should think of the house that he inhabits all year long as a *sukka* as well: "That I made the Children of Israel dwell in booths, when I brought them out of the land of Egypt" (Lev. 23:43).

From all this we learn that Sukkot is not a festival that embraces two distinct meanings, the agricultural meaning as *Ḥag HaAsif* and the historical meaning as *Ḥag HaSukkot*. Rather, the meaning of Sukkot is solely agricultural. Even in its identity as *Ḥag HaSukkot* it remains the Festival of Ingathering. The mitzva of *sukka* is not an independent commandment that serves to remind us of the booths in the wilderness. Rather, the purpose of the mitzva of *sukka* is to define the nature of the Festival of Ingathering. On *Ḥag HaAsif* we dwell in booths, and express thereby that it was not our power or the might of our hand that made us this wealth, but rather, it was God who gave us the power to make this wealth. He who caused us to dwell in booths in the wilderness is He who caused us to dwell in the Land of Israel to eat of its fruit and be sated with its good. Therefore, we eat and are sated, and we bless God for the good land which He has given us.

According to this, we can understand why Deuteronomy refers to the festival as *Ḥag HaSukkot* even though the festival recorded in that passage fits the description of *Ḥag HaAsif* ("when you have gathered in your corn and your wine") and the mitzva to rejoice is mentioned there twice. The mitzva of *sukka* is one of the mitzvot of *Ḥag HaAsif* – and *Ḥag HaAsif* is itself *Ḥag HaSukkot*.

IV. THE *SUKKA* OF THE FARMER

We have established that a parallel exists between Pesah and Sukkot, one that is deeply rooted in the character and nature of the two holidays. But just how far does this parallel go? Should we suggest that every element that we find in Sukkot has an equivalent counterpart in Pesah? If we accept this proposition, we would see dwelling in a *sukka* on Sukkot and eating *matza* on Pesah (the eponymous mitzvot of their respective holidays) as basically parallel; just as there is a mitzva to eat *matzot* on Pesah in order to remember the *matzot* of the Exodus, there is a mitzva to dwell in a *sukka* on Sukkot in order to remember the booths from the time of the wilderness. But this similarity between eating *matza* and dwelling in a *sukka* does not find expression in the wording of the Torah. Pesah is mentioned in the Torah in seven different places,[8] and in each of those seven places it is stated explicitly that there is a mitzva to eat *matzot* during the seven days of the festival. In five of those seven places, it says that the mitzva is a reminder of the Exodus from Egypt.[9] The Festival of Sukkot is also mentioned in the Torah in seven places.[10] However, the mitzva to dwell in a *sukka* is mentioned only once: "You shall dwell in booths seven days; all that are home-born in Israel shall dwell in booths" (Lev. 23:42). Only there is it stated that the *sukka* is a reminder of the booths in the wilderness. This difference between the mitzvot of *matza* and *sukka* is especially striking in the passages from Leviticus and Numbers, and, to a lesser degree, the passages from Deuteronomy. Let us first analyze the two parallel verses in Leviticus:

Pesaḥ	Sukkot
And on the fifteenth day of the same month is the Festival of *Matzot* to God; seven days you must eat *matzot*. (23:6)	The fifteenth day of this seventh month shall be the Festival of Sukkot for seven days to God. (23:34)

---

8. Exodus 12:14–20; 13:3–10; 23:15; 34:18; Leviticus 23:6–8; Numbers 28:17–25; Deuteronomy 16:3, 4, 8.
9. This reason is given in all four sources from Exodus and in the source from Numbers.
10. Exodus 23:16; 34:22; Leviticus 23:33–36; 39–43; Numbers 29:12–38; Deuteronomy 16:13–15; 31:10–13.

In both of these verses, mention is made of the name of the festival: *Ḥag HaMatzot* and *Ḥag HaSukkot*. But in the context of Pesaḥ, mention is also made of the mitzva of eating *matzot*. On the other hand, regarding Sukkot there is no hint of the mitzva of dwelling in a *sukka*.

We find a similar disparity in Numbers:

Pesaḥ	Sukkot
And on the fifteenth of this month is the festival: Seven days shall *matzot* be eaten. (28:17)	And on the fifteenth day of the seventh month you shall have a holy gathering…and you shall keep a feast to God seven days. (29:12)

Neither of these two verses mentions the name of the festival. Nevertheless, the first verse mentions the mitzva of eating *matza*, whereas the second verse does not even hint at the mitzva of dwelling in a *sukka*.

This phenomenon appears in Deuteronomy as well. The passage here does not mention *Ḥag HaMatzot* by name, but only describes the Paschal offering. Nevertheless, this passage too commands the people to eat *matza* for seven days. It also explicitly states that the *matzot* serve as a reminder of the Exodus. In contrast, this passage does refer to *Ḥag HaSukkot*, but still neglects to mention the mitzva of dwelling in a *sukka* or its significance as a reminder of the booths in the wilderness.

The reason that the Torah offers for the mitzva of dwelling in a *sukka* – remembering the booths of the wilderness – raises a problem. This reason resembles the reason the Torah offers for the mitzva of eating *matza*, the common denominator being that the Torah relates both of them to an event connected to the Exodus. However, only the reason given for eating *matza* is readily understandable, for we were told in the story of the Exodus that the dough of those leaving Egypt did not have time to rise, and therefore they baked it as *matzot*. In contrast, dwelling in a *sukka* was never described previously in the Torah. It seems that the booths were not an essential element of the journey in the wilderness. It is therefore difficult to understand why it was precisely dwelling in a *sukka* that the Torah chose to symbolize the journey in the wilderness.[11]

Based on this, it appears that dwelling in a *sukka* must have an additional meaning, one that is not connected to its function as a mitzva, nor associated with the booths of the wilderness. This meaning is apparently so simple and self-evident that there was no need for the Torah to explicate it.

It is the way of farmers to dwell in booths when they gather in their crops, as their fields and vineyards are far from their houses. During the harvest, people leave their homes and set up "a shelter in a vineyard, a lodge in a garden of cucumbers" (Is. 1:8). They remain in these booths for many days over the course of the hot months of the summer. When the ingathering comes to the end, they celebrate the Festival of Ingathering in those booths, in which they had lived during the entire period of ingathering. In this way their work site becomes transformed into a place of celebration. It was in these booths that the farmers saw that God had blessed the work of their hands. From there they went out each morning to gather in God's blessing, and it was to there that they returned each evening to rest from the day's work. It is therefore only natural that they should later celebrate God's festival in those booths, thanking Him who sent them His blessing. Just as it is only possible to relate the story of the Exodus when the *matza* and *maror* "rest before you" (*Mekhilta DeRabbi Yishmael, Bo* 17; and the Haggada), so too it is only possible to recite a blessing over the ingathering when a person dwells in the booths of the ingathering and all the blessing of the ingathering "rests before you."

This explanation for the significance of the *sukkot* of the festival is self-evident, and there was no reason for the Torah to spell it out explicitly. The Festival of Ingathering is the most natural festival of every people. The agricultural ingathering is the foundation of every human

---

11. This question resolves itself according to the view of Rabbi Akiva that "the booths were clouds of glory" (Sifra on Leviticus 23:42). It is possible that Rabbi Akiva said this in order to answer this question. It stands to reason, however, that the plain sense of the verse follows the viewpoint of Rabbi Eliezer, in that midrash, that "they were booths, literally."

society; it is, therefore, self-evident that the people should celebrate a national festival at the end of the period of ingathering. It is also self-evident that the ingathering celebration should be conducted in the booths of the ingathering. These are all things that the Torah did not have to state explicitly, because the natural conditions that arise on their own from human nature are not decreed by the Torah, but are sanctified with its commandments. They are the givens of the mundane world, upon which the Torah builds its holy edifice. It was also unnecessary to say that the Festival of Ingathering is also the Festival of Sukkot, and that it is celebrated in booths. But the Torah did have to say that Sukkot should be celebrated as a holy festival for God. For in the mundane world, Sukkot is celebrated as a festival for man, as it is man who conquered nature and harnessed it to his ends; by the sweat of his brow he worked his land, until it bore him fruit. When natural man gathers the produce of his land, he is proud of his power and of the might of his hand, which made this wealth for him. Thus he dwells in his mundane booth and celebrates the festival of ingathering – for himself. In the Torah's holy world, however, Sukkot is celebrated for God. The celebrants know that it is God who gives them the power to make this wealth. It is He who blessed the fruit of their land, and it is only by virtue of this blessing that the land yielded its produce and the trees of the field sent out their fruit. They dwell in the booths of ingathering, they eat, drink, and rejoice, and they bless God who blessed the work of their hands. In this way these mundane booths are transformed into holy *sukkot*, in which the *Shekhina* dwells.

In light of this, we can understand why the Torah did not explain the meaning of the *sukka* in most of the passages dealing with Sukkot. What is more, the very mention of the mitzva of *sukka* is neglected in these passages, for the *sukka* of the festival is fundamentally a mundane booth, in which the Festival of Ingathering would have been celebrated even in the absence of a mitzva. Just as the ingathering itself is not an inherently sanctified act, so too the act of dwelling in a *sukka* during the period of the ingathering and during the Festival of Ingathering is not inherently sanctified either. It is precisely because the *sukka* is fundamentally a mundane booth that it becomes a resting place for the sanctity of the day and it becomes sanctified as a result. For Sukkot is entirely a festival for the Land of Israel; on it the People of Israel thank God for having brought them to a comely land to eat of its fruit and be sated with its good.

V. THE SACRED AND THE PROFANE

Indeed, dwelling in the Land of Israel itself is a fundamentally mundane act. Israel dwells in it the same way that every nation dwells in its land. Nowhere does the Torah say that the Land of Israel is holier than all the other lands: The Torah does not call the Land of Israel a king's palace, or claim that its climate makes one wise, or that it is uniquely disposed for prophecy and the presence of the *Shekhina*. Rather, the Torah praises the Land of Israel, saying that it is a land flowing with milk and honey, that it has abundant water and exemplary fruit. All these virtues are in the realm of the mundane, and similar virtues are found in other lands in which other nations dwell. It is precisely because the Land of Israel is fundamentally a mundane land that it is more sanctified than all other lands, that it becomes the dwelling place of the *Shekhina*, and that prophets and holy men issue from it. God does not rest His *Shekhina* on a people whose sanctity is only evident in holy places and in holy times and in people specially designated for holiness. Rather, the *Shekhina* rests on a people who sanctify mundane life and whose sanctity is evident in mundane times and places. For this reason, the Torah only lists the virtues of the Land of Israel as a mundane land, for these trees and these stones, among which the people lead their mundane lives, become the chariot for the *Shekhina*, and it is in them that the holiness of the Land of Israel finds expression.

Consequently, this mundane nature of the Land of Israel applies equally to Sukkot, the festival of the Land of Israel. It is celebrated in connection with the mundane ingathering, and on it people dwell in mundane *sukkot*. But these fruits that were gathered and these *sukkot* in which the people dwell are, in fact, holy fruits and holy *sukkot*, for they symbolize Israel's ability to elevate mundane life and imbue it with holiness. The *sukka*, in which the festival of the Land of Israel is celebrated, is itself the Land of Israel in miniature. In it one eats and drinks and performs mundane acts, and all these acts become sanctified with the sanctity of the *sukka*, which is nothing less than the sanctity of the Land of Israel.

We can now understand the single passage in which dwelling in a *sukka* is described as a mitzva that serves to remind us of the period of the wilderness. This passage seems to contradict the explanation that we just delineated. The *sukka* is not described here as a booth of ingathering, in which one voluntarily dwells in order to celebrate the Festival of Ingathering. The *sukka* is now described as the booth of the wilderness, and we are commanded to dwell in that *sukka* in order to remember the booths that the People of Israel inhabited during the period of the wilderness. In truth, there is no contradiction, for the *sukkot* of ingathering are themselves the booths of the wilderness. Our existence in the Land of Israel is actually a continuation of our sojourn in the wilderness: He who caused us to dwell in booths in the wilderness is He who caused us to dwell in the booths of ingathering in the Land of Israel. And in the same way that He fed the People of Israel from heaven and caused water to issue forth for them from the rock of flint, He also continues to feed them from the fruit of the land and sates them with its good.

This idea helps to explain the relationship between the various passages that deal with Sukkot. In most of these passages, the *sukka* is merely a booth of ingathering, in which people dwell of their own volition. These passages express the deep meaning of Sukkot, that mundane dwelling in the Land of Israel is simultaneously holy dwelling, and that the mundane booths of the festival of ingathering are simultaneously holy *sukkot*. However, this notion assumes that Israel dwells in the land in full faith of the sanctity of Israel's mundane life, and that they recognize that their power and the might of their hands did not make this wealth, but rather, God gave them the power to make this wealth. When they dwell in the *sukkot* of ingathering in the Land of Israel they remember God, who fed and sustained them in the wilderness in a land that was not sown. Only when this assumption is true is the mundane *sukka* of ingathering transformed into a holy *sukka*, and the voluntary dwelling in this *sukka* turns into a sanctified dwelling of mitzva.

The Torah knows, however, that this assumption is not always valid, and there is great danger that Israel's *sukka* of ingathering will resemble the ingathering booths of the nations of the world, who on their ingathering festivals bow down to their own might and power and attribute their success to their own wisdom and understanding. For this reason, the Torah added a special mitzva in one of the passages dealing with Sukkot. In this passage the Torah itself turns the mundane booth of dwelling in the Land of Israel into a *sukkat mitzva* that reminds us of the period of the wilderness. The Torah does not completely rely on Israel to understand independently that the ingathering booth is but a continuation of the *sukkot* in the wilderness. Rather, it expresses this idea in the form of an obligating mitzva – the mitzva to dwell in a *sukka* on the Festival of Ingathering. By way of this mitzva, the *sukka* of the festival is transformed from a mundane *sukka* to a *sukkat mitzva*. The *sukka* of ingathering becomes the *sukka* of the wilderness, not just by virtue of the faith of those dwelling in it, but by virtue of the mitzva cast upon them.

VI. "THAT YOUR GENERATIONS MAY KNOW"

The mitzva of *sukka* is different in one respect from all the other mitzvot in the Torah. In the case of other mitzvot, a person fulfills his obligation even if he does not know the reason for the mitzva. In the case of *sukka*, however, a person can only fulfill his obligation properly if he knows why he dwells there. *"That your generations may know* that I made the Children of Israel dwell in booths, when I brought them out of the land of Egypt."* This distinction between *sukka* and the rest of the mitzvot is easily understood in light of all that we explained above. In all the other mitzvot, had the mitzva not been written in the Torah, people would not observe it. This principle applies not only to the received commandments, but even to the rational ones. Even rational mitzvot were written in the Torah on the assumption that people would be negligent in their observance were those mitzvot not recorded in the Torah as God's commandments. *Sukka* is different: It is clear that people would still dwell in a *sukka* on the Festival of Ingathering even had there been no mitzva to do so. The Torah itself assumes that the festival is observed in the booth of ingathering, which is why it is called Ḥag HaSukkot. Nevertheless, the Torah makes sure to explicate the mitzva of *sukka* in Leviticus 23:42. This command did not change anything on the practical level. Rather, it transformed the nature of the *sukka* and the reason for dwelling in it. It is no longer a booth of ingathering, in which people dwell in order to gather in the blessing of ingathering. Instead, it is the *sukka* of the wilderness, in which we dwell in order to remember that period in our people's history. From this it follows that a person only fulfills his obligation if he fulfills this novel component as well. One must dwell in the *sukka* not merely in order to collect the blessing of the ingathering of the Land of Israel, but in order to remember the booths that our forefathers inhabited during their sojourn in the wilderness.[12]

Let us recall that all of this is an expansion of Rashbam's viewpoint cited above. Rashbam understood that *sukka* is not an independent mitzva, detached from the agricultural meaning of *Ḥag HaAsif*. It comes to teach us that our houses that are filled with all that is good are merely a continuation of the *sukkot* in the wilderness. According to our modification of this view, the mitzva of *sukka* is not connected to the houses that we have filled with the blessing of the ingathering, but rather to the *sukkot* from which we went out to collect the produce. These booths of ingathering – and not our houses of plenty – are the continuation of the booths of the wilderness. When we dwell in these *sukkot* in the Land of Israel, we see ourselves as living in booths in a land that is not sown. And when we go out from these booths to gather in the produce of our land, we see ourselves as going out to collect manna and drink water issuing forth from the rock of flint. These mundane booths of ingathering, in which we dwell as a natural result of an agricultural lifestyle, are the very same booths that sheltered us long ago during our forty-year trek through the wilderness, when we left the bondage in Egypt to become God's people in the Land of Israel.

---

12. See *Baḥ, Oraḥ Ḥayim* 625:1, who derives from the language of the *Tur* that a person does not properly fulfill the mitzva of *sukka* unless he knows the reason for the mitzva. However, the reason for the mitzva that we proposed cannot be assigned to the *Tur* himself, for it is clear that the *Tur* explains the mitzva of *sukka* in line with Ramban, the first position cited above. According to this view, the mitzva of *sukka* is not at all connected to the agricultural aspect of Sukkot.

The Festivals of God: Mikra'ei Kodesh

Rav Baruch Gigi

The Torah discusses the festivals in several different places. Since each discussion presents different details regarding these laws, one who wishes to study the holidays must analyze all the sections in order to obtain a complete picture. This rigorous analysis lies beyond the scope of this essay; however, we may reasonably assume that each individual discussion of the festivals emphasizes a particular aspect of the Jewish holidays. Here we will try to understand the unique contribution of Leviticus 23, described by Ḥazal as "the order of Mo'adim" (Sifrei, Parashat Re'eh, 127). We will examine its place within the parashot dealing with the festivals, as well as within Leviticus.

I. DIFFICULTIES IN THE CHAPTER

The first difficulty presents itself at the outset of the parasha – the chapter opens with a discussion of Shabbat. The Rabbis ask, "What does Shabbat have to do with the festivals?" To this question we may add that the verses themselves indicate quite clearly that Shabbat should not be considered as one of the festivals. Firstly, the chapter ends, "These are the *festivals* of God...apart from the Shabbatot of God" (vv. 37–8). Furthermore, whereas the discussion of each festival receives its own introduction of "God spoke to Moses," only one such introduction appears for the first three together – Shabbat, Pesaḥ, and *Ḥag HaMatzot*. Seforno on verse 9 notes that in the Torah, the phrase "the Festival of the Pesaḥ" refers not to what we colloquially call "Pesaḥ," but to what we consider "Erev Pesaḥ" – the fourteenth of Nisan, on which the Paschal sacrifice is offered. The next seven days are exclusively referred to by the Torah as "*Ḥag HaMatzot*." Apparently, only *Ḥag HaMatzot* belongs to the category of the festivals, and the new speech to Moses relates to specifically that discussion.

Another indication that we should consider Shabbat differently from the festivals lies in the absence of the phrase, "You shall bring an offering by fire to God" regarding Shabbat. This brief mention of the *musaf* sacrifice appears with regard to each festival, but is absent in *Parashat Emor* regarding Shabbat.

Finally, there is the simple fact that Shabbat cannot be called a "*mikra kodesh*" – an occasion "*declared* sacred." The sanctity of Shabbat does not depend upon the declaration of the New Moon by the *beit din* (Jewish court); Shabbat is fixed, every seven days, regardless of when the court determines that the new month should begin. A *mikra kodesh* – a "declaration of sanctity" – is a day made holy by the court, and thus Shabbat seems to have no place in this chapter.

Among other difficulties, verse 5 mentions the Paschal sacrifice, offered on the fourteenth of Nisan (i.e., one day *before* the festival of *Ḥag HaMatzot*). This day, too, seems inappropriate in this context, as it is not a *mikra kodesh*. As well, the *parasha* omits all details regarding the *musaf* sacrifices of each festival, sufficing with a generic expression that repeats itself throughout: "You shall bring an offering by fire to God." As we know, the details are presented later in *Parashat Pinḥas*. Why not here?

Ramban claims that the *musaf* sacrifices were not offered in the wilderness, and therefore these laws appear only towards the end of Numbers, as *Benei Yisrael* prepared for entry into the Land of Israel. Later commentaries challenge his premise based on a statement in Talmud Menaḥot that implies otherwise.

The classical commentaries (Rashi, Ramban, and others) raise other issues, including the strange opening word of the discussion of Yom Kippur – "*akh*" ("however"), and the division of the section of Sukkot into two distinct sections, so that the verses dealing with Sukkot are interrupted by a concluding section: "These are the set times of God that you shall celebrate as sacred occasions" (37–38).

II. CHAPTER 23'S PLACE WITHIN LEVITICUS

The key to resolving these issues lies in the understanding of how this chapter relates to the rest of Leviticus. As a whole, Leviticus can be divided into two parts. The first deals with the laws of *korbanot* (sacrifices) along with *tum'a* and *tahara* (impurity and purity), thus rendering Leviticus worthy of the name Ḥazal assigned to it – "*Torat Kohanim*" (The Law of the *Kohanim*). The second half deals with issues of *kedusha* – holiness – in the more general sense of the term. It is within this framework that our chapter must be understood.

Chapters 19–22 deal with personal sanctity, dividing it into three levels:

1. The regular Jew: "You shall be holy, for I, HaShem your God, am holy" (19:2), continuing through the concluding verse, "You shall be holy to Me, for I, God am holy" (20:26);
2. The special sanctity of the *kohanim* (21:1–9);
3. The high level of sanctity of the *Kohen Gadol* (21:10–16). The Torah then elaborates on this level, enumerating the laws of *kohanim* unfit for service due to physical defects (end of chapter 21), the laws of *tum'a* as applied to *kohanim*, the *kedusha* of *kohanim* as relevant to the laws of *teruma*, and then, as an aside, the laws of animals unfit for sacrifice due to physical defects. This section of the sanctity of the human being concludes, "You shall not profane My holy Name … for I am God who sanctifies you" (22:32).

Chapter 23 brings us from the sanctity of the individual to the sanctity of time.

III. THE FESTIVALS OF GOD – SACRED OCCASIONS

In light of this analysis, it seems clear that our chapter intends merely to list those festivals whose sanctity results from the *beit din's* determination of the calendar – "These are My festivals … *which you shall proclaim as sacred occasions."* Therefore, the verses here present only those features that directly relate to this quality of *mikra kodesh* – having been declared sacred by the people. As such, three main points appear in the discussion of each festival:

1. *"mikra kodesh"*;
2. the prohibition of work;
3. a brief reference to the *musaf* sacrifice.

The essence of a *mikra kodesh*, which embodies the concept of the active sanctification of time, includes: (1) the prohibition of performing work; (2) festive attire and feasts (see Ramban, citing the Sifrei). The *musaf* sacrifices, however, do not reflect this quality, as a *musaf* sacrifice is required even on Rosh Ḥodesh, which does not constitute a *mikra kodesh* (see Arakhin 10b). Therefore, rather than presenting the *musaf* sacrifices in detailed fashion, our chapter merely makes a general allusion: "You shall make an offering by fire."

It should be noted that these elements are *components* of a *mikra kodesh*. The *definition* of a *mikra kodesh*, however, lies in its having been established by the *beit din*, which creates the sanctity and infuses it within a given time frame. Once the *beit din* has done so, these days turn into festivals of God, *"mikra'ei kodesh."*

IV. A SHABBAT OF COMPLETE REST – *MIKRA KODESH*

This distinction can help us understand the conceptual relationship between Shabbat and the festivals. Shabbat contains all the *components* of a *mikra kodesh*, but, fundamentally, it cannot be classified as such. The basic definition of this term involves a day declared holy by the Jewish court. In spite of this, the discussion of the festivals opens with Shabbat, since this section's theme is the sanctity of time. Such a concept is made possible only by the sanctity with which God Himself infused Shabbat during Creation. If not for the fact that "God blessed the seventh day and declared it holy," man would be totally incapable of sanctifying even a brief moment.

"You shall be holy, for I, HaShem your God, am holy." God is the source of *kedusha* in the world. Therefore, the sanctity of time draws its strength, as it were, from the sanctity of Shabbat that God Himself initiated. This may be the intent of Ḥazal, cited by Rashi (v. 3): "Whoever desecrates the festivals is considered as if he desecrated the Shabbat, and whoever observes the festivals is considered as if he observed the Shabbat." By extension, the recognition of the sanctity of the festivals automatically involves the recognition of the sanctity of Shabbat.

If this is how we are to understand the relationship between Shabbat and the festivals, then it stands to reason that the sanctity of the holidays is inferior to that of Shabbat. Shabbat constitutes the *source* of the *kedusha*; the sanctity of the festivals is merely derivative. This accounts for the more severe punishment meted out to Shabbat violators, as well as several other leniencies regarding Yom Tov.

The clearest expression of this hierarchical relationship between Shabbat and Yom Tov appears in the writings of the medieval talmudic commentator, Ra'avan (Pesaḥim, chapter 10):

> They therefore instituted [the text for *havdala* after Shabbat which occurs on a festival], "You separated between the sanctity of Shabbat and the sanctity of Yom Tov." This means that the sanctity of Shabbat is greater, since the Almighty sanctified it Himself, as opposed to Yom Tov, which Israel themselves sanctify, as it is written, "which *you* shall proclaim as sacred occasions." The festivals of God require the sanctification of *beit din*.

V. "IT SHALL BE A SACRED OCCASION FOR YOU; YOU SHALL AFFLICT YOUR SOULS"

As stated earlier, the essence of a *mikra kodesh* features, among other elements, festive eating and drinking. Therefore, the inclusion of the fast of Yom Kippur in our chapter seems, at first glance, problematic. Its inclusion underscores the fact that the critical issue involves the determination by the *beit din* of the festival, a point certainly as relevant to Yom Kippur as to any other festival. The fact that it lacks a critical component – eating and drinking – may account for the Torah's peculiar introduction to Yom Kippur, "*akh*" – "however." The added emphasis may be understood as teaching us that although not all the components of a *mikra kodesh* apply on Yom Kippur, nevertheless, "It shall be a sacred occasion for you." This unique dichotomy of Yom Kippur may also explain the Torah's emphasis regarding the two conflicting components of Yom Kippur – the prohibition of work (representing the *mikra kodesh*) and the requirement of fasting (the seeming antithesis of the *mikra kodesh*): "Indeed, any person who does not practice self-denial *throughout that day* shall be cut off"; "and whoever does any work *throughout that day*" (vv. 29–30). The Torah stresses that throughout this day, these two contradictory prohibitions apply.

VI. THE PASCHAL SACRIFICE

Earlier, we raised Seforno's question regarding the fourteenth of Nisan, the day of the offering of the Paschal sacrifice. The verses here in *Emor* mention this festival, despite the fact that this day seems not to belong to the category of *mikra kodesh*. One simple answer might be that this day appears here only by association with *Ḥag HaMatzot*, the seven-day festival that follows the Pesaḥ. This claim may be supported by the fact that no new introduction of the phrase, "God spoke to Moses saying," interrupts between *Ḥag HaPesaḥ* and *Ḥag HaMatzot*.

However, we may explain the inclusion of *Ḥag HaPesaḥ* differently, based on the first mishna of the fourth chapter of Pesaḥim (40b): "A place where the custom is to perform work on Erev Pesaḥ before noon – one may do work; a place where the custom is not to – one may not." After midday, however, one may certainly not engage in work. Tosafot there (citing the Talmud Yerushalmi) say that since the Paschal sacrifice may be offered from midday, performing work during such time would be highly inappropriate, and is thus forbidden. Although Ran questions whether this prohibition is of biblical or rabbinic origin, the simple reading of the passage in the Yerushalmi implies that the prohibition is, in fact, biblical.

If so, then the fourteenth of Nisan, the day on which the people offered the Paschal sacrifice, features at least one *mikra kodesh* quality, namely, a prohibition of work. However, since the prohibition of work does not evolve directly from the proclamation of the *beit din*, but rather from the concurrent offering of a sacrifice, it cannot be considered a *mikra kodesh* in the full sense of the term. Therefore, the Torah does not employ this expression in the context of the fourteenth of Nisan. Nevertheless, the Torah does see fit to make mention of this quasi-festival among the other festivals, as it does reflect one element of a *mikra kodesh*. (Another possible manifestation of the "festival" quality of the fourteenth of Nisan may be the "*ḥagiga*" sacrifice offered on that day; see Exodus 23:18.)

VII. THE *OMER* AND *SHETEI HALEḤEM* SACRIFICES

If the Torah chooses not to relate the *musaf* offerings here, why does it include the *omer* and *shetei haleḥem* sacrifices in this chapter? The answer relates to the fact that *Yom HaBikkurim* (the holiday we call "Shavuot") has no fixed calendar date; it occurs fifty days after the fifteenth of Nisan (Pesaḥ). In order to establish the festival of Shavuot as *mikra kodesh*, the Torah needs to record the entire process: the offering of the *omer* sacrifice on the sixteenth of Nisan, the counting of forty-nine days, and the offering of the *shetei haleḥem* sacrifice on the fiftieth day.

VIII. THE TWO MENTIONS OF SUKKOT

Finally, we must account for the peculiar division of the Torah's discussion regarding the Festival of Sukkot. It seems that only the first half – verses 33–36 – relate to the central theme of the chapter. These verses establish the first and eighth days of Sukkot as *mikra'ei kodesh*, during which work is forbidden. This information effectively concludes the discussion of this chapter – the concept of *mikra kodesh*. Naturally, then, these verses are followed by a concluding formula for the *mikra'ei kodesh* section. However, since the *omer* and *shetei haleḥem* sacrifices were previously mentioned, the Torah must, for purposes of literary consistency, record as well the "gathering sacrifice": "On the first day you shall take the product of *hadar* trees."

This second section does not relate at all to the concept of *mikra kodesh*, as clearly indicated by the absence of this phrase in these verses. For the same reason, the *musaf* sacrifice and the prohibition of work are also omitted. Since the Torah returned to the issue of the festivals after having already formulated a conclusion passage, a second conclusion is required: "Moses declared the festivals of God to *Benei Yisrael*." However, the term "*mikra kodesh*" does not appear in this second conclusion, but rather only in the initial conclusion: "These are the festivals of God that you shall celebrate as sacred occasions [*mikra'ei kodesh*]."

Holiness and Assault

Rav Mosheh Lichtenstein

P arashat Emor's central theme is the motif of *kedusha* – holiness – and its various manifestations. The idea of *kedusha*, as exhibited in the *kohanim* and offerings, on the one hand, and the sanctity of time itself (*kedushat hazman*) as expressed in the holidays on the other hand, is the basic concept developed throughout the *parasha*. Though each individual element represents a different aspect of divine sanctity, the overarching concept which informs them all and serves as the unifying principle which forges our *parasha* into a single entity is the manifestation of holiness within the human world. As the Torah itself proclaims: "*venikdashti betokh Benei Yisrael Ani HaShem mekadishkhem*." Even without attempting in our limited space to enter into the details of the *parasha*'s internal organization or to offer an explanation for its sequence, it may be claimed that there is a distinct topic which organizes the *parasha* into a single unit and integrates it into the broader scheme of Leviticus. Clearly the issues of *kedusha* and *Mikdash* are the connection between *Emor* and the preceding sections of Leviticus from the opening sections of *korbanot* in *Parashat Vayikra* and through the halakhot of the *kohanim* and holidays in *Emor*.

However, one part of the *parasha* – the concluding section – doesn't seem to fit at all into this pattern. The end of the *parasha* deals with the law concerning a person who assaults a fellow Jew, resulting either in murder or bodily injury, or inflicts damage upon his friend's livestock. These laws, which detail the punishment of the murderer and establish the requirement of monetary compensation in cases of violent assault, belong to the category of laws "*bein adam leḥaveiro*" – between a person and his fellow person – and seem to be totally unrelated to the context of *Parashat Emor* and its topic of *kedusha*. The logical place for these halakhot should be *Parashat Mishpatim*, the *parasha* which incorporates within it (almost) the entire corpus of *Ḥoshen Mishpat*, civil law. Torts, banking, civil law, commercial law, etc. are all dealt with at length in *Parashat Mishpatim*; the inclusion of these issues within *Parashat Emor* is puzzling.

Additionally, since all of these halakhot do in fact appear in *Mishpatim*, the question is not only whether they can be integrated into *Emor* or not, but also the issue of redundancy. All that is stated here has already been written there. Why then repeat the exact same verses? Even were we to grant that the issues of damages may have a place in Leviticus, there should still be no need, since they have already been covered previously.

Moreover, we must ask ourselves why the Torah appends the discussion of bodily damages to the story of the *megadef* – the blasphemous son of the Egyptian woman. Unlike the violent attacker, the *megadef* clearly belongs to *Parashat Emor*. Even though the story is a historical episode and not a halakhic dictate, unlike the rest of Leviticus (with the exception of the Nadav and Avihu episode), its purpose is to illuminate the concept of *kedushat HaShem*, its importance and gravity, and to highlight the dangers and difficulties involved in observing and respecting it. As such, it is an appropriate, if tragic, sequel to the *parasha*'s directive to lead lives of holiness and a vivid reminder of the need for constant vigilance in this endeavor. However, the transition, or rather the continuity, in the Torah from God's verdict regarding the *megadef* to the systematic exposition of the laws of physical assault is extremely difficult, since blasphemy and bodily harm would seem to be unrelated issues.

In order to resolve these questions, which mutually reinforce each other, we must adopt an entirely different perspective regarding the issue of violent assault. Though it is true that physical injury is an issue concerning the relationships between human beings and a crime committed against the injured party for which compensation is due, this is not the only element involved in murder or assault, nor is this the aspect which the Torah is relating to in Leviticus. The Torah is making the point that assaulting a human being is an assault upon God Himself. Man was created in God's image and his likeness is an expression and representation of the divine. The Divine Wisdom which willed the entire created world endowed Man with a unique charisma and entered into a special relationship with him. Not only was Man created in God's image, he also received the essence of his soul directly from God and his existence is by virtue of this contact with his Creator. (See Genesis 2:7 and Ramban's commentary there.)

Moreover, the unique and intimate relationship between God and Israel as His people, expressed and amplified in Tanach by means of the marital and conjugal metaphor, adds an additional dimension to the Jew as His representative within the created world.

Thus, Man, created by God in His image, endowed with the faculties of reason and spirit, is the supreme expression of the Divine Presence in the material world, so that he who strikes a blow against a fellow man is also striking a blow against his Creator. Therefore, the Torah deals with this issue in Leviticus, in addition to its previous treatment in *Parashat Mishpatim*. There the emphasis was upon the civil element and the injury inflicted upon the assaulted person is treated from the perspective of an injured party seeking compensation and remuneration; here, though, the focus is upon the sinner who has mutilated the divine image and sinned against God. The attack upon a human being is considered an act of desecration, *ḥillul hakodesh*, a prime topic of *Parashat Emor*.

This highlights the transition which the Torah makes from the *megadef* to the person who assaults a fellow human. Rather than being an abrupt and incomprehensible switch from an issue involving the human-divine relationship to a human-human relationship, they are both an expression of a blasphemous act which the Torah prohibits. The transition between the two is smooth and readily achieved, since they both address the same issue.

Though we are dealing with this issue at the hermeneutical level, it should be added that there are halakhic ramifications as well. The permissibility of suicide or self-inflicted wounds, the nature of the payment which one is obligated to give to the injured party, and various other details regarding these halakhot are all a function of this duality.

Actually, this concept which is explicitly formulated by the Gemara in Sanhedrin (58b), which states that "He who strikes the jaw of a Jew is like one who strikes the jaw of the *Shekhina*," expresses itself in many other halakhic instances, aside from the above-mentioned laws of assault. Thus, the Mishna in Sanhedrin (46a) interprets the prohibition of *halanat hamet* (delaying burial) along these lines, explaining that any diminution of human life is a diminution of the *Shekhina* itself and that any abuse of the human image is a defilement of the image of God which is reflected within Man. This same explanation is also true of *bal tashḥit*, the biblical injunction prohibiting wanton destruction. It is not only the ingratitude and thanklessness exhibited by unappreciative man towards the bounty awarded him by the compassionate Master of the world, but also the attitude displayed towards the Creator and His handiwork by the vandal which the Torah outlaws. The world is the concrete material expression which embodies the divine ideals as represented to us, and as such is deserving of our respect.

In conclusion, we must draw attention to the fact that if our analysis has so far been correct, then we must follow the Torah and ascribe certain value, above and beyond the monetary worth, to animal life. For the Torah did not conclude the *parasha* with the issue of assault committed against a human being, but added in the same group cases of a human striking an animal, and drew a clear parallel between the two. In the same manner that it distinguishes between assault (23:19) and murder (23:21), it distinguishes between killing and injuring an animal, "*makeh nefesh beheima*" (23:18) and "*makeh beheima*" (23:21). Though the practical bottom line – compensation – is the same in both instances, they are treated separately due to the fact that the issue is not an exclusively monetary issue, since there is the fact that he has killed the *nefesh beheima*. Any evil committed against God's handiwork reveals Man overstepping his boundary and challenging his God, be it a major or minor infraction.

It is this same arrogance and egocentrism of Man that the *parasha* of "*hovel umazik*" shares in common with *megadef* and it is this which places this *parasha* squarely within the framework of Leviticus, since the issue that the Torah is dealing with in this context, as in all of Leviticus, is the manifestations of *kedusha* within the human world and our reactions to them. The *megadef* and the *hovel*, the *ba'al hakorban* and the *kohen*, are all a response to the divine challenge to invest our world with *kedusha* and are, therefore, coupled together in the same *parasha*.

The Law of the Blasphemer

Rav Amnon Bazak

I. INTRODUCTION

Our *parasha* is the continuation of several chapters containing many commandments, a section that begins immediately after the sin of Nadav and Avihu in chapter 10. Suddenly, in the middle of chapter 24, the long list of commandments is interrupted for a moment, and the Torah reverts to its historical narrative with the case of the blasphemer:

> The son of an Israelite woman, being also the son of an Egyptian man, went out among *Benei Yisrael*. And this son of the Israelite woman quarreled with an Israelite man in the camp. The son of the Israelite woman blasphemed God's Name, and cursed. They brought him to Moses, and his mother's name was Shlomit, daughter of Divri, from the tribe of Dan; and they placed him in custody so that they could consult God. (24:12)

Following this episode, we find further chapters of commandments and instructions in *Parashot Behar* and *Beḥukkotai*, with the Torah once again leaving chronological history. This phenomenon raises the question: What is the meaning of this story, and why does it appear specifically here?

Further questions arise as we examine the incident more closely. From the description in the text, it would appear that the main problem was the cursing of God's Name, and that it was for this reason that the sinner was placed in custody.[13] The beginning of God's instruction to Moses seems to convey this impression:

> God spoke to Moses, saying: Remove the blasphemer from the camp, and let all those who heard place their hands upon his head, and let the entire congregation stone him. And speak to *Benei Yisrael*, saying: Any person who curses his God will bear his sin. One who blasphemes will surely be put to death, the whole congregation shall stone him. Stranger and native born alike – when he blasphemes, he shall be put to death. (vv. 13–16)

Surprisingly, following these words, there is a sudden transition to the laws of one who kills another person and one who kills an animal:

> One who kills any person shall be put to death. And one who kills an animal shall pay compensation: an animal for an animal. And one who maims his neighbor – as he has done, so shall be done to him – a fracture for a fracture, an eye for an eye, a tooth for a tooth; as he has maimed the person, so shall be done to him. And one who kills an animal shall pay compensation, while one who kills a person shall be put to death. There shall be one law for you, identical for the stranger as for one who is native born; for I am HaShem your God. (vv. 17–22)

---

13. Rashi understands this sin (*"vayikov"*) as "uttering a curse," as in, "How shall I curse (*mah ekov*)" (Num. 23:8); see Sanhedrin 56a. Ibn Ezra, on the other hand, raises two possibilities: "Some say that this means that he uttered God's Name explicitly, as in 'which God's mouth will express (*yikavenu*)' (Is. 62:2), or 'who were indicated (*nikvu*) by their names' (Num. 1:17). Others say that it is to be understood as in 'how shall I curse' (Num. 23:8); but the first [interpretation] is more accurate, in my view." In other words, to Ibn Ezra's view, the sin involved here is the actual utterance of God's name. From the context, however, Rashi's interpretation seems more logical; Rashbam concurs.

Only thereafter do we find the conclusion of the story:

> Moses spoke to *Benei Yisrael,* and they brought the person who
> had cursed outside of the camp, and they stoned him with stones.
> And *Benei Yisrael* did as God had commanded Moses. (v. 23)

What are the laws of damages doing in the middle of the story?

II. THE SON OF AN EGYPTIAN MAN

The verses emphasize the issue of nationality. The story of the blasphemer does not start out as a quarrel between two regular members of
Benei Yisrael; rather, the parties are "the son of an Israelite woman, being
also the son of an Egyptian man" and "an Israelite man." Perhaps the dispute erupted over money matters, and then the parties came to blows,
and for this reason the laws of civil damages and the laws of injuries are
bound together here. But then something unexpected happens – in the
heat of the argument, the son of the Egyptian man becomes enraged,
and he curses the Israelite man in God's name. In order to understand
the severity of this situation it must be noted that the only mention of
a similar incident in all of Tanach appears in the battle between David
and Goliath: "The Philistine said to David: Am I then a dog, that you
come at me with sticks? And the Philistine cursed David in God's name"
(1 Sam. 17:43).[14] What caused the blasphemer to act as he did?

The utterance seems to have emerged specifically because of the
blasphemer's problematic parentage – the fact that he was the son of
an Egyptian man. Attention should be paid to the fact that the Torah
does not identify the two quarreling men by name; the only name that
is mentioned is that of the woman who gave birth to a son fathered
by an Egyptian man. The price for this deed is paid by her son who, it
would appear, harbored a degree of alienation towards the nation that
had caused his father's people to suffer such terrible punishments. In a

---

14. This parallel seems to have guided R. Levi who teaches (Midrash Tanḥuma, *Emor,*
siman 23): "'The son of an Israelite woman ... went out' – from where did he go out?
R. Levi taught: He left his world, as it is written, 'a champion man went out' (1 Sam.
17:4)" – referring, obviously, to Goliath the Philistine.

moment of fury, his frustration exploded with such force that he cursed in God's name.

III. "IDENTICAL FOR THE STRANGER AS FOR ONE WHO IS NATIVE BORN"

Apparently it was specifically the blasphemer's complicated parentage that lay behind the initial uncertainty that led *Benei Yisrael* to place him in custody. Ramban engages in a lengthy discussion regarding the person's national identity, raising several possibilities – however, the very existence of this discussion proves that the status of the Egyptian's son was unclear. As a result of this complex status, then, it was not immediately obvious that he should be punished for his sin as any regular Israelite would be. For this reason, in the response to Moses, God emphasizes that the death penalty for blaspheming applies to any person dwelling in the Israelite camp: "One who blasphemes will surely be put to death, the whole congregation shall stone him. *Stranger and native born alike*; when he blasphemes, he shall be put to death" – just as all the laws of interpersonal relations apply to him as well: "There shall be one law for you, *identical for the stranger as for one who is native born*, for I am HaShem your God."

IV. THE BLASPHEMER AND THE GATHERER

There are several similarities between the incident of the blasphemer and that of the "gatherer of wood" in Numbers:

> While *Benei Yisrael* were in the desert they found a man gathering wood on the Shabbat day. Those who found him gathering wood brought him before Moses and Aaron and all the congregation. They placed him in custody, for it had not been declared what should be done with him. Then God said to Moses, "The man shall surely die; let the entire congregation stone him outside of the camp." So the entire congregation took him outside of the camp and stoned him with stones, and he died, as God had commanded Moses. (15:32–36)

Each of the stories describes a different sin, but in both cases, when the sinner is brought to Moses, he is placed in custody until his punishment is clarified. In both cases God tells Moses that he is to receive the death penalty, which is to be carried out outside of the camp by means of stoning at the hands of the entire congregation. Both stories conclude with a description of the execution: "They took the blasphemer outside of the camp and stoned him with stones, and *Benei Yisrael* did as God had commanded Moses" (Lev. 24);[15] "The entire congregation took him outside of the camp and stoned him with stones, and he died, as God had commanded Moses" (Num. 15).

Nevertheless, there are several differences between the two incidents. The most important and most obvious difference is that the story of the blasphemer includes a list of laws that Moses is commanded to transmit to the nation ("You shall speak to *Benei Yisrael*, saying"), concerning both the specific sin involved and the general framework of interpersonal laws, while the story of the gatherer of wood contains no such list, and Moses is not instructed to teach *Benei Yisrael* anything.

This difference appears to arise from what we have noted above. The principal innovation of the story of the blasphemer is that the laws of the Torah – both those between man and God and those between man and his fellow – apply to a stranger as well; therefore there is a need to repeat the laws relevant to the incident of blasphemy and to note that they apply to the stranger as well. In the story of the wood-gatherer, on the other hand, the doubt apparently concerned the specific question of whether gathering wood was considered a *melakha* (forbidden activity) on Shabbat; the verdict gave a clear answer to this question.

At this point we must take note of another difference between the two stories. Concerning the blasphemer, we are told: "Take the

---

15. Ramban perceives an important message in the mention of the execution of the punishment "as God had commanded Moses": "Thereafter the text repeats once again that *Benei Yisrael* did [as commanded]. The reason for this is in order to teach us that when Moses spoke to *Benei Yisrael*, they immediately took the blasphemer out [of the camp] and stoned him; all of Benei Yisrael did this with a view to observing and fulfilling as God had commanded Moses, *not out of hatred for the son of the Egyptian who had quarreled with the Israelite, but rather with a view to removing that which was rotten from amongst them.*" Seforno adds: "[Teaching] that they did not stone him out of *hatred for being a stranger* who quarreled with an Israelite, but rather they did it in order not to deviate from God's command."

blasphemer outside of the camp; let *all those who heard place their hands upon his head,* and let all the congregation stone him." When it comes to the wood-gatherer, we are told only, "The man shall surely be put to death; let all the congregation stone him with stones outside of the camp." What is the significance of having all those who heard placing their hands upon the head of the blasphemer?

Generally, the placing of hands is a symbolic gesture, "transferring" the sin, as it were, from the one who places his hands to the one upon whose head the hands are placed. This is the case concerning sacrifices, such as the burnt sacrifice: "He shall place his hand upon the head of the burnt sacrifice, and it shall be accepted from him, to atone for him" (Lev. 1:4). The same idea is expressed in the sacrificial service of the *Kohen Gadol* on Yom Kippur: "*Aaron shall place both his hands upon the head of the live goat,* and recite over it all the sins of *Benei Yisrael* and all their transgressions, for all their iniquities, and he shall place them upon the head of the goat, and send it by the hand of an appointed person to the desert. *And the goat shall bear all their sins* to a barren land, and he shall let the goat go in the desert" (Lev. 16:21–22). It seems that a similar action was required in the episode of the blasphemer, too. In contrast to the story of the wood-gatherer, in which the public was not involved in any way by the deed, in the case of the blasphemer, the effect of hearing his utterance was in itself harmful and required atonement. Through the "placing of hands" upon the blasphemer, he "assumed" the sin of the hearers, as well, and the damage of hearing his curse was thereby atoned.

This idea fits well with the stipulations of the *Torah Shebe'al Peh* concerning a blasphemer, as Rambam writes (*Hilkhot Avodat Kokhavim* 2:10):

> Anyone who hears a cursing of God must tear his garments (even for a curse by one of God's other names he must tear). This applies to one who hears it uttered by a Jew; both the person that hears and one who hears [second-hand] from the person who heard must tear…. All of the witnesses and the judges, one by one, place their hands upon the head of the blasphemer and say to him, "Your blood is upon your hand, for you have brought this upon yourself." Among all those who are put to death by the *beit din*

there is no other instance in which hands are placed upon some-one's head, except in the case of the blasphemer, as it is written, "all those who heard shall place their hands."

This brings us to the third difference. In the story of the blas-phemer, the people appeal to Moses alone – "They brought him to Moses" – whereas the wood-gatherer is brought before "Moses and Aaron and all of the congregation." I would like to suggest that bringing the blasphemer to Moses alone suggests a special reason to discuss this incident. We may note the connection between the beginning of the story – "The son of an Israelite woman, being also the son of an *Egyptian man, went out* among *Benei Yisrael*, and the son of the Israelite woman and [another] Israelite man *quarreled* in the camp," and the previous occasion of two men quarreling:

> And it was, during those many days, that Moses grew up *and went out* to his brethren, and he saw their suffering, and he saw *an Egyptian man* striking a Hebrew man, one of his brethren. He turned this way and that and saw that there was no-one, and he struck the Egyptian, and buried him in the sand. He went out on the second day and behold, two Hebrew men *were quarreling*. He said to the guilty party, "Why are you strik-ing your neighbor?" He answered: "Who made you a prince and judge over us? Do you mean to kill me, as you killed the Egyptian?" So Moses feared and said, "Indeed – the matter is known." (Ex. 2:11–14)

Many years previously, Moses had encountered two incidents of dispute between people. By nature, he was unable to remain silent in the face of injustice – neither when it came to blows by an Egyp-tian, nor when it came to aggression displayed by an Israelite. In the argument described in our *parasha*, Moses encounters the son of an Egyptian man who also adopts negative behavior in his argument with the Israelite. Perhaps, then, *Benei Yisrael* brought the man specifically before Moses, since they were aware of his sensitivity towards this type of behavior.

V. LOCATION OF THE *PARASHA*

We can now address the location of the story at this point in the text. Our *parasha* concludes the collection of chapters on sanctity in Leviticus (19–23), dealing with the sanctity of *Benei Yisrael*, of the *kohanim*, and of various occasions. Many verses in these chapters have emphasized the sanctity of the nation specifically in its distinction from other nations. For example, "You shall be holy to Me, for I, God, am holy, and I have distinguished you from the nations to be Mine" (Lev. 20:26); "You shall not desecrate My holy name, and I shall be sanctified amongst *Benei Yisrael*; I am God who sanctifies you, who has brought you out of the land of Egypt, to be your God" (22:33–34). Interestingly, one of the clear expressions of the sanctity of *Am Yisrael* concerns guarding speech and avoiding cursing:

> You shall sanctify yourselves and be holy, for I am HaShem your God. You shall observe My statutes and fulfill them; I am God who sanctifies you. For any person who curses his father and his mother shall surely die; he has cursed his father and his mother; his blood is upon him. (20:7–9)

A direct, practical expression of the command to *Benei Yisrael* to be holy is the prohibition of cursing one's parents, and the death penalty for this sin. The same idea applies even more strongly when it comes to God. The sanctity of *Benei Yisrael* finds expression in having been taken out of Egypt. Now, in our *parasha*, the son of an Egyptian man comes and curses God.

In order to illustrate briefly the significance of Israel's inherent holiness, the Torah records the unfortunate story of one who was not included in that sanctity, and the price for his mother's damage to the sanctity of Israel. The story of the blasphemer, then, is a tragic description of the phenomenon of intermarriage and assimilation.

Parashat Behar

The Structure of Shemot and Vayikra

Rav Menachem Leibtag

Shouldn't *Parashat Behar* be in Exodus? After all, the opening verse informs us that these mitzvot were given on Mount Sinai! Why did the Torah postpone it for Leviticus instead?

To complicate matters, *Parashat Behar* is only one example of many *parashot* towards the end of Leviticus that appear to belong in Exodus. The law to light the Menora, recorded at end of *Parashat Emor* (24:1–3), is almost a direct quote from *Parashat Tetzaveh* (Ex. 27:20–21).

To answer these questions, we shall investigate the possibility of an underlying structure that may explain what otherwise seems to be the random progression of *parashot* and topics in Leviticus.

I. INTRODUCTION

Leviticus contains primarily mitzvot, and neatly divides into two distinct sections – chapters 1–17 contains laws for the *kohanim* relating to the *Mishkan* itself, and chapters 18–27 contain laws relating to living a life of sanctity, *kedusha*, even outside the *Mishkan*. This reflects God's words to *Benei Yisrael* before Sinai, "You will be a nation of priests (*kohanim*) and a holy nation (*goy kadosh*)." However, while this definition neatly explains the progression of mitzvot between *Parashot Aḥarei Mot* and

Kedoshim, many of the laws in *Parashat Emor* appear to contradict this definition.

As the following summary shows, most of the mitzvot in *Parashat Emor* relate to the *Mishkan* itself, and hence should have been recorded in the first half of Leviticus.

- Chapter 21 – Laws pertaining to *kohanim;*
- Chapter 22 – Animals not fit for offering;
- Chapter 23 – Special offerings offered on the holidays;
- Chapter 24 – Oil for lighting the Menora; and baking the *leḥem hapanim.*

Based on the above outline of Leviticus' two halves, these topics would apparently fit better in the first half.

To complicate matters, at the very end of *Emor,* we find a different type of difficulty. In 24:10–23, we find a narrative – the story of an individual who cursed God's name in public and was subsequently punished. Not only is this story totally unrelated to either half of Leviticus, it is the only narrative in the entire book (aside from the story of the dedication of the *Mishkan* and the aftermath found in chapters 8–10, as it relates to the *Mishkan* itself).

Similarly, *Parashat Behar* is no less problematic. Even though the laws of *Shemitta* and *Yovel* fit nicely into our definition of the second half of Leviticus (see Ibn Ezra 25:1), the opening and closing verses present us with two different problems. The first verse informs us that these mitzvot were given on Mount Sinai (rather than at the *Ohel Mo'ed*), and hence suggests that this entire section should belong in Exodus! More disturbing is *Parashat Behar*'s conclusion, where three powerful verses appear, seemingly out of context with what has been discussed:

> For *Benei Yisrael* are servants to Me, they are My servants whom I freed from the land of Egypt, I am HaShem your God. Do not make for yourselves any other Gods…. Keep My Sabbath and guard My temple, I am your God. (25:55–26:2)

While the first verse forms a nice summary to the laws of that unit (25:47–54), the last two laws are totally unrelated! Furthermore, all three verses contain echoes of the first four of the Ten Commandments.

The above questions appear to shake the very foundation of our understanding of the two halves of Leviticus. Should we conclude that Leviticus is simply a random collection of mitzvot? The solution I will suggest is based on an amazing idea that I heard many years ago from Rav Yoel Bin-Nun.

II. THE STRUCTURE

To answer the above questions, we must first re-examine each of the *parshiyot* (mentioned above) to determine where each of these out-of-place sections really does belong, starting with the first topics in chapter 24.

1. The *Ner Tamid* (24:1–4)
   The four verses describing the mitzva to light the Menora with olive oil are almost an exact repetition of the first two verses of *Parashat Tetzaveh* (Ex. 27:20-21).

2. The *Leḥem HaPanim* (24:5–9)
   These verses describe how to prepare the *leḥem hapanim* (showbread) that was to be placed on a weekly basis on the table located inside the *Mishkan*. Even though this is the first time that we find the details of this mitzva in the Torah, the general mitzva to put *leḥem hapanim* on the table was already mentioned in *Parashat Teruma* (see Exodus 25:30).

3. The *Mekallel* (24:10-23)
   Even though this section begins with a story (see 24:10–12), this short narrative leads directly into a small set of civil laws, that are almost identical with Exodus 21:12, 23–25 in *Parashat Mishpatim*.

4. The Laws of *Shemitta* and *Yovel* (25:1-25:54)
   As we explained above, these mitzvot were given to Moses at Mount Sinai. However, in Exodus, we find many other laws recorded in *Parashat Mishpatim* that were given at Mount Sinai. In fact, the basic laws of *Shemitta* have already been mentioned:

"Six years you shall sow your land and gather your produce and the seventh year" (Ex. 23:10-11).

5. The "Mini-Commandments" (25:55-26:2)
   We noted that the three verses at the very end of *Parashat Behar* echo the first four Commandments. If so, then these verses belong in *Parashat Yitro* (Ex. 20:1–9).

III. BACK TO EXODUS

We see that not only do all of these sections belong thematically in Exodus, they progress in backward order, from *Tetzaveh*, to *Teruma*, to *Mishpatim*, to *Yitro*. Even though this order may seem to be simply coincidental, the next chapter in Leviticus (chapter 26 – the *Tokheḥa*) provides additional circumstantial evidence to suggest that this pattern may be intentional. The *Tokheḥa* explains the reward (or punishment) that *Benei Yisrael* receive should they obey (or disobey) God's laws. This constitutes an integral part of the covenant between God and *Benei Yisrael* that was enacted at Mount Sinai (see Deut. 28:69).

Even though this covenant is detailed in *Parashat Beḥukkotai*, its basic principles were first recorded in *Parashat Yitro* in the Torah's account of the events that took place at Mount Sinai: "And now, if you shall listen to Me and keep My covenant faithfully, then" (Ex. 19:5-6, compare carefully with Lev. 26:3, 12, 23).

Therefore, even though this section is thematically consistent with the theme of Leviticus' second half, nonetheless, it was given to *Benei Yisrael* on Mount Sinai, and could easily have been included in *Parashat Yitro*, most probably in chapter 19. (See also *Ḥizkuni* on Exodus 24:7 and Ibn Ezra on Leviticus 25:1, where they explain that the *Tokheḥa* was actually read at the giving of the Torah at Sinai.)

IV. COMPLETING THE STRUCTURE

In addition to the above, we see that previous sections in Leviticus fit into this pattern. The Torah presents the holidays (*Parashat HaMo'adot*, 23:1-44) in chapter 23, together with the laws of Shabbat. Again, although these laws relate thematically to the theme of *kedusha* in the second half of Leviticus, they also relate to the laws of Shabbat that conclude the *parshiyot* concerning the *Mishkan* (see Exodus 31:12-17, 35:2-3), and could have been recorded in *Parashat Ki Tissa* together with the laws of Shabbat.

Before this, we find a discussion of animals that cannot be offerings (22:17-33), including an animal with a blemish, or an animal less than eight days old. This commandment clearly should have been recorded in *Parashat Vayikra*, belonging thematically in the book's first half, for it discusses the various types of animals which one can bring as an offering.

Finally, *Parashat Emor* opens with laws that explain when a *kohen* may and may not become *tamei* (21:1–22:6). Though these laws thematically relate to the second half of Leviticus (for they govern the daily life of the *kohanim* outside the *Mishkan*), nonetheless the mitzvot that follow should have been recorded in *Parashat Tzav*, for they concern who can and cannot eat the meat of the sacrifices.

In summary, even though each of the above *parshiyot* may be thematically related in one form or other to the theme of the second half of Leviticus, nonetheless each section could also have been recorded either in the second half of Exodus (or early in Leviticus) as well.

What we discover is a literary style known as a chiastic structure (A-B-C-B1-A1). This structure is common in the Tanach, and serves to emphasize unity of theme and accentuate a central point. Therefore, to uncover the structure's significance, it is usually critical to identify its central axis. To accomplish this, we will first summarize the basic units of mitzvot (in Exodus) which *Benei Yisrael* receive from the time of their arrival at Mount Sinai, and then their parallels in the latter *parshiyot* in Leviticus. The following chart illustrates the resulting structure:

A. *Brit* – before *Matan Torah*
B. Commandments
C. Mitzvot – given at Mount Sinai, after *Matan Torah*
D. *Mishpatim* – civil laws
E. Construction of the *Mishkan*
F. Shabbat (and holidays)
G. Offerings of the individual
H. *Kohanim* – how to sacrifice
I. The *Shekhina* rests on the *Mishkan* during its dedication

I1. The *Shekhina* rests on the camp due to the holy behavior of the people

H1. *Kohanim* – who cannot offer

G1. Offerings – what cannot be an offering

F1. Holidays

E1. Menora and *Shulḥan*

D1. *Mishpatim* in aftermath of the *Mekallel* incident

C1. Mitzvot at Mount Sinai, *Shemitta* and *Yovel* (*Behar*)

B1. "Mini-Commandments"

A1. *Brit* – the *Tokheḥa* (*Beḥukkotai*)

It should come as no surprise that at the thematic center of this structure – part I – lies the dual theme of Leviticus – i.e., its two sections: (1) the *Shekhina* dwelling on the *Mishkan*, and (2) its subsequent effect on the nation.

This model reflects how the intense level of *kedusha* in the *Mishkan* impacted on the spiritual character of the entire nation, in all realms of daily life. Furthermore, this idea reflects the basic theme of *Maʿamad Har Sinai* in Exodus, the opening leg of the chiastic structure. When the Jews first entered into a covenant before they received the Torah at Mount Sinai, God spoke as follows:

> And if you listen to Me and keep My covenant…then you shall be for Me, a kingdom of priests and a holy nation (*mamlekhet kohanim vegoy kadosh*). (Ex. 19:5-6)

The achievement of this goal – to become God's special nation – as detailed in the "bookends" of this structure (A and A1), is made manifest by the dwelling of God's *Shekhina* in the *Mishkan* (I) – at the center of this structure; and is achieved by the fulfillment of God's commandments as detailed throughout this entire unit of Exodus and Leviticus.

The thematic significance of this chiastic structure is strengthened by its closing. Just as *brit Sinai* – the covenant at Mount Sinai – is the opening *parasha*, the details of that covenant – the *Tokheḥa* of *Beḥukkotai* – constitutes its closing *parasha*. Additionally, the *Tokheḥa* explains how the Promised Land will serve as God's agent to reward

Benei Yisrael, should they be faithful to His covenant, while the Land will punish (and ultimately expel them) should they go astray.

Finally, we note how the mitzvot of Leviticus (G, H, I) – that were given from the *Ohel Mo'ed* (see 1:1) – are surrounded by mitzvot that were given *"beHar Sinai"* (A, B, C, D, E, F). Considering that the entire purpose of the *Mishkan* was to serve as a vehicle to perpetuate the fundamentals of *Ma'amad Har Sinai*, this unique structure beautifully reflects the eternal goal of the Jewish nation.

Shabbat and Sanctuary:
Holy Time and Holy Place

Rav Chanoch Waxman

I. INTRODUCTION

Parashat Behar begins with the command of the *Shemitta* year. Upon entering the land, *Benei Yisrael* are to work the land for six years at a time, ceasing their labors during the seventh year.

> When you come to the land which I shall give you, the land shall rest (*veshavta ha'aretz*) a Sabbath to God (*Shabbat LaShem*). Six years you may sow your field and six years you may prune your vineyard and gather in the yield. But in the seventh year the land shall have a Sabbath of complete rest (*Shabbat Shabbaton*), a Sabbath to God (*Shabbat LaShem*); you shall not sow your field nor prune your vineyard. You shall not reap the aftergrowth of your harvest nor gather the grapes of your untrimmed vines; it shall be a year of complete rest (*shenat Shabbaton*) for the land. But you may eat the produce of the Sabbath of the land (*Shabbat ha'aretz*). (25:2–6)

Even the most casual reading of the verses above should be enough to make us realize that Torah is interested in emphasizing the term "*Shabbat*" and the verb stem *sh-b-t* (ש. ב. ת). The term appears *seven* times in the text (25:2, 2, 4, 4, 4, 5, 6), the very number of Shabbat itself.

Moreover, factoring in the doubling of the stem in the phrase "*Shabbat Shabbaton*" (25:4), the six phrases containing the stem *sh-b-t* form an interlocking chiastic structure of the following form:

Type	Hebrew Phrase	Location
A	*Veshavta ha'aretz*	25:2
B	*Shabbat LaShem*	25:2
C	*Shabbat Shabbaton yiheye la'aretz*	25:4
B	*Shabbat LaShem*	25:4
C	*Shenat Shabbaton yiheye la'aretz*	25:5
A	*Shabbat ha'aretz*	25:6

While this may be just another way of emphasizing the stem, a mere demonstration of literary artistry, this kind of structure may also possess conceptual significance. The point seems to be the emphasizing of the "interior" of the "A" frame. The agricultural Sabbath, the resting of the land (A), finds its import in the intertwining of the "*Shabbat Shabbaton*" of the land (C) and the concept of "*Shabbat LaShem*" (B).

Interestingly enough, these are the exact phrases used previously in the Torah to command resting on the seventh day. In the Ten Commandments, the Jews are told that the seventh day is a "Sabbath to God" – *Shabbat LaShem* (Ex. 20:10). Likewise, Exodus 35 refers to a "Sabbath of complete rest to God" – *Shabbat Shabbaton LaShem* (35:2). In other words, just as the seventh day Sabbath is both "*Shabbat Shabbaton*" and "*Shabbat LaShem*," so too the seventh year Sabbath is "*Shabbat Shabbaton*" and "*Shabbat LaShem*."

But is this more than word games? After all, it seems more than logical to utilize the language of the seventh day Sabbath, the Sabbath of creation, to formulate the seven-year agricultural cycle. Both involve working six units and resting on the seventh. The term "*Shabbat*" seems to be a biblical word meaning to cease, desist, rest, and the like. Why claim that the language and structure of Leviticus 25:2–6 possesses any special significance?

I would like to argue that the language is striking, especially in comparison to the previous mention of the seven-year agricultural cycle, back in Exodus. Chapter 23 states the following:

> And six years you shall sow your land, and shall harvest its fruits. But the seventh year you shall let it rest (*tishmetena*) and lie fallow, and the poor people of your nation may eat, and what they leave the beasts of the field shall eat. So you shall do with your vineyard and with your olive grove. Six days you shall do your work and on the seventh day you shall rest (*tishbot*). (Ex. 23:10–12)

Shocking, isn't it? In its very first mention of the seven-year agricultural cycle, the Torah refrains from utilizing any "Shabbat" imagery. Despite the logical structure and literary form of "six x shall you ... and on the seventh you shall not," despite the mention of the seventh day Sabbath immediately afterwards, the Torah does not term the seventh year a "Sabbath." In place of the term "*shabbat*" for cease, rest, and desist, the Torah utilizes the term "*shamot*," from the stem sh-m-t (ש. מ. ט). In other words, in Exodus 23, the seventh year is not a "*shabbat*." It is just "*shemitta*," the ceasing of work during the seventh year.

If so, the text of the beginning of *Behar* appears in a new light. Leviticus 25:2–6 performs a radical transformation of the image and nature of the seventh year. The language and structure that we may have been wont to dismiss seem to be a deliberate attempt to link the seventh year with the biblical concept of the Sabbath.

This leads to two questions. First, beyond the level of language, what comprises the philosophical link between the Sabbath of the seventh day and the Sabbath of the seventh year? Second, why here and why now? Why does the Torah connect the imperative to leave the land fallow in the seventh year with the concept of Shabbat here in this place, near the end of Leviticus? What is the connection between the Sabbath of the land and Leviticus?

II. A "SHABBAT" FRENZY

At first glance, some of the standard conceptions of Shabbat could help extricate us from our difficulty. The fourth commandment follows its definition of the seventh day as "Sabbath to God" (*Shabbat LaShem*) with an explicit imperative and an explanation:

> You shall not do any work – you, your son or daughter, your manservant or your maidservant, or your cattle, or the stranger who is within your gates. For in six days God made the heavens and the earth and sea and all that is in them, and He rested on the seventh day. (Ex. 20:10–11)

In the case of the weekly Sabbath, working six days and resting on the seventh echoes the divine act of fashioning the world. As such, the Israelites' resting on the seventh day constitutes testimony to God's creation of the world.

Moreover, the requirement to refrain from "working" on the seventh day entails refraining from providing for one's existence, i.e., food, clothing, and shelter. The Israelites in the desert were prohibited from gathering manna on the Sabbath and forced to depend upon the "miracle" of the non-decaying double portion of the sixth day provided by God (see Exodus 16:22–29). By this means they developed a consciousness of their dependence upon God and the miraculous quality of even their daily existence. Likewise, not working on the seventh day, not providing for one's own sustenance, symbolizes dependence upon God. It emphasizes the "miraculous" quality of even our daily sustenance and builds consciousness of dependence upon God.

These themes should help explain the usage of "*Shabbat*" imagery for describing the seven-year cycle. Just as resting on the seventh day echoes God's rest and testifies to creation of the world in six, so too ceasing agricultural labor in the seventh year serves as witness to God's "working" six and resting on the seventh. In a similar vein, the seven-year agricultural cycle picks up on the "dependence" theme implicit in the Sabbath. He who leaves his field fallow in the seventh year depends upon divine mercy and the divinely promised bounty of the sixth year to make it through (see 25:20–22). He depends upon God's goodness rather than the labor of his own hands.

But this is insufficient. Admittedly, the thematic overlap between not working on the seventh day of the week and the cessation of agricultural labor in the seventh year does resolve the problem of the philosophical link between the weekly Sabbath and the seventh year Sabbath. Nevertheless, it does little to resolve the issue of the connection to Leviticus. We are still left wondering why the Torah chooses only here to introduce the "*Shabbat*" imagery and explicate the philosophical overlap between the seventh day and the seventh year.

In point of fact, the latter part of Leviticus seems almost obsessed with the image of "*Shabbat*," introducing it at rather surprising junctures. Starting in chapter 23, almost every segment contains the term. For example, chapter 23, "*Parashat HaMo'adot*," the delineation of the holidays, opens with the commanding of the Sabbath of the seventh day (23:1–3), even though the Sabbath is not itself a festival day.

Moreover, throughout the *parasha*, the term "*Shabbat*" is used in conjunction with every single holiday mentioned (see 23:24, 23:32, 23:38–39). In fact, it seems to be this predilection that leads to the usage of the obscure phrase "on the morrow of the Sabbath" (*mimaharat haShabbat*) in the dating of the waving of the first cuttings and the calculation of the date of the holiday of Shavuot (23:15–16). In short, the rabbinic position identifying "the morrow of the Sabbath" as the day after the holiday of Pesaḥ, rests on good literary foundations.

But this is just part of the story. The next *parasha* found after the holiday segment, the donation of oil for the lamp and flour for the showbread (*leḥem hapanim*, 24:1–9), also mentions Shabbat. The bread is switched weekly, on the Sabbath day (24:8). In fact, except for the mention of Shabbat, there appears to be no good reason for the citation of a "donation" or "*Mishkan* functioning" *parasha* at this point. Exodus would be the more logical option.

Shifting from *Parashat Emor* to *Behar-Beḥukkotai* further highlights the emerging trend. The main body of *Parashat Behar* (25:1–54), best thought of as the *Shemitta* year-Jubilee cycle and associated laws, opens with the defining of the fallow seventh year as a Sabbath to God and a complex literary emphasis of the term "*Shabbat*" (25:2–6), as we have seen. Likewise, in the other half of *Parashat Behar*, a short two-verse segment at the end of the *parasha* states the following:

> You shall not make idols for yourselves, or set up carved images … in your land … for I am HaShem your God. You shall keep My Sabbaths and venerate My sanctuary; I am HaShem. (26:1–2)

Of all possible precepts, the Torah once again mentions Shabbat.

Finally, the obsession theory under development also "explains" the strange conjoining of the horrible punishments of *Beḥukkotai* with one particular sin. By logic and according to indicators in the text, the terrors of war and exile should hinge upon general abrogation of the covenant with God. The punishment section opens with an "if" clause:

> But if you do not obey Me and do not observe all these commandments, if you reject My laws, and spurn My rule, so that you do not observe all My commandments and you break my covenant. (26:14–15)

The punishments result from general abrogation of the covenant.

Yet later on, after the starvation, plagues, and exile, the Torah teaches that all the punishment has come for a particular purpose:

> Then shall the land make up for its Sabbath years throughout the time that it is desolate and you are in the land of your enemies; then shall the land rest and make up for its Sabbath years. Throughout the time that it is desolate, it shall observe the rest that it did not observe in your Sabbath years while you dwelt upon it. (26:34–35)

The exile comes by virtue of the violation of the *Shemitta* year. It allows the land to make up the lost Sabbath years. Once again, and rather unexpectedly, the Torah chooses to utilize and emphasize the term and concept of "*Shabbat*."

This must be more than just style, and this must be more than just a literary frenzy.

III. HOLINESS IN TIME

Let us return to very first mention of the term "*Shabbat*" in the latter part of Leviticus. As mentioned above, "*Shabbat*" first crops up as the first "*mo'ed,*" the first festival (23:2–3). Although this seems rather mysterious, our previous discussion of *Parashat Emor* should help clear things up.

Analyzing "*Parashat HaMo'adot,*" and its connection to the preceding portions of Leviticus, I argue that "*mo'ed*" should not be understood so much as "festival," but rather literally as a "holiday," i.e., a holy day. The "*mo'adim*" are sanctified times. As examples of holiness, they fit right into the theme of Leviticus.[1]

The weekly Sabbath constitutes the arch-paradigm of time-based sanctity. The Torah introduces the Sabbath of the seventh day with the following text:

> Thus the heaven and earth were finished, and all their array. On the seventh day God finished the work that He had been doing, and He ceased (*vayishbot*) on the seventh day from all the work that He had done. And God blessed the seventh day and declared it holy. (Gen. 2:1–3)

While the Torah of course mentions the cessation of "work" on the seventh day and alludes to the contrast between the previous six days and the seventh, the primary thrust of the text is upon blessing and sanctity. God's blessing and sanctifying of the seventh day constitutes the conceptual crescendo of the origins of the Sabbath.

If so, we no longer need wonder why the Sabbath appears as the first holiday. If the Torah wishes to discuss the sanctity of time, the meeting with God in time, then the Sabbath is the obvious place to begin. Likewise, we need no longer wonder why the Torah utilizes the term "*Shabbat*" as a recurring motif throughout "*Parashat HaMo'adot,*" and as a means of referring to the various holidays (23:24, 23:32, 23:38–39). In a *parasha* that is really about the sanctity of time, the term "*Shabbat*" is a way not just to say "a day on which work is forbidden," but also to allude to the essence of the *parasha*. The symbol of "*Shabbat*" constitutes the natural choice.

---

1. Waxman, "Of Space and Time," http://www.vbm-torah.org/parsha.62/28emor.htm

All of this can be phrased far more radically. It is not just that Leviticus wishes to discuss the sanctity of time and hence introduces "*Parashat HaMo'adot*" and its Sabbath preface. Rather, Leviticus initiates a fundamental shift in its concern. Until chapter 23 and the introduction of the holidays, Leviticus has been about matters related to the holiness of *place*, meeting God in space, and hence dealt with the Sanctuary, sacrifices, and priests. But from here on, Leviticus is about the holiness of *time* and its literary symbol, the "*Shabbat*." The latter part of Leviticus deploys the term "*Shabbat*" not just out of literary motivations, but as signaling a shift in focus, a new general theme and a concentration on a different type of holiness than previously elaborated.

In utilizing the phrases "*the Sabbath of the land*," "*a Sabbath to God*," and "*Shabbat Shabbaton*," the beginning of *Parashat Behar* (25:2–6) telegraphs that we have stumbled upon another example of the sanctity of time. Like the weekly Sabbath and the holidays, the seventh year constitutes a case of holiness in time. In the worldview of Leviticus, it is another opportunity, just like Sanctuary and Shabbat, for meeting with God. Hence the Torah, here in Leviticus, links the laws of the seventh year with the symbol of "*Shabbat*" and defines the *Shemitta* year.

IV. TWO WAYS OF ENCOUNTERING GOD

Earlier, I listed six seemingly problematic contexts in which the Torah utilized the term "*Shabbat*" in the course of the latter part of Leviticus. The chart below should help provide a recap.

Context	Problem	Verses
Laws of the holidays	Mention of Shabbat as the first festival	23:1–3
Laws of the holiday	Utilization of term "*Shabbat*" for each festival	23:15–16, 24:32,38–39
Donation of oil and flour	Inclusion of the *parasha* in Leviticus and not Exodus	24:1–9
The *Shemitta* year	"*Shabbat*" imagery and transformation into a Sabbath	25:2–6
Segment of laws at the end of *Behar*	The mention of the precept of Shabbat	26:1–2
The curses of *Beḥukkotai*	Exile seems connected to the violation of the *Shemitta* year	26:34–35

While the theory propounded until this point, the shift to the sanctity of time and hence the symbol of "*Shabbat*," easily handles the first five contexts, the last one is not so simple. To put this a little bit differently, it still seems unclear why exile hinges upon violation of the *Shemitta* year.

But this is only part of the problem. A quick review of the fifth context mentioned above, the tail end of *Behar*, raises a more fundamental problem. The text preceding the covenantal promises and punishments of *Behukkotai* reads:

> You shall not make idols for yourselves, or set up carved images ... in your land ... for I am HaShem your God. You shall keep My Sabbaths and venerate My Sanctuary; I am HaShem. (26:1–2)

Apparently, the sanctity of place, the holiness of fixed space, has not completely faded out of the story line of Leviticus. Here, as a preface to the "If-Then" and "If not-Then" covenant of *Behukkotai* (see 26:3–4, 14–16), the Torah presents the obvious prohibition of idol worship, the now obvious precept of Shabbat, and the now slightly surprising and vague requirement to "venerate the Sanctuary." But what is the sanctity of space doing here in the part of Leviticus that has already shifted to the sanctity of time?

The answer lies in that the shift in Leviticus from the sanctity of place to the sanctity of time comprises not so much a revolutionary movement, but a dialectical motion culminating in synthesis of the two types of holiness.

In plainer and more concrete terminology, the Torah recognizes two distinct types of holiness. After focusing for most of Leviticus on the first type, namely the sanctity of space and Sanctuary, the Torah then introduces the second, the holiness of time, beginning in chapter 23. While the former, the sanctity of place, is symbolized by the term "Sanctuary," the latter, the sanctity of time, is expressed in the term "*Shabbat*." As a preface to the covenant that closes the book of holiness, the Torah links the two ways of finding holiness and meeting God. It conjoins "*Shabbat*" and "*Mikdash*," and places them after the prohibition of idol worship, i.e., the requirement of loyalty to God. In this succinct summary, the Torah reminds the Israelites what it is all about.

V. "SHABBAT" AND "MIKDASH"

To close, let us return to the last unresolved detail, the connection of the punishments of *Beḥukkotai* with the violation of the *Shemitta* year. In reality, the synthesis of holiness of time and holiness of place happens not so much in the fifth context, the preface to the covenant, but back in the fourth, the introduction of the *Shemitta* year. Let us take one last look at the text.

> When you come to the *land* which I shall give you, the *land* shall rest (*veshavta ha'aretz*) a Sabbath to God. Six years you may sow your field and six years you may prune your vineyard and gather in the yield. But in the seventh year the *land* shall have a Sabbath of complete rest, a Sabbath to God; you shall not sow your field or prune your vineyard. You shall not reap the aftergrowth of your harvest or gather the grapes of your untrimmed vines; it shall be a year of complete rest for the *land*. But you may eat the produce of the Sabbath of the *land* (*Shabbat ha'aretz*). (25:2–6)

The segment begins with the phrase, "*when you come to the land*" (25:2), and mentions the term "*land*" six times. As pointed out earlier, it is "the land" that "rests," and the "A" frame of the structure previously outlined consists of the conjoining of the term "*Shabbat*" and the term "*aretz*" (land). In sum, the *Shemitta* year is not just about time, but also about place. It already fuses the holiness of place and the holiness of time together. It is only in the Holy Land that the seventh year is holy.

Put differently, the *Shemitta* year contains within it both "*Mikdash*" (Sanctuary) and "*Shabbat*." It in fact constitutes the expansion of each type of holiness to the largest possible units of each dimension. The holiness of time expands from the standard unit of one day, a single day out of a cycle of seven, to fill an entire year. Likewise the holiness of place expands beyond its normal and assumed parameters. It also exists beyond the walls of the Sanctuary; it in fact fills the entire Land of Israel. The entire land is a holy place.

This resolves the textual and symbolic connection between violation of the *Shemitta* year and exile. Like the covenant preface of "*Shabbat*" and "*Mikdash*" (26:1–2), the *Shemitta* year is also about the holiness of time and the holiness of place. Like the covenant preface, it is about the opportunity for encountering sanctity and meeting with God. Like the preface, it succinctly contains the religious ideal of Leviticus, and the goal of entry into the Land of Israel. But if *Benei Yisrael* violate the *Shemitta* year, if they fail to understand and exploit the sanctity of time and place, if they fail to encounter God, what is the point? Hence, the punishments and exile of *Parashat Beḥukkotai*. *Benei Yisrael* have understood neither the sanctity of time nor the sanctity of place, and have violated the meanings of both "*Mikdash*" and "*Shabbat*." Exile is the result.

You Shall Dwell in the Land in Security

Rav Yair Kahn

I. SHEMITTA ETZEL HAR SINAI

On the third month of the first year after leaving Egypt, *Benei Yisrael* arrived at Sinai (Ex. 19:1). On the following day, Moses ascended the mountain and God called to Moses from Mount Sinai (ibid., 19:3). From that day until the first month of the second year, when the *Mishkan* was built, Moses received the divine word from Mount Sinai. However, once the *Mishkan* was assembled, God called to Moses from within the *Mishkan*, as is written, "And God called unto Moses and spoke unto him out of the Tent of Meeting" (Lev. 1:1). The mention of Mount Sinai at the beginning of *Parashat Behar* is therefore puzzling:

> God spoke to Moses on Mount Sinai, saying: Speak to *Benei Yisrael* and say to them: When you come into the land that I give you, the land shall observe a Sabbath rest for God. (25:1)

This difficulty was noted by our Sages, who posed the famous question: "*Ma inyan Shemitta etzel Har Sinai?*" Why is *Shemitta* found alongside Mount Sinai?

In truth, Mount Sinai defines the parameters of the closing unit of Leviticus. Aside from the mention of Mount Sinai at the beginning of this *parasha*, the Torah similarly concludes the covenant in *Parashat Behukkotai*:

> These are the statutes and ordinances and laws that God made between Him and the Children of Israel at Mount Sinai, by the hand of Moses. (26:46)

Leviticus concludes with the words:

> These are the commandments that God commanded Moses for the Children of Israel at Mount Sinai. (27:34)

Thus, although *Shemitta* and *Yovel* continue the theme of sanctity of time that was introduced in *Parashat Emor*, *Parashot Behar* and *Behukkotai* form an independent unit.

The anachronistic mention of Mount Sinai at the end of Leviticus prompted Ibn Ezra to apply the principle of "*ein mukdam ume'uhar baTorah*" – the Torah does not necessarily correspond to chronological sequence:

> "*BeHar Sinai*" – *Ein mukdam ume'uhar baTorah*. This occurred before *Vayikra* and all the *parashot* that follow, for the speech was at Mount Sinai, and here the [Torah records] the covenant written in *Parashat Mishpatim*. It was recorded at this point in order to connect the [various] conditions of the land. Just like it says regarding forbidden relations that they are the cause that the land shall vomit you, so too it says in *Parashat Behukkotai* regarding the Sabbath of the land. (Ibn Ezra 25:1)

II. THE SINAITIC COVENANT

Ibn Ezra identifies the *Behar-Behukkotai* unit with the Sinaitic covenant recorded at the end of *Parashat Mishpatim*:

> And Moses wrote all the words of God and rose up early in the morning, and built an altar under the mount, and twelve pillars for the twelve tribes of Israel. And he sent the young men of

Benei Yisrael, who offered burnt offerings, and sacrificed peace offerings of oxen unto God. And Moses took half of the blood, and put it in basins, and half of the blood he splashed against the altar. And he took the book of the covenant, and read it to the people, and they said: "All that God has spoken will we do and obey." And Moses took the blood and sprinkled it on the people, and said: "Behold the blood of the covenant, which God has made with you in agreement with all these words." (Ex. 24:4–8)

This covenant took place around the time of *Ma'amad Har Sinai*, but its content is nevertheless recorded at the end of Leviticus. Ibn Ezra explains that the Torah wanted to connect the various conditions that are necessary to ensure the settlement in the Land of Israel.

Ramban was much more hesitant than Ibn Ezra in applying the principle of *"ein mukdam ume'uḥar,"* and, as in other instances, he argues on its application here as well. Ramban agrees with Ibn Ezra that *Behar-Beḥukkotai* is a record of the covenant forged at Sinai. However, Ibn Ezra identifies it with the covenant of the first *luḥot*, while according to Ramban, that covenant was annulled by the sin of the Golden Calf. Ramban thus claims that the covenant of *Behar-Beḥukkotai* is a second covenant that was forged along with the second *luḥot*. When Moses descended with the second *luḥot*, the most pressing task was to build the *Mishkan* and to teach the *Mishkan*-related laws. At the end of Leviticus, Moses finally had the opportunity to inform *Benei Yisrael* of the new covenant of the second *luḥot*.

At first glance, the covenant that Ibn Ezra and Ramban are referring to is essentially the blessings and curses of *Parashat Beḥukkotai*. *Benei Yisrael* accept the mitzvot of the Torah, and God, as it were, commits to award Israel with various blessings. If *Benei Yisrael* do not adhere to the mitzvot, then God will punish them. Similarly, the blessings and curses in *Parashat Ki Tavo* conclude as follows:

These are the words of the covenant which God commanded Moses to make with *Benei Yisrael* in the land of Moab, *aside from the covenant which He made with them at Horeb*. (Deut. 28:69)

This relates to *Parashat Beḥukkotai*. It would seem that the location of *Parashat Behar*, which contains the laws of *Shemitta* and *Yovel*, is merely tangential to the covenant.

Ibn Ezra noted that observance of *Shemitta* is one of the conditions necessary for Israel to remain in the Land of Israel.

> Then shall the land be appeased for her Sabbaths, as long as it lies desolate and you are in your enemies' land; even then shall the land rest, and appease her Sabbaths. (Lev. 26:34)

The Torah therefore introduced the laws of *Shemitta* prior to the conditions of the covenant, even though they are not part of the covenant itself.

III. SHEMITTA AND BERAKHA

On the other hand, we might claim that *Shemitta* and *Yovel* are integrally related to the covenant. In order to illustrate this point, let us consider the following:

> And you shall perform My statutes, and keep My ordinances and do them; and you shall dwell in the land in safety. And the land shall yield her fruit, and you shall eat until you have enough, and dwell therein in safety. (25:18–19)

When taken out of context, these verses seem to belong to the *berakhot* section at the beginning of *Beḥukkotai*. However, these verses are actually found in the middle of the *Shemitta* and *Yovel* section in *Parashat Behar*. In fact, if we compare them to the opening lines of *Beḥukkotai*, the similarity is startling:

> If you shall walk in My statutes, and keep My commandments, and do them, then I will give your rains in their season, and the land shall yield her produce, and the trees of the field shall yield their fruit. And your threshing shall reach unto the vintage, and

the vintage shall reach unto the sowing time; and you shall eat your bread until you have enough, and dwell in your land in safety. (26:3–5)

The *Behar* section continues:

And if you shall say: "What shall we eat the seventh year? Behold, we may not sow, nor gather in our increase." Then I will command My blessing (*berakha*) upon you in the sixth year, and it shall bring forth produce for the three years. And you shall sow the eighth year, and eat of the produce, the old harvest; until the ninth year, until her produce shall come in, you shall eat the old harvest. (25:20–22)

The *berakha* that we shall eat from the old harvest relates specifically to the commandments of *Shemitta* and *Yovel*. Surprisingly, we find a parallel at the beginning of *Behukkotai*: "And you shall eat old store harvest" (26:10).

What is the Torah telling us by drawing these parallels? I think the Torah is saying that *Shemitta* and *Yovel* are not just mitzvot; they are an opportunity. They form a vision of a utopian society, based on the awareness that Israel are the servants of God (25:55), living in *Eretz Yisrael*, the land of God (25:23). They describe a religious ideal of human faith reciprocated by divine providence. In a word, *Shemitta* and *Yovel* are more than just commandments – they are a context for attaining the *berakhot* of the covenant.

This idealistic view of *Shemitta* may be connected to the *hak'hel* ceremony that takes place within the context of *Shemitta*, when the king gathers the nation and reads to them from the Torah. The *hak'hel* ceremony is a re-enactment of *Ma'amad Har Sinai*, which itself is called "the day of *hakahal*." Once every *Shemitta* cycle, there is a renewal of the covenant that was forged at Sinai. Might not the timing of this renewal be connected with understanding that *Shemitta* is the context for achieving the blessings of the Sinaitic covenant?

IV. *KOL YOSHVEHA ALEHA*

The Gemara in Arakhin (32b) quotes a very interesting *baraita*:

> Upon the exile of the tribe of Reuben and the tribe of Gad and half the tribe of Manasseh, *Yovel* was annulled, as it is written: "And you should proclaim freedom unto the land for all its inhabitants" – during the time that all its inhabitants are on it, and not at a time that some have been exiled. Perhaps if they were all on it, however mixed together, the tribe of Benjamin with Yehuda, and the tribe of Yehuda with Benjamin, *Yovel* should be observed? We learn from what is written, "For all its inhabitants" – at a time that its inhabitants are settled properly, but not when they are mixed.

According to most opinions, this halakha is unique to *Yovel*. Other mitzvot that are specific to *Eretz Yisrael* are dependent on *kedushat ha'aretz* (the halakhic consecration of *Eretz Yisrael*) achieved at the time of Joshua through conquering and settling the land. Many claim that this sanctity was nullified when the Babylonians conquered *Eretz Yisrael*. *Yovel*, on the other hand, ceased when the Assyrians exiled the tribes that had settled east of the Jordan, over a hundred years earlier, even though the halakhic sanctity of the land was still extant. Similarly, there are many who accept the position that *kedushat ha'aretz* was reinstated upon the return of Ezra, following the Babylonian exile. Nevertheless, most *Rishonim* agree that *Yovel* did not apply according to biblical law, during the time of the Second Temple, as the inhabitants were not settled properly. What is the meaning of this unique halakha?

One possible explanation is that other mitzvot specific to *Eretz Yisrael* are primarily focused on agriculture, and the *kedusha* of the land is therefore critical. *Yovel*, however, contains a social component as well as an agricultural one. On the one hand, agricultural work is prohibited on *Yovel*, just as it is prohibited on *Shemitta*. On the other hand, all Hebrew slaves are set free at *Yovel*, and land that was sold returns to its original owner. The laws of *Yovel* allow those who suffered economically, and were consequently forced to sell their property or themselves, to regain that which they lost. This aspect of *Yovel* is not rooted in the soil, but rather in an ethical, social ideal.

The ethical sensitivities that inspire these laws apply at all times. However, *Yovel* and its laws are binding only when the vision of *Yovel* can be fully realized. When some of the tribes are no longer in *Eretz Yisrael*, the nation can no longer function as an organic whole, and the vision of "freedom unto the land for all its inhabitants" is no longer attainable. The socio-ethical component cannot be achieved, and *Yovel* as a complex idea cannot be implemented. Put simply, the agricultural component cannot be applied independently of the social component. Therefore, there is no *Yovel* when freedom for all the land's inhabitants cannot be fulfilled.

Another possible explanation is based on our suggestion that *Shemitta* is the context for attaining the *berakhot* of the covenant. If this is true regarding *Shemitta*, how much more so with respect to *Yovel*! The *pesukim* in *Parashat Behar* (25:18–19) that parallel the *berakhot* of *Beḥukkotai* are written within the context of *Yovel*.

> If you walk in My statutes, and keep My commandments, and do them, then I will give your rains in their season, and the land shall yield her produce, and the trees of the field shall yield their fruit. And your threshing shall reach unto the vintage, and the vintage shall reach unto the sowing time; and you shall eat your bread until you have enough, and dwell in your land in safety. (26:3–5)

Perhaps this lofty vision of *Yovel* requires optimal conditions. Members of all the tribes, representing the nation as an organic whole, must be in *Eretz Yisrael*, each tribe in the portion allotted to it. Only then can ultimate freedom be proclaimed for all its inhabitants.

Between Shemitta and Beḥukkotai

Rav Yonatan Grossman

Parashat *Behar* opens by informing us where it was conveyed: "God spoke to Moses *at Mount Sinai,* saying" (Lev. 25:1). Many commentaries address this emphasis on location. Rashi, for example, derives from this verse that *all* of the commandments and their related details were communicated by God to Moses at Mount Sinai; Ramban disagrees. Rashbam explains "at Mount Sinai" to mean "before the erection of the Tabernacle." According to the straightforward reading of the text, Rashbam understands that the Torah sections dealing with the *Shemitta* and *Yovel* (the *Shemitta* year and the Jubilee year) mentioned here were actually transmitted to Moses at Mount Sinai, before the remainder of Leviticus was communicated to him.

In *Parashat Beḥukkotai* we read of the blessings that the Jewish people will merit "if you follow My decrees and observe My commandments to fulfill them," and in contrast, the curses that will transpire "if you will not listen to Me and will not fulfill all of these commandments." The ensuing maledictions revolve around the number seven:

> "And if you will not listen to Me, I will chastise you *sevenfold* for your transgressions." (26:18)

"And if you walk with Me with indifference and will not hearken to Me, I will strike you *sevenfold* according to your transgressions." (26:21)

"I will also strike you *sevenfold* for your transgressions." (26:24, 26:28)

These expressions stressing the number seven require some explanation. Why do these curses strike in multiples of seven and why does the Torah have to repeat this fact over and over? This directs us to the commandments of *Parashat Behar*, which immediately precede the blessings and curses. The commandments of *Behar* are also arranged in multiples of seven. The *Shemitta*, for instance, is to be fulfilled every seventh year: "In the *seventh year* there shall be a year of complete rest for the land, a Shabbat to God. Do not plant your field nor prune your vineyard" (25:4). The commandment of *Yovel* is even more pronounced: "You shall count *seven Shemitta* years, *seven cycles of seven years*. These *seven Shemitta* years shall equal forty-nine years. You shall sound a blast of the shofar in the *seventh month*" (25:8–9). In other words, the *Yovel* year is to be inaugurated by the shofar in the seventh month, after a count of seven times seven years. The remaining commandments of *Parashat Behar* also deal, in one way or another, with these central observances of *Shemitta* and *Yovel*.

In light of this, we may suggest that the blessings and curses in *Parashat Behukkotai*, which immediately follow these laws, are in fact referring specifically to the observance of *Shemitta* and *Yovel*. If the Jewish nation refrains from agricultural pursuits during the *Shemitta* year, then they will merit the blessings; if not, then the curses will ensue. Therefore, the *Tokheha* (reproof, i.e., the section of the curses) emphasizes the number seven over and over. This is the fundamental digit for the counting of the seventh year – the *Shemitta*, and the fiftieth year of the *Yovel* which occurs after seven countings of seven years.

According to this reading, the blessings and curses do not address the general issue of Torah observance, but rather the specific mitzvot of *Shemitta* and *Yovel*. Although the number seven which is common to both sections is not sufficient to prove this connection, additional points reinforce this interpretation.

After God warns the people that exile will ensue if they will not obey the commandments, the verse states:

> I will scatter you among the nations and will unsheathe the sword to pursue you. Your land will be desolate and your cities in ruins. The land shall be appeased for its Sabbaths while it is desolate and you are in the land of your enemies; the land shall rest and have appeasement for its Sabbaths. All the days of its desolation it shall be at rest, according to the rest that it did not enjoy while you dwelt in it. (26:33–35)

Here it is abundantly clear that the curses – at least the punishment of exile – are meted out for the non-observance of the *Shemitta*. Since the Jewish people failed to observe this obligation while they dwelt in their land, they must suffer exile and will therefore cease working the land against their will. Similarly, the Torah later states: "The land will be abandoned of them and will be appeased of its Sabbaths in desolation. The people, too, shall be forgiven their transgression" (26:43). It is difficult to maintain that the blessings and curses address all the mitzvot, and that the *Shemitta* is here stated as an arbitrary example. It seems much more plausible that the curses, in fact, specifically address the mitzva of *Shemitta*.

An additional point which lends credence to the assumption that the blessings and curses refer specifically to the observance or non-observance of the mitzvot of *Shemitta* and *Yovel* is one which we mentioned at the outset: the setting in which they were communicated. As is well known, Leviticus was transmitted to Moses in the Tabernacle, the *Ohel Mo'ed*, as is clearly stated at its outset: "God called Moses and spoke to him in the Tabernacle" (Lev. 1:1). In contrast, the beginning of *Behar*, which introduces the mitzvot of *Shemitta* and *Yovel* (at least according to Rashbam's reading, which we earlier adopted), indicates that the communication took place earlier: "God spoke to Moses *at Mount Sinai*."

If in fact the Torah relates here a collection of items that were actually communicated at an earlier date at Mount Sinai, then we must determine the extent of this collection. Where does it end and when is the chronological order resumed? The concluding verse of the blessings and curses provides the answer to this question: "These are the decrees, laws, and observances which God concluded between Himself and *Benei Yisrael* at Mount Sinai, by Moses' hand" (26:46). In other words, what we have here is a self-contained unit that was transmitted to Moses at Mount Sinai, and for whatever reason was recorded at the conclusion of Leviticus. This unit includes the *Shemitta* and *Yovel* as well as the blessings and the curses, which are here recorded as the direct consequence of Israel's observance or non-observance of these laws.

The obvious question which arises is, why does the Torah depart from the chronological sequence, and suddenly introduce at the end of Leviticus commandments and a covenant which had been communicated to the Jewish people much earlier? R. Avraham Ibn Ezra provides an answer at the beginning of *Parashat Behar* (25:1):

> The Torah is not necessarily arranged chronologically. This section in fact precedes the *parasha* of *Vayikra* and all the sections that follow it.... The reason for its mention here is to connect the various conditions for dwelling in the land [of Israel]. Just as it was stated concerning the forbidden sexual unions that their non-observance would lead to the land spewing the people out, so too was it stated concerning the observance of the *Shemitta*.

Ibn Ezra understands that the Torah delayed mentioning the commandments of *Shemitta* and *Yovel* as well as the blessings and curses until now, in order to establish a connection with the section dealing with sexual immorality. Here also, the Torah states that non-observance will lead to expulsion from the land (see Leviticus 18:28, 20:22), just as exile is promised for failing to observe *Shemitta* and *Yovel*.

I would like to adopt the view of Ibn Ezra but to apply it elsewhere. Leviticus, especially in its first half, deals with the various aspects of the Temple – the laws of sacrifice, the *kohanim*, *tum'a* and *tahara*, etc. Even seemingly unrelated topics are viewed through the prism of the Temple and its sanctity. The sanctity of time, for example, is presented in the context of the *Kohen Gadol's* service on Yom Kippur. The sanctity of man is presented in the context of the service of the *kohanim* in the

Temple. In other words, both the sanctity of time and that of man are presented against the backdrop of the sanctity of place – the Temple!

Lest a person incorrectly assume that the service of the Deity is to be confined to the "place which God shall choose," the second half of Leviticus emphasizes that sanctity is relevant in all places. The behavior of a servant of God is to be conditioned by sanctity even while he is in his home and not directly present in the precincts of the Temple. The Torah therefore emphasizes that the three central elements of place, time, and the individual are meaningful not only in the Temple, but everywhere.

1. Sanctity of Persons:

    Leviticus relates much information about the election of the *kohanim* and their unique responsibilities, but it goes on to state, "Be holy" (19:2), as an imperative addressing all of the people. The *kohanim* may have unique laws which govern permitted marriages (such as the disqualification of a divorcee, etc.), but the rest of the people are also commanded to desist from sexually immoral practices, wherever they may lie. (This point was stressed by Ibn Ezra.) The *kohanim* may have been chosen to serve God in the precincts of the Temple, but there is a similar notion of sanctity that can apply to all people who are prepared to observe the dictates of the Torah. This in fact explains the common expressions that occur in commands addressed to the *kohanim* as well as to the people.

2. Sanctity of Time:

    Although we may already have read about the service of the *Kohen Gadol* on Yom Kippur (18:1–34), we later read about all of the holidays which are to be designated as "holy gatherings" on which labor is to be curtailed (23:1–44). The sanctity of time is thus expanded beyond the precincts of the Temple to embrace the world at large.

3. Sanctity of Place:

    Now, at the very conclusion of Leviticus, the Torah re-emphasizes this in a clear and direct manner by introducing the laws of the *Shemitta* and *Yovel*. Here the discussion concerns the sanctity of place, and necessitates specific conduct.

There may be a specific place where God causes His presence to be manifest, but by the same token "the whole earth is Mine." Through these laws, every tiller of the land must realize that the entire world belongs to God and that by His will alone it is given to man to work it and to derive sustenance. When the nation as a whole desists from working the land every seventh year, it indicates God's ownership of the whole earth, and not only the place of the Temple where His presence is manifest.

The mitzvot of *Shemitta* and *Yovel,* together with the blessings and curses that relate to them, are recorded here even though they were transmitted at Mount Sinai. This is in order to emphasize the above point at the conclusion of the book which deals more than any other with service of God in His Temple. The commandments are placed upon the Jew wherever he may be; he desists from working the earth because "the whole earth is Mine."

The Third Tablets

Rav Meir Spiegelman

A number of *parashot* in the Torah parallel the Ten Commandments, the most obvious example being *Parashat Kedoshim*. In *Parashat Kedoshim*, several of the commandments are paralleled in full (such as honoring parents and Shabbat), while others find only a partial repetition (such as the prohibition, "You shall not stand idly by your neighbor's blood," parallel to "You shall not steal [i.e., kidnap]"). Accepting this parallel as a given, I wish to understand its significance, and reveal the connection between it and our *parasha*.

I. BOUNDARIES OF THE PARALLEL

Before discussing the parallel itself, we must first identify its boundaries. In other words, where does the literary unit corresponding to the "Ten Commandments" begin, and where does it end?

It is clear that the unit corresponding to the Ten Commandments does not begin before chapter 18. Most of the preceding commands pertain to the *Mishkan*, and are addressed to Aaron. Starting from chapter 18, however, the commands do not necessarily relate only to the *Mishkan*, and they are conveyed to Moses. (Even when the commands are addressed to the *kohanim*, Moses receives the command from God and passes it on to Aaron.) Indeed, the opening verses of chapter 18 represent a classic introduction to a new section:

> God spoke to Moses, saying: "Speak to *Benei Yisrael* and say to them: I am HaShem your God. You shall not follow the customs of the land of Egypt, where you dwelled, nor shall you follow the customs of the land of Canaan to which I bring you, nor shall you walk in their statutes. You shall fulfill My laws and observe My statutes, to walk in them, I am HaShem your God. And you shall observe My statutes and My laws, which a person shall follow and live by them; I am HaShem." (Lev. 18:1–5)

Moreover, these verses also echo the continuation of *Parashat Kedoshim* (for example, 20:22).

In contrast to the beginning of the section, which is easy enough to identify, the conclusion is more difficult to locate. The end of chapter 20 would seem a suitable place to conclude the section, for this chapter ends with concluding verses reminiscent of the beginning of *Parashat Kedoshim* (and they are followed immediately by the start of a section meant only for *kohanim*):

> And you shall keep all My statutes and all My laws, and fulfill them, that you may not be expelled by the land to which I bring you, to dwell in it. You shall not follow the statutes of the nation which I cast out from before you, for they did all this and I have detested them…. You shall be holy unto Me for I, God, am holy, and I have separated you from the nations to be Mine. (Lev. 20:22–26)

Despite this, however, it appears that the unit corresponding to the Ten Commandments concludes much later on. The opening verses of *Parashat Behar* connect us directly to the Revelation at Sinai, and the verses concluding this *parasha* complete the parallel to the beginning of *Parashat Kedoshim* and to the Ten Commandments:

For *Benei Yisrael* are My servants; they are My servants whom I took out of the land of Egypt, I am HaShem your God. You shall not make for yourselves pagan gods, nor shall you build for yourselves an idol or a statue, nor shall you place a carved stone in your land to bow down upon it, for I am HaShem your God. You shall observe My *Shabbatot* and you shall revere My Sanctuary; I am HaShem. (25:55–26:2)

However, it would seem that the end of *Parashat Behar* is also not the end of the unit parallel to the Ten Commandments; rather, I propose that the unit concludes either in the middle of *Behar* or at the end of *Parashat Behukkotai*. I arrive at this conclusion based on the fact that after the conclusion of the curses in *Behukkotai* (as well as at the end of the *parasha*), the Torah explicitly closes the framework that opened at the beginning of *Parashat Kedoshim*:

These are the statutes and the laws and the teachings that God placed between Himself and *Benei Yisrael* at Mount Sinai by the hand of Moses. (Lev. 26:46)

In summary, we may say that there is a large unit of chapters – starting at the beginning of *Parashat Kedoshim* (or a little before then) and concluding at the end of Leviticus – that corresponds to the Ten Commandments and the *parashot* that follow. In fact, since the Torah states that this unit was conveyed to Moses at Mount Sinai, the parallel is not incidental; rather, this unit is conveying an alternative formulation of the Ten Commandments told to Moses at Sinai.

Two questions now arise: First, why does the Torah repeat the Ten Commandments once again in these *parashot*; and second, why is the formulation of the Ten Commandments here different from the one we find in *Parashat Yitro* and in *Parashat Va'ethanan*?

II. FOLLOWING THE SIN OF THE GOLDEN CALF

In order to answer these questions, we must return to the Revelation at Sinai and the sin of the Golden Calf. The impression that arises from the Sages' description of Moses' ascents and descents of the mountain may be misleading – we imagine that Moses came down from the mountain, then – after a short time – ascended once again, and *Am Yisrael* received the second tablets after just one hundred and twenty days. This description does match the historical facts, but does not fully reflect the intervening drama.

When Moses descended Mount Sinai for the second time, after praying to God to forgive the nation, the future looked quite gloomy to *Benei Yisrael*. The most blatant signs of their lowly situation were the fact that the *Ohel Mo'ed* now stood outside the camp, following God's declaration that He would not dwell amidst the nation. In general, we are accustomed to thinking that Moses' words to God, "See – You tell me, Bring up this nation," were uttered as part of his prayer on behalf of *Benei Yisrael*, but this is not necessarily so. God did not completely forgive the nation following Moses' prayer, and *Benei Yisrael* were left in a sort of interim situation, in which God was not prepared to go on amongst them. Had Moses not prayed once again on their behalf, this situation would have continued. Only after Moses prays a second time – "See – You tell me, Bring up this nation" – only then does God answer him, promising to go up amongst the nation.

It appears that Moses shattered the first tablets for the sake of the Jews, since acceptance of the tablets would represent agreement with their content. Moses wanted to avoid the more serious punishment that would have been appropriate had they committed their sin while at the same time accepting the tablets; therefore he broke them. The shattering of the tablets expressed Moses' view that *Benei Yisrael* were not worthy of receiving them. Therefore, the nation had to receive the Ten Commandments a second time – this time with their consent. Indeed, in *Parashat Ki Tissa*, in the section describing the second tablets, there are verses that are almost identical to those in *Parashat Mishpatim*, describing the first tablets.

III. THE THIRD TEN COMMANDMENTS

In light of the above, we may ask what would have happened had Moses not beseeched God on behalf of *Benei Yisrael*, or had his request – that the nation be *completely* forgiven – not been accepted. On the face of it, it would seem that God would have had to forge a new covenant with *Benei Yisrael*, now that the first tablets had been broken. It is reasonable to assume that God would not have given a second set of tablets, but some way would have been found to give *Benei Yisrael* the Commandments that they had not agreed to accept the first time.

It is possible that this is precisely the role of the unit beginning in *Parashat Kedoshim*. The Sages teach that Moses ascended Mount Sinai three times, each time remaining there for forty days and forty nights. This is not stated explicitly in the Torah (although it may be hinted at in the verses in Deuteronomy), but its basis may be discerned in our *parasha*. Since on two occasions Moses ascended the mountain, remained there for forty days, and received a set of tablets – it is logical to posit that the third time, too, he remained for forty days, and received the Torah. This third "receiving of the Torah" is what is described in the section under discussion, which begins with the giving of the Torah, continues with the three pilgrim festivals, and concludes with the forging of the covenant in *Parashat Behukkotai*. It appears that every time there was any change in the status of *Benei Yisrael*, it became necessary for a new covenant to be made, which would reflect this change. In particular, following the sin of the Golden Calf, there was a need for the covenant of *Parashat Behukkotai*.

IV. THE COVENANT

What is a covenant? Simply put, a covenant is an agreement between two parties. Within the framework of the covenant in *Parashat Behukkotai*, *Am Yisrael* was committed to observe the mitzvot, and God committed Himself to help them. A similar covenant appears in *Parashat Mishpatim*: God gives *Benei Yisrael* laws, statutes, and commandments, and promises them reward for their fulfillment: "None shall miscarry nor be barren in your land; I shall fill the number of your days. I shall send the fear of Me before you." (Ex. 23:3). The covenant of *Parashat Mishpatim* was forged through the sprinkling of blood and the nation's acceptance of the "contract" (the second set of tablets).

The covenant in our *parasha* includes some elements that are very similar to those of the covenant in *Parashat Mishpatim*. *Benei Yisrael* receive the Commandments (in *Parashat Kedoshim*), and then receive a collection of mitzvot including the three pilgrim festivals (*Parashat Emor*) and the laws of damages. At the beginning of *Parashat Behar*, the Torah takes us back to Mount Sinai, in a *parasha* that includes the description of reward that is similar to the reward promised in *Parashat Mishpatim*:

"And the land shall give its fruit and you shall eat to satiety, and you shall dwell upon it in security" (Lev. 25:19). Finally, at the end of the *parasha*, the Torah brings the obligations of both parties to the covenantal agreement – the blessing and the curse.

However, despite the similarity, the covenant in *Parashat Behukkotai* is substantially different from the one in *Parashat Mishpatim*. First, in *Parashat Mishpatim*, God's commitment to help *Am Yisrael* is almost independent of their observance of the Torah, while in *Parashat Behukkotai* the condition is explicit. Second, in *Parashat Mishpatim* God's promises to *Am Yisrael* are given prior to the forging of the covenant (the sprinkling of the blood upon the nation), and prior to their acceptance of the contract (the second tablets). In *Parashat Behukkotai*, in contrast, the two parties to the covenant are mentioned successively, and the fulfillment of the covenant is conditional upon the actions of *Benei Yisrael* ("and I shall establish My covenant with you"). Third, the covenant in *Parashat Mishpatim* is not formulated in terms of "sin" and "punishment" (except for the warning not to sin), while *Parashat Behukkotai* emphasizes the aspect of reward and punishment more strongly.

Why such a great difference between these two covenants? It appears that the difference is a result of the sin of the Golden Calf. Following this sin, a new covenant is required, including two possibilities – the possibility of reward, and the possibility of punishment, heaven forbid. Following the episode of the Golden Calf, the possibility of *Benei Yisrael* sinning and being punished can no longer be ignored. Therefore, there is a clear correspondence between the "reward" in the covenant of *Behukkotai* and the covenant of *Parashat Mishpatim*.

In light of this explanation, another question arises. If the commandments in our *parasha* were indeed given to *Benei Yisrael* between the first and the second tablets, why does the Torah mention them only at the end of Leviticus? Why does this unit not appear in its natural place – at the beginning of *Parashat Ki Tissa*?

It would seem that the Torah wanted to preserve the continuity between the command to build the *Mishkan* and its execution. There are a number of differences between the structure of the *Mishkan* in *Teruma-Tetzaveh* and its structure in *Vayak'hel-Pekudei*. The Torah seeks, on the one hand, to emphasize these differences by juxtaposing the command to build the *Mishkan* and its fulfillment, while on the other hand teaching that despite these changes, the *Mishkan* that was ultimately built was a direct continuation of the *Mishkan* that was commanded. The sin of the Golden Calf is recorded in *Parashat Ki Tissa*, in the middle of the subject of the *Mishkan*, for it was the cause of the differences between the command and the execution.

V. FORMULATION OF THE COMMANDMENTS

If the *parashot* of *Kedoshim*, *Behar*, and *Behukkotai* contain a form of "third set of commandments," then why is there such a glaring difference between the formulation of this unit and the formulation of the first and second tablets, in *Yitro* and *Va'ethanan*?

One possible direction involves paying attention to the fact that the reason that the Torah gives for the obligation of observing the mitzvot in *Parashat Kedoshim* is different from the one offered in *Parashat Yitro*. In *Parashat Kedoshim*, we are obligated to observe the mitzvot because we are holy. At the giving of the Torah, in contrast, the concept of holiness, *kedusha*, is almost entirely absent. In *Parashat Yitro*, observance of the mitzvot is a function of the relationship between God and *Am Yisrael* ("You shall be chosen to Me from all the nations"; "You shall be unto Me a kingdom of priests and a holy nation"; etc.).

This explanation serves to solve another problem. At the beginning of our *parasha*, after God promises to shower *Am Yisrael* with all manner of blessings when they will be dwelling securely in their land, the Torah adds: "and My soul shall not abhor you." Would anyone have thought that while God blesses the fruits of the ground and the nation, He abhors *Benei Yisrael*?

In light of the above thesis, we have a way to understand this statement. As mentioned, the covenant of *Parashat Behukkotai* was made in between the first and the second tablets, while God was not dwelling amongst the nation. In this situation, God promises that the situation will return to what it was – "My soul shall not abhor you, and I shall walk in your midst and I shall be your God." As an aspiration for the future, God insists that even had Moses not asked God to make His Presence dwell amongst the nation, if *Benei Yisrael* would behave as they should – He would once again dwell amongst them.

Parashat Beḥukkotai

The Two Dibburim of Beḥukkotai

Rav Yehuda Rock

In the Torah, mitzva units are generally introduced with the phrase "*Vayedabber*" – "God spoke to Moses, saying," or some variation thereof, so that each unit is known as a "*dibbur*" (plural, *dibburim*). A *dibbur* can consist of anything from a short paragraph to a series of commands spread over several portions. In the case of *Parashat Beḥukkotai*, we find both. Its first half continues from *Parashat Behar*, which begins: "God spoke to Moses at Mount Sinai, saying: Speak to the Israelites and say to them" (Lev. 25:1–2). This lengthy monologue continues all the way until the end of chapter 26, in the middle of *Parashat Beḥukkotai*. The first part of this *dibbur* (chapter 25) speaks about the laws of *Shemitta* and *Yovel*, the Sabbatical and Jubilee years; the sale and redemption of land and homes; interest; and the indentured servant. The second part (starting from 26:3) promises blessings upon the land if the commandments are observed, and curses if God's covenant is violated. In between the two parts there are two verses concerning idolatry, Shabbat, and the proper reverence to be shown towards the Sanctuary (26:1–2). This first monologue concludes at 26:46: "These are the statutes, judgments, and teachings which God gave between Himself and the Israelites at Mount Sinai, by Moses' hand." The second *dibbur* begins immediately afterwards, at the beginning of chapter 27: "God spoke to Moses, saying: Speak to the Israelites and say to them." It covers the subjects of valuations (for vows), property dedicated to God, and tithes. This speech, too, features a concluding verse (27:34): "These are the commandments which God commanded Moses for the Israelites at Mount Sinai."

Both *dibburim*, we are told (in the very first verse, at the beginning of *Behar*; and in the concluding verses in the middle of and at the end of *Behukkotai*), were stated at Mount Sinai. We may ask, when exactly were these two monologues stated, and why are they located at the end of Leviticus? We shall examine the context and function of each of these two *dibburim*, and the significance of their respective introductory and concluding verses.

Let us begin with the first *dibbur*. Concerning the introduction to the first speech (25:1), Ibn Ezra writes:

> "At Mount Sinai" – the Torah follows no chronological order. This actually took place prior to [that which is recorded in] *Parashat Vayikra* and all the portions that follow it, for it was stated at Mount Sinai. This is the covenant that is written in *Parashat Mishpatim*, and it is mentioned here in order to connect it to the condition for [receiving] the land. Just as God said, concerning sexual immorality, that because of it the land would expel them (Lev. 18:28), so He says the same, in *Parashat Behukkotai*, concerning the Sabbaths of the land; [therefore] He first sets forth the details of these Sabbaths.

Ibn Ezra understands the matter as follows: As this monologue was stated at Sinai – and bearing in mind that since the inauguration of the *Mishkan* (Tabernacle), God has spoken from the Tent of Meeting, as explicitly stated in Leviticus 1:1 – we must therefore conclude that the occasion of the speech recorded here must have preceded all of Leviticus. Ibn Ezra asserts further that the Torah sets forth here the details of the covenant which is forged at the end of *Parashat Mishpatim*, in Exodus 24:1–11, the covenant of the basins. Ibn Ezra does not explain his reasoning for this latter assertion.

Since, according to Ibn Ezra's view, this monologue precedes the first twenty-four chapters of Leviticus, he must explain why it appears here rather than in its proper place, in *Parashat Mishpatim*. He explains that the Torah seeks "to connect it to the condition for [receiving] the land." As we understand from the continuation of his explanation, he views the blessing and the curse in the second part of the monologue as the essence of what God is saying. The blessing and the curse set out the conditions for the existence of the Jewish nation in the Land of Israel. The Torah presents these conditions before describing the preparations for the entry into the land in Numbers.

Ibn Ezra's unstated assumption – that the crux of the *dibbur* here is its second part, i.e., the blessings and curses – requires that he explain why the *dibbur* also includes the first part. He resolves this by explaining that since the curses include (26:34–35, 43) the land expelling those who violate "its Sabbaths," i.e., *Shemitta* and *Yovel*, the Torah precedes the blessings and curses with the laws of these Sabbaths.

Ramban, as we know, consistently maintains that the Torah is written in accordance with the chronological order of events. Here too, Ramban maintains that the monologue that starts in *Parashat Behar* and continues through the first part of *Beḥukkotai* is conveyed by God to Moses when he ascends Mount Sinai to receive the second set of tablets (Ex. 34). Moses does not have a chance to pass these commandments on to the nation immediately, since he has to command them concerning the *Mishkan* and then supervise its construction. Immediately upon completion of the *Mishkan*, God gives Moses all the commands documented in Leviticus. It is only at their conclusion that Moses has the opportunity of conveying to the Jewish people the rest of what he had heard at Sinai. While Ramban agrees with Ibn Ezra that God gave this to Moses prior to the events of Leviticus, he distinguishes the time of God's command from the time of its transferral to the nation and maintains that this latter stage occurs at the present stage in the narrative.

This interpretation fails to produce a narrative continuity on the basis of the literal text. However, Ramban gains consistency in claiming that the redaction and ordering of the Torah follows the chronological development of events, rather than being based on thematic messages. His hypothesis of the two-stage commandment (God to Moses at one point in time, and Moses' conveying it to the nation at a later time) suggests that the formulation of the narrative speaks about God's original command to Moses, while its location at the end of Leviticus reflects the time when Moses conveys it to the people.

Ramban's view is problematic specifically when we view this unit as having been recorded in its proper chronological position; it is then that the formulation "God spoke to Moses" raises a difficulty in terms of narrative continuity. What the literal reading of the text suggests is that now, at this stage of events, with the *Mishkan* already assembled and functioning, God speaks to Moses on Mount Sinai – which is clearly impossible. Were Ramban correct, then it would make far more sense for the Torah, at this stage, to record Moses' speech to the nation rather than God's speech to Moses. There are other instances of the Torah describing Moses as commanding the nation concerning matters which he had heard previously from God (Ex. 35:1; Lev. 8:5). In such cases the Torah quotes Moses, and in his words the original command is attributed to God. In this way, the reader learns that God had previously commanded Moses. Similarly, in our case, the Torah could have said something like: "Moses spoke to the people and said to them, These are the things which God commanded me at Mount Sinai." This option would have preserved both the narrative continuity and the principle of chronological redaction, and the reader would immediately have understood the two stages involved.

It seems to make more sense to propose that the general chronological order of the Torah is based not on a strict principle of chronology, but rather on narrative-literary continuity. When the literary form is that of a story, it is expected that every event that is recorded takes place at the point where it appears in the text. Accordingly, wherever the Torah gives no indication to the contrary (as in, for example, the commands concerning the *Mishkan*), the text should be understood as following the order of events. However, it is certainly possible that there could be a unit that is written somewhere other than its chronological place – on the condition that the Torah states this explicitly. This would seem to be the case in our *parasha*. The Torah states explicitly that this *dibbur* took place "at Mount Sinai" – i.e., at the time when divine commands still issued from Mount Sinai (and not from the Tent of Meeting). Within the framework of the narrative-literary form, this represents a sort of "flashback" to an earlier time, with the Torah informing the reader of this jump by means of the words, "at Mount Sinai," which serve – in the literary context – as an indication of time. For this reason it seems that we should accept the view of Ibn Ezra, maintaining that this does indeed represent a jump back to an earlier time, and that what is postponed is not the command but only the place where it is recorded in the Torah.

As we have seen, Ibn Ezra does not only assert that the commandments in our *parasha* were given prior to the events of Leviticus, but adds that the Torah is setting forth here the conditions of a covenant, as described at the end of *Parashat Mishpatim*. Ramban also takes pains to place the original *dibbur* within the context of a covenant. To his view, these commandments represent the renewal of the covenant, in the wake of the sin of the Golden Calf. Ramban's motive in proposing this is clear; he needs to locate God's original *dibbur* as late as possible, since he goes on to explain why Moses has not had the opportunity until now to convey it to the people. Nevertheless, there is a more fundamental question here. On what basis do both commentators assume that God's *dibbur* here constitutes a covenant?

The answer to this question is to be found at the end of Ramban's commentary on this verse:

> The same happened concerning the covenant on the Moabite Plains – they accepted the Torah with those oaths and curses, and that was the covenant, as it is written: "These are the covenantal matters which God commanded Moses to forge with the Jewish people in the land of Moab, aside from the covenant which He forged with them at Horeb." (Deut. 28:69)

Ramban bases his view on a verse that appears after the blessings and curses in *Parashat Ki Tavo*. That verse tells us that there were covenantal matters related to Horeb (Sinai), and there were covenantal matters at the Moabite Plains. Since the covenant in *Ki Tavo* includes blessings and curses, both Ramban and Ibn Ezra conclude that "covenantal matters" mean blessings and curses. Blessings and curses from Sinai appear only in our *parasha*, and therefore the reference in

Deuteronomy ("aside from the covenant *which He forged with them at Horeb*") would seem to refer to our *parasha*. Rashi arrives at the same conclusion, and writes: "'Aside from the covenant' – meaning, the curses in Leviticus, which were stated at Sinai."

Here we encounter a problem. If our *parasha* contains the "covenantal matters" at Horeb, then the original story of the forging of the covenant seems to be missing something. It lists the commandments concerning which the covenant is made – "all of God's words and all of the judgments" (Ex. 24:3) – and it describes their inscription in a scroll (v. 4), the ceremonial aspects of the forging of the covenant (vv. 4–8), and the nation's acceptance of the covenant (v. 7). However, on the basis of the verse in *Ki Tavo*, there is supposed to be another central element of the forging of the covenant – the promises and threats, the blessings and curses. Yet this element is entirely absent from *Parashat Mishpatim*! Ibn Ezra explains that the postponement of this unit until long after its chronological place in the Torah is "in order to connect it to the condition for [receiving] the land," by juxtaposing the relevant sections. However, we must ask ourselves: Does this seemingly minor consideration really justify the omission of such a fundamental element from the record of the forging of the covenant – especially when this element is so integral that it is referred to in *Parashat Ki Tavo* as "*the covenant* which He forged with them at Horeb"?

Immediately following the above verse in *Ki Tavo*, Moses gathers the people together and speaks to them: "Moses called to all of Israel, and he said to them" (Deut. 29:1). His speech continues until the end of *Parashat Nitzavim* and is portrayed as the forging of a covenant (29:9–13):

> You are all standing today... to pass you into HaShem your God's covenant and His oath .... Not with you alone do I forge this covenant and this oath.

Ibn Ezra explains (28:69–29:1):

> This is the covenant of God's command at the Moabite Plains – "Moses called to all of Israel" – to forge the covenant. Therefore it says afterwards, "You are all standing today."

It appears that Ibn Ezra means to connect the two sources, so that the forging of the covenant in *Nitzavim* is a continuation of the covenant of the blessings and curses in *Ki Tavo*. However, the very fact that Moses needs to call all of Israel together would seem to show that the gathering had already broken up after the previous divine speech, and now Moses is calling a separate gathering. It makes no sense that the "covenantal matters" – i.e., the content of the covenant – would be conveyed at one gathering, while the actual forging of the covenant would take place at a different gathering.

The solution appears simple. The phrase "These are the covenantal matters" refers not to the preceding speech, but rather to the one that follows. In other words, the "covenantal matters" are not the blessings and curses in *Ki Tavo*, but rather the matters that Moses conveys after he has called together all of the Jewish people – i.e., the final verses of *Ki Tavo* and all of *Nitzavim*. "These are the covenantal matters…. Today you are standing…to pass you into [the] covenant."

According to this understanding, there is no reason to define the blessings and curses of *Ki Tavo* as a "covenant." Consequently, it is in no way surprising that the "covenantal matters" are transmitted on a different occasion, at another gathering of the entire nation.

It follows that there is no need to define the "covenantal matters" in general as blessings and curses. This brings us back to the question of the definition of a "covenant," and we will return to this question below. In any event, "the covenant which He forged with them at Horeb" refers, quite simply, to the covenant at the end of *Parashat Mishpatim*, concerning God's words and the judgments that had been transmitted prior to them. It has nothing to do with our *parasha*.

We previously asked: If the divine speech in our *parasha* was delivered at Sinai, why was it not written in its proper place? The answer to the question is now clear. God did say this at Sinai, but not as an integral part of the Sinai Covenant. He stated this as an independent matter, which may be connected to the Sinai Covenant (after all, the curses in *Beḥukkotai* relate to the violation of the covenant), but is an addition to it rather than part of it. For this reason it is not vital that the Torah convey this *dibbur* in its place; it could be postponed until our *parasha* – even for a relatively minor thematic reason.

If the blessings and curses are not the "covenant," what is the essential content of the Sinai Covenant and the Moabite Plains Covenant?

In the Moabite Plains Covenant, which, according to the understanding we have proposed refers to *Parashat Nitzavim*, we find the following (Deut. 29:9–12):

> You are all standing here today before Hashem your God…to pass you into Hashem your God's covenant and His oath, which HaShem your God forges with you today, in order that He might establish you today to be His nation and He your God, as He has spoken to you and as He swore to your forefathers – to Abraham, to Isaac, and to Jacob.

The essence of the Moabite Plains Covenant is that He will be Israel's God and they will be His nation. Since the Torah itself draws a parallel between the Moabite Plains Covenant and the Sinai Covenant, it would seem that this is the essence of the latter as well. Indeed, the language in the above verses echoes God's words to Moses in *Parashat Va'era*, in the planning for the Exodus (Ex. 6:6–7):

> Therefore say to the Israelites…"I shall take you to be My nation, and I shall be your God, and you will know that I am HaShem your God, who brings you out from under the burdens of Egypt."

In other words, the entire Exodus leads up to the forging of the covenant, and the relationship which the covenant is meant to cement is supposed to be based on the consciousness of God as having brought Israel out of Egypt.

After the Exodus, when the nation reaches the wilderness, God indeed proposes the covenant to them (Ex. 19:5–6):

> And now, if you will diligently obey Me and observe My covenant, then you will be My treasure from among all the nations, for all of the earth is Mine, and you will be for Me a kingdom of priests and a holy nation.

The Jewish people accept the offer and commit themselves to the covenant. Following the necessary preparations, God is revealed on Mount Sinai, declaring himself their God, who redeemed them from slavery (Ex. 20:2–3):

> I am HaShem your God, who brought you out of the land of Egypt, from the house of slavery. You will have no other gods besides Me.

As noted above, the *dibbur* in our *parasha* comes from Sinai, but it is not as an integral part of the "Sinai Covenant." For this reason it is not vital that it be recorded in its place, and it makes sense that the Torah postpones presenting it until our *parasha*.

What is the reason for the delay? We have already noted the approach of Ibn Ezra, maintaining that the purpose of the delay is "to connect it to the condition for [receiving] the land." We also noted the difficulties arising from this interpretation – it has no clear support in the literal text, other than the juxtaposition itself, and even this seeming continuity is broken by the second *dibbur* in our *parasha*.

Now we are in a position to suggest a different solution. As we have seen, in *Parashat Va'era* the Torah defines the ultimate purpose of the Exodus from Egypt as the forging of a relationship between the nation and God, as well as a consciousness of this covenant on the part of the nation: "And you will know that I am HaShem your God, who brings you out from under the burdens of Egypt." We find that the mechanism for inculcating this consciousness amongst the nation is the dwelling of God's Presence in the *Mishkan*, and that this is the original plan for the Exodus (Ex. 29:43–46):

> I shall meet there with the Israelites … I shall dwell amongst the Israelites, and I shall be their God, and they will know that I am HaShem their God, who brought them out of the land of Egypt to dwell in their midst. I am HaShem their God.

In other words, the *Mishkan* is a direct and necessary continuation of the Exodus from Egypt and of the Sinai Covenant. For this reason, the next narrative recorded following the story of the Sinai Covenant is the command to build the *Mishkan* and the process of its construction (with a break for the story of the covenant's violation, the sin of the Golden Calf). As Ramban explains, once God's Presence dwells in the *Mishkan*, there must be a series of commands that issue from the Tent of Meeting, pertaining to the Divine Presence and the proper observance of the sanctity that this entails.

Hence, it is for this reason that the unit is relocated from its chronological place in the Torah. The reason is not, as Ibn Ezra proposes, in order to place it in close proximity to Numbers; nor is it, as Ramban would have it, simply a result of Moses not having had time, until now, to transmit the message to the nation. Rather, on the literary level, had the unit appeared in its chronological place, it would have broken the literary continuity of the story of the Exodus with its objectives – the Sinai Covenant and the *Mishkan*.

As noted, the second *dibbur* in our *parasha* also emanates from Sinai, as evidenced by its conclusion: "These are the commandments ... at Mount Sinai." Apparently, the purpose of this verse is to delineate the end of the deviation from the chronological narrative. After the Torah indicates to the reader that at this point the narrative presents a "flashback" to events that happened earlier, the Torah signals, at the end of the book, the return to a chronological timeline, in preparation for Numbers. The concluding verse of Leviticus should be read together with the first verse of Numbers. "These are the commandments which God commanded Moses for the Israelites at Mount Sinai" ends the parenthetical unit of commandments from Sinai which remained to be conveyed. We now return to the flow of the story. The exact point of return, in time and space, is: "God spoke to Moses in the wilderness of Sinai, at the Tent of Meeting, on the first day of the second month, in the second year of their departure" – i.e., the departure of "the Israelites," who are mentioned in the previous verse – "from the land of Egypt."

The function of the verse that concludes the first monologue – "These are the statutes, judgments, and teachings (*ḥukkim, mishpatim,* and *torot*) which God gave between Himself and the Israelites at Mount Sinai, by Moses' hand" – is less apparent. Rashbam and Seforno explain that this verse sums up only the preceding section (*Parashat Behar* and the blessings and curses of *Parashat Beḥukkotai*). We can certainly accept that the "statutes" refer to the laws of *Shemitta* and *Yovel*, shunning idolatry, Shabbat, and the Sanctuary, while the "judgments" refer to the monetary matters listed in *Parashat Behar*; but what are the "teachings"? In the terminology of the Torah, "teachings" usually refers to lengthy series of detailed instructions, such as the "teachings" of the sacrifices. In the *dibbur* in *Parashat Behar* there are no such "teachings." We are therefore inclined to adopt the explanation of Ibn Ezra (on this verse) and of Ramban (at the beginning of *Parashat Behar*) that the verse is meant to sum up the halakhic sections of Exodus, which were also given at Sinai.

This explanation gives rise to the question of why the second *dibbur* in our *parasha* is not included in this summary. From the perspective of Ibn Ezra and Ramban, the reason is clear – the verse summarizes only those matters that are part of the Sinai Covenant. According to our hypothesis, however, even the first *dibbur* is not part of that covenant. If this is so, why does the verse bring together the first *dibbur* in our *parasha* and previous sections from Exodus, but not include the second *dibbur* in our *parasha*?

Seemingly, although the first *dibbur* is not defined as part of the covenant, it still belongs to the general subject of the relationship between Israel and God. We may say that the matters in it – the proper behavior towards the land and towards Israelite servants, and the conditions for the Jewish people's existence in the land – belong to the category of what "God gave between Himself and the Israelites." The laws of valuations for vows and of dedicated objects, on the other hand, merely define the proper handling of certain types of vows, and the Torah does not include these vows within the defining features of the relationship between God and Israel. For this reason, they belong to the general category of "the commandments ... at Mount Sinai," but not to "the statutes, judgments, and teachings which God gave between Himself and the Israelites at Mount Sinai."

Vayikra 26: Concluding the Covenant

Rav Tamir Granot

I. PARASHAT BEḤUKKOTAI AS THE CONCLUSION OF A COVENANT

Parashat Beḥukkotai opens: "If you will follow My statutes and observe My commandments, and perform them." The Torah goes on to warn: "But if you will despise My statutes and your soul abhor My judgments, such that you will not perform all of My commandments, thereby violating My covenant."

This two-sided formulation bears the general character of a covenant. Following the enumeration of several commandments, there are some verses of summary which define the reward that awaits the nation if it fulfils the commandments – i.e., upholds the covenant – and the punishment that will befall the people if they violate them. As the second verse quoted above explicitly states, observance of the statutes and the judgments itself represents upholding the covenant, and the opposite is likewise true – failure to observe them constitutes a violation of the covenant.

The *parashot* preceding *Beḥukkotai* are indeed crammed with statutes and commandments, and it is these that the Torah refers to here as the substance of the covenant. Thus, there can be no doubt that we have here, at the beginning of *Beḥukkotai*, a formulation of conclusion of the covenant. Proof of the extent to which this form is typical of a covenant may be found in the parallel covenant in Deuteronomy, where once again we find promises of reward and punishment at the end of the covenant, as part of the conditions (chapter 28), preceded by a long list of commandments.

But a comparison with Deuteronomy also shows what is missing in Leviticus. In Deuteronomy, the blessings and curses follow a description of a *covenantal ceremony* that is destined to take place upon Mount Gerizim and Mount Eival. In other words, first there is the actual ceremony of the forging of the covenant, which is set out in the text after the chapters containing the commandments over which the covenant is forged, and only afterwards is there the appendix, as it were, with the blessings and curses.

The order in Deuteronomy may be summarized as follows:

1. Declaration of the future covenant: "Behold, I set before you this day a blessing and a curse" (Deut. 11:26).
2. The substance of the covenant, including chapters of commandments: "These are the statutes and the judgments which you shall observe to perform" (12:1).
3. The covenant ceremony, including its summary: "This day HaShem your God commands you to perform these statutes and the judgments" (26:16), and later: "These shall stand to bless the nation upon Mount Gerizim" (27:12).
4. Appendix: Reward if the covenant is upheld; punishments for its violation: "And it shall be, if you will diligently listen … to observe to perform all of His commandments" (chapter 28).

If we compare the covenant presented in Leviticus with that described in Deuteronomy, we find that two elements appear in both: number 2 (the substance of the covenant), and number 4 (the appendix of reward and punishment). The other two elements that appear in Deuteronomy are missing: number 1 (the introductory declaration that what follows is a covenant) and number 3 (the ceremony). How can Leviticus conclude with the verses of the covenant if there is no preceding announcement of it, nor any actual event in which the covenant is forged?

Chapter 26 of Leviticus therefore appears to be wedged in the wrong place, because it is the conclusion of a covenant that has no beginning.

II. PROBLEM OF THE STATUS AND LOCATION OF THE COVENANT IN *PARASHAT BEḤUKKOTAI*

Let us examine the location of this covenant in chapter 26 from a more general perspective. The beginning of *Parashat Beḥukkotai* is not a real introduction; it is a continuation of a speech whose beginning and end we need to find. A quick review leads us to the verse at the beginning of chapter 25, and to the end of chapter 26.

The beginning of the speech reads as follows: "God spoke to Moses at Mount Sinai, saying: Speak to *Benei Yisrael* and say to them, When you come to the land...then the land shall lie fallow." This is followed by the laws of *Shemitta* (the Sabbatical year) and *Yovel* (the Jubilee year).

The end of the speech, following all of the curses, reads: "These are the statutes and the judgments and the teachings that God set forth between Himself and *Benei Yisrael* at Mount Sinai, by the hand of Moses."

Rashi questions why specific mention is made of Mount Sinai in this regard, while the other commandments in Leviticus are recorded as having been given in the Tent of Meeting. He deduces that just as these laws (concerning *Shemitta* and *Yovel*) were given in all their details at Sinai – so were all the others. But this distracts our attention from a different – perhaps more important – question: Why is Mount Sinai mentioned in connection with the Tent of Meeting at all? Our problem is not one of location. After all, the Tent of Meeting stood at the foot of Mount Sinai. The problem concerns chronology. God promised Moses that if *Benei Yisrael* would build a *Mishkan*, He would dwell in their midst and would speak with Moses from above the covering of the Ark, from between the two *keruvim* (Ex. 25). The building of the *Mishkan* was completed, and as the beginning of Leviticus indeed testifies, "God spoke to him in the Tent of Meeting, saying." From that point onwards, God speaks to Moses only in the Tent of Meeting; it is a metaphysical fact that the Divine Presence rests in the *Mishkan*.

The introduction to *Parashat Behar* is most surprising, because it means that this *parasha* was given while Moses stood atop Mount Sinai. From a literary perspective, this places the *parasha* in Exodus, which records commandments given at Sinai, rather than in Leviticus, which records commands given in the Tent of Meeting. Why does this *parasha*, which by all appearances was conveyed to Moses long ago, appear here, at the end of Leviticus, as though forgotten and only now inserted as an afterthought?

III. THE CONNECTION BETWEEN CHAPTER 25 AND CHAPTER 26

Rashi's question emphasizes the fact that the laws of *Shemitta* (chapter 25) were given at Sinai, and he explores the significance of this fact. But, as we have concluded above, not only the unit on *Shemitta* but in fact the entire section on the covenant – and particularly its blessings and curses – was also given at Sinai. In other words, what we have is an organic unit comprising two main parts:

1. Chapter 25 – laws of *Shemitta* and *Yovel*;
2. Chapter 26 – promise of reward and punishment for upholding the covenant.

This unit as a whole was given at Sinai. What is the connection between these two parts, causing them to appear here as a single unit?

The answer – or, at least, the beginning of an answer – appears explicitly in the verses of the curses:

> Then the land will enjoy its Sabbaths, so long as it lies desolate and you are in the land of your enemies; then the land will rest and enjoy its Sabbaths. So long as it lies desolate it shall rest, for not having rested during your Sabbaths while you dwelled upon it.... Then the land shall be forsaken by them and shall enjoy its Sabbaths while lying desolate from them, and they will make amends

for their sin, because – truly because – they have despised My judgments and their soul has abhorred my statutes. (26:34–43)

The Torah establishes here that the number of years to be spent in exile – i.e., the punishment for violating the covenant – is the number of *Shemitta* years during which the land did not lie fallow as it should have. In fact, Israel's exile is presented as a process of making amends, whereby the land receives that which is owed to it. This may perhaps be the reason why the curse also mentions that "it shall be desolate for your enemies who dwell upon it." What kind of a curse is this? *Ḥazal* explain that this curse contains a measure of blessing, and in practical terms this is certainly the case. But the reason for this peculiar "blessing" is that exile is described here as a process that takes place for the sake of the land, as if to restore its spiritual strength.

The symbolic and inherent connection to the matter of *Shemitta* – which is actually not referred to as "*Shemitta*" but rather as "*Shabbat ha'aretz*," "the Sabbath of the land" – is clear. The Shabbat of the land is an expression of its sanctity; the fact that it is God's land: "For the land is Mine." The fact that we live in the land and that it is given to us is part of the fulfillment of the covenant – "For you are strangers and residents with Me." The Jubilee year turns this metaphysical ideal into an all-embracing legal principle – everything returns to its original place, there is no absolute acquisition. This metaphysical and legal perception lies at the foundation of the covenant. The land does not belong to us. It is given to us, as part of the covenant. It may not be taken for granted. Violation of the covenant is a reflection of the mistaken perception that the land is ours no matter what. Exile returns everything to its natural state – the land returns to its original Owner, and then, obviously, it rests; i.e., it is not worked by any human hand, and we live outside of it, so that we may be able to receive it as reward for the covenant when we become worthy.

This leads us to the understanding that the crux of this unit, given at Mount Sinai, is in fact the covenant, while the matter of the Shabbat of the land is juxtaposed to it because the ideal that underlies the commandment of *Shemitta* – the divine status of the land – also determines the substance of the curses in the covenant.

IV. LOCATION OF THE UNIT ON *SHEMITTA*
AND THE COVENANT AT MOUNT SINAI

In Exodus, we note the sense of a jump from *Parashat Mishpatim* to *Teruma*. This impression arises both from the sudden preoccupation with the *Mishkan*, which was never mentioned in any of the previous *parashot*, and that the giving of the Torah at Sinai lacked the usual conclusion in the form of promised reward for those who uphold it and punishment for those who violate it.

If we compare the covenant in Deuteronomy, as the complete model, to the covenants in Exodus and Leviticus, we make an interesting discovery:

	Deuteronomy Model	Exodus Model – (Giving of the Torah)	Leviticus Model
Declaration	Beginning of *Parashat Re'eh* (12)	"And now, if you will diligently listen … and observe My covenant" (ch. 19)	omitted
Commandments	*Parashot Re'eh-Ki Tavo* (ch. 12–26)	"And these are the judgments" (ch. 20–23)	Section on *Shemitta* and *Yovel*, and perhaps also the preceding laws (ch. 25–26)
Ceremony	Ch. 27 – Mount Gerizim and Eival	"And he took the book of the covenant" (ch. 24)	omitted
Reward and punishment	Ch. 28 – blessings and curses	omitted	*Parashat Behukkotai*

We see that the elements of the covenant in Exodus and Leviticus actually complement each other. Since the Torah tells us explicitly that the element of the covenant in Leviticus came from Sinai, we need only take one further step to conclude that in fact it is the same covenant, with a literary division into two parts. We propose the following structure:

1. Declaration of establishment of covenant – Exodus 19;
2. Commandments (substance of the covenant) – Exodus 20–23;
3. Ceremony – Exodus 24;
4. Reward and punishment (blessing and curse) – *Parashat Behukkotai* (perhaps introduced by *Parashat Behar*, including the laws of *Shemitta* and *Yovel*).

In other words, the covenant known as the Covenant of Sinai or the Covenant of Horeb (for example, in Deuteronomy 28:69 – "Aside from the covenant which He forged with them at Horeb") includes the text in Exodus from chapter 19 onwards, as well as chapters 25–26 of Leviticus. Theoretically, this proposition seems logical. But is there any indication, in the course of the description in Exodus, hinting at the missing portion which we find later in Leviticus?

The answer would appear to be in the affirmative:

> God said to Moses: Come up to Me to the mountain, and be there, and I shall give you the tablets of stone and the Torah [teaching] and the commandments which I have written, to instruct them. (Ex. 24:12)

The Holy One promises Moses that He will convey to him, on the mountain, in addition to the tablets of stone also the "Torah and the commandments." But the continuation of the text contains neither teaching nor commandments; there is only the command to build the *Mishkan*, which is clearly not what was referred to. Where, then, are the promised Torah and commandments? The commentators offer various explanations:

Targum Yonatan suggests that the reference was only to the Ten Commandments, which hint to (or represent general categories that include) all of the other commandments. But the literal reading of the text clearly indicates that the "Torah and the commandments" means more than just the Ten Commandments (as Rav Sa'adia Gaon and Rashi point out).

Ibn Ezra proposes a different interpretation:

"The Torah" – This refers to the Written Law; "and the commandments" – this refers to the Oral Law, for all of the commandments were given to Moses at Sinai during the days when he stood atop the mountain.

Ibn Ezra adopts the view of *Ḥazal* that the reference here is general rather than pointing to any specific list of commandments. Essentially, this interpretation represents a declaration of faith that the entire Torah originated at Sinai.

In his introduction to the *Mishneh Torah*, Rambam treats this rabbinic teaching as the source for the principle that the Oral Law was conveyed at Sinai. However, on the literal level, the text gives no indication of this.

Let us try to understand what is being referred to here by analyzing the terms "Torah" and "commandments." First, let us go back to Leviticus. The first verse of the curses reads, "If you will not listen to Me, and not perform all of these commandments (mitzvot), and if you despise My statutes (*ḥukkotai*) and your soul abhor My judgments (*mishpatai*) so as not to fulfill all My commandments, thereby violating My covenant" (26:14–15).

An examination of these verses shows that the term "commandments" is meant in the general sense, and is used as a generic term ("all of these commandments") which is then defined as "My statutes" and "My judgments." Hence, "My commandments" = "My statutes" + "My judgments."

Attention should also be paid to the fact that in many verses, the term "commandment" or "commandments" appears alone as a general concept, while the terms "statutes" and "judgments" appear together, as a complementary pair of categories of commandments.

In light of the above, let us now examine the closing verses of the curses.

These are the statutes and the judgments and the teachings (*torot*) that God set forth between Himself and *Benei Yisrael* at Mount Sinai, by the hand of Moses.

Now that we have established that *"statutes and judgments"* may be summarized in a word as *"commandments,"* we may say that the Torah is telling us here, "These are the *commandments* and the *teachings.*" Appearing here as a summary of the unit describing the curses, the reference is obviously also to all of the commandments and teachings that preceded this unit – i.e., the covenant in its entirety. Now, if we compare what we are told when Moses ascends the mountain, in Exodus, with what we find at the end of Leviticus, we find that the conclusion echoes the introduction:

Exodus 24 – Introduction:	Leviticus 26 – Conclusion:
1. "Ascend to Me to the mountain"	1. "At Mount Sinai"
2. "And I shall give you"	2. "Which God gave"
3. "and the teaching"	3. "and the teachings"
4. "and the commandments"	4. "the statutes and the judgments" (= the commandments)

The conclusion that arises here is that in inviting Moses to ascend the mountain, God intends to teach him the laws of *Shemitta* and *Yovel*, and only afterwards, the appendix of blessings and curses. The teachings are the laws of *Shemitta* and *Yovel*. For reasons that we have not yet established, this *parasha* (Lev. 25–26) does not appear in its proper place, following chapter 24 of Exodus, as the closing section of the covenant (as we find, for example, in chapter 28 of Deuteronomy); rather, it is postponed to the end of Leviticus.

Why? The Torah contains three major collections of commandments:

1. The list in Exodus, given at Sinai (20–23);
2. The list in Leviticus, given in the Tent of Meeting (18–25);
3. The list in Deuteronomy, given at the Plains of Moab (12–26).

The rest of the Torah consists of narratives or historical (genealogical etc.) lists, and a large section devoted to the *Mishkan* and its service (end of Exodus and beginning of Leviticus, as well as part of Numbers).

The first collection of laws (Exodus) appears as part of the covenant at Sinai.

The third collection (Deuteronomy) is part of the covenant forged on the Plains of Moab.

The middle collection (Leviticus) does not appear to be part of either of these two covenants. There are two covenants, but three sets of laws.

The transfer of the conclusion of the covenant and the appendix of blessings and curses to the end of Leviticus serves to include the second collection of laws within the covenant of Sinai. Hence the covenant of Sinai includes not only the commandments in the *parashot* of *Yitro* and *Mishpatim*, but also the chapters of laws in Leviticus. From a historical point of view, the covenant in its entirety was given to Moses at Sinai. From a literary and legal perspective, the transfer of the summary of the covenant to the end of Leviticus serves to include the Leviticus commandments.

Indeed, the introduction to Leviticus 18 testifies that it is an introduction to the covenant in *Parashat Behukkotai*:

> God spoke to Moses, saying: You shall not follow the behavior of the land of Egypt, where you dwelled; nor shall you follow the behavior of the land of Canaan to which I bring you, nor shall you follow their statutes. You shall perform My judgments and observe My statutes, to walk in them; I am HaShem your God. You shall observe My statutes and My judgments, which a man shall perform and live by them; I am HaShem…that the land not expel you when you defile it, as it expelled the nation that was before you.

The characteristic formulations "observe My statutes," "perform My judgments," and the threat throughout that the land will expel the nation, are all typical (linguistically and thematically) of chapter 26 – the curses. In other words, the Torah includes all the lists of commandments in the second part of Leviticus within the framework of the covenant that concludes it.

V. EXODUS AND THE MISSING METAPHYSICAL LINK

Our main question, in discussing the location of the concept of the *Mishkan* in Exodus, concerned the thematic jump between the *parashot* related to the Exodus from Egypt – which assume God's revelation at Sinai and His appearance from the heavens, but not that God dwells on earth – and the *parashot* concerning the *Mishkan,* which assume God's presence within the camp of Israel, on earth.

I propose that Leviticus 25–26 belongs immediately following chapter 24 (the covenant) of Exodus, and prior to the command concerning the *Mishkan.* This leads us to the missing metaphysical link.

Observance of the covenant ensures that *Am Yisrael* will enjoy all kinds of benefits, abundant wealth, security, and peace. But the crux of the divine promise, in the wake of the covenant, is to be found in the following verses:

> And I *shall set My dwelling place among you,* and My soul shall not abhor you. And I shall walk among you, and *I shall be your God, and you will be My nation.* (26:11–12)

There are two promises here:

1. That God's Presence will rest in the midst of the nation and land of Israel;
2. That He will be our God and we will be His nation.

While the second promise lies at the foundation of the Exodus from Egypt ("I shall take you as My nation and I shall be your God" [Ex.] 6), the first promise has no mention in Exodus until the sudden command to build the *Mishkan.* The two promises are obviously connected – the Judge and Leader acts from within His nation, for only if God dwells in our midst can He lead us directly. This is the significance of God's declaration following the debacle of the Golden Calf: "I shall not ascend in your midst, for you are a stiff-necked nation – lest I consume you on the way." If God is in our midst, He leads, decides, and judges immediately. This can certainly be to the nation's detriment, if they are sinful.

If we pursue our assumption that these verses were given to Moses at Sinai, prior to the building of the *Mishkan,* the Torah is then conveying an explicit message:

"If you follow My statutes and observe the covenant, I shall dwell in your midst." The promise of the Divine Presence is not a condition for the covenant, nor the foundation upon which the covenant is presented.

Rather, it is its result; we may also say, its climax. God's promise here to allow His Presence to rest among us assumes the fundamental principle that God is not in heaven, revealing Himself from time to time, but rather that He may choose to actually dwell upon earth. This is the necessary foundation for the concept of the *Mishkan*. The command to build the *Mishkan* closes the gap between the promise of the covenant – which, by its own terms, can be fulfilled only on earth – and the reality of *Benei Yisrael* in the desert, encamped at the foot of Mount Sinai. God promises that He will dwell amongst the nation meantime, along the way, too – and not only when they reach the land of Canaan – if they will build Him a *Mishkan*.

If we summarize what we have said above, the following picture emerges: Divine service, in its most fundamental sense, does not require that God dwell amongst the nation. The metaphysical model that is presented up until the chapters of the covenant is that God remains in His heavenly abode, and He reveals Himself in the world as necessary, or leads us through some emissary – an angel. This is exactly what we are told in the unit describing the earthen altar and the unit on the angel (Ex. 20, 23).

Divine service may be aimed heavenward; such is the religious worship of every nation. But the Exodus also includes the idea of a covenant, meaning that God will be our King – "I am HaShem your God." Every nation has its king, but for *Benei Yisrael*, "God is your King" (as Samuel tells the people [1 Sam. 8]). Entering into and accepting the covenant – "We shall do and we shall hear" – represents an invitation to God to rule over us. Therefore, immediately after the ceremony of the covenant, God promises that if the covenant is indeed upheld, He will be able to dwell in our midst, on earth. The nation, on the other hand, is not able to fulfill the covenant in its entirety, for they have not yet reached the land. Therefore God tells Moses, "Let them make Me a Sanctuary that I may dwell in their midst." In other words, it is enough to enter into the covenant for God to agree to make His Presence rest among us. Obviously, actual violation of the covenant will lead to its cancellation. But even the cancellation of the covenant does not necessarily mean a cancellation of any relationship at all. God may no longer be our King in direct practice; He may lead us from afar, through an angel. He may not rest amongst us, but we still serve Him. The possibility of maintaining "religious relations" outside of the framework of the covenant, when it is violated, continues to exist. Hence, although the historical ideal is the fulfillment of the covenant and the establishment of the *Mishkan*, great importance is still attached to the more primal religious model, expressed in the verse, "In every place where I cause My Name to be mentioned, I shall come to you and bless you."

Historically and logically, then, the covenant with its climax – "I shall set My resting place in your midst" – precedes the command to build the *Mishkan* and provides its metaphysical foundation.

Arakhin and Shemitta

Rav Avraham Walfish

T he two chapters of our *parasha* divide neatly into two separate topics: the blessings and curses of chapter 26 and the laws of vows and consecrations of chapter 27. The first of these topics would seem, upon cursory reading, to provide a fitting conclusion to Leviticus; indeed, the chapter's concluding verse could readily serve as the book's summary: "These are the statutes and the ordinances and teachings which God gave, between Him and the Israelites, at Mount Sinai by the hand of Moses." It is puzzling that the Torah does not conclude Leviticus with this chapter, but instead chooses to tack on a chapter dealing with a topic which has no clear connection to its immediate context and appears to be a kind of addendum, providing an anti-climactic finale to the book.

Let's examine a different question. The Torah remarks, at the height of the *Tokheḥa* (admonishment/curses, 26:34–35): "Then shall the land repay (*tirtzeh*) its *Shabbatot*, all the days of its desolation, while you are in the land of your enemies; then shall the land rest and repay its *Shabbatot*. During all the days of its desolation it shall rest, all that it did not rest during your *Shabbatot*, when you dwelt upon it." The striking anthropomorphic image of the land as "owing" Sabbatical years which it needs to "repay" by means of exile is as surprising in its theological explanation of the exile as in its personification of the Land of Israel. Nothing in the opening and sequence of the *Tokheha* would seem to have prepared us for this single-minded focus on the violation of *Shemitta*. Rather, the Torah explained that the *Tokheha* results from Israel's wholesale and thorough-going rejection of *all* of HaShem's commandments (14–15): "But if you don't hearken unto Me and don't do all these commandments. And if you reject My statutes and if your soul abhor My ordinances, so that you don't do all my commandments, but abrogate my covenant."

If the curses result from rejection of all the commandments and abrogation of the covenant, why does the Torah focus upon *Shemitta* as the focal point of the *Tokheha*? To paraphrase Rashi: "What is *Shemitta* doing in the context of the *Tokheha*?" Examination will reveal that the Torah's emphasis on the centrality of *Shemitta* in the *Tokheha* is not an arbitrary or isolated phenomenon. The Torah has carefully, if subtly, prepared us for this idea by the way in which it presents the mitzvot of *Shemitta* and *Yovel*, in *Parashat Behar*. Let us examine the concluding verses of the Torah's presentation of *Shemitta* and *Yovel* and compare them to the blessings which open *Parashat Behukkotai*:

Behar – Chapter 25	*Behukkotai* – Chapter 26
And you shall do *my statutes* and *my ordinances you shall observe*	If you shall walk in *my statutes* and *my commands you shall observe*
and you shall dwell on it securely	you shall live securely in your land
The land shall give its fruit	*The land* shall give its yield and the tree… *shall give its fruit*
And *you shall eat to satiation*	*you shall eat* your bread *to satiation*
And if you shall say: What will we eat in the seventh year? Behold we don't sow and we don't gather our produce! I will appoint my blessing to you in the sixth year and it will provide produce for the three years.	
And you shall sow the eighth year and eat of the old produce until the ninth year, until its produce comes, *you shall eat old.*	*and you shall eat old,* long-kept and shall bring out old from before new.

The passage in *Behar* establishes clearly that *Shemitta* is a mitzva unique both in its demand and in its promise. The demand that an entire society abandon their agricultural livelihood for an entire year – and when *Shemitta* and *Yovel* come back to back (forty-ninth and fiftieth years), for two successive years – presents a unique challenge to the halakhic man of faith. The Torah responds by proclaiming a unique promise. God will insure that those who observe *Shemitta* and *Yovel* will not go hungry. Observance of *Shemitta* carries with it an iron-clad guarantee of divine blessing. The divine blessing of the pre-*Shemitta* year is similar to the divine blessing promised in *Beḥukkotai* to those who observe the commandments – overabundant yields of crops, which ensure continuity between the lengthy consumption of "old" produce and the arrival of "new" produce. Paradoxically, the Torah declares, our secure dwelling in the land is guaranteed not by intensive economic activity, but rather by refraining, at God's behest, from exploitation of the land.

Why has the Torah singled out *Shemitta* and *Yovel* in this way? I believe that the answer resides in the Torah's conceptual summary of the laws of *Shemitta* and *Yovel* at the conclusion of the passage we cited above (25:23): "and the land shall not be sold in perpetuity, because the land is Mine, for aliens and settlers (*gerim vetoshavim*) are you with Me." Two conclusions emerge from the Torah's characterization of the Jewish people as *gerim vetoshavim* on God's land:

1. Our right to exploit and dispose of the land is restricted, inasmuch as we are not the full owners, but rather tenants on land whose title is retained by God. The laws of *Shemitta* and *Yovel* express these limitations in the fullest and most dramatic fashion (*Parashat Behar*).

2. Our very presence on the land is contingent upon our fulfilling the conditions of our "lease," namely the mitzvot which God has commanded us. Hence the ultimate punishment for violation of the mitzvot is exile, leaving the land desolate (26:32 = *Beḥukkotai*). *Behar* and *Beḥukkotai* embody two different ramifications of the idea that Israel are no more than *gerim vetoshavim* on God's land.

If we examine the matter in greater depth, we can arrive at a fuller understanding of the blessings and curses, as well as the centrality of *Shemitta* and *Yovel*. The Torah's depiction of the mitzvot connected with the *Shemitta* year presents a further, very interesting parallel to the *berakhot*, as well as to the *kelalot*:

> *Parashat Behar* 25:7 – And for your animals and for wild beasts in your land, and all the produce shall be for them to eat.

> *Parashat Beḥukkotai* 26:6, 22 – And I shall abolish evil wild beasts from the land … and I shall send upon you wild beasts of the field and shall bereave you.

Just as the Torah taught us that, paradoxically, we must refrain from exploitation of the land in order to secure our hold upon it, so here the Torah teaches an equally paradoxical lesson. In order to free our land from the danger of wild beasts we must refrain, every seventh year, from closing our fields to domestic animals and wild beasts.

The Torah's perception is that man may achieve completely harmonious relations with his environment, as described in detail in the *berakhot* of *Beḥukkotai*: "and I will give peace in the land" (26:6) refers both to the absence of human enemies and to the banishing of evil wild beasts. In *Beḥukkotai*, the land, vegetation, wild beasts, and human society are all at peace within the Land of Israel. The Edenesque ambience of the *berakhot*, in which man lives in harmony with his environment, is reinforced by a literary allusion: "and I will walk (*vehit'halakhti*) among you and I will be your God and you will be My people" (26:12). The verb *hit'halekh*, described by R. David Zvi Hoffmann as meaning "walking here and there [without a specific destination], lingering here and there in order to examine things encountered along the way," is normally used by the Torah to refer to man's relationship with God (Gen. 6:9, 17:1). Only in Eden does the Torah apply this verb to divine activity, expressing the intimacy of God's relations with man. The complete harmony between Israel and their environment, in the holy land, culminates in a harmonious relationship between Israel and God. God can *mit'halekh* only in a setting in which man and his environment are at peace, just as

Adam in primeval Eden lived at peace with the land, as well as with its flora and fauna.

The harmony promised by *Beḥukkotai* between man, his environment, and God is bestowed by divine blessing upon the people which have carried out the divine precepts. Of these precepts, the mitzvot of *Shemitta* and *Yovel* exemplify the harmony between man and environment which is promised in the *berakhot*. In the *Shemitta* year man allows the earth to rest: "and the land shall keep a *Shabbat* for God" (25:2), refraining from working the land and exploiting its produce. All men and beasts are afforded equal access to the free-growing *Shemitta* produce (25:6–7). In the *Yovel* year, all land is returned to its rightful possessor – and all possessors return to their land and family (freeing of slaves – 25:41) – because we recognize, just as Adam did in Eden, that we are not truly landowners, but only custodians of land belonging to God. The *Shemitta* is also called "God's *Shabbat*," because the *Shemitta* harmony between man, land, and his fellow creatures is rooted in the same premise: the land is HaShem's, and He periodically requires us to surrender our custodial rights and express His sovereignty by effacing the barriers which symbolize our human control over the land.

Shemitta and *Yovel* periodically re-create within the Land of Israel an Edenesque relationship between man, his environment, and God. More than any other mitzvot, these two demand of man the fullest recognition and expression of the divine sovereignty, the source of all mitzvot, as well as all the *berakhot* which God has promised. Transgressing these two mitzvot is a double failure, a failure to recognize the true nature of his relationship with God, as well as a failure to understand the relationship with his environment which is thereby implied. God will punish Israel for their failure for failing to live in proper harmony with their environment. The Torah personifies the land. Israel must allow it to observe a *Shabbat* for God (25:2, 4), or else it will exact repayment by lying desolate while Israel is scattered among the nations (26:34–35). This personification gives powerful expression to the idea the Torah is trying to convey – man is not master of his environment. As custodian of God's land, he needs to maintain a dialectical relationship with his environment, of control and surrender, acted out in the rhythm of six work years and one *Shemitta*, seven *Shemittot* and one *Yovel*.

Here we return to our opening question: After this powerful conclusion, why does the Torah tack on a group of laws dealing with vows and consecrations (chapter 27), concluding once again with a closing summation (27:34): "These are the mitzvot which God commanded Moses [to convey] to the Israelites, on Mount Sinai"?

The repeated mention of Mount Sinai in this verse indicates that chapter 27 is connected to chapters 25–26. A further connection of this chapter to chapters 25–26 is the repeated reference to *Yovel*, and indeed the Bible scholar M.Z. Segal (*Mavo HaMikra*, p. 94) suggested that chapter 27 serves as a kind of appendix to the laws of *Yovel* – redemption of objects, persons, or land which have been consecrated, rather than sold to a person. Other scholars have suggested explanations of the location of our chapter within the context of Leviticus as a whole, rather than the context of chapters 25–26. Rav Samson Raphael Hirsch suggests that the optional mitzvot of chapter 27 serve as a fitting supplement to the mandatory mitzvot of the rest of the book. In a similar vein, some contemporary scholars have suggested that the theme of chapter 27 is the ability of man to create new obligations, supplementing the divinely-ordained mitzvot of Leviticus with the humanly-created "mitzvot" listed in the chapter.

A brief comment by Rav D.Z. Hoffmann points to a way of understanding the placement of our chapter which will account both for its relationship to chapters 25–26 and for its relationship to Leviticus as a whole. Rav Hoffmann (vol. 11, p. 269) suggests that our chapter comes as a "supplement to the statutes of holiness, laws were given regarding people and things which were consecrated to the Temple." We may note that "the statutes of holiness" begin in chapter 19 and culminate in *Parashat Behar*, in which the holiness of the Israelite person is integrated with the holiness of space (Land of Israel) and of time (*Shemitta* and *Yovel*). Consecration to the Temple, on the other hand, harks back to the opening section of Leviticus, which discusses the sacrificial service in the Sanctuary. Chapter 27 concludes Leviticus by weaving together the two main themes of the book: (1) the sanctity derived from the indwelling Divine Presence, symbolized and embodied by the Sanctuary; and

(2) the sanctity of the Israelite individual and community, embodied in all walks of life, but achieving its chief expression in the way in which Israel realizes the sanctities of space and time. In chapter 27, the Israelite expresses his sanctity by consecrating his person, other persons, animals, objects, or land to the Sanctuary. The forms that this humanly-created sanctity takes, as well as the relationship of this sanctity to the sanctity of the *Yovel* year, round out Leviticus by showing the highest form of interaction between the sanctity of persons and the sanctity of the indwelling Divine Presence in the Sanctuary.

The Value of Man

Rav Amnon Bazak

I. INTRODUCTION

The *parasha* of *arakhin* (estimated values, for the purposes of a vow made to God) deals with the estimated values of a man, an impure animal, a house, a field of possession (one's portion of the land of Israel), and a field that is purchased. In most cases, the value is estimated in accordance with the specifications of the object that is sanctified to God. In certain cases it is determined at the discretion of a *kohen*. Concerning an impure animal, we read: "The *kohen* shall assess it, whether it is good or bad; as the *kohen* values it, so shall it be" (27:12), and similarly concerning a house: "The *kohen* shall assess it, whether it is good or bad; as the *kohen* values it, so shall it stand" (v. 14). A field is assessed based on objective considerations – the amount of seed that can be sown in it and the number of years remaining until the *Yovel*: "Its value shall be according to the seed required to sow it, a *homer* of barley shall be valued at fifty shekels of silver. If he dedicates his field from the *Yovel*, it shall stand according to the estimation. But if he dedicates his field after the *Yovel*, then the *kohen* shall calculate the money according to the years remaining until the *Yovel*, and deduct that from the estimation" (vv. 16–18).

However, there is a noticeable deviation in the manner of calculation when it comes to the value of a person. There are no subjective considerations; only the person's age and sex are relevant. For instance, every man aged anywhere between twenty and sixty years has the same value. This fact alone indicates the system's uniqueness.

II. THE KING'S DECREE

Let us begin by drawing up a table of the estimated values found in verses 3–7:

Age of the subject	Gender: Male	Gender: Female
Twenty until sixty	50 shekels of silver, in the currency of the *Mishkan*	30 shekels
Five until twenty	20 shekels	10 shekels
One month until five years	5 shekels	3 shekels
Sixty years and older	15 shekels	10 shekels

This table illustrates two fundamental principles regarding the rating of a person's value:

1. In each of the four stages of a person's life, the estimated value of a male is higher than that of a female.
2. A person's value is estimated in accordance with his stage of life. The highest value is attached to the period during which he is "at his peak"; the next highest level corresponds to the years preceding this period, from the age of five until the age of twenty; following this is the period of old age; and the lowest value is given to the years of infancy and early childhood.

At first glance, it appears that the person's value is estimated according to his ability to work. This is based on the assumption, especially during biblical times, that a higher monetary value is attached to a male than to a female, and the value of each is determined in accordance with his/her age and productive capacity. However, this assumption raises a number of questions:

1. We must question the affirmation that a person's best years are up to the age of sixty. The Torah indicates that the age for labor

is up until fifty, as we read concerning the *levi'im*: "From the age of fifty he shall return from the ranks of divine service, and he shall serve no more" (Num. 8:25).

2. It is also surprising that the worth of a person during his most productive years is calculated at fifty shekels, which is much higher than the actual value of a slave: "If the ox gores a slave or a maidservant, he shall give the sum of thirty shekels to the master" (Ex. 21:32).

3. During two stages of life the ratio between the value of a male and that of a female is 5:3 (between the ages of twenty and sixty and from one month until five years). Why, then, is this ratio not maintained between the ages of five and twenty, and, more importantly, why is the value of a man over the age of sixty (fifteen shekels) lower than his value between the ages of five and twenty (twenty shekels), while in the case of a female there is no difference between these two stages of life, and in both cases the value is ten shekels? Rashi addresses this problem and comments (Arakhin 19a): "Upon reaching old age, a woman is closer in value to a man; therefore a man loses more than one-third of his value in his old age, while a woman loses only one-third of her value. As people say: 'An old man in the house is like an obstacle in the house; an old woman in the house is a good sign in the house.'" This is a charming teaching in and of itself, but it does not provide an altogether satisfying answer to our question. Is it really true that in the case of a woman there is no difference between the stages of 5–20 years and 60 years plus, while when it comes to a man such a difference does exist?

It is apparently these questions and others that lead Ibn Ezra to his unequivocal statement in this regard:

> The generally accepted view is that this is *a decree of the King* – that [for a boy aged] from one month until five years he gives five shekels; if he is even one day over a month old he gives five shekels…the principle here is a *decree of the Torah*, for if [the calculations] followed the principle of a male being worth more

than a female, after the age of sixty one-third should be added, while from the age of five until twenty one-half should be added. And from the age of a month up until five years, and from twenty until sixty, one-tenth of the value should be added to that half.

III. ITS VALUE SHALL BE ACCORDING TO ITS SEED FOR SOWING

It appears that there is indeed a difference in the scale of values for a male and a female. We questioned above why a person's "best years" are up until the age of sixty, rather than fifty, the "retirement age" for *levi'im*. Interestingly, the age of sixty appears in Tanach in a different context – not in relation to work capacity, but rather in relation to fertility:

"Isaac was sixty years old when they were born" (Gen. 25:26);

"Then Ḥetzron came to the daughter of Makhir, the father of Gilad, and he married her – when he was sixty years old, and she bore him Siguv" (1 Chr. 2:21).

The only two places in Tanach where a person is mentioned as being sixty years old both deal with people who bore children in their later years. The verses emphasize the age in order to indicate the unusual nature of this phenomenon. Thus, it would seem that the age of sixty represents the end of the usual period of fertility, and our *parasha* conveys the same idea.

In light of this we can also explain the significance of the sum attached to a person at his peak – fifty shekels of silver. This sum is mentioned in the Torah in one other place:

If a man finds a young virgin who has not been betrothed, and he takes hold of her and lies with her, and they are found, then the man who lay with her shall give the girl's father fifty pieces of silver, and she shall be his wife, since he mistreated her; he shall not send her away all the days of his life. (Deut. 22:28–29)

In several places (Ketubot 33a and elsewhere) the significance of paying fifty shekels is defined as the "benefit from lying [with her]." This act, representing the man's vigor and fertility, is therefore estimated as a benefit of fifty shekels, and symbolically this is then the value of a man at the peak of his fertile years.

Let us now try to understand why the second highest value is accorded to the stage between five and twenty years, rather than from sixty years upwards. At both stages a man is able to attain fertility, but the stage at which he is on the way to reaching his physical peak is not the same as the stage of becoming old. In a person's later years, sexual intercourse is no longer considered as having fertile potential, and for this reason the person's value drops. Interestingly, the sum of fifteen shekels is found elsewhere in the context of sexual relations that are not meant to lead to conception:

> God said to me: Go, further, and love a woman who is loved by someone else and commits adultery, like God's love for *Benei Yisrael* who have turned to other gods and who love raisin cakes. So I brought her to me for *fifteen pieces of silver,* and a *ḥomer* of barley and a *letekh* of barley. (Hos. 3:1–2)

Rav Hai Gaon notes this connection (as quoted by Rashi in his commentary, ad loc.):

> In the name of Rav Hai Gaon, I found the Gaon's explanation: "'I brought her to me' – I allotted a small sum of money in exchange for her. As the one who says, 'my own value [is obligated] upon me' – if [the person is] sixty years or older, the exchange is fifteen shekels."

In light of this, the value of a person between the ages of one month and five years clearly does not reflect any commercial ability. This, then, must be the minimum value of any child from the age of one month – exactly the same as one pays the *kohen* for a firstborn at a *pidyon haben*. Once again, we may say that the fact that the child has any value at all arises from the potential inherent in him.

In the same way, we may address our original question: Why the estimation of the male is determined only according to his age, rather than by his subjective worth. If indeed the scale according to which a person is valued is his fertile capacity, then in fact his work capacity is of no significance. All people during their most fertile years, regardless of their physical abilities, education, or occupation, are equal in this regard.

The idea of a person's value being determined in accordance with his fertility exists in the Oral Law, as well. Concerning the verse, with regard to a Hebrew servant, "Let it not be hard for you, when you send him away from you, free, for he has been worth double a hired servant to you for six years" (Deut. 15:18), Rashi comments, "From here [the Rabbis] taught: A Hebrew servant works both in the day and in the night; this is the sense in which he is worth double a hired servant. What is meant by 'work at night'? His master gives him a Canaanite maidservant, and their children belong to the master." The work of this Hebrew servant is considered "double the worth of a hired servant" because of his ability to sire children, who then belong to the master.

In fact, our thesis is hinted at further on in the chapter, concerning the estimated worth of a field:

> If a person dedicates part of a field of his possession to God, *its estimation shall be according to the seed required to sow it,* a homer of barley shall be worth fifty shekels of silver. (v. 16)

Concerning a field we are told explicitly that its value is estimated according to its fertility, "according to the seed to sow it." But, in contrast to a person, when it comes to a field the Torah does take into consideration the discrepancy in the fertile potential of different fields (on the basis of the quality of the ground, the size of the field, etc.). Therefore, the basic unit to measure the fertile capacity of the field is "a homer of barley seed" which is worth "fifty shekels of silver," just like a person. But in the case of a field, this unit may be multiplied many times over, depending on its changing value.

IV. VALUE OF A WOMAN

Let us now address the various estimated values of a woman. Obviously, the criterion for a woman is different than that for a man, since from the biblical perspective a woman has no "seed"; she is considered a passive

442

participant in the process of conception. Therefore, we must explain the differences in the monetary estimations in a different way.

We have already mentioned above that the sum of thirty shekels, the maximum value of a woman at the strongest stage of her life, is noted in the Torah in a different context: "If the ox gores a servant or a maid-servant, he shall pay the sum of *thirty shekels* to the master" (Ex. 21:32). We may deduce from this that when it comes to a woman, her value is indeed determined in accordance with her capacity for work. We noted above that the "retirement age," as mentioned with regard to the *levi'im*, is fifty; it is reasonable to posit that the division of ages was determined according to this criterion for men, and the Torah saw no reason to create a different division for women. Therefore age remains as the only factor, and for women, once again, there is no discussion of subjective categories of work capacity, etc.

We now have a satisfactory answer concerning the discrepancy in the ratio between the values of men and women at different stages of life. The entire problem proceeds from the assumption that the scale for both is the same. But if in fact there are two separate scales – fertility, in the case of men, and work capacity in the case of women – then it is indeed logical that the same ratio is not maintained at every stage of life. It is quite conceivable that work capacity does not diminish after the age of sixty in as drastic a fashion as fertility does.

The Surrogate and the Sacrifice

Rav Itamar Eldar

T
he Book of Leviticus concludes with the laws of *arakhin*, valuations. The Torah in chapter 27 codifies how one may vow to donate various items – houses, fields, people, and animals – and the prices at which they may (or, in some cases, must) be redeemed. The location of this passage demands an explanation. One approach is based on the fact that the method used for calculating the value of a field is tied into the upcoming *Yovel* (Jubilee) year, as this is the time when ancestral property is returned to the original family. Thus, this approach argues, the passage of *arakhin* could only have been written after the passage of *Shemitta* (Sabbatical) and *Yovel* in *Parashat Behar* (Ramban, ad loc.: "for it is among the statutes of *Yovel*").

However, this answer is less than fully satisfying. This passage does not immediately follow the commandments of *Yovel* in *Parashat Behar* (chapter 25); rather, it comes after the blessings and curses detailed in the first half of *Parashat Beḥukkotai*. In fact, it is the passage of *arakhin* which concludes the Book of Leviticus as a whole.

R. David Zvi Hoffmann answers that the curses immediately follow the legal discussion of *Shemitta* and *Yovel* because they come as punishment for neglecting these mitzvot in particular (26:34–35, 43). Alternatively, he suggests that it is the Torah's desire to conclude the

Book of Leviticus not with curses but with laws. The *Keli Yakar* offers an original proposal – *arakhin*, after all, are a class of vows, and it is human nature to make vows when in distress, as Jacob did in his time. What greater time of distress could there be than the calamities of the curses?

A similar approach, connecting *arakhin* in chapter 27 to the curses of chapter 26, is advanced by Rav Mordechai Yosef Leiner in *Mei HaShilo'aḥ*, ad loc.:

> When a man makes a special vow, it shall be according to your valuation of souls to God – this means that, after the *Tokheḥa*, God grants Israel a safe haven, giving them the passage of valuations, indicating that a person can redeem himself from anything. Four types of redemptions are written – houses and fields, people and animals – and they parallel the four times that the number seven appears in the reproof, for seven symbolizes that God is exacting even to a hair's breadth. This is why God mandates four types of redemption.

It appears that the key to understanding the decision to conclude the Book of Leviticus with the passage of *arakhin* is to grasp the relationship of this last passage to the very first.

Let us compare the opening of the first chapter of Leviticus to the opening of the last:

> Speak to the Israelites and say to them: "When a person (*ish*) from among you brings an offering to God – from the animals, from the cattle, and from the flocks you shall bring your offering." (1:2)

> Speak to the Israelites and say to them: "When a man (*adam*) makes a special vow, it shall be according to your valuation of souls to God." (27:2)

The book thus begins with an offering brought by "a person," and it concludes with a valuation vow made by "a man."

The beginning of Leviticus deals with the nature and characteristics of offerings. One can discern there a theme of substitution, a human being offers an animal in place of himself. This concept of substituting an animal for a person is first found in the case of Abraham and Isaac, in Genesis 22. Abraham is told to bring his son up as an elevation-offering, but at the last minute, the slaughtering-knife is sheathed and he takes a ram in place of his son. In this story we learn that God does not want human sacrifice.

However, despite this unambiguous message, we find throughout the generations biblical personages who seek to express their religious service by offering their children. Indeed, Jeremiah (19:5) expresses God's lament:

> They have built the high places of Baal to burn their children in the fire as offerings to Baal – which I had not commanded, nor spoken, and which had not come into My mind.

The Sages interpret this in the following way (Ta'anit 4a):

> And further, it is written, "Which I had not commanded, nor spoken, and which had not come into My mind" – "I had not commanded" refers to the sacrificing of the son of Mesha, the King of Moab, as it says (II Kings 3:27): "And he took his first-born son who would reign in his stead and he brought him up as an elevation-offering." "Nor spoken" refers to Yiftach. "Which had not come into My mind" refers to Isaac son of Abraham."

While the Israelites incinerate their children and perhaps rely on the precedent or near-precedents of the son of King Mesha of Moab, the daughter of Yiftach and, of course, Isaac son of Abraham, the prophet absolutely condemns both the act and the precedents. Under no circumstances does God desire human sacrifice.

We have rendered the verse from chapter 1 as "When a person from among you brings an offering to God," but the verse is actually structured "When a person *brings from among you* an offering to God," which can be understood as a literal reference to human sacrifice. However, the conclusion, "from the animals, from the cattle, and from the flocks you shall bring your offering" invalidates this approach. This phrasing alludes to the fact that offering an animal sacrifice suffices to fulfill the intent of "bring[ing] from among you an offering" by offering a substitute.

However our passage, the passage of *arakhin*, does not deal with sacrificing a human, but with consecrating one. We will now try to understand the meaning of this special vow and what the valuation of a human being truly means. First of all, we must distinguish between redeeming a field, house, or animal, as described in this portion, and redeeming a person. While as regards the others there is a possibility of consecrating an object, human beings cannot be consecrated in the physical, monetary sense. Rather, the vow basically obligates one to give an amount of money equivalent to their valuation to God, and thus the Torah comes and sets the valuation of each human being based on gender and age.

Thus, a human being cannot be consecrated, according to the Torah, and therefore, the consecration is the amount of money corresponding to the valuation of the person.

Nevertheless, we do find a case of vowing to consecrate a person for the Temple, as it were – Hannah, mother of Samuel:

> And she made this vow: God of hosts, if You look with pity on the hardship of Your servant, if You remember me and do not forget me, if You give your handmaid a male child, I will give him to God all the days of his life. No razor shall ever touch his head. (1 Sam. 1:11)

Indeed, Hannah fulfills her vow and after Samuel's birth, she gives him to Eli in the *Mishkan*, and she says: "Now I, in turn, give him to God; as long as he lives, he shall be dedicated to God" (v. 28). Hannah asks God for a son, and then she gives him back to God.

The passage of *arakhin* determines that a person may not consecrate himself or another to the Temple, but only the worth of a soul. Just as an animal offering includes, to a certain extent, the sacrifice of the one bringing it as well, so too dedicating a sum of money equivalent to the valuation of a person includes the person himself, to some extent, in the dedication. The person gives himself to God, just as Hannah does to her son in practice.

When Hannah consecrates Samuel for the *Mishkan,* she intends that this is his place, this is where he belongs. This is how one who dedicates his valuation to the Temple is supposed to feel. This is not a donation but an exchange. One would have wanted to ask to work in the Temple, to be dedicated to it, to serve in it, but since one is not able to do so, one gives an amount of money according to the dictated valuation, which comes into the holy precincts as a surrogate for the human soul.

This passage concludes Leviticus, the book in which the narrative action of the Torah comes to a hiatus. The Book of Exodus concludes with the building of the *Mishkan* and the Divine Presence residing it. In terms of the plotline, this narrative continues only in Numbers, as the nation prepares to leave and finally departs from Mount Sinai. The *Mishkan* is a "traveling Mount Sinai," and its construction allows the Israelites to leave Mount Sinai and to continue on their way to the Land of Israel with God in their midst. They leave Exodus and Mount Sinai and set out on their travels in Numbers. But for a moment, the Torah stops, with the wondrous expression which opens Leviticus (1:1), "And He called to Moses, and God spoke to him from the Tent of Meeting, saying."

Before we continue, God is saying to Moses, the fact that I descended to reside among you is not relevant only to the continuation of this specific journey. Your holiness in the dimensions of time, place, and person now becomes existential and regular – "When a person from among you brings an offering."

Leviticus, the book of holiness, opens and concludes with the relationship of man to the Temple, to the *Mishkan* – as expressed through the voluntary impulse to connect to the Temple, to holiness. At its outset and dénouement, Leviticus designates channels for the person who wishes to come to the gates of the Temple and to lend himself or sacrifice himself to the Holy. The Holy One residing in Israel demands that a person sanctify himself, that he be a part of this endeavor. However, at the beginning and the end of Leviticus, we find how the Torah lifestyle distinguishes itself from other cultures, by advocating not only the sanctity of Tabernacle and Temple but also the sanctity of man.

In both passages, at Leviticus' commencement and consummation, the Torah deals with sacrifice, belonging, and the desire to devote oneself, on the one hand; and on the other hand, surrogacy and substitution. The offering and the valuation teach us that the Torah views positively the desire to be dedicated to the holiness which resides among us; but at the same time, the person, the "man" who sacrifices and vows, remains a person and human being – with life, with the world, with a body, with the material, with liberty and freedom, with the mundane. All of these elements are delivered deliberately, by thought and by action, to that which is Holy, but without losing themselves, their essence, their value: a person brings, a man vows, but the human soul and self is inviolable.

Contributors

Rav Amnon Bazak serves as a *Ram* in Yeshivat Har Etzion and teaches Tanach at Herzog College and at the SKA Beit Midrash for Women in Migdal Oz. He has authored a number of books, among them *Shemuel Aleph: Melekh BeYisrael, Shemuel Bet: Malkhut David*, and *Ad Hayom Hazeh*, on fundamental issues in modern Tanach study.

Rav Ezra Bick teaches Talmud and Jewish Philosophy at Yeshivat Har Etzion, and is the Director of the Israel Koschitzky Virtual Beit Midrash. He is the author of *In His Mercy: Understanding the Thirteen Midot* and a forthcoming volume on the *Shemona Esrei*.

Rav Yoel Bin-Nun studied at Yeshivat Merkaz HaRav and Yeshivat Har Etzion, where he was among the founders. He was *rosh yeshiva* of Yeshivat HaKibbutz HaDati, and currently teaches Bible and Jewish Philosophy in Herzog College.

Rav Mordechai Breuer *zt"l* taught at Yeshivat Har Etzion for over thirty years, where he trained a generation of younger scholars. He was the originator of the method of Biblical interpretation known as *"shitat habeḥinot."* He authored two volumes of *Pirkei Moadot* and important works on the *mesorah.* Two volumes of his articles on Genesis (*Pirkei Bereshit*) appeared after his death, as well as a volume on the Book of Isaiah.

Rav Itamar Eldar studied at Yeshivat Har Etzion and currently serves as the head of the Beit Midrash le-Torah ule-Hayyim in the Golan and head of adult education at Yeshivat Orot Shaul in Kfar Batya, Ra'anana. He has authored VBM series on the *Kuzari, Hasidut* and Kabbala.

Rav Baruch Gigi studied at Yeshivat Har Etzion and since 5766 has served as its *rosh yeshiva*. He also teaches at SKA Beit Midrash for Women in Migdal Oz and other *batei midrash* for women, as well as at Herzog College. For over twenty years he has trained *to'anot beit din*, and is currently writing a multi-volume series entitled *Talelei Shabbat*.

Rav Tamir Granot studied at Yeshivat Har Etzion and earned a doctorate in Jewish Philosophy from Bar Ilan University. He is *rosh yeshiva* of Yeshivat Orot Shaul in Kfar Batya, Ra'anana, and also teaches Talmud and Jewish Philosophy at Herzog College. His VBM series on Jewish thought and the Holocaust was recently published as *Emunah Veadam Lenokhaḥ HaShoah*.

Rav Yonatan Grossman studied in Yeshivat Har Etzion and received a doctorate in Bible from Bar Ilan University. He has taught at the Yeshivat Har Etzion since 1998 and currently teaches Bible at Bar Ilan University and Herzog College. He is author of a number of VBM series and the recent book *Esther: Megillat Setarim*.

Rav Yair Kahn has been a *Ram* at Yeshivat Har Etzion since 1987 and is head of its Overseas Students Program. Rav Kahn is also the editor of the *Shiurei HaGrid* series, published by the Toras Horav Foundation and Mossad Harav Kook.

Rav Menachem Leibtag headed the Overseas Program at Yeshivat Har Etzion for over a decade. He founded the Tanach Study Center, a comprehensive program for the study of Tanach on the Internet. He